THEFT, LAW AND SOCIETY

SECOND EDITION

BY

JEROME HALL

Professor of Law, Indiana University

INDIANAPOLIS

THE BOBBS-MERRILL COMPANY, INC.

PUBLISHERS

PREFACE

A notable increase of interest in legal science since the first publication of this book, important developments in other social disciplines, and the generous reception of the book, here and abroad, have encouraged me to provide a second edition.

I have tried to improve upon the first edition in several respects. The whole work has been carefully gone over with a view to effecting a closer coherence of the various chapters. A substantial portion of the text, especially of Part Two, has been revised. The discussion of receiving stolen property was reorganized and amplified, and other parts of the book have been brought up-to-date, especially in order to test the validity of certain generalizations which I ventured to express in the 1935 edition. A new chapter, that on embezzlement, has been added, while the one on petty larceny was omitted because it seemed to be incongruent with the rest of the book. And in the Introduction I discuss problems which, I think, are very important for the progress of socio-legal studies in general.

The time and effort required to produce this edition (more than six months went into the preparation of the chapter on embezzlement, alone) have given me some insight into the reasons for the lack of such studies. Without the opportunities provided by the Columbia University Law School from 1932 to 1934, it would not have been possible to do the necessary research and to write this book in the first place. And without the facilities and funds for research and other assistance provided by Indiana University, I could not have gotten out this edition of it. I also wish to thank various public officials and executives of insurance companies and protective associations for giving me the benefit of their many years of experience and thoughtful observation in special fields.

JEROME HALL

Bloomington, Indiana.

INTRODUCTION

The need for scientific knowledge of interpersonal conduct in relation to law has become urgent in an age of tensions, conflicts, and expanding controls. This book represents an effort to supply a small portion of that very great need and to do so in ways that may have some general significance.

Theories of social science, especially those concerning methodology, are often presented very abstractly and in technical vocabularies which seem remote from the actual problems of research. This does not imply that theory should be abandoned or subordinated to practical guidance on research. What is involved is precisely the question of cogent, critical, realistic social theory. Under the circumstances, it occurred to me that a report and discussion of methods and theories employed in this research on theft might be of interest.

The general approach to the problems studied was simply one of curiosity about many phases of law, an attitude conditioned by strong intellectual currents in the social sciences. That movement in the United States was not, of course, unique; and an account of the origins of recent socio-legal studies in various countries would take us back at least to Maine and to earlier developments on the continent, e.g., the German historical school. The above influence, joined to an interest in the criminal law, led to certain decisions regarding this research.

The first major decision was to concentrate upon a specific socio-legal problem in the field of crime. This reflected the view that progress in the social disciplines depends upon intensive research in narrow areas—a judgment transmitted by scholars in reaction against philosophical social science. At the same time, it had become evident by 1930 that this approach could degenerate into a mere grubbing for facts. The decision to explore a narrow field was qualified by a taste for social theory, which was first directed toward such questions as—

which segment of the criminal law should be investigated and why, how can it be done, what data are required, what data are probably available, can the research on such and such an inquiry be carried to assured conclusions, what records should be provided to permit another investigator to retrace the steps taken in order to check the validity of the findings, and so on.

For several reasons the law of theft was selected as the most inviting area in which to apply and test social theory. That law is intimately tied to interests which have stimulated considerable speculation among social theorists. This suggested some very broad questions, e.g., what is the relationship between the law of theft and property? Is there a one-way process, i.e., of impact of economic institutions on law or of legal controls molding the institutions; or is the relationship more complex? This sort of question represented the most general reference of social theory to the problems of theft.

Social theory was thus the dominant perspective; but there was another important source of questions and ideas. As a lawyer working with the rules of the law of theft, I had encountered many peculiarities in modern statutes, e.g., provisions that a dog and a negotiable instrument can be stolen and special legislation regarding growing crops and property owned by railroad companies. These raised both technical and social problems.

In the case-law there were many nice distinctions regarding, e.g., larceny by trick and obtaining property by false pretenses, custody and possession, and interpretations of statutes which clearly opposed ordinary canons of construction; indeed, some of the decisions seemed to be utter nonsense. Yet, on the assumption that our predecessors in the Bar and on the Bench were thoughtful persons, there must have been some reason in their doings. In any case, these phenomena raised fundamental questions involving the meaning and functions of law. In all of this, statutes and case-law were inter-connected, and it was important to determine their respective roles in the development of the law of theft. Issues debated in the early thirties in this country regarding the judicial process, similar to those discussed on the continent as *libre recherche* or *Freirechtslehre,* were plainly relevant to the solution of these problems. With reference to the above questions and many others, the law of theft promised to be a fertile field for investigation.

Shortly after the study of the law of theft was begun, the need to engage in extensive historical research became insistent. In no other way could it be determined why such terms and notions as *ferae naturae,* breaking bulk, chose-in-action, larceny by trick, larceny by servant, and so on are found in the present law and what they mean; indeed, the principal divisions of theft (larceny, embezzlement, fraud, and receiving stolen property) cannot be understood unless one knows how and why they entered the law. Specifically, it was necessary to start with simple larceny and to trace the emergence of several differentiated crimes from that primitive legal form as social need sought a more refined set of instruments.

In order to apply and test questions of social and legal theory as they were focused on theft, it was essential to know the history of 18th century England. For that was the age of the Industrial Revolution. I did not know, though perhaps I should have, that the 18th century was also the period when practically the entire modern law of theft was made. It was anticipated, however, that with reference to theories of cultural change, institutional interaction, the functioning of laws, problem-solving by judges, and so on, there would be significant data at the time and place of the impact of the Industrial Revolution. Finally, it would obviously be a great advantage to work in a period which had left an abundance of records and documents about whose genuineness there was no doubt. Thus, in sum, both in order to answer technical questions and to discover persuasive solutions of larger theoretical issues, it was necessary to engage in certain historical research.

Eighteenth century England proved to be an excellent laboratory. The functioning of the social and legal institutions was so pronounced in that century, the problems met were obviously related to unmistakable cultural changes, and the methods taken to solve them are so readily discernible that it is easy to see what happened, what was done, how it was accomplished, and what the motivations were. If those problems, processes, and methods should turn out to be substantially like the ones which confront and characterize present law, judicial process, and legislation, discoveries in the 18th century laboratory might rise to the level of knowledge which could defensibly be included in a science or sociology of law.

Pollock and Maitland's *History of English Law* remains an inspiration to anyone who enters the realm of legal history. But another kind of legal history was wanted for the purposes in hand. Whether in fact each generation writes its own version of legal history or whether the problems raised in this study of theft were peculiar ones, in either case a history was needed which would be relevant to social and economic questions and to current legal theories of the judicial process. It therefore had to be discovered and supplied.

A detailed history of at least one case was also essential to the progress of the research. All history, including that of law, is composed of individual events; hence knowledge of law or of any other institution is knowledge of series of such events. There are many ways of getting at the significance of historical legal events, and statistics and the case-method of the law schools are among the more important ones. But another kind of case-analysis was required, namely, a case-history of at least one case. This, it was believed, might go some distance toward satisfying the need for insight into the actualities of legal events by describing concrete facts, rules, persons, pressures, and objectives which cannot be derived from case-analysis, statistical statements, and scientific generalizations. Unfortunately, not enough was known about the selected case to allow attainment of that objective as fully as was desired.

In addition to serving the above purpose, the case-history, presented in the first chapter, describes forces and ideas which may be viewed as variables of continuous operation. Such "conditions," abstracted from many specific events, provide criteria for generalization. In short, the Carrier's Case is interpreted as a concrete legal event involving the principal types of data discussed throughout the book. Thus, specific description and abstraction represent ways of looking at legal events. But the descriptions carry distinctive reports which, eluding generalization, render possible the reconstruction of past situations and experiences and exhibit the bonds between past legal institutions and our own.

There was another reason for investigating the Carrier's Case. I had read in 18th century cases, to which I first turned, emphasized references to a certain 15th century case—that of a carrier—and learned that ideas expressed in the decision of that case were important in 18th century law. In addition, economic history revealed the substantial coincidence of the Carrier's Case with the rise of modern commercial economy, the precursor of the Industrial Revolution. The need to understand both 18th century law and problems concerning the interrelations of economy and law indicated the desirability of exploring the Carrier's Case. Unexpectedly, there developed an intriguing mystery about some of the facts of the case, e.g., regarding the contents of the bales and the king's relations to the judges.

The framework of the 18th century history of theft was built in chapter 2 by specifying the main lines of legal change as simply and definitely as possible, with unavoidable sacrifice of detail. The object was to provide a clear structure of the new law upon which the currents of concomitant social change, the contemporary ideologies, and reform movements could be directed. The explication of interacting changes, where everything is in flux, requires that some phases of the dynamic process be regarded as fixed for a time. Later, in chapters 3 and 4, the substantive law was treated not as a given structure but, instead, as a guide and product of judicial and legislative problem-solving.

Relevant theory concerns the ways in which various factors interact, the conditions of legal growth, the qualities of legal problem-solving, the underlying perspectives which guide interpretation, the extent to which generalizations regarding these processes are verified, and so on. With reference to such questions, the text of the book must speak for itself. Some explicit indications of basic viewpoints are offered, e.g., in the chapter headings and subheadings. These suggest a reliance upon both institutional changes viewed as operating causally, i.e., as externally determined, and upon problem-solving, the discovery of solutions which cannot be fully accounted for by antecedent causes or conditions. Stated otherwise, the writer tried to function both as an observer of cultural changes and as a participant in the solution of socio-legal problems. This interpretation of what was done involves important problems which have long been the subjects of polemics regarding the social disciplines, and it will be discussed shortly.

The first and second chapters of the book were planned to form a unity in two respects. The first chapter, the case-history of a case, delineates and reconstructs a socio-legal microcosm, while the second chapter gathers together data abstracted from a multiplicity of such events and organizes them. The two chapters, combined, also give an account of the development of the basic categories of the modern law of theft and of their "material" components.

So, too, though designed on other lines, the third and fourth chapters are intended to comprise a single discussion. The latter, dealing with administration, explores the functional meaning of substantive laws described in the preceding chapter. An account of 18th century criminal law would be very incomplete, indeed, it might be misleading, if only one of those phases of law were considered. Accordingly, chapter 3 describes certain laws with little involvement of administration; while chapter 4 selects some of those laws, adds many others, and feeds them all through the process of adjudication operating in problematic situations raised by the impact of new forces, economic and ideational, on the legal structure—the substantive rules.

The separate presentation of substantive law and administration, though it may be regrettable from a theoretical viewpoint, facilitated the analysis of certain problems traditionally associated with each of these phases of law. For example, in chapter 3 the pressure of various groups on the legislature can easily be traced as well as the correlation of the products of the farms and crafts with legal protection of them by Parliament. The limitations on those pressures are met in the fourth chapter, e.g., in social forces opposing the drive for repression, which often included the efforts of economic classes which had used their influence to secure the enactments; but now, members of these groups, as individuals, confront individual offenders in the harsh grip of the legal apparatus.

In each of the above chapters (3 and 4) a departure was made from the historical narrative in order to discuss a current problem. In chapter 3 certain technical aspects of contemporary legislation are considered immediately after the history of the law on the subject-matter of larceny. And the last part of chapter 4 is a discussion of recent administration of criminal law in Chicago, involving waiver of the felony charge. In neither instance was the addition of the current problem felt to be incongruous or to interrupt the flow of thought engendered by the historical narrative. Indeed, it may be hazarded that few better illustrations can be found of the continuity of history, revealing the past law, legal institutions, and legal methods in present law, legal institutions, and legal methods. This also suggests the relations between the historical part of this book and Part Two, the analysis of current problems.

With reference to the historical research, the reader will note that there was considerable use of 18th century documents such as parliamentary debates, committee reports, current pamphlets, statistical data, comments of philosophers and reformers and, of course, the usual legal materials. Obviously, there was much reliance on social and economic history. In making use of such a variety of materials, I merely extended an important development of recent history. A goodly number of distinguished historians, though they were apt to neglect legal data, had already established the desirability of inclusive presentation emphasizing social and economic factors, as a more valid reconstruction of the past. What needs emphasis, however, is the use of history to provide insights without which the most carefully devised methods and techniques of research are not fruitful.

History is entirely omitted in Part Two—unless the presentation of short series of decisions is viewed as history. In Part Two, two kinds of knowledge, broadly speaking, were sought —valid generalizations and accurate descriptions of efforts to solve legal problems. The latter approximate history in character but greatly contract the temporal dimension, aiming not at continuity but at acquaintance with detailed facts. We cannot here discuss the question whether such description is a kind of knowledge. It must suffice to call attention to the description of dealing in stolen goods, the activities of protective associations and insurance companies, the characteristics of automobile thieves and embezzlers, the practices used in disposing of the cases of these offenders, and so on. If the description of these and many other situations and patterns of behavior helps one to understand the social processes dealt with, that is sufficient for the present purpose. The relation of description to scientific generalization and the independent function of description in social science are important questions, and it is hoped that some partial solutions are suggested by this study.

The generalizations in this study extend from a very high level to relatively narrow descriptions which are distinguishable from specific ones. Some of the theories employed were not explicitly formulated, e.g., a pluralistic view of socio-legal change, indicated in the consideration of both institutional interactions and problem-solving, a theory of legal sociology implied in giving rules of law the central place, "culture lag," and others.

Among the theories which were rather definitely expressed are the following:

(a) The functioning of courts is significantly related to concomitant cultural needs, and this applies to the law of procedure as well as to substantive law.

(b) The chronological order of the principal phases of legal change is (1) a lag between the substantive law and social needs, (2) spontaneous efforts ("practices") of judges, other officials, and laymen to make successful adaptations, and (3) legislation.

(c) Technicality and legal fiction function both as formal links between the old law and the emerging law and also as indexes to solutions of legal problems.

(d) The "law-process," represented in the norm-oriented and directed conduct of large sections of the population, provides the conceptual framework of legal sociology.

These and other "high level" generalizations mark the outer limits of the inquiry and they influenced the investigation of particular problems. In varying degrees they seem to have been themselves verified, though they were not formulated in the rigorous way in which the narrower generalizations, to which we shall shortly refer, were expressed.

Certain notions, implying various theories, were employed in this study as "constructs." For example, one construct frequently used in this book is the triangular relationship envisaged between a social problem at one base angle, the relevant substantive law at the other, and administration at the apex. Another is implied in the restriction of inquiry to the conduct of offenders, officials, specialized lay groups, and "the public." The relevant premises are that this construct denotes a fair sample of the important types of conduct involved and that the principal problems can be adequately treated in the given context. Still another construct, employed, e.g., in the chapters on automobile theft and embezzlement, consists in the interrelation of law, mores, and objective values, which are examined in different combinations.

With regard to more rigorously formulated generalizations, attention is directed to a number of propositions which approximate scientific laws in structure and are also supported by considerable data (but are not systematized). Among these are the generalizations expressing the co-variation of rate of automobile theft and size of population, the percentage of arrests for automobile theft and the same variable, and several propositions stating the interrelations of certain variables in embezzlement.

With reference to the question whether these generalizations are "social laws" or are merely statistical descriptions (assuming that there is an essential difference), it will be noted that the indicated generalizations on automobile theft and embezzlement are unlimited while statistical statements regarding, e.g., the age of automobile thieves and embezzlers, the percentage of convictions of professional receivers as compared with that of lay offenders, the relative frequency of probation for embezzlers as compared with that in other offenses, the percentage of automobiles recovered within a short time, and so on, do not generalize beyond the given data. Nor do they express a co-variation of factors. Even if the former, the "social laws," must be distinguished from laws of physical science it would also seem necessary to set them apart from general descriptions of limited fields of data.

Finally, many postulates are implied throughout the discussion, and some validity is attributed to practically all of them. For example, it is assumed that there are degrees of rationality in legal controls, that "better" solutions of socio-legal problems can be discovered. Another postulate is that the substantive law should represent the salient facts of social problems. And some elementary value judgments were implied without any effort to establish their validity.

The various types of knowledge indicated above—empirical, valuational, specific, and general—fuse at many points, revealing the complexity of social science.

That is also reflected in recurrent interest in the integration of the social disciplines; and this research on theft may have some significance for that problem since several social disciplines were utilized in the course of the investigation. It is important to note that the inquiry on theft was directed not toward the social sciences, but toward certain socio-legal problems. Yet, there certainly seems to be a coherence of the social knowledge employed in this study. From the perspective of

the present research, integration of the social disciplines results from their relevance to the solution of a problem. And
that is readily distinguishable from the logical unification of
the disciplines, viewed as forms of discourse.

Integration of the social disciplines by way of their relevance
to the solution of a social problem is like looking at an object
from different positions—the specific perceptions cumulate and
fuse into an integrated perception of the object. So, too, as one
explores a social problem from the perspectives of the various
disciplines, his knowledge accumulates and it fuses into a
"total" knowledge of the problem. Sustained, deliberate efforts
to achieve such an integration of knowledge might consist in
articulating the various approaches, planning the course and
types of investigation required for a "total" solution of certain
problems, and ordering the respective solutions in relation to
each other.

There is another way of viewing the integration of social
disciplines. From this approach, the basis of unification may be
found in the common features of social problems and processes.
The integration of the social disciplines would thus be the
consequence of discovering their distinctive subject-matter.

The difference between social science and reform, i.e., better
solutions, is a crucial one, but it is not possible to keep them
wholly apart in actual research. Thus, several reforms were
discovered in the course of this research, and there is also
advocacy of certain reforms, e.g., with reference to the control
of dealers in stolen goods, embezzlement, etc. The discovery
of these reforms, but not the advocacy of them, seemed inseparable from the research. And, as noted above, numerous other
value judgments were expressed or implied throughout the
study. All of this involves a major question of contemporary
social theory.

A strongly represented viewpoint excludes all valuation from
social science. On the authority of eminent scholars who sought
a "value-free" social science and because of the prestige of
physical science, as well as for other reasons, it is maintained

that the social researcher must completely eschew evaluation. But here is a specific study, a socio-legal research on theft, regarding which some pertinent questions may be raised.

To facilitate that, a few instances of the value judgments made in the course of this study may be noted. It was implied and stated, e.g., that 18th century criminal statutes were very harsh, and the efforts of the reformers were approved as well as the later statutes which eliminated the capital penalty. Value judgments were expressed regarding current administration of the law in connection with waiver of the felony. Others were made in comparison of the harms committed by professional automobile thieves with those of "joy-riders," of dealers in stolen goods and lay receivers, of "white collar" criminals who take many thousands and the petty thief or embezzler, and so on. Indeed, every analysis of specific decisions and legislative enactments involved some evaluation. And the valuational postulates, noted above, will be recalled. If social science excludes evaluation on substantial, not merely formal, grounds, such judgments as the above ones are no part of it and, at best, can elicit only toleration as condonable lapses. But the evidence at hand does not support such a disposition. Studied avoidance of even any suggestion of evaluation would have inhibited inquiry. It would have revealed a rigid predilection for a doctrine and raised obstacles to communication. There are important reasons for this.

To understand a problematic situation, it is necessary to reconstruct and re-live it with all the doubts, assurance, insights, sense of obligation, and aspirations experienced by the original actors in it. Moreover, the inescapable fact is that social problem-solving, especially when legal controls are involved, includes efforts to find the best solutions. That is why it is impossible actually to exclude the Ought from an Is-Ought process. That is also why an adequate understanding of legislative and judicial processes includes an estimate of the valuations represented in the efforts to attain goals and to discover and experience "higher" values. It is the central, though not the only, point in insistence on empathy, participation in problem-solving, discovery of the actors' meanings, and the like.

When petty thieves and murderers were subjected to the same capital penalty, and criticism spread to ever-widening groups until drastic legal revisions were made, how can one understand what went on in the courts, among the public, or in Parliament unless he evaluates the conduct, debates, valuations, and decisions at every step of the process? Can one understand the functioning of the Chicago judges *vis a vis* youthful "joy-riders" and a statute imposing 1 to 20 years imprisonment unless, whatever else he explores and comprehends, he also appraises the moral considerations that influenced their judgments?

In the above instances one is apt to approve the solutions reached. But many problematic situations do not terminate successfully, and these are especially revealing with reference to the discovery of reforms. But, regarding both types of situation, we must ask: Is it possible to participate in actual problem-solving without the least thought of better values or insights or sounder answers than those reached? I doubt very much that criticism can be so contained. It seems to me that discovery of needed reforms, in the above sense, is unavoidable in social inquiry. Such discovery, however, must be contrasted with efforts *primarily directed* toward discovery of reforms and, of course, with advocacy of reforms or other practical enterprises. The difference is describable in terms of motivations, primary objectives, and attitudes.

If scientific inquiry differs from efforts to reform but necessitates valuation at many points, including the discovery of better solutions, the consequences for social science are bound to be rather complex. In my opinion and, it seems to me, on the evidence of this study of theft, the question of the normativity of social facts, the "Is-Ought problem," has been oversimplified. On the one side, for reasons stated above, there has been oversimplification regarding the place of valuation in social science.

On the other side, it has not been sufficiently recognized that the normative element in on-going social processes does not ban descriptive generalizations. For that purpose, the problematic situations are viewed as *past* events, and ends are "fixed" as results; they are taken as given facts. For example, suppose it is agreed that there is an "ought" element in the conduct of a judge who construes a statute very strictly in order to avoid the imposition of a severe penalty. Instead of participating in his problem-solving efforts, we can view them as a past situation, "fix" the end he sought, e.g., transportation instead of capital penalty, or probation for "joy-riders" instead of long terms as felons in the penitentiary, and describe his conduct in terms of movement toward those specific results. It is also possible to generalize regarding selected recurrent phases of such situations and to correlate them with significant variables, e.g., the prosecution of embezzlers in relation to restitution, the rate of automobile theft in relation to size of population, the expansion of larceny in relation to economic changes, and so on. In this way valid empirical generalizations regarding past problem-solving processes can be discovered. Certainly such generalizations have significance not found in case-histories or in the most vivid participation in any number of specific instances of problem-solving.

These observations, which I think can be fairly tested in the following study, may be restated as follows:

One essential type of social interpretation is presented *as though it were simultaneous with the process that is being interpreted,* i.e., the problem-solving situation is reconstructed and it is re-lived. Such knowledge includes an appreciation of the meanings conceived and experienced by the actual participants as well as criticism of their value judgments.

The re-living of an experience in problem-solving *is necessarily restricted to specific concrete situations.* The case-history of the Carrier's Case is an inadequate illustration of this method of interpretation because detailed data regarding the judges' thinking, their motivations, and the actual process of arriving at the decision are lacking. If the aid of sympathetic judges could be enlisted so that detailed autobiographical documents and accounts of the judges' reflections and conferences became available to supplement transcripts of evidence, lawyers' arguments, extra-forensic investigations, and so on, it would be possible to push much farther in this direction.

There is another basic type of social knowledge, namely, generalization regarding recurrent facts. To generalize means to abstract, to select certain elements from actual complex events. One can view these events (e.g., instances of legal problem-solving) as past movements toward known results. It is both possible and significant to select certain components of these events and to generalize regarding their co-variation with other factors.

This study of the law of theft, it seems to me, is an illustration of the thesis that both of the basic perspectives described above, together with their representative methods of research, are needed to provide an adequate explanation of socio-legal processes.

TABLE OF CONTENTS

CHAPTER THREE

CHAPTER FOUR

BOOK TWO
CURRENT PROBLEMS

CHAPTER FIVE

CHAPTER SIX

CHAPTER SEVEN

EMBEZZLEMENT 289

APPENDIX

BOOK ONE

HISTORICAL PERSPECTIVE

Theft, Law and Society

CHAPTER ONE

THE CARRIER'S CASE

Every legal problem arises within the framework of a particular set of social institutions. The interrelations of these institutions and the interaction between them and the body of legal sanctions existing at any given time create innumerable problems, in the solution of which the materials of legal history are made. In these problem-situations, one sees an interplay of impersonal forces as well as the unceasing efforts of man directed at the considered use of means to gain ends, and applied in the actuality or under the illusion of power to modify his course of life.

The law of theft provides a superb opportunity to study these problems. Related immediately to the development of property interests and characterized by its concern with relatively refined methods of illegal acquisition, this body of law has a long and well-marked history which can be definitely and significantly traced. For each ultimate link in the chain of its history is a specific case or statute.

The report of any law case is a human document. Illuminated with but a bit of imagination, even the technical words written in a musty volume portray a vivid drama. The dead awaken, contestants battle hotly for the things they value; and powerful forces penetrate the courtroom, driving the actors to extend themselves to their uttermost limits. The final opinion, deliberately expressed, may conceal within its austere form a life-struggle. Most cases, to be sure, are merely cumulative in their effect, moving in well beaten paths, with some inevitable deviation but by and large within the lines laid down. Occasionally, however, comes a case of tremendous

3

importance. It affects the gentlemen on the bench greatly; despite their efforts to preserve the appearance of conformity to precedent, it is clear that they struck out in a definitely new direction.

Such a case, decided in 1473, was designated the Carrier's Case.

I. THE FACTS AND THE LAW

The facts are simple enough: the defendant was hired to carry certain bales to Southampton. Instead of fulfilling his obligation, he carried the goods to another place, broke open the bales and took the contents. He was apprehended and charged with felony.

The case was discussed at length, at least on two occasions, before and by the most illustrious judges of the time, among whom were Brian, the Chief Justice, Choke, and Nedham; attorneys Hussey and Molineux represented the Crown.[1]

Brian, one of the soundest of English judges, contended throughout the proceedings that no felony had been committed. The defendant had possession, said Brian, "by a bailing and delivery lawfully"; and "what he himself has he cannot take with *vi et armis* nor against the peace; therefore it cannot be felony nor trespass."

Against this position, it was argued:

1. There was no bailment but, instead, "a bargain to take and carry" which did not vest possession if the carrier's intention was unlawful at the time he received the goods.

---

[1] The Carrier's Case, Y. B. 13 Edw. IV. f. 9, pl. 5, is interesting from a procedural point of view for several reasons: First, it was heard in the Star Chamber (and later in the Exchequer), although the beginning of the Court of the Star Chamber is generally set at 1487, fourteen years after the Carrier's Case was decided. Second, the trial of a felony in the Star Chamber was extraordinary. Finally, its later hearing in the Exchequer, an inferior tribunal, is also unusual. Possible reasons for the appearance of the case in the Star Chamber are (1) the fact that an alien merchant was involved. There are numerous cases in which foreigners appear as parties in the early history of the court; (2) the question of waif, to which the king might have a right, although it was actually decided otherwise. As to the date of the case with reference to the origin of the Star Chamber, it is indicated that the statute of 1487 (3 Hen. VII, c. 1) did not create a new tribunal but that the court was in process of formation for some years prior to the passage of the act. *Cf.* Dicey, The Privy Council (1887) 95.

2. Granted that there was a bailment, felony was committed by subsequently taking the property *animo furandi.*

3. The bailment was terminated by taking the goods to a place other than Southampton and "breaking bulk," that is, opening the bales.

4. The defendant had possession of the containers or wrappers only but not of the contents of the bales.

5. The case should be decided not according to common law but "according to the law of nature" (this was urged by the Chancellor).

The defendant was finally held guilty of felony by a majority of the judges. In order to understand the meaning of the decision and its effect upon the law of theft, it is necessary to project an inquiry in several directions. The traditional professional approach runs in terms of an analysis of the law existing at the time of the trial. Since the *corpus juris* was well known to the judges and was, avowedly at least, given particular consideration, this approach suggests itself quite naturally as the necessary initial investigation.

It must, however, be borne in mind that in 1473 *stare decisis* was not the solid structure that it has become, if for no other reason than that the number of past cases was relatively small and the reporting of them was still a rather haphazard affair. No abridgement had yet been published (Statham's was printed in 1490); but, on the other hand, the Year Books had been compiled for two centuries, and the judges were undoubtedly familiar with the important cases. Moreover, despite the fact that the Chancellor's remark regarding the law of nature went unchallenged, it is perfectly clear that the judges regarded themselves as bound by the common law. Such difference, then, as existed regarding the extent of precedent and the attitude of the judges with reference to the binding effect of past cases, was one of degree.

We may start with the fact that it was agreed that:

1. Trespass is an essential element of larceny.

2. A person in possession of property cannot commit a trespass upon that property.

3. A bailee has possession.

Trespass as an essential element of larceny simply meant taking a chattel from one who had possession of it. It is as clear as anything can be that, prior to the Carrier's Case, "taking", as an element of larceny, had no artificial meaning. Anglo-Saxon and early Norman economic conditions limited both the objects and the methods of theft. Movable property consisted of cattle, farm products, and furniture. "To carry it [movable property] away manually was, in practice, the only way by which he was likely to be deprived of it." [2]

Since theft of cattle by armed bands was by far the most important crime against property,[3] it requires no stretch of imagination to see what was meant by "trespass" in the early law.[4] Quite appropriately, the old form of indictment charged "that J. S. on etc. one etc. of the goods and chattels of J. N. feloniously did steal, *take and carry away against the peace*," etc.[5] Theft was either "manifest" or "non-manifest," depending upon whether or not the offender was caught in the act of stealing. In either event, the trespass was identical. The final effect was likely to be the same if the property taken was worth more than a fixed minimum amount; but the manifest thief was disposed of on the spot. This distinction between types of theft persisted into the thirteenth century when new procedural developments introduced by the Normans gradually established a different classification.[6]

When we turn to the professional literature we find no use or interpretation of the word "trespass" as an element of theft,

---

[2] Stephen, General View of the Criminal Law of England (1863) 51.

[3] See *infra* p. 82.

[4] "The most striking fact about the use of *cum vi* (*sua*) *et armis* and kindred expressions in the early appeals is that they were used only in connection with an invasion of land by an armed force, never of the act of an individual of and by himself." Woodbine, *Origins of the Action of Trespass* (1925) 34 Yale L. J. 361.

[5] "In truth, the limitation [that felony required a taking from the possession of the owner without his consent] seems to have been inherent in the nature of a common law felony. That act alone was punishable by appeal or indictment which was done *contra pacem regis*, or, in other words, *vi et armis*." (Citing Brian J. in Carrier's Case, and in 3 Hen. VII, 12, pl. 9.) Beale, *The Borderland of Larceny* (1892) 6 Harv. L. Rev. 245.

[6] 2 Pollock and Maitland, H. E. L. (2nd. ed. 1911) 496.

which fitted the facts in the Carrier's Case. Glanvil, the first author of a text of the procedural common law, stated specifically that "the party, indeed, shall be absolutely excused from the imputation of Theft, by reason that his possession of the thing detained originated through the owner of the property."[7] Bracton, influenced by his Latin training, emphasized the *animo furandi*,[8] and provided the basis for one of the arguments made in the Carrier's Case. The definition of theft in the *Mirror of Justices*, though embedded in considerable irrelevancy, particularly emphasized the "taking . . . for bailment or livery excludes larceny."[9]

As for actual case materials, there were only two or three very fragmentary decisions in point. In an early anonymous case[10] the defendant was indicted because *"felonice abduxit unum equum rubrum price de tant."* In the King's Bench, to which the case had been removed from the sheriff's tourn, it was held that the indictment could not lie because it did not appear whether the defendant had *taken* the horse feloniously or whether he had led it away *after* he had come lawfully into possession of it.[11]

In the debate on the Carrier's Case there was also some suggestion of another legal principle which was in the process of formation. It referred to larceny by a servant. A special rule applicable to servants only was mentioned as early as 1339, but was disregarded in 1344–1345.[12] The earliest case which presented the doctrine in some detail was reported in the Year Books[13] where it was stated:

"If a taverner serve a man with a piece, and he take it away, it is felony, for he had not possession of this piece; for it was put on the table but to serve him to drink: and so it is of my

---

[7] Book X, c. 13 (*circa* 1187)
[8] Vol. 2, Twiss ed. 509.
[9] Sel. Soc. ed. 25.
[10] 2 Edw. III, p. 1, no. 3 (1328).
[11] In commenting on the case, Stephen writes: "This is a judicial recognition of part of the doctrine of the *Mirror* as to the proper definition of theft." 3 History of the Criminal Law of England (1883) 136.
[12] Y. B. 18, 19 Edw. III (R. S.) 508.
[13] 49 Hen. VI, Mich. pl. 9.

butler or cook in my house; they are but ministers to serve me, and if they carry it away it is felony, for they had not possession, but the possession was all the while in me; but otherwise peradventure if it were bailed to the servants, so that they are in possession of it."

Although this decision was discussed, apparently with general approval, in Carrier's Case, the doctrine was repudiated several years later by Brian and his associate judges.[14] Not until 1506 was it held that property in or about the house of the master was in his possession, and that his servant had mere custody of this property and was guilty of felony if he converted it.[15]

I have extended the discussion of the emerging distinction between custody and possession somewhat beyond 1473 to indicate the full implications of existing legal sanctions as they might have appeared to the judges who decided Carrier's Case. The point was argued in the Exchequer Chamber, and the case of a servant was definitely distinguished from that of a bailee, it being agreed that the latter had possession and not mere custody. It must be concluded that this rule played no part in the decision of the case.

Finally, it may be noted that modern scholars agree that trespass as an element of larceny meant, prior to the Carrier's Case, a direct, simple, overt taking from another's possession.[16]

---

[14] "HUSSEY put a question. If a shepherd steals the sheep which are in his charge, or a butler the plate which is in his charge, or servants other things which are in their charge, whether it shall be called felony. And it seemed to him that it would. And he cited a case which was, that a butler had stolen certain stuff which was in his charge, and was hanged for it. HAUGH (J.) cited the case of Adam Goldsmith of London, who had stolen certain stuff which was in his charge, and was hanged for it. BRIAN (C. J.)—It cannot be felony, because he could not take *vi et armis*, because he had charge of it. And the justices were of the same opinion, and so no discussion, etc." Note, Mich. Y. B. 3 Hen. VII, f. 12, pl. 9 (1487).

[15] Hil. Y. B. 21 Hen. VII, f. 14, pl. 21. The point, about which there apparently remained some doubt, was finally settled by 21 Hen. VIII, c. 7 (1529). *Cf.* 1 Hale, P. C. 667; 3 Stephen, H. C. L. 151–2.

[16] "There can we think be little doubt that the 'taking and carrying away', upon which our later law insists, had been from the first the very core of the English idea of theft. 'He stole, took and carried it away': this is the charge made against the thief. The crime involves a violation of possession; it is an

How, in the face of such a definite legal rule, was it possible to hold a bailee guilty of larceny? The judges were too well versed in the law to concur in Hussey's argument that a subsequent taking *animo furandi* (following Bracton) was sufficient. Nor did Vavisour's point that there was "a bargain to take and carry" rather than a bailment, lie any better (except with Laicon, J.).[17] An additional, quite ingenious theory was suggested which finally carried the day for the Crown. Choke J.,[18] advanced this argument:

"I think that where a man has goods in his possession by reason of a bailment he cannot take them feloniously, being in possession; but still it seems here that it is felony, for here the things which were within the bales were not bailed to him, only the bales as an entire thing were bailed *ut supra* to carry; in which case if he had given the bales or sold them etc., it is not felony, but when he broke them and took out of them what was within he did that without warrant, as if one bailed a tun of wine to carry, if the bailee sell the tun it is not felony nor trespass, but if he took some out it is felony; and here the twenty pounds were not bailed to him, and peradventure he knew not of them at the time of the bailment. So is it if I bail the key to my chamber to one to guard my chamber and he

---

offence against a possessor and therefore can never be committed by a possessor." 2 Pollock and Maitland, H. E. L. 498.

"This change of possession has from the earliest times been essential to larceny; so that there can be no larceny where there is no trespass." 3 Holdsworth, H. E. L. 361.

"If there was a delivery by the owner, the opinion of Brian, C. J., is the only one that can be supported on principle." Beale, *op. cit*. 251.

[17] As Professor Beale has suggested, if the carrier took the bales before he was authorized to do so under the agreement, the case might be supported on principle. Beale, *op. cit*. 251.

[18] Little is known about the judges except the steps in their legal careers. About Choke, who provided the principal theories upon which the decision was based, we are told "that he was a useful judge, and did not unnecessarily interfere with the violent politics of the time, may be presumed from his successive reappointments on the temporary restoration of Henry VI in 1470, on the return of Edward IV in the following year, and on the accessions of Edward V and Richard III in 1483. . . .

"By the inquisition taken after his death it appears that besides Long Ashton he possessed several other manors and lands in the same county, and also the manor of Randolveston in Dorcetshire." 4 Foss, Judges of England 486–7.

takes my goods within this chamber, it is felony, for they are not bailed to him."

No comment is reported regarding Choke's argument concerning the contents of the bales. The decision, expressing an attempted reconciliation with precedent, was that "breaking bulk" terminated the carrier's possession and that "where a man has possession and that determines, he can then be felon of the things, as if I bail goods to one to carry to my house, and he bring them to my house and then take them thereout it is felony; for his possession is determined when they were in my house."

Holmes called this "an unnecessary as well as inadequate fiction." "The rule," said he, "comes from the Year Books, and the theory of the Year Books was, that, although the chest was delivered to the bailee, the goods inside of it were not, and this theory was applied to civil as well as criminal cases. The bailor has the power and intent to exclude the bailee from the goods, and therefore may be said to be in possession of them as against the bailee."[19] In any event, it was held that "breaking bulk" terminated the bailment. Somewhat simplified, the theory was that the property at once reverted to the constructive "possession" of the bailor, and the removal of it from the bales supplied the "trespass." By this refinement the door was opened to admit into the law of larceny a whole series of acts which had up to that time been purely civil wrongs.[20] The

[19] The Common Law 224.
Cf. "That [opinion] of Choke J., though it rested upon a rule then well established, seems hardly justified by the facts. It may well be that when a chest is delivered, there is no delivery of the goods within the chest; but this can be true only if the chest is an article of sufficient importance in itself to be the subject of delivery. One cannot say as a matter of fact that bagging in which a bale of goods is wrapped, or paper about a parcel, or twine with which a bundle of clothes is tied, is delivered, while the goods thereby inclosed are not delivered; and these bales appear to have been of that sort. The view of Choke, J., seems, however, now to be the prevailing one, and to have been carried to extreme lengths." (Citing Com. *v.* James, 1 Pick, 375; Reg. *v.* Poyser, 2 Den. C. C. 233.) Beale, *op. cit.* 251.
[20] Professor Beale points out (*id.*) that later treatises did not adopt Choke's rationale but placed the decision upon the more persuasive, though unprecedented, ground that, "There are some tortious acts before the regular completion of a contract, on which goods are delivered, which may determine the priority of it, and amount in law to a new taking from the possession of the owner." 2 East, P. C. 695.

case also provides an illuminating example of legislation by judges who assert that they are applying the principle of *stare decisis* in all its rigor![21] The judicial technique involved in such decisions has been discussed at length.[22]

The discussion has been confined thus far to legal analysis and the traditional professional technique employed in such analysis. Such an approach can only lead to one conclusion—that the decision in a particular case is or is not in accord with precedent. This type of analysis is not designed to explain the *causes* of any departure from precedent or, for that matter, of adherence to precedent. Its function ends when it appears that a departure *exists*. The demonstration that new law has been made is obviously important; but the very assertion that a decision is *new* law is tantamount to alleging that it was not found among existing legal rules or deduced from them.

Modern legal scholars agree that the Carrier's Case was an important innovation in the law of larceny.[23] The difficulty of formulating an objective standard to determine the existence and extent of departure from precedent which any case represents, arises from the fact that it is impossible to fix the meaning of many decisions with a high degree of precision.[24] Moreover, for various reasons, but chiefly because of a felt need to perpetuate traditional theories of the judicial function, the courts almost invariably assume, if their opinions are to be taken at face value, that their decisions necessarily result

---

[21] The ease with which a fiction, once invoked, may be expanded can be seen from an early American case. In Commonwealth *v.* Joel Brown, 4 Tyng. 580 (Mass. 1808), the defendant, who was employed to carry several articles, converted one entire package. The defendant was held guilty on two grounds: first, that he was a servant and not a carrier; and, second, that *by removing one package from several,* he was "breaking bulk."

That the Carrier's Case is very much alive today may be seen in Rupert Cross, *Larceny De Lege Lata* (1950) 66 L. Q. R. 499, and J. Edwards, *Possession and Larceny,* in Current Legal Problems (Keeton and Schwarzenberger eds. 1950) 139.

[22] See Maine, Ancient Law c. 2 and 3; Pound, *Spurious Interpretation* (1907) 7 Col. L. Rev. 379; Pound, Interpretations of Legal History (1923) 131 ff.; L. L. Fuller, *Legal Fictions* (1930–31) 25 Ill. L. Rev. 363, 513, 877.

[23] Stephen writes: "This has always appeared an extraordinary decision.... This [decision] required a deviation from the common law, which was accordingly made." 3 H. C. L. 139. Holdsworth writes: "That this was a departure from principle is obvious." 3 H. E. L. 366. Beale, *op. cit.* 251.

[24] Oliphant, *A Return to Stare Decisis* (1928) 14 A. B. A. J. 73.

from the logical application of prior rules. We have seen the expression of this judicial assumption in the Carrier's Case. Indeed, if this case be read and accepted literally, it represents no change in the law. Trespass was and trespass remained an essential element of the law of larceny. There was a "trespass." *Quod erat demonstrandum!*

As suggested, it may be stated, in general, that a court departs from precedent when it redefines a concept or adopts and introduces into its decision a proposition of law which can neither be found among existing legal rules nor logically derived from them. Clearly, however, the *application* of this standard is difficult because of the infinite variation of facts and the consequent opportunities for expansion or contraction of concepts.[25]

If Carrier's Case represents a purely formal compliance with precedent and a substantial departure from it, our problem becomes more complicated. For we are then confronted by a *change* in law which cannot be explained in terms of precedent and the continuity thereof; by definition, we are seeking to understand a *departure* from, and, in effect, *a renunciation* of precedent.

This type of problem may be approached from many points of view.[26] If we ask the specific question, *why* did Carrier's Case (or any other event) occur when it did, we turn quite naturally for an explanation to the events which *preceded* it.[27] Such explanations have been provided by narratives of events

---

[25] The opinion may be hazarded, however, that, in fact, as a result of the conditioning of legal specialists over a period of many years, a relatively high degree of uniformity (for the purpose in hand) in the interpretation and application of legal rules has been attained. Thus the unanimity of expert opinion regarding the Carrier's Case is evidence of the existence of sufficiently objective criteria to insure a relatively high degree of uniform judgment in many cases. See Hall, General Principles of Criminal Law (1947) 32–50.

[26] *Cf.* Pound, Interpretations of Legal History (1923).

[27] "Answers to questions Why? can only therefore be found in the antecedents of the developments under consideration; and if we want to know why the Reformation took place in the sixteenth century, why America was discovered in 1492, why learning came to its new birth at the end of the fifteenth century, we must search the records of preceding generations." Pollard, Factors in Modern History (1907) 34.

occurring between a chosen point of "origin" and the phenomenon for which an explanation was sought.

Historians have recently broadened the scope of their inquiry to include *thorough* consideration of social, economic,[28] political and religious conditions.[29] This approach is based upon (*a*) the alleged fact that the behavior of any people is, by and large, uniform, standardized, and habitual,[30] and that, as a result, social life may be thought of in terms of "institutions" which denote such behavior; and (*b*) that social change (departures from institutional modes of behavior which are generally recognized as permanent and important) is to be explained as a result of conditions determined by and arising from a large network of institutions which are closely interrelated and the impact of these institutions upon each other. An institutional interpretation of history[31] does not

---

[28] ". . . from the lawyers the historical method passed to the economists." Ashley, English Economic History and Theory, Preface ix.

[29] This raises interesting questions regarding history and sociology. "When he begins to generalize, the historian is no longer a historian, but becomes, in a large way, a sociologist." J. W. Swain, *What Is History?* (1923) 20 J. of Phil. 282.

Cf. "The controversy turns, in first instance, on the question of what is the proper province of the historian; whether History should concern itself only with unique and hence unrepeatable phenomena, or whether it may not also be concerned with studying the underlying forces and influences that condition social growth and which, by their very nature, seem to be constantly operative . . . As a matter of fact, the two points of view are not mutually exclusive. It would seem folly to deny that there are two aspects of the history of man. One consists of the exceptional or extranormal happenings; the other of the common or persistent factors." Schlesinger, *History*, Research in the Social Sciences (Gee, ed. 1929) 227.

And *cf.* Teggart, Theory of History; and R. L. Schuyler, *Law and Accident in History* (1930) 45 Pol. Sci. Quar. 273.

[30] *Cf.* Cooley, Social Organization 313ff.; Allport, Institutional Behavior, and K. N. Llewellyn, *The Constitution As An Institution* (1934) 34 Col. L. Rev. 1.

[31] Three limitations are apparent. (1) The interpretation will obviously be incomplete. All of the facts are not known, and of those which were known at one time, only a few have been recorded. Yet even this very incomplete history which has come down to us is of enormous proportions, despite the disinclination of historians to delve into fifteenth century England. It will, therefore, be necessary to condense the existing, incomplete history very considerably.

(2) History is not only incomplete, but it is also conditioned by accepted ideas about the importance and relevancy of the factors regarded as causal, and by the selection and interpretation of particular data by certain individuals. "But it is the historian in every case who presents the evidence; strive for

ignore human factors but emphasizes common and recurring, rather than infrequent or individual, modes of human behavior.[32]

II. THE POLITICAL CONDITIONS

Carrier's Case was decided in England in 1473. A glance at the political scene immediately preceding Edward IV's accession indicates the nature and extent of the change in government which he introduced. In 1450 Cade's Rebellion occurred. In 1452 the Hundred Years' War terminated with the English driven from France. The War of the Roses started in 1455 and lasted until 1459; then, after a short truce, the

---

impartiality as he may, his presentation and arrangement of the evidence will have something to do with the verdict given." J. W. Swain, *op. cit.* 284. *Cf.* "But even under these auspicious circumstances, with the student seeking objective truth as his only goal, the preconceptions of the age, as well as his own human shortcomings, almost certainly refract the historian's vision and affect the result of his researches." A. M. Schlesinger, *op. cit.* 211. This difficulty is increased in the following discussion due to the fact that an explanation is sought for specific legal developments. This renders it impossible merely to reproduce or summarize sections of the commonly accepted history, but requires a further special selection of data which can be significantly related to the criminal law and Carrier's Case.

(3) Most important is the question, how far does an institutional interpretation of changes in law provide a satisfactory "explanation" of these changes? It would be fatuous to expect an explanation for the *precise form* that changes in the law have taken. It may accordingly be argued that this type of analysis does not *explain* change at all, but merely describes the antecedent and concomitant conditions of change. In any event, all that will be attempted is to discover the *various possibilities for certain changes* in the law which were determined by the conditions established by existing, interrelated, interacting institutions.

[32] It is possible to write a history of law in terms of great judges and lawyers. Such phenomena as dissenting opinions, reversals by upper courts, and other changes *within a short period of time* suggest the operation of individual, unique influences, or at least make such a hypothesis defensible. Certainly it seems clear that judges like Brian, Choke, Coke, Mansfield, and Buller have left many distinctive marks upon the law and have greatly influenced its development. These judges and all the others functioned in a milieu which was determined very largely by existing legal, social, political and economic institutions and their interaction. The interpretation of the law of theft that follows emphasizes this latter aspect of the complex pattern set by the operation of many converging forces. *Cf.* Vinogradoff, *Aims And Methods Of Jurisprudence* (1924) 24 Col. L. Rev. 1; and L. K. Frank, *An Institutional Analysis Of The Law* (1924) 24 Col. L. Rev. 480.

The two views indicated above are represented by Carlyle's Heroes And Hero Worship at one extreme and, at the other, by Tolstoy's War And Peace.

war again broke out and continued intermittently until 1471, when Edward defeated the Lancastrians at Tewkesbury and recaptured the throne. These and many similar events provide the basis for the uniform conclusion of historians of Lancastrian England that the entire period was marked by disorder and discontent.[33] This chaotic condition was due chiefly to the existence of a powerful baronial class which the Lancastrians were impotent to hold in check. That the instability and turbulence of the times affected the administration of the criminal law is also clear. "The livery of a great lord was as effective security to a malefactor as was the benefit of clergy to the criminous clerk." [34] The subserviency of the courts to the militant power of the nobility became a commonplace.[35]

This, then, provides the central basis for contrasting Lancastrian impotence and "administrative anarchy", as Pollard characterized it,[36] with the powerful New Monarchy of Edward. With Edward's victory came the annihilation of Warwick, whom Hume called "the last of the barons", and of the most powerful family in England, except the king's. The Church was reduced to its lowest level of influence; enormous confiscations brought about by wholesale attainders severed the treasury from the will of the Commons. For several years Edward hardly summoned Parliament at all. [37]

So extreme was the concentration of power in the king that several historians have severely condemned his reign as despotism. Green maintains that the liberty from arbitrary government which the English had won over a period of many

[33] For a brief account of the lawlessness during this period, see V. B. Redstone, *England During the War of Roses* 16 (n. s.) Trans. of the Royal Hist. Soc. 186–90.

[34] 3 Stubbs, Constitutional History 533.

[35] "Nothing is more curious than the way in which it is assumed that it is idle to indict a criminal who is maintained by a powerful person; (quoting from 1 Paston Letters 190) 'ther kan no man indyte him for Sir T. Todenham mayteynyth him.'" Plummer, Introduction to Fortescue, The Governance of England 29. See Plummer's Introduction, 20–25, for à description of lawlessness in the fifteenth century.

[36] *Op. cit.* 71.

[37] 1 Innes, A History of England and the British Empire (1913) 461–2.

years was lost at the end of the War of the Roses.[38] Hallam is even bitter. To him "the reign of Edward IV was a reign of terror." [39] "No laws favorable to public liberty, or remedial with respect to the aggressions of power, were enacted, or, so far as appears, even proposed in Parliament during the reign of Edward, the first since John to whom such a remark can be applied." [40]

This leads directly to the next factor to be considered, namely, the relationship of the judges to the Crown. The sharp struggle for independence of the judiciary and the supremacy of law did not arise until a century and a half later in Coke's desperate battle with James over Peacham's Case. There had been, to be sure, an occasional expression of discontent by a courageous judge; and we are told that Sir William Hussey, who had represented the Crown in the Carrier's Case, "in the first year of this reign [Henry VII's] successfully protested against the King's practice of consulting the judge beforehand upon Crown cases which they were subsequently to try." [41] Coke was dismissed in 1614, and the Crown's practice of "consulting" the judges beforehand continued for a long time after that.[42] Indeed, contemporary sources reveal Edward's domination of public officials generally. Thus, Charles Plummer, relying on the Paston Letters,[43] declares that occasionally royal letters were sent to justices or to sheriffs ordering them to show favor to a particular person.[44]

---

[38] "Parliamentary life was almost superceded, or was turned into a mere form by the overpowering influence of the Crown. The legislative powers of the two Houses were usurped by the royal Council.

"The old English kingship, limited by the forces of feudalism or of the religious sanctions wielded by the priesthood, or by the progress of constitutional freedom, faded suddenly away, and in its place we see, all-absorbing and unrestrained, the despotism of the new Monarchy." J. R. Green, A Short History of the English People (1899) 290.

[39] 3 Constitutional History 198.

[40] 1 Id. 10.

[41] Y. B. 1 Hen. VII. p. 26, quoted in Foss, Lives of the Judges.

[42] Independent judges were dismissed. This was the fate of Crew in 1626, of Walter in 1629, and of Heath in 1634.

[43] Vol. 3, 428.

[44] Op. cit. 22.

Cf. "He (Edward) also exercised very freely what was called the dispensing

Green, whose dislike of the new despotism militates against his impartiality, declaims against the degradation of justice brought about by "servility of the judges, [and] by the coercion of the juries." [45] He charges that "it was to Edward that his Tudor successors owed the introduction of an elaborate spy system, the use of the rack, and the practice of interfering with the purity of justice." [46]

The Carrier's Case was heard first in the Star Chamber [47] and later in the Exchequer; conceivably, the judges in these august tribunals might have been free from royal interference. On the contrary, we are informed on every hand that Edward reduced the formerly powerful Council to complete subservience to his wishes. The inclusive and undifferentiated function of this tribunal,[48] the special interests of the Crown together with the relations that existed between the judges of the Star

---

power, that is the power to suspend the law in certain cases, and in other ways asserted the royal prerogative as no previous king had done for two hundred years." Cheyney, An Introduction to the Industrial and Social History of England (1916) 137.

[45] Op. cit. 290.

[46] Id. 293, and 3 Stubbs, op. cit. 282.

Cora L. Scofield, the biographer of Edward, supplies additional evidence which leaves little doubt regarding Edward's domination of his judges: "The day came when Edward disgraced himself by dismissing a man whom he should have rewarded, not punished, for the fearless stand he had taken on behalf of justice and right. Chief Justice Markham's only offense consisted in charging the jury to bring a less severe verdict against Sir Thomas Cook than was desired. . . . he lost his office. Again, the trial of Burdett, Stacy and Blake in 1477 is painful evidence how far it lay within the power of the king to control the courts and to pervert justice to serve his own ends . . . and evidently it was not merely in such important cases as that of Burdett, Stacy and Blake that Edward stooped to interfere." 2 The Life and Reign of Edward the Fourth (1923) 372–3.

[47] "It is, indeed, perhaps not generally known, that crimes of a very ordinary nature, such as would now come before a police magistrate, occupied the attention of the Star Chamber. Charges of robbery, murder, sheep stealing, theft . . . were investigated by Councillors." Dicey, The Privy Council (1887) 105, and cf. 56–62.

"The jurisdiction of the Council was not, however, confined to cases in equity or cases in error. It exercised original jurisdiction over cases which specially concerned the King, or which exceeded the competency of the ordinary courts." Scofield, A Study of the Court of Star Chamber (1900) xxv.

[48] Dicey selects as "the most characteristic feature of the period . . . the inseparable combination in the Council of political and judicial authority." Op. cit. 106.

, the king, and his chief representative, the Chancel-
the likelihood of royal control extremely probable.
accept the opinion of the leading authority on the
subject, that, "Instead of a ruling or guiding council there was
at every step an emphasis of the royal authority." [49]

The above changes, ushered in with the Yorkist reign,
present nothing short of a profound transformation in both
the state and the judiciary. This in itself might provide, for
some purposes, a sufficient explanation of the decision of the
judges in the Carrier's Case. Indeed, so great a master of the
criminal law as Stephen, in commenting upon Carrier's Case
asserts, "I think it obvious from the report that the decision
was a compromise intended to propitiate the chancellor, and
perhaps the king." [50]

The "will of the king" long provided a sufficient explanation
of the conduct of the king's servants. The "new" history,
reflecting social and economic evolution, has broadened the
range of investigation and secured acceptance of the necessity
for dealing with a more varied and complex aggregate of
phenomena. Even if the essential technique is the same as
that found in the older history, its emphasis upon social and
economic data and, more important yet, the concomitant
changes in thought which are reflected by this literature, compel us to push the quest further if an explanation which will
more adequately satisfy current intellectual requirements is to
be had.

III. The Economic Conditions

We find, on comparison of the Year Book report with Pollock
and Wright's translation of it, [51] which has been generally followed, that two very important parts of the judges' opinions

---

[49] Baldwin, The King's Council in England During the Middle Ages 426.
[50] 3 H. C. L. 139.
  Cf. ". . . the judges, perhaps to please the king . . . reported to the
chancellor . . . that it was felony." 3 Holdsworth, H. E. L. 366.
[51] Possession In The Common Law (1888) 134–7.

have been ignored. The first is contained in the statement by the chancellor that "This is the case of an alien merchant *who comes here with a safe conduct.*" The portion italicized is omitted by Pollock and Wright. The second passage is the last paragraph in the decision (all of which is omitted by Pollock and Wright), which supplements the above as follows:

"And though it is a felony the goods may not be claimed as waifs, for it appears here that the man who demands the goods here is a foreigner, and the King has granted him 'safe and sure conduct for himself and his goods', which is a covenant between him and the King. Hence if a felon takes his goods that is no reason why this foreigner should lose them, leaving him only his right to sue the felon, but he may sue the King on this covenant. And thus it seems that the King himself may not have such goods as waifs, and for the same reason he may not grant them to another person, nor may another person claim them by prescription. And note the case was such that the Sheriff of London claimed these goods as waifs, etc., and alleged a prescription to have waifs, etc."

It appears, also, that it was certain "bales" which were broken into, but the contents of the bales are nowhere stated. The only significant remark was that of Choke J., who said that "the twenty pounds were not bailed to him." Lastly, it is reported that the bales were to be carried to Southampton.

We have, therefore, the following intrinsic, specific information to suggest further exploration, namely, that

1. the complainant was an alien merchant;

2. he had a covenant with the king which provided safe passage for him and his goods;

3. the property taken is described as being within bales, and as weighing twenty pounds;

4. the defendant was a carrier;

5. and he was to deliver the merchandise at Southampton.

In order to strike the general note which, in a word, characterizes much of the following interpretation, it is necessary to recall that one of the most important movements in all of modern history was taking place during this time, namely, the Renaissance.[52] It is not necessary to decide with reference to the thesis here presented whether the Renaissance was a rebirth of the old learning or whether, on the contrary, it represented a decline from the achievements of mediæval scholarship. In either event, it is the revolutionary changes in social institutions which are significant.

Despite the continuity of historical processes, it is possible to recognize certain periods of accelerated social change, and thus to fix an important point in the early development of the Renaissance at the middle of the fifteenth century. Mediæval Europe was being transformed into a relatively modern Europe. Commerce was undergoing radical change along with the rest of the older culture.[53] Many historians select the capture of Constantinople by the Turks in 1453 as the most apt date for the commencement of modern history, while others emphasize the discovery of America. Although all such specifications are somewhat arbitrary, it is defensible, nevertheless, to contrast the essential character of the mediæval world with that of the modern world, and conclude that there are several reasons "why modern history as distinct from mediæval, begins towards the end of the fifteenth century." [54]

A mass of data supports this view. In England the economy of the middle ages was almost exclusively agricultural and rural.[55] "At the time of the great Survey there were hardly any

---

[52] "One cannot say when the Middle Ages gave way to the Renaissance. Indeed, in some respects, the Middle Ages are not over yet. . . . So, one must not expect to find the Renaissance, or any other important era, inaugurated by a striking event or a violent revolution. Only very gradually did the new dispensation take form and shape." E. M. Hulme, The Renaissance, The Protestant Revolution and The Catholic Reformation in Continental Europe (1914) 3.

[53] "Rational commerce is the field in which quantitative reckoning first appeared, to become dominant finally over the whole extent of economic life. . . .

"The first books on computation usable by merchants come from the 15th century, the older literature, going back to the 13th, not being popular enough." Max Weber, General Economic History (Knight's transl.) 223.

[54] Pollard, op. cit. 31.

[55] "Till nearly the end of the fourteenth century, England was a purely agricultural country. Such manufactures as it possessed were entirely for consumption within the land; and for goods of the finer qualities it was dependent

commercial towns." [56] By the fifteenth century, however, a series of important changes had become manifest.[57] Thus, "in the time of Edward III the wealth of England still consisted mainly in raw products, and her industry was but little advanced, but in the fifteenth century manufacturing was springing up in every town." [58] With the growth of manufacturing in the fifteenth century came marked changes in the manorial system and numerous departures from its mediæval form. Came also the decay of serfdom and the rise of a new class of tenants whose rights were gradually recognized by the courts. But most important of all is the fact that during this period the old feudal relationships gave way before a rising middle class which owed its influence to the development of a rapidly expanding industry and trade.[59] For example, in the middle of the fourteenth century there were only 169 important merchants, but at the beginning of the sixteenth century there were more than 3000 merchants engaged in foreign trade alone.[60] We may summarize these tremendously important fifteenth century changes by quoting the scholarly editors of a detailed study on this period:

---

on importation from abroad. The only articles of export were the raw products of the country, and of these by far the most important was the agricultural product, wool. To understand, therefore, the life of rural England during this period, is to understand nine-tenths of its economic activity." Ashley, An Introduction to English Economic History and Theory (3rd ed. 1894) 5–6.

[56] "Even in a place like Cambridge, which had a fairly advanced municipal life, the burgesses were engaged in rural pursuits . . . the people of the towns were still engaged in agriculture." 1 Cunningham, The Growth of English Industry and Commerce (1910) 3.

[57] "Old institutions of every kind, in town and country, were falling to pieces; new attempts were being made to regulate industry and encourage commerce." Id. 459.

[58] A. Abram, Social England in the Fifteenth Century (1909) 1.

[59] "Now, the industrial and commercial system of modern history requires two factors which feudalism did not provide; it requires a middle class and it requires an urban population. Without these two there would have been little to distinguish modern from mediæval history. Without commerce and industry, there can be no middle class; where you had no middle class you had no Renaissance and no Reformation."

"So in one way or another, before the end of the fifteenth century a new middle class, a new social force had been created, and this force is one of the greatest factors in the making of modern history." Pollard, op. cit. 41, 48. Cf. 1 Cunningham, op. cit. 387.

[60] Cheyney, op. cit. 162.

"It was obviously in the course of the later middle ages, and more particularly in the fifteenth century, that there took place the great transformation from mediæval England, isolated and intensely local, to the England of the Tudor and Stuart age, with its world-wide connections and imperial designs. It was during the same period that most of the forms of international trade characteristic of the middle ages were replaced by methods of commercial organization and regulation, national in scope and at times definitely nationalistic in object, and that a marked movement towards capitalist methods and principles took place in the sphere of domestic trade." [61]

The cumulative effect of the new economic organization of society and the changed political institutions, already described, becomes clear upon the presentation of certain interesting facts. Indeed, so interrelated are the institutions of any period that it would be remarkable if there were no connection between the Crown and the new mercantile class. Our expectations in this regard are more than fulfilled, for we are informed that "Philip de Commines says that Edward IV owed his restoration to the aid of the rich burgesses of London, and however this may be, it is certain that he depended largely upon the support of the traders and merchants, and favored them greatly . . ." [62] Apparently Edward realized "that Richard (II's) failure to protect English shipping alienated the merchants from his side." [63] Certainly Edward cultivated the business interests assiduously.

It may, however, be objected that the merchant in Carrier's Case was an alien. We are led, therefore, both by the internal evidence in the case and the importance of the question, to an

---

[61] Studies in English Trade in the Fifteenth Century (ed. Eileen Power and M. M. Posten, 1933) xvii.

[62] Abram, *op. cit.* 212.

[63] 1 Cunningham, *op. cit.* 409.

". . . the weak Lancastrian sovereign, Henry VI, took little thought of commerce, with the result that in the ensuing Wars of the Roses, London and the other leading commercial cities were on the side of the Yorkists . . . Thus Edward IV was the first avowedly mercantilist King of England." S. A. Cudmore, History of the World's Commerce (1929) 124.

examination of English foreign trade in the fifteenth century.[64]

As a matter of fact, in the middle of the fifteenth century feeling was very strong against alien merchants. Frequent repressive measures were taken against them. So numerous and skillful were they that local traders felt themselves unable to compete successfully. The complaint was made in 1455 that " 'merchant strangers Italians' bought woolen cloth, wool, woolfells and tin in every port of the kingdom with ready money, and so made their purchases at reduced prices." [65] Bitter attacks against the foreign traders were common. Hostility rose to the point where riots occurred, stimulated by rival merchants; [66] many Italians were assaulted in 1456 and 1457. This was followed by threatened withdrawal of all relations and a decree of the Italian Senate prohibiting trade with London.[67]

The general insecurity of the times made any transportation hazardous.[68] The special risks to which the alien merchant was subjected gave rise to the royal practice of issuing formally executed covenants of safe conduct through the realm.[69] The

---

[64] See Studies in English Trade in the Fifteenth Century (1933, ed. E. Power and M. M. Posten).

[65] Quoted by 1 Lipson, *op. cit.* 469–70.
"Regarding Italian merchants the 'libille' complains that they brought in trifles and take away 'oure best chaffore, clothe, wolle, and tynne.'" Quoted by Abram, *op. cit.* 36.

[66] 1 Lipson, *op. cit.* 463.

[67] *Id.* 470.

[68] "Even recognized associations of merchants frequently indulged in practices which can only be characterized as piracy. Commerce, in fact, was deeply imbued with the spirit of lawlessness, and in these circumstances it is probable that the depredations of pirates did not excite the same alarm nor discourage trade in the same degree as would be the case in more law-abiding times." 2 Traill, Social England 337–8.

[69] "The merchants of Venice complained that they dare not avail themselves of the permission to resort to England, unless they had a special safe-conduct as well. The existence of a commercial treaty, therefore, was no guarantee that merchants would be allowed to pursue their calling unmolested." *Id.* 404.
Cf. "The requirements to which these relations gave rise among the merchants, looked first in the direction of personal protection. Occasionally this provision took on a sacerdotal character, the foreign merchant being placed under the protection of the gods or of the chieftain. Another form was the conclusion of safe conduct agreements with the political powers of the reign, as in upper Italy during the middle ages. . . .
"The second great requirement of commerce was legal protection. The merchant was an alien and would not have the same legal opportunities as a

extraordinary importance of the covenant of safe conduct is indicated by the holding in Carrier's Case denying the Crown's right to waif—this by the king's judges sitting in the king's court and applying the king's law! In two reports of Carrier's Case, other than the principal one given in the Year Book, emphasis is placed on the safe conduct. Kelyng writes, "a merchant alien, who has the king's *securum e salvum conductum tam in corpore quam in bonis*;" [70] and Richard Crompton dwelt upon the fact that "a Merchant Stranger (which) came into England by the King's safe conduct." [71]

The combined force of the hazards of transporting goods and of attacks on alien merchants was unable to stem the tide of foreign trade. [72] Indeed, "the rise in English foreign trade, and the consequent interest in national shipping, distinguishes the fifteenth from any previous century." [73] Numerous commercial treaties were made during this period; [74] and the Merchant Adventurers who had secured their charter in 1407 were already enjoying a large international trade and had become wealthy and influential. [75]

---

member of the nation or tribe, and therefore required special legal arrangements." Weber, *op. cit.* 212.

In England, as long ago as Magna Charta, c. 30, "safe and sure Conduct" was assured to foreign merchants.

[70] 145 Eng. Rep. 92.

[71] Crompton reports further, "And it seemeth by the booke that a Merchant shall not loose the Merchandizes, because hee comes hither with the kings safe conduct *ut supra*, 13 *Ed.* 4. 9. And it is said there that it was adjudged that notwithstanding the statute which giveth that the safe conduct shall be enrolled, and the number of the Marryners, and the name of the ship, that where safe conduct is, and hath not his due circumstances according to this, yet it shall be allowed, for Aliens say that they are not bound to know our statutes for they come by reason of the Kings privy Seale upon his safe conduct: . . . It is held by the Chancellor in the first case, that a Merchant stranger which comes by safe conduct is not bound to sue by the Law of the Land, to try a thing by twelve men, but that it shall bee determined according to the Law of nature, in the Chancery." Star Chamber Cases, reprinted from the Edition of 1630 or 1641 (Soule and Bugbee, 1881) 51–2.

[72] "Notwithstanding this drawback, however, there can be no doubt that trading connections increased in number, and that greater uniformity and equality of commercial privileges was the outcome of the numerous commercial treaties between the countries of Europe." 2 Traill, *op. cit.* 404.

[73] Abram, *op. cit.* 31.

[74] 1 Cunningham, *op. cit.* 414.

[75] 2 Traill, *op. cit.* 401.

This trade was stimulated by the king's cordiality to foreign traders. Two instances are especially suggestive. First is his relationship to the Hanse. In 1465 Edward accepted from the Hanse "a present of a large sum of money for the renewal of their charter" to deal in wool export.[76] The Crown's usual financial distress made such "loans", as they were called, attractive to Edward and profitable for the Hanse. This did not stop the constant altercations between the Hanseatic League and English merchants which culminated in 1468 in the cessation of all trade and in actual war. Edward's loss of the throne and his subsequent efforts to regain it gave the Hanse the greatest possible opportunity for expanding its commerce. Appraising the situation with excellent business acumen, the Hanse merchants rallied to Edward's support. "When Edward in his turn began to plan an expedition to England, he was able to do so with the assistance of the Hanse . . . it was on Hanseatic boats and under Hanseatic escort that Edward sailed to England, there to resume the war and to emerge victorious on the battlefield of Barnet. For these services he promised to satisfy the Hanseatic complaints and demands, and these services were alleged as the official motive for the far-reaching concessions made to the Hanse at the conference at Utrecht."[77] Negotiations between the English Crown and the Hanse were begun in 1472,[78] and in 1474 the Treaty of Utrecht restored full privileges to the Hanseatic traders with the understanding that English merchants would be permitted to trade in the dominions of the League. Accordingly, if the merchant in Carrier's Case was a Hanseatic trader, his case could hardly have been heard at a more favorable time. Edward was under heavy obligations to the Hanse; he needed and desired their good will; he had established friendly contacts with them, and he was anxious for the success of the pending negotiations to renew commercial intercourse.

---

[76] M. Dobb, Capitalist Enterprise and Social Progress 256.
[77] M. M. Posten, op. cit. 136.
Cf. 1 Lipson, op. cit. 497; 1 Cunningham, op. cit. 422.
[78] M. M. Posten, op. cit. 136.

The bales in question were, however, to be carried to South-ampton. This city had commanded the trade with the Latin countries for many years. It "was the chief port on the south coast, and the great emporium for imported wines and mis-cellaneous goods." [79] As far back as 1297 an ordinance had "enjoined that wool and other merchandise should have no passage out of the realm save at the following ports . . . Southampton where collectors of customs were appointed." [80] The likelihood, therefore, that the merchant in Carrier's Case was Italian is further supported by the fact that the Italians concentrated their trade in Southampton. After the riots of 1456 and 1457, the Venetians, Genoese, and Florentines decided to cease trade with London; prior to that, "a Genoese mer-chant urged upon the king to make Southampton the seat of traffic, and was assassinated through the jealousy of the Lon-don traders." [81] Italian merchants and financiers were very numerous in England during this period, and they had become so firmly entrenched [82] that they dominated English finance for centuries. [83] The history of the period is replete with recitals

---

[79] Abram, op. cit. 50.

Cf. 1 Cunningham, op. cit. 425–6; and J. S. Davies, A History of South-ampton (1883) 250–1, 254, 255.

"The stately vessels of Venice and Genoa, bringing the luxuries of the Mediterranean and of the Far East to the shores of England, there to exchange them for her more homely wares—wool and tin and cloth—deigned not to visit Bristol. In London, in Southampton and in Sandwich they unloaded silks and . . . and there they were privileged to ship staple English goods to southern Europe and the Levant." E. M. Carus Wilson, The Overseas Trade of Bristol, in Studies in English Trade in the Fifteenth Century (Power and Posten ed.) 224.

[80] Quoted by 1 Lipson, op. cit. 472.

[81] 1 Lipson, op. cit. 462–3.

[82] "The Florentine branches (of the Medici) in Bruges and London had from early days been closely connected. As late as 1470 Benedetto Dei says of them: 'They rule these lands, having in their hands the lease of the trade in wool and alum and all the other state revenues, and from thence they do business in exchange with every market in the world, but chiefly with Rome, where they make great gains.' This statement is rather boastful, but we have evidence from other sources as to the continued predominance at this time of the Florentine financiers both in England and the Netherlands." R. Ehren-berg, Capital and Finance in the Age of the Renaissance 196.

[83] Tawney, writing even of the middle of the sixteenth century, states: "But financial business continued to be largely in the hands of Italians.

of transactions between the king and the Italian traders.[84]
Edward's obligations and his intimacy with them resulted in
the grant of many privileges.[85] Accordingly, whether the merchant in Carrier's Case was a Hanseatic trader or, as seems
more likely, an Italian (and these two groups were practically
the only foreign traders in England at the time), royal support might well have been forthcoming.

But Edward's interest in commerce was not a purely personal one arising from his need for financial support; indeed,
his greatest reputation lies as much in his intelligent encouragement of trade [86] as in his arbitrary rule. The most important legislation passed during his reign was commercial, and
the treaties he concluded to facilitate trade were numerous.
It was to be expected that a king who was so definitely and

When in 1553, Cecil prepared a programme for controlling the exchanges,
what he emphasized most was the necessity of keeping a tight hold on the
Italians who 'go to and fro and serve all princes at once . . . work what
they list and lick the fat from our beards.'" *Introduction* to Wilson's Discourse Upon Usury 64.

[84] "The commercial and political dignity of the family of Medici was now
supported by Lorenzo the Magnificent, the grandson of Cosmo. King Edward,
who was perpetually in want of money, had now borrowed £5000 from him
and his brother Guiliano, together with Thomas Portunary, and others, stiled
merchants of Florence, probably agents of the Medici, for which, as usual,
he gave an assignment upon the customs to fall due." (692.)

". . . Quanvese, one of Cosmo's agents was the chief instrument in supporting Edward IV by furnishing him at a time above 120,000 crowns. . . .
(Portunary) another of Cosmo's agents . . . became security for King Edward to the duke of Burgundy for 50,000 crowns and at another time for
24,000. Comines' hint of the damage sustained by delay of payment is supported by a grant of King Edward, dated 30th November 1466, whereby it
appears that £5,254:19:10 of the money lent him by Gerald Camzian (whom
Comines calls Quanvese) still remained due for payment of which Edward
permitted him to berd, clock and clean, any wool whatsoever, and export it,
or any other wool, to the Mediterranean, and also to export woven cloth, in
grain or without grain, to any country whatever, and to retain in his own
hands all the customs . . . till they should amount to the sum owing to him
. . . (Rymer's unpublished records, Edw. IV, Vol. 1, 467.) . . . Edward
was forever borrowing; and we shall again find him receiving further supplies
from the house of Medici." 1 Macpherson, Annals of Commerce (1805) 677-8.

[85] "They enjoyed very special privileges about arrest for debt and in regard
to the tribunals before which they should plead." 1 Cunningham, *op. cit.*
425-6.

[86] "The practical interest of Edward IV in trade is familiar", writes C. K.
Kingsford, Prejudice and Promise in XVth Century England (1925) 124.

so greatly indebted to mercantile interests, both native and foreign, would be sympathetic to these interests; but that he should bring considerable ability to his participation in the economic life of the country and that he should persistently foster its development were rare qualities in an English monarch.

There was still another reason, important and unusual, for Edward's close attention to business matters: he was himself a merchant, carrying on many private ventures. The Croyland Chronicle reports his activities in this direction: "Having procured merchant ships, he put on board of them the finest wools, cloths, tin, and other products of the kingdom, and like one of those who lived by trade, did exchange merchandise for merchandise by means of agents both among Italians and Greeks." [87] In most of these business transactions, which appear to have been numerous, Edward employed foreign factors to represent him.[88] Some of the highest officials in the land, including George Neville, Bishop of Exeter and Chancellor of England, likewise engaged in private foreign trade.[89] However, not Neville but Booth was the solicitous chancellor

---

[87] Quoted by Vickers, England in the Later Middle Ages 483, who also writes, "Despite the splendour of his court and his delight in costly trappings, he was the first English King for many a long year to die free of debt." *Ibid.*

[88] "In this age it was customary for sovereigns to be concerned in merchandize. . . . But King Edward went beyond all the contemporary sovereigns in commercial transactions: he owned several vessels, and like a man whose living depended upon his merchandize, 'exported the finest wool, cloth, tin, and the other commodities of the kingdom to Italy and Greece, and imported their produce in return by the agency of factors or supercargoes.' . . . But the trade of these royal merchants, when they carried it to a great extent, as King Edward actually did, must have been very oppressive to the real merchants, who could not possibly compete with rivals, who paid no customs, and had the national force to protect their trading speculations." 1 Macpherson, *op. cit.* 695.

If we were interested in explaining Carrier's Case in terms of specific events which preceded it, instead of in terms of the changing institutions of the times, the report of a certain transaction of Edward IV would be most intriguing, for we are informed "that a carrack sailing from Southampton on 30th April, 1473, carried 114½ sacks and 13 cloves of wool which belonged either to Edward or his mother, whose attorney Peter de Casasse, made the shipment. . . ." Scofield, *op. cit.* 411. Here, by a curious turn of circumstances we have almost all of the facts in Carrier's Case: a foreign merchant (the factor), a shipment of wool, from Southampton, and in 1473.

[89] 2 Scofield, *op. cit.* 419.

in Carrier's Case who argued that the "alien merchant . . . is not bound to sue according to the law of the land nor await the trial of twelve men nor other formalities of the law of the land, but should sue here where it will be determined in chancery according to the law of nature." [90]

A final inquiry, projected from the internal evidence of the case itself, adds considerable weight to the conclusions reached thus far. What, in fact, was the merchandise taken? In none of the reports of the case do we find this stated, probably because the goods were so common that it was thought unnecessary even to name them. The Year Book report simply noted "certain bales with etc. and other things." In Choke's opinion, however, we have a clue in the remark that "the twenty pounds were not bailed to him."

The principal articles of trade at this time were wool, cloth, hides and tin. Tin would hardly have been packed in bales; nor is it likely, even from the bit of internal evidence regarding the merchandise taken, that hides were contained therein. A case heard before the King's Council in 1439 [91] is suggestive in this connection. John Forde, the defendant, on examination confessed that he attempted to evade customs duties by disguising his shipment "so that it would be appraised by all as a pack of woolen cloth and not of any wool." Certain similarities in the case are strikingly parallel. Forde had sold the merchandise to a foreign trader and had employed a carrier to deliver it. He described his method of . . . "binding together the said pack all around with linen cloth *after the fashion of packs of woolen (goods)* so that" etc. All this fits in well with the reference to the merchandise in Carrier's Case being in *"bales"*, a Norman-French word which might with equal propriety have been translated as "packs." [92] The

---

[90] *Cf.* "Frequently petitioners (foreign merchants) declared that juries had been unfair to them. Francis Dore, merchant of Genoa, stated that the jurors said they would credit no Lombard." Quoted by Abram, *op. cit.* 47, from Early Chancery Proceedings, etc.

[91] Sel. Soc. Select Cases Before the King's Council, 1243–1482 at 103–4.

[92] "Bale, ball, *a pack, a bale.*

"Ballots, *little packs*" Robert Kelham, A Dictionary of the Norman or Old French Language (1779) 27.

weight of the goods taken (twenty pounds) lends additional support to this view.

The relevant extrinsic evidence strongly reënforces the conclusion that wool, cloth, or both, were the goods taken from the bales in Carrier's Case. So overwhelming in quantity was the trade in wool and cloth that the probabilities are enormously in this direction. Raw wool was the leading commodity of trade in England since at least Norman times,[93] and English cloth had been exported as early as 1265.[94] The Merchant Adventurers, the principal organization of its type for many years, engaged exclusively in the exportation of woolen cloth.[95] The expansion of the wool industry was by no means uniform; a definite depression started in the early part of the fourteenth century.[96] By the middle of the fifteenth century, however, business had revived,[97] the manufacture of cloth had become well established, and the entire textile industry was expanding very rapidly. "There is abundance of evidence to show that the manufacture of cloth had increased with such extraordinary rapidity, that it had grown to be a very important trade . . . the one industry which was already organized on modern lines was flourishing greatly . . ."[98] With this development came the familiar concomitants of business enterprise—the use of large amounts of capital and of credit facilities,[99] the appearance of numerous middlemen, a division of labor, the employment of hundreds of persons

---

"Bale, a Pack, or quantity of Goods or Merchandise, as a *Bale* of Silk, Cloth, etc. the word is used in 16 R. 2 Chap. 1 and still in use." Th. Manley, The Interpreter (of) Words and Terms Etc. (1684), first compiled by Dr. Cowel.

[93] 1 Cunningham, *op. cit.* 2.
[94] 2 Traill, *op. cit.* 399.
[95] *Id.* 401.
[96] 1 Lipson, *op. cit.* 397.
[97] Kingsford, *op. cit.* 124.
[98] 1 Cunningham, *op.* cit. 434, 439.
". . . the conditions of the English cloth trade facilitated the growth of capitalism on a large scale, and opened up a new stage in the evolution of industrial organization." 1 Lipson, *op. cit.* 412.
[99] "A wool-exporting firm, like the Celys in the fifteenth century, bought from the growers on six months' credit, and paid them when the wool was sold abroad." Tawney, *op. cit.* 46.

by single firms, and the growth of industrial urban areas which penetrated into the rural districts.[1]

Of cumulative significance are the records of the export of wool and cloth in very large quantities from Southampton.[2] They show that this city was one of the most important ports for the shipment of these goods. The conclusion that the merchandise taken in Carrier's Case was very probably wool or cloth means no less than that *the interests of the most important industry in England were involved in the case.*

Transportation of merchandise in England developed alongside of the expanding commerce. But the carrying trade was crude and unreliable.[3] The need for regulation and for raising the standards of honesty resulted from the increasing necessity of the merchants to rely upon professional carriers rather than upon their own servants. Entirely apart from any personal pressure brought by the Crown, the interests of English and foreign merchants were identical in so far as security of transportation of goods was concerned.

IV. THE CONJUNCTION OF LEGAL SANCTIONS WITH POLITICAL AND ECONOMIC CONDITIONS

There is reason to believe, indeed, that a foreign merchant stood in an especially favorable legal position. For, during this period, as we have seen, except for the emerging rule regarding theft by a servant (based upon his having mere custody), the common law recognized no criminality in a person who came legally into possession of property and later converted it. Apparently it was thought that the owner should have protected himself by selecting a trustworthy person. Since, presumably, this could readily be done, the owner must

---

[1] 2 Traill, *op. cit.* 399.

[2] See *Tables of Enrolled Customs and Subsidy Accounts 1399 to 1482*, Power and Posten, *op. cit.* 356–8.

[3] "This last letter Makyn sent by the Oxford carrier (about 1465) by whom he desired Marchall to send back 40s. However, he was not too trustful of such a conveyance, so he bade Marchall 'buy a pound of powdered pepper to carry the money privily or else two pounds of rice, for that makes great bulk.'" Quoted by Kingsford, *op. cit.* 33.

have been negligent if he delivered his property to a person who absconded with it. An alien merchant, however, would obviously be handicapped in his selection of a carrier whom he did not know, but with whom he was compelled to deal nonetheless. The situation made the application of the common law rule a hardship, and this may have suggested the chancellor's observation that a foreign merchant "is not bound to sue according to the law of the land. . . ." [4] Moreover, the civil liability of a carrier in the early common law was absolute.[5] He was virtually held to be liable as though he were an insurer, and this principle of stringent civil liability might have operated to extend criminal liability. In any event, the fact that the carrier followed a public calling would stimulate efforts to penalize him.

The state of the common law in 1473 explains the direction in which the departure from precedent was made. In the absence of any other even remotely relevant sanction in the criminal law, the only choice was—guilty of larceny or not guilty of any offense.[6]

But it may be a matter of some wonder why the change in law did not come from the legislature rather than from a court which was compelled to disguise its decision in fictitious terms in order to save the face of the existing doctrine. The respective roles of court and legislature in the creation of new law will be discussed later.[7] Here it must suffice to recall

---

[4] "The chancellor, who seems to have had regard rather to the position of the owner of the goods than to the criminality of the carrier, seems to have wished to make the matter turn upon the moral character of the act of misappropriation." 3 Stephen, H. C. L. 139–40.

[5] "The extraordinary liability of a common carrier of goods is an anomaly in our law." Joseph Beale, *The Carrier's Liability: Its History* (1897) 11 Harv. L. Rev. 158–68; *cf.* Holmes, The Common Law, Lecture V; and G. M. Fletcher, The Carrier's Liability (1932) esp. 2, 13, 21, 25–6.

"One outstanding feature of bailment as soon as English law emerged from the realm of speculation was the absolute liability of a bailee to answer to the bailor for the thing bailed. This feature was common to all forms of bailment, and its existence in the period of the Norman Conquest is generally assumed. It is more doubtful whether the rule had any clear continuous history throughout the 13th, 14th and 15th centuries." Fletcher, *op. cit.* 2.

[6] See Chapter Two for the development of embezzlement.

[7] Chapters Three and Four.

first, that Edward rarely summoned Parliament; second, that the sharp distinctions we are accustomed to draw regarding a division of powers cannot be applied accurately to the political instrumentalities of fifteenth century England; and, lastly, that the method actually used was, because of the relationship between the Crown and the Star Chamber, by far the simplest.

We are now in a position to visualize the case and the problem presented to the judges as a result of the legal, political, and economic conditions described above. On the one hand, the criminal law at the time is clear. On the other hand, the whole complex aggregate of political and economic conditions described above thrusts itself upon the court. The more powerful forces prevailed—that happened which in due course must have happened under the circumstances. The most powerful forces of the time were interrelated very intimately and at many points: the New Monarchy and the *nouveau riche*—the mercantile class; the business interests of both and the consequent need for a secure carrying trade; the wool and textile industry, the most valuable, by far, in all the realm; wool and cloth, the most important exports; these exports and the foreign trade; this trade and Southampton, chief trading city with the Latin countries for centuries; the numerous and very influential Italian merchants who bought English wool and cloth inland and shipped them from Southampton. The great forces of an emerging modern world, represented in the above phenomena, necessitated the elimination of a formula which had outgrown its usefulness. A new set of major institutions required a new rule. The law, lagging behind the needs of the times, was brought into more harmonious relationship with the other institutions by the decision rendered in the Carrier's Case.

CHAPTER TWO

THE GROWTH OF THE LAW OF THEFT IN THE EIGHTEENTH CENTURY

I. THE COURSE OF THE LAW AS AFFECTED BY THE EXISTING LEGAL SANCTIONS

Except for Carrier's Case and two important developments in the early sixteenth century, which will be described shortly, practically the entire modern law of theft has been a product of the eighteenth century.[1] There were, of course, many intervening developments both in law and in the output of professional literature. But growth in the eighteenth century is so accelerated that it protrudes conspicuously from the pattern of the whole course of the criminal law. Not only does the eighteenth century loom up in the number of new laws[2] and the amount and quality of legal literature produced,[3] but also as regards the nature of the changes which occurred. For it is in this century that one comes upon the law of receiving

---

[1] Dr. Leon Radzinowicz' History of English Criminal Law and its Administration from 1750 (1948) provides excellent detailed descriptions of subjects treated in Chapters 2, 3, and 4 of this book.

[2] "Thus, then, stands the case—A century has passed away, marked by nothing so extraordinary in our legislation, as the rapid growth of criminal laws. In that century, the criminal law of England has increased to fourfold dimensions. Of the twenty bulky volumes of the statutes on your table, three contain the statutes prior to the year 1700; for all the rest, we are indebted to the industrious spirit of legislation which has prevailed in later times." F. Buxton, *Debate in House of Commons on the Forgery Punishment Mitigation Bill,* 5 Hansard, Parliamentary Debates (1821) 902.

[3] Perhaps it requires innovation to inspire interest. At any rate, the professional literature dealing with the criminal law is very meager during the preceding two centuries. Staunford's Pleas of the Crown appeared in 1557 and presented the most systematic statement of the criminal law in existence until Hale's work appeared in 1736. Coke's Third Institute added very little to Staunford. In the eighteenth century, however, and immediately thereafter, concomitant with the enormous development in the criminal law, there appeared a series of scholarly works, the most important of which, in addition to the posthumous publication of Hale's Pleas, were those by Hawkins (1716), Foster (1762), Blackstone (1769), East (1803) and Russell (1819).

stolen property, larceny by trick, obtaining goods by false pretenses, and embezzlement. Here, for the first time, the modern lawyer finds himself in contact with a body of substantive criminal law which he feels is essentially his own.

In the eighteenth century embezzlement, larceny, and false pretenses converge at several points. At times the concept of "possession" as used in the traditional definition of larceny becomes so fine-spun that it threatens to obliterate entirely the distinctions between the three crimes. Finally, these offenses become merged in some jurisdictions in a single statutory crime of theft.

To understand this body of substantive criminal law, three lines of inquiry must be projected: first, the most important developments in the law of theft; second, the most significant concomitant economic and social changes; and, third, the effect of these changes on the law of theft.

1. *Embezzlement*

It will be recalled that in the Carrier's Case reference was made to the then emerging norm of larceny by servant, and that the early, uncertain development of this rule [4] was definitely settled in 1529 (21 Hen. VIII, c. 7) with regard to property which the servant received from his master or which he took from his master's house. The rule became fixed that (a) property received from the master remained in his possession, the servant securing "mere charge or custody" of it; but that (b) property received from a third person for the master was in the servant's possession, and he was therefore not guilty of felony if he converted it.[5]

---

[4] "The anomalous distinction according to which, if the servant receives the thing from another person for his master, the servant has the possession, and so cannot commit theft, is made more rational by the old cases. For the distinction taken in them is, that, while the servant is in the house or with his master, the latter retains possession, but if he delivers his horse to his servant to ride to market, or gives him a bag to carry to London, then the thing is out of the master's possession and in the servant's." Holmes, The Common Law 226.

[5] The rule is stated in 1 Hale, P. C. 668.

The distinctions thus drawn between custody and possession, however tenuous in appearance, were by no means academic in effect. The early rules of law which required that a trespass be committed before there could be felony had prevented prosecution of servants as well as of bailees. There was available a civil action for breach of trust,[6] but this, quite obviously, would be worthless against most servants. A civil action would avail little against irresponsible bailees, for that matter. After Carrier's Case and the statute of 1529, however, bailees who "broke bulk" and servants who converted goods received from their masters could be prosecuted for felony.

Violation of public trust is probably one of the oldest notions in history, e.g. Aristotle refers to the embezzlement of funds by road commissioners and other officials.[7] In England, the Articles of Edward I provided for the investigation of "overseers of works" who converted stone or timber which should have gone into public construction.[8] In the *Mirror of Justices* similar offenses are expanded to include "those who receive more from their bailiwick than they answer for to the king." The offense is called "perjury against the king," indicating that the false report rather than conversion is the gist of the crime.[9] "Larceny" included "open thieves . . . tricksters . . . bailiffs, receivers, and administrators of other persons' goods, who steal in rendering account."[10] Apparently there was considerable embezzlement "by the highest officials . . . in the fourteenth century. . . ."[11] An Elizabethan statute was directed against "persons who embezzled munitions of war . . . which had been entrusted to them."[12] And

---

[6] "It may have been based on the sentiment that against open violence people ought to be protected by law, but that they could protect themselves against breaches of trust by not trusting people,—a much easier matter in simple times, when commerce was in its infancy, than in the present day." 3 Stephen, H. C. L. 151.

[7] Pol. 1305^{b13}, 1308^{b16}; Ath. Const. 54^2.

[8] 2 Bracton (Twiss ed.) 593. Hale refers to a statute of Richard which made "embezzling of a record . . . a great offense." 1 Hale, P. C. 646.

[9] The Mirror of Justices, Selden Soc. VII, 18-19 (1895).

[10] *Id.* 25.

[11] 1 Pike, A History of Crime in England (1873) 261.

[12] 31 Eliz. c. 4. 1589; 1 Hawkins, P. C. 48; 4 Holdsworth, H. E. L. 501.

a statute of James I (7 Jac. 1.7) made it criminal for any person in the wool industry to "imbezil any Wool or Yarn delivered to him to be wrought." [13] Except for this seventeenth century statute, the above instances of embezzlement concerned public property and, in England, especially officials who had violated the king's trust.[14] But while the idea of embezzlement is ancient, and instances of its incidence are continuous in the criminal law, legal control of the type of criminal behavior which has become a commonplace in modern times—the violation of private financial trust—dates definitely from the eighteenth century.

The eighteenth century law of embezzlement grew out of the need to overcome the limited utility of the custody concept. The rule that a servant who converted goods or money received from a third person for his master committed merely a civil breach of trust, provided a constantly recurring problem until 1799. Only then was the required legislation enacted. Prior to that time, indeed, the courts were narrowing this area of trust considerably. The technique was to expand the "possession of the master" at every conceivable opportunity. Thus, if the servant placed the money or goods received from a third person into any receptacle owned by the master, that was held enough to constitute possession in the latter, and subsequent conversion larceny.[13] There were limits, however, beyond which even the constructive possession of the master could not be extended, while for over two centuries business increased very rapidly and "servants" became clerks and cashiers who dealt constantly with third persons.

The climax of this situation was reached in the case of The King v. Joseph Bazeley in 1799.[16] Bazeley was the principal teller for a firm of bankers. In that capacity he received for deposit a note for one hundred pounds which, after crediting

---

[13] 1 Hawkins, P. C. 92.

[14] There was a linguistic usage whereby "larceny by servant," was designated "embezzlement" in some of the treatises. 1 Hale, P. C. 506. And see N. 11 *infra*.

[15] R. v. Chipchase (1795) 2 East, P. C. 567. Spear's Case (1798) 2 East, P. C. 568-9. Abrahat's Case (1798) 2 East, P. C. 569.

[16] 2 East, P. C. 571; 168 E. R. 517.

it to the customer's account along with additional sums deposited, he put into his pocket and used to meet a personal obligation. In deciding this case the court said:

"It is clear that the prosecutors had not, upon the present occasion, the actual possession of the Bank-note, and therefore the inquiry must be, whether they had the constructive possession of it? or, in other words, whether the possession of the servant was, under the circumstances of this case, the possession of the master? . . . The prosecutors in the present case had only a right or title to possess the note, and not the absolute or even qualified possession of it. It was never in their custody or under their control . . . At the time, therefore, of the supposed conversion of this note, it was in the legal possession of the prisoner. To divest the prisoner of this possession, it certainly was not necessary that he should have delivered this note into the hands of the prosecutors, or of any other of their servants personally; for if he had deposited it in the drawer, kept for the reception of this species of property, it would have been a delivery of it into the possession of his masters; but he made no such deposit . . . After these determinations it cannot be contended that the possession of the servant is the possession of the master; for, independently of these authorities, the rule that the possession of the servant is the possession of the master, cannot be extended to a case in which the property never was in the master's possession, however it may be so construed in cases where the identical thing stolen is delivered by the master, or where the question is between the master and a third person."

The case was argued on April 24, 1799 and the defendant was discharged shortly thereafter. That same year, 39 Geo. III, c. 85, the first general embezzlement statute,[17] was passed.

---

[17] ". . . if any servant or clerk, or any person employed for the purpose in the capacity of a servant or clerk, to any person or persons whomsoever, or to any body corporate or politick, shall, by virtue of such employment, receive or take into his possession any money, goods, bond, bill, note, banker's draft, or other valuable security, or effects, for or in the name or on the account of his master or masters, or employer or employers, and shall fraudulently embezzle, secrete, or make away with the same, or any part thereof, every such offender shall be deemed to have feloniously stolen the same."

This statute applied only to servants and clerks. Though it extended beyond employees of bankers, it still bore the mark of Bazeley's Case. Accordingly, when in 1812 one Walsh, a stock broker—no servant, but an agent—converted a large sum of money which formed the proceeds of a check given him to invest, it was held that his conduct did not come within the statute. It was a "mere breach of trust." [18] Parliament promptly passed legislation to cover such cases in the future. From 1812 on through the nineteenth century additional enactments extended piece by piece the scope of embezzlement.[19]

There had indeed been three embezzlement statutes passed prior to the general law of 1799 which were very important. But all three were special, not general. The first (15 Geo. II, c. 13) enacted in 1742, related to embezzlement by officers and servants *of the Bank of England*. This was a true embezzlement statute (the word was used sometimes to refer to larceny by a servant), for it included the conversion of property delivered to the servant or officer by third persons.[20] An identical enactment passed in 1751 (24 Geo. II, c. 11, s. 3) applied to officers and servants *of the South Sea Company*. The third special embezzlement statute (5 Geo. III, c. 25) passed in 1765, contained similar provisions with reference to employees *of the post office*. Out of the pressure of particular interests which reached far enough to affect the public grew gradually an understanding of general interest in private protection. But this

---

[18] Rex v. Walsh, 168 E. R. 624.

[19] 52 Geo. III, c. 63 (1812); 6 Geo. IV, c. 94 (1825); 20 & 21 Vict. c. 54 (1857); 31 and 32 Vict. c. 116 (1868).

Stephen summarized the law as follows: "The fraudulent misappropriation of property is not a criminal offence, if the possession of it was originally honestly acquired, except in the case of (1) Servants embezzling their masters' property, who were first excepted in 1799. (2) Brokers, merchants, bankers, attorneys, and other agents, misappropriating property intrusted to them, who were first excepted in 1812. (3) Factors fraudulently pledging goods intrusted to them for sale, who were first excepted in 1827. (4) Trustees under express trusts fraudulently disposing of trust funds, who were first excepted in 1857. (5) Bailees stealing the goods bailed to them, who also were first excepted in 1857. The original rule is tacitly assumed, and all the exceptions to it are expressly reënacted in a wider form in the Larceny Act of 1861." 3 Stephen, H. C. L. 158–9.

[20] For later additions to this statute, see 2 East, P. C. sec. 19, 578–9, and 2 Russell on Crimes (10th ed. 1950) 1286.

transpired by slow stages. Bazeley was a clerk. Walsh was a broker.

2. *Larceny by Trick*

Two very important extensions of the definition of larceny had been made by Carrier's Case and the concept of "custody" by servants. The third major development in the early law referred to a different type of behavior but, because of its relationship to larceny by trick, it became, with the others, part of the same intricate pattern of the eighteenth century law of theft. This change was ushered in by the statute of 33 Hen. VIII, c. 1 (1541) which enlarged the law on cheating.[21] The early rules on cheating [22] were confined to frauds upon the general public perpetrated by the use of false weights and measures, against which ordinary prudence was deemed to be no safeguard. The statute of 33 Hen. VIII extended the law of criminal fraud to cases of less general application and retained the requirement that an objective device (a seal, letter, etc.) be employed by the defendant.

Again, for two relatively quiescent centuries, there was no important development in the law of criminal fraud. Then in 1757 came the statute of 30 Geo. II which provided that "Whereas divers ill-disposed persons, to support their profligate way of life, have by various subtle strategems, threats and devices, fraudulently, obtained divers sums of money, goods . . . all persons who knowingly and designedly, by false pretence or pretences, shall obtain from any person or persons, money, goods, wares, or merchandizes, with intent to cheat or defraud any person or persons of the same . . . shall be deemed offenders", etc.[23] More than a quarter of a century elapsed,

---

[21] It was made a misdemeanor to "falsely and deceitfully obtain, or get into his or their hands or possession, any money, goods, chattels, jewels, or other things of any other person or persons, by colour and means of any privy false token or counterfeit letter made in another man's name, to a special friend or acquaintance, for the obtaining of money, &c. from such person. . . ."

[22] For an excellent discussion, see W. Hamilton, *The Ancient Maxim Caveat Emptor* (1931) 40 Yale L. J. 1133.

[23] The offense was made punishable by fine and imprisonment, or being put in the pillory, or publicly whipped, or transportation for seven years, "as the court . . . shall think fit and order."

however, before this statute was interpreted broadly enough to take on its modern meaning. (The reason for this will be noted shortly.) In the meantime, the law of false pretenses became so intimately related to the law of larceny by trick that the two must be considered together.

Larceny by trick was not, like most other major eighteenth century developments in the law of theft, the product of legislative enactment. It may, in fact, be attributed entirely to Pear's Case,[24] decided in 1779. Pear was indicted for stealing a horse. Having hired the horse to go to Sutton and back, he sold it the same day the agreement was made. On his trial, the jury returned a special verdict that "he hired the horse with a fraudulent view, and intention of selling him immediately." The issue on appeal was whether the conversion of the horse was a mere breach of trust or whether it was felonious. There was considerable difference of opinion among the judges.[25] The majority finally found that since it was established by the jury's verdict that the hiring was fraudulent, "the parting with the property [possession] had not changed the nature of the possession, but that it remained unaltered in the prosecutor at the time of the conversion; and that the prisoner was therefore guilty of felony."[26]

Professor Joseph Beale, in an interesting article on Pear's Case, has severely criticized this judgment. "That this decision," says he, "was a novelty, and an unwarranted modification of the law of larceny appears upon an examination of the authorities cited by the court."[27] These authorities were Rex v. Chissers[28] and Tunnard's Case.[29] Chissers had entered a shop ostensibly to make a purchase, and was given two cravats to examine. He immediately absconded with the cravats; and on his trial was found guilty of felony. Tunnard hired a horse to ride a distance of three miles; instead, he rode to London where he sold it. On being tried, he was found

---

[24] 2 East, P. C. 685.
[25] Seven held it to be felony; two held contrariwise; and two were doubtful.
[26] 168 E. R. 209.
[27] *The Borderland of Larceny* (1892) 6 Harv. L. Rev. 248.
[28] T. Raymond 275 (1678).
[29] 2 East, P. C. 687 (1729).

guilty of felony, but "if there had been no special agreement the privity would have remained, and it could not have been felony."[30] As to Chissers' Case, Professor Beale states that he was never given possession of the goods; and that, on the other hand, Tunnard's Case was an application of the rule in Carrier's Case, for there was no intention to steal at the time of the hiring. His conclusion that neither case was properly applicable to Rex v. Pear seems well taken, although it is not certain that Tunnard did not have a felonious intention at the outset.[31] If the felonious intention arose after the hiring, as the judge's remarks indicate, Tunnard's Case must itself have been an innovation because there was, of course, no breaking of bulk, and larceny by bailee was still far in the future.

As Professor Beale points out, the crux of the decision in Pear's Case turns upon the Carrier's Case. The judges commented on the Carrier's Case and concluded that "it was settled by old authorities that the taking need not be by force." Thus, a decision, based specifically on the fact that there was a breaking of bulk, was extended to mean that there need be no force in any case. This interpretation removed the ancient vi et armis much farther from the operative facts of larceny and gave rise to larceny by trick. Fraud in securing possession joined breaking bulk and custody in servants to extend the definition of larceny far beyond its original traditional meaning.[32]

---

[30] 168 E. R. 209(a)².

[31] The jury's verdict is ambiguous—"the prisoner rode away with the horse with intent to steal it."

[32] "In one point of view there is much public convenience in this doctrine, without any injustice to the criminal. It is easier to guard property from open violence than secret fraud, the latter crime is of a more mischievous description; its moral guilt is greater, from adding falsehood to theft, and falsehood often of a most falsitious kind, to make, therefore, fraud a felony, and thus oppose it to the penalties that are opposed to larceny, is just as beneficial. On the other hand, by removing, not in every instance, but in certain cases only, the plain distinction between the two offenses, a prosecutor is frequently under difficulties (arising from analogical reasonings) as his mode of proceed-

Particularly significant in revealing the effect of available sanctions on the judicial process are several cases which were decided after Pear's Case but prior to Rex v. Young et al.,[33] which in 1789 radically changed the law of false pretenses. These decisions, which relied upon Pear's Case, cast much light also upon the distinction drawn between larceny by trick and obtaining property by false pretenses. Thus, in the case of The King v. Patch, decided in 1782, where property was obtained from the prosecutor by means of the ring-dropping swindle,[34] "it was objected that this amounted only to a fraud." But the defendant was held guilty of larceny on the ground "that the possession was obtained by fraud, and the property [title] was not altered; for the prosecutor was to have it again." In another case of "finding" an imitation diamond ring and securing a deposit of money from the prosecutor,[35] it was again argued that this amounted only to fraud. Although some of the judges took that view because it was not contemplated that the identical money should be returned, the majority held, on the authority of Pear's Case, that the defendant was guilty of felony (larceny) because the money was delivered as a pledge "so that though the possession was parted with, the property was not." Despite the dubious application of the principle,

---

ing, litigation is multiplied, the authorities are divided, and criminals escape." 1 Hammond, The Criminal Code (1828) 6–9.

Cf. "This is the only operation the cases cited have upon my mind, and they confirm me in the opinion that the old rule should be most sacredly regarded. If we once begin to depart from it, we shall gradually include in the definition of felonious stealing, acts that are at present deemed very far from its comprehension, until at length perhaps, the boundaries between fraud and felony, shall be no longer discernible; and the lives of many citizens sacrificed improperly, before the law can be again brought back to its ancient simplicity and certainty." Note to State v. Long, 1 Haywood 159 (1795); 2 No. Car. 210.

A survey of the rules is presented by J. Scurlock, *The Element of Trespass in Larceny at Common Law* (1948) 22 Temple L.Q. 12.

[33] This case is discussed *infra* pp. 50–51.

[34] The defendants, in the company of the prosecuting witness, pretended to find a valuable diamond ring, which was, in fact, a cheap imitation and they persuaded him to take charge of the ring and to deposit his watch and money as security. 2 East, P. C. 678–9.

[35] Moore's Case, 2 East, P. C. 679 (1784).

there is no doubt that this became the basis for differentiating fraud from larceny by trick.[36]

Professor Beale takes strong exception to the soundness of the rule and maintains that "if the contract, being fraudulent in its inception, was not to be considered in Pear's Case, it should equally be disregarded if it had attempted to bestow the property as well as the possession on the defendant."[37] He states also that the rule distinguishing larceny by trick from false pretenses is defective on both sides, "for there are instances of false pretenses where the title does not pass to the defendant and instances of larceny where it does pass." To which it might be replied that the *intention* of the prosecutor to surrender title rather than the actual transfer of title is the distinction to be made.[38] But the cases are sufficiently confusing to raise serious questions regarding the validity of the distinction drawn between larceny by trick and obtaining property by false pretenses.[39] In any event, it is generally agreed that Pear's Case was a sharp departure from precedent.[40] It can, however, be explained on grounds of policy relevant

---

[36] "Upon reviewing the authorities there collected it will appear that the distinction so far as regards the subject of the present inquiry turns mainly upon the consideration whether or not the owner deceived by appearances intended to part with the absolute *property,* and not barely with the *possession* or *temporary use* of the thing at the time of the delivery, rather than upon any actual difference in the degree of fraud meditated by the taker, the intent in both instances being dishonestly to acquire and convert to his own use the property of another without any or an adequate consideration." 2 East, P. C. 816.

[37] *Op. cit.* 253.

[38] To which effect see Bishop, Criminal Law (9th ed.), sec. 808ff.; 37 Yale L. J. 1048. *Cf.* East's remarks in footnote 36, *supra,* and Atkinson's Case where "on reference to the Judges after conviction, all present held that it was no felony; on the ground that the property was intended to pass by the delivery of the owner." 2 East, 673 (1799). Note that this case was decided after R. *v.* Young (1789).

But *cf.* "It is therefore, submitted that the true ground for distinguishing between larceny by trick and obtaining property by false pretences, is not, whether or not the owner delivered the goods with the intent to pass title, but whether or not, as a matter of law, title did pass to the defendant." Citing West Virginia *v.* Edwards, 51 W. Va. 220 (1902). Note (1924) 9 Iowa L. Bull. 210.

[39] *Cf.* Beale, *op. cit.* 256.

[40] For a discussion of what is involved in such an estimate, see *supra* pp. 11–12.

to the conditions of the time, which will be described later.

At this point it is important to recall the legal sanctions which existed at the time Pear's Case came up for decision, so that the various alternatives before the court may be seen. At the present time, a lawyer who considered the facts in Pear's Case would think immediately of larceny by bailee. But it was not until 1857 that larceny by bailee became a criminal offense.[41] Embezzlement, of course, was out of the question for the defendant was neither clerk nor agent, and the general embezzlement statute was still twenty years in the future. There were, therefore, only two possible solutions: larceny and obtaining property by false pretenses. The statute on false pretenses had been passed twenty-three years prior to Pear's Case, and it may well be thought that the refusal to apply it was arbitrary. Certainly the distinction between the delivery of title and delivery of possession only, seems narrowly conceived. It has been constantly criticized. In both cases the intention of the defendant is identical—to secure the chattel and deprive the owner of it permanently. In both cases the harm done is identical. In both cases fraudulent representations are made. How, then, can the decision in Pear's Case be defended?

3. Obtaining Property by False Pretenses

This brings us directly to a consideration of the law on criminal fraud in the eighteenth century. Hawkins, writing at the beginning of the century, was able to say:

"It seemeth to be the better opinion, that the deceitful receiving of money from one man to another's use, upon a false pretence of having a message and order to that purpose, is not punishable by a criminal prosecution, because it is accompanied with no manner of artful contrivance, but wholly depends on a bare naked lie; and it is said to be needless to provide severe laws for such mischiefs, against which common prudence and caution may be a sufficient security."[42]

---

[41] 20 & 21 Vict. c. 54 superseded by 24 & 25 Vict. c. 96, s. 3.
[42] 1 Hawkins, P. C. Ch. 71, sec. 2.

There were many cases to support Hawkins' statement.[43] What is particularly important, however, is that *after the enactment of 30 Geo. II,*[44] *the same rule was applied.* In Rex *v.* Wheatly, a leading case decided in 1761,[45] the defendant sold sixteen gallons of malt liquor, representing that there were eighteen gallons. He was not even indicted under the statute of 1757 for obtaining property by false pretenses, and the court held that he was not guilty of any offense. Lord Mansfield stated the rules as they were then interpreted:

"The offence that is indictable must be such a one as affects the public. As if a man uses false weights and measures, and sells by them to all or to many of his customers, or uses them in the general course of his dealing: so, if a man defrauds another, under false tokens. For these are deceptions that common care and prudence are not sufficient to guard against. So, if there be a conspiracy to cheat: for ordinary care and caution is no guard against this.

"Those cases are much more than mere private injuries: they are public offences. But here, it is a mere private imposition or deception; no false weights or measures are used; no false tokens given; no conspiracy; only an imposition upon the person he was dealing with, in delivering him a less quantity instead of a greater; which the other carelessly accepted. It is only a non-performance of his contract: for which non-performance, he may bring his action." [46]

---

[43] Rex *v.* Bryan, 93 E. R. 903 (1730) is typical of cases which, prior to 30 Geo. II (1757) were not criminal. In this case, the defendant came to the prosecutor's shop and falsely stated that she was a servant of the Countess of P. who sent her to get some silks. The court held that this was "no more than telling a lie", and the judgment was arrested.

[44] See *supra* p. 40.

[45] 97 E. R. 746.

[46] As late as 1775, Mansfield held likewise. In R. *v.* William Bower (98 E. R. 1110), he said: "The prosecutor swore that he bought the chain at the defendant's shop, of Thomas Jones the defendant's servant, and asked him [very little was made of the agency] if it was real gold. He said it was: that he carried it to be examined when he found it to be under the standard weight and not marked. . . . It is certainly an imposition; but I incline to think it is one of those frauds only which a man's own common prudence ought to be sufficient to guard him against; and which, therefore, is not indictable; but the party injured is left to his civil remedy."

Nothing was said about false pretenses, and apparently none of the judges thought that the false pretense statute (30 Geo. II) passed four years prior to Wheatly's Case, had any application. Mr. Justice Dennison cited the ruling in The Queen *v.* Jones [47] where, upon similar facts it was said, "It is not indictable, unless he came with false tokens; we are not to indict one man for making a fool of another." [48]

It becomes clear, therefore, why the judges in Pear's Case paid scant attention to 30 Geo. II. As they said, it was at that time, like 33 Hen. VIII, "confined to cases where credit was obtained in the name of a third person; and did not extend to cases where a man on his own account got goods with an intention to steal them." In short, 30 Geo. II was interpreted as being modeled after 33 Hen. VIII. The token or counterfeit letter was supplemented by false pretenses; the receiving of money or goods "in other men's names" was carried over by the judges to limit the later statute.

But the above words of the earlier statute were not repeated in 30 Geo. II, and it therefore became possible to expand this statute by judicial interpretation. It was, however, not until nine years after Pear's Case that the next step was taken and the law was extended in Rex *v.* Young *et al.*[49] to impart its modern meaning. Indefensible, therefore, as Pear's Case might be with reference to strict application of *stare decisis*, the departure from precedent appears to have been reasonably taken (assuming for the moment that the end reached was desirable, about which, more later) in light of the available sanctions. For, as put by the reporter, "the question . . . referred to the

---

[47] Salk. 379 (1704); 91 E. R. 330.

[48] In Reg. *v.* Mackarty *et* Fordenbourgh, 92 E. R. 280 (1705), two defendants had represented certain wine to be real Lisbon wine, when, in fact, it was not. They were held guilty of conspiracy. "But the true ground of that judgment, which was given by Mr. Justice Dennison in Wheatly's case, was that it was a *conspiracy;* and not the ground alluded to in the printed report of Govers's case; where speaking of Mackarty's case Lord C. J. Ryder is made to say, (borrowed probably from the report in 6 Mod.) 'that *the pretending to be a merchant* was there holden to be a false token.' Yet what was that but a false affirmation simply?" 2 East, P. C. 824.

[49] See *infra* pp. 50–51 for a discussion of this case.

Judges [was] whether the delivery of the horse by the prosecutor to the prisoner, had so far changed the possession of the property, as to render the subsequent conversion of it a mere breach of trust, or whether the conversion was felonious?"

There were several reasons why the court in Pear's Case inclined toward holding the defendant guilty of larceny. The effects of the economic and social conditions of the time will be here passed over. They will be discussed later in some detail.[50] But there is intrinsic evidence of importance. For example, the case involved the conversion of a horse, theft of which was for centuries regarded as one of the most serious offenses and made the subject of considerable special legislation. Thus, the origin of larceny by trick can be attributed, in part, to the desire of the judges to mete out a severer punishment than was possible for false pretenses.[51] This would account not only for the court's meeting the above situation by extending the criminal law, but also for the redefinition of larceny rather than of the statute on false pretenses. Larceny had originally included a real trespass *vi et armis*. When in 1541 obtaining goods by the use of false tokens or counterfeit letters was made criminal, that offense, probably because it did not include an act of force, was made a misdemeanor. Likewise obtaining property by false pretenses was made a misdemeanor in 1757. Such seeming emphasis upon the *means* of acquiring property in 1541 is understandable. Less so in 1757, unless by the mere inertia of moving within a category once laid down: thus, indeed, many of our present statutes are similarly constructed. But the evil being the same, the means used (short of that personal violence involved in robbery) are to modern thinking of minor consequence; and it has accordingly been suggested that the judges in Pear's Case might well have taken this view.[52]

---

[50] See *infra* p. 62 *ff*. For an instance of current use of this legal history, see State *v*. Healy, 95 N. E. 2d 258–259 (Ohio, 1950).

[51] Hammond, Introduction to The Criminal Code (1828).

[52] "The object gained, with all its attendant mischiefs, being identically the same in fraud as in larceny, good sense naturally induced a disposition to treat as a theft the privation of property through deceit. This disposition inclined the authorities to listen to a refinement in reasoning, which proves that a de-

Pear's Case is significant, also, because it marked the beginning of the most accelerated expansion of the law of theft. The case, itself, considerably broadened the definition of larceny, and the frequent prosecutions for larceny by trick that followed evidence its important effects.

The very strong movement to extend the law of theft which is unmistakable from 1779 on was, interestingly enough, given its next great judicial impetus by a civil case—Pasley v. Freeman, decided in 1789.[53] This case would have to be included among the half dozen most important cases in the field of torts. It was the first case which held that an action of deceit could be brought for damages resulting from false representations made by a person who was not a party to a contract induced thereby.[54] The opinions of the judges clearly indicate the sharp shift in attitudes regarding false representations, which had occurred since Wheatly's Case was decided in 1761.

Pasley sued Freeman for damages. He alleged that "the said Joseph Freeman . . . did wrongfully and deceitfully encourage and persuade the said John Pasley . . . to sell and deliver to the said . . . Falch divers other goods . . . value 2634 £ 16 s. 1 d. upon trust and credit; and did for that purpose then and there falsely, deceitfully, and fraudulently, assert and affirm . . . that the said [Falch] . . . was a person safely to be trusted and given credit to in that respect." The plaintiff, relying on the defendant's representations, sold the merchandise and sustained a heavy loss. The defendant had no business or other connection with Falch, the buyer. He personally did not stand to gain by the transaction. In a lengthy decision rendered in the Hilary Term of 1789, judgment was given for the plaintiff, with one of the four judges dissenting.

---

livery of property is no delivery at all; and thus establishes (the definition of Larceny) a taking from the owner without his consent: a doctrine which being at variance with the common apprehensions of mankind, and the creature of mental reservation, is with much propriety called legal construction." Hammond, Introduction to Report of the Select Committee on The Criminal Law of England (1824) 9.

[53] 3 Durn. & East 51; 100 E. R. 450.
[54] Harper, Law of Torts (1933) 445.

Grose J., the dissenter, stated that "this action is as novel in principle as it is in precedent, that it is against the principles to be collected from analogous cases, and consequently that it cannot be maintained." Buller J. replied, "I agree that an action cannot be supported for telling a bare naked lie . . . but a deceit is more than a lie on account of the view with which it is practised, it's being coupled with some dealing, and the injury which it is calculated to occasion, and does occasion, to another person." Ashurst J., holding with Buller J., added: "Where cases are new in their *principle*, there I admit that it is necessary to have recourse to legislative interposition in order to remedy the grievance: but where the case is only new in the *instance*, and the only question is upon the application of a principle recognized in the law to such new case, it will be just as competent to Courts of Justice to apply the principle to any case which may arise two centuries hence as it was two centuries ago." And Kenyon, the Chief Justice, who was inclined to take a broad view of the cases and to add a bit of moral philosophy to his opinions, stated: "All laws stand on the best and broadest basis which go to enforce moral and social duties. . . . There are many situations in life, and particularly in the commercial world, where a man cannot by any diligence inform himself of the degree of credit which ought to be given to the persons with whom he deals. . . . The law of prudence leads him to apply to them [other persons] and the law of morality ought to induce them, to give the information required. . . . It is admitted that the defendant's conduct was highly immoral, and detrimental to society."

Within a week [55] after judgment was rendered in Pasley *v.* Freeman, there was decided on the seventh day of February, 1789, the case of Young *et al.* against the King.[56] *The same four judges sat upon the bench.*[57] In this case the defendants had

---

[55] The reports do not state the exact date that Pasley *v.* Freeman was decided. It seems rather certain, however, that the case was decided between the first and fourth of February, 1789. See the order of the cases in 3 Durnford and East's reports.

[56] 3 Durn. & East 98; 100 E. R. 475.

[57] Ashurst J. was one of the judges who decided Pear's Case in 1779. It seems that Mansfield and Buller also formed the bench that rendered the decision in Pear's Case. *Cf.* 168 E. R. 204 and 208.

falsely represented to the complainant that a certain race was to take place upon which, they said, they had placed bets, and they persuaded him to do likewise. Prosecution was brought against them under the statute of 30 Geo. II,[58] and the judges unanimously held that a conviction was proper. Even Grose J., who in Pasley *v.* Freeman had argued that reliance on the defendant's representations was gross negligence (quite in line with the attitude of the judges in Wheatly's Case), was now "clearly of opinion that this case comes within the Act of Parliament." Buller J. pointed out, significantly, that very few cases had been brought on this false pretense statute; and he was able to remember only one, tried in 1778, which apparently did not enter the reports. He indicated the line that was to be taken in the future development of the crime: "Barely asking another for a sum of money is not sufficient; but some pretense must be used, and that pretense must be false . . ." Ashurst's remarks stand out in bold contrast to those of such an outstanding jurist as Mansfield, who had written a quarter of a century earlier in R. *v.* Wheatly, "I may be sorry for it in the present case, as circumstanced", but nevertheless argued that the prosecutor was negligent and held no crime had been committed.[59] Said Ashurst now: "The Legislature saw that all men were not equally prudent, and this statute was passed to protect the weaker part of mankind." And Kenyon, the Chief Justice, again took the position that it was an excellent thing to have the law coincide with morals.[60]

Within one week, therefore, in February of 1789, a bench consisting of some of the most eminent of English judges made two very important departures from the past law. They decided that a civil action for damages could be brought for false representations against a person who had gained nothing by his de-

---

[58] *Supra* p. 40.

[59] Mansfield sensed the social problem. But *cf.* Dennison's quotation: "We are not to indict one man for making a fool of another."

[60] "I admit," he said, "that there are certain irregularities which are not the subject of criminal law. But when the criminal law happens to be auxiliary to the law of morality, I do not feel any inclination to explain it away. Now this offense is within the words of the Act; for the defendants have by false pretenses fraudulently contrived to obtain money from the prosecutor; and I see no reason why it should not be held to be within the meaning of the statute."

ceit. They thereupon decided further that a false pretense need not be in the name of a third person in order to be within 30 Geo. II. Another step toward the modern law of false pretenses was taken in 1805 when it was held that the conduct of a person without any oral representation on his part could constitute false pretenses.[61]

Once Young's Case had been decided, the necessity to choose between larceny and immunity from criminal prosecution disappeared.[62] It naturally follows that when the resulting rules of the law of theft are arranged in a series of propositions, a number of inconsistencies exist.[63] When, however, these same rules are arranged in the chronological order of their appearance, when the derivation of each is related to the specific legal problem confronting the court at the particular time, when it is remembered that the possibilities of solution are limited and determined at any moment by the established sanctions, the behavior of the courts loses all appearance of arbitrariness.

4. Receiving Stolen Property

The final and, in some ways, the most important development in the modern law of theft was that concerning the receipt of stolen property. Its origins can be traced to medieval England, e.g. in the laws of Ine against "harbouring stolen cattle." [64] Apparently, officials under Athelstan frequently instigated the

---

[61] R. v. Story, 168 E. R. 695; and R. v. Freeth, 168 E. R. 718 (1807).

[62] Cf. Atkinson's Case, 2 East, P. C. 673 (1799), footnote 38, supra, and Rex v. Patch and Rex v. Moore, 2 East P. C. 678–80 and supra n. 34.

[63] "The decision in Pear's Case was not merely contrary to authority; it was not carried to its logical conclusion by subsequent cases. If the contract, being fraudulent in its inception, was not to be considered in Pear's Case, it should equally be disregarded if it had attempted to bestow the property as well as the possession on the defendant. . . . And it would seem that the court meant to carry its rule to the extreme, and thus render useless the statutes which punished the obtaining of goods by false tokens and by false pretenses." Beale, op. cit. 253.

[64] "When one man charges another with stealing cattle, or harbouring stolen cattle, he shall deny (the charge of) theft by (an oath of) 60 hides, if he is allowed to produce an oath." (about 690 A.D.) Attenborough, The Laws of the Earliest English Kings, sec. 51 at 3.

theft of cattle by their vassals and concealed them and their booty; [65] and it was common for nobles to do likewise throughout the late middle ages.[66] But Bracton speaks of "receivers of bad men," not of receivers of stolen goods.[67]

The persistence of this attitude toward receivers into the seventeenth century is shown in Dawson's Case,[68] where an action in slander was brought for the words:

"Thou art an arrant knave, for thou has bought stolen swine, and a stolen cow, knowing them to be stolen. And adjudg'd against the plaintiff, for receipt or sale of goods stolen is not felony, nor makes any accessory, unless it is joined with a receipt or abetment of the felon himself."

By the end of the seventeenth century this ancient law has become burdensome and we find Hale discussing somewhat despairingly the possibility of prosecuting the receiver of stolen goods as an accessory after the fact to the theft.[69] After pointing out that there cannot be an accessory after the fact to petty larceny because it is not a felony punishable by death, he adds that the mere receiving of stolen goods with knowledge does not make the receiver an accessory after the fact in any case.[70]

---

[65] *Id.* secs. 129, 131 at 6.

[66] 1 Pike, History of Crime in England 250–1.

[67] ". . . if any one has knowingly fed such a person after his outlawry and expulsion, and received and held communication with him in any way, or harboured or concealed him, he ought to be punished with the same punishment with which the outlaw is punished . . ."

"And likewise he who knowingly receives robbers, who is termed a receiver of bad men, and neglects to give them up to justice, shall be punished . . ." 2 Bracton (Twiss ed.) 337, 339.

[68] 80 Eng. Rep. 4 (1602).

[69] 1 P. C. 618–22.

[70] Thus he writes: "A. hath his goods stolen by B. who sells them to C. upon a just value, tho C. knows them to be stolen, this makes not C. accessary, unless he receives the felon. *Dalt. Cap.* 108, p. 288.

"But by some opinions, if he buy them at an under value, it makes him accessary, *per Crompt.* 43. *b.* and Sir *Nich. Hyde, Dalt. ubi supra;* but it seems this makes not an accessary, for if there be any odds, he that gives more, benefits the felon more than him that gives less than the value, but it may be a misdemeanor punishable by fine and imprisonment, and the buying at an under value is a presumptive evidence, that he knew they were stole, but makes him not accessary.

"If A. hath his goods stolen by B. and C. knowing they were stolen, receives

It is clear that Hale was making considerable effort to bring such receiving within the only available legal category of importance. But the very fact which is now admissible and important in proving guilty knowledge, namely, the payment of a price below the market, is necessarily rejected by Hale. He is forced to have in mind aid rendered to the felon.

The desired end was not brought about until 1692 when it was enacted (3 & 4 W. and M. c. 9, IV) that:

"And forasmuch as thieves and robbers are much encouraged to commit such offences, because a great number of persons make it their trade and business to deal in the buying of stolen goods; be it therefore enacted by the authority aforesaid, That if any person or persons shall buy or receive any goods or chattel that shall be feloniously taken or stolen from any other person, knowing the same to be stolen, he or they shall be taken and deemed an accessary or accessaries to such felony after the fact, and shall incur the same punishment, as an accessary or accessaries to the felony after the felony committed."

For several years thereafter, prosecutions were instituted solely upon the theory that had been enacted into the law, namely, that a receiver of stolen goods was an accessary after the fact. But the weakness in thus modelling the measure upon the mere extension of existing categories was that under the still prevailing law as to accessories it kept the prosecution of the receiver dependent upon the *prior* conviction of the thief as principal. The thief's self-interest together with the wealth and influence of the receiver were generally sufficient to thwart the Crown's efforts to convict the former. It was therefore exceed-

---

them, this simply of itself makes not an accessary, and therefore it hath been often ruled, that to say, *J. S. hath received stolen goods, knowing them to be stolen,* is not actionable, because it imports not felony, but only a trespass or misdemeanor, punishable by fine and imprisonment, for the indictment of an accessary *after,* is that he received and maintained *the thief,* not *the goods.*

"But yet it seems to me, that if *B.* had come himself to *C.* and had delivered him the goods to keep for him, *C.* knowing that they were stolen, and that *B.* stole them, or if *C.* receives the goods to facilitate the escape of *B.* or if *C.* knowingly receives them upon agreement to furnish *B.* with supplies out of them, and accordingly supplies him, this makes *C.* accessary, and with this seems to agree the preamble of the statute of 2 & 3 E. 6 *cap* 24. *Crompt.* 41*b.* for it is relieving and comforting." 1 Hale, P. C. 619–20.

ingly difficult to reach the latter.[71] In an effort to remedy this situation it was enacted by 1 Anne c. 9, that criminal receivers could be prosecuted "as for a misdemeanor . . . although the principal felon be not before convicted, of the said felony." 5 Anne c. 31 (1706) which superceded 1 Anne c. 9, substituted for the above clause, the provision to punish "as for a misdemeanor if the principal felon cannot be taken." [72]

The theory that the receiver was an accessory remained unchanged, but the new statute removed a practical obstacle in the way of prosecution. However, the very language of the statute, the reference to the "principal felon" in the new proviso in 5 Anne c. 31 and the unchanged situation if the thief were apprehended showed the extent to which the statute was still caught in tradition.

The case of The King v. Evans [73] reveals that the receiver was still regarded as an accessory in the middle of the eighteenth century. Prosecution of Evans for feloniously receiving a silk handkerchief of the value of 12 pence resulted in the discharge of the defendant although the thief was found guilty of larceny. The jury apparently wished to make sure that the thief would be punished only for petty larceny and fixed the value of the goods at 10 pence. The court therefore discharged Evans.[74] Thus the theory was extended to its logical conclusion even in a case where there had been a conviction of the thief.[75] The accessory theory was still in vogue in 1827 but it was then recognized that

---

[71] "The receiver, who is generally the employer and patron of the thief, very often escaped with impunity; for if he could keep the thief out of the way, he, the receiver, could not be tried, and therefore went unpunished." 2 East, P. C. 744–5.

Cf. Foster, Crown Law (1762) 373.

[72] *Cf.* Foster and East, *infra* footnote 79.

[73] 168 Eng. Rep. 37 (1749).

[74] Note this undesirable by-product of the growing humanitarianism in the eighteenth century. The desire to avoid a capital penalty for the thief results in the *complete* discharge of the receiver under the rule.

[75] *Cf.* "So, too, in petit larceny, and in all crimes under the degree of felony, there are no accessories either *before* or *after* the fact; but all persons concerned therein, if guilty at all, are principals; the same rule holding with regard to the highest and lowest offences, though upon different reasons. In treason all are principals, *propter odium delicti;* in trespass all are principals, because the law, *quæ de minimis non curat,* does not descend to distinguish the different shades of guilt in petty misdemeanors." 4 Bl. Comm. 36.

the evil was great and the offense was made a felony.[76] Yet so
dominating is the accessory theory that the offense is made a
felony only where the prior crime is felony, and misdemeanor
when the prior crime is misdemeanor.

By the end of the first quarter of the eighteenth century the
basic pattern for this type of criminal behavior was complete.
We find the courts during the remainder of that century inter-
preting the statutes in a manner intended to facilitate dealing
with this problem, as may be seen from a brief survey of English
decisions in the last half of the century. The statutes, 3 & 4 W.
and M. c. 9, sec. 4 and 5 Anne c. 31, had already been extended
in the case of The King v. Pollard and Taylor.[77] The defendants
were indicted "as for a misdemeanor" for receiving goods stolen
by one Foster, knowing them to be stolen. After conviction, a
motion in arrest of judgment was made upon the ground that
the receiver could be prosecuted for misdemeanor only if the
thief could not be taken; that if the thief could be apprehended,
the prosecution must be for felony as accessory and that, as a
matter of fact, the thief in this case had been arrested, tried and
acquitted.[78] But the judges held that the prosecutor had his
election to prosecute either for felony or misdemeanor. That this
decision required "interpretation" of 5 Anne c. 31 is apparent,
for this statute provided specifically that a receiver was to be
prosecuted for felony as an accessory unless the principal felon
"cannot be taken so as to be prosecuted."

Foster, writing in 1762, criticized the above ruling, insisted upon a stricter interpretation of the statutes, and accounted for
the decision upon technical procedural grounds.[79] The courts,
however, continued to interpret the statutes in order to facilitate

---

[76] 7 & 8 Geo. IV, c. 29.
    It is noteworthy that as early as 1769 provision was made by 10 Geo. III,
c. 48 that receivers of jewelry, stolen plate or gold should be punished as felons.
[77] 92 Eng. Rep. 392 (1724).
[78] Which would make impossible conviction of the receiver as an accessory.
[79] He wrote: "I know Attempts have been made under various shapes to
prosecute the Receiver as for a Misdemeanor while the Principal hath been in
Custody and Amenable, but not Convicted. But I think all Devices of that
kind are utterly illegal. For though the 1st of Q. Anne in the strict letter of it
seemeth to be confined to the single Case of the Non-Conviction of the Principal, yet the subsequent Statute, in order to make them Both consistant, must
be understood as explanatory of the Former. Since Both Acts plainly provide

prosecution of the receiver. In Thomas' Case,[80] it was objected for the defendant, charged with being an accessory after the fact, that the principal felon was not named. But the judges upheld the indictment unanimously on the ground that it was the purpose of the statutes " to reach the receivers where the principal thieves could not easily be discovered." The court added that, where the principal is known, that fact should be set forth in the indictment.

The difficulty was more definitely adjudicated in the case of The King v. Wilkes.[81] Here the receiver was indicted for misdemeanor and, after conviction on 5 Anne c. 31, the legality of the verdict was assailed on the ground that the principal felon could have been taken. The facts, indeed, appeared conclusive on this point. The thief had approached the prosecutor and confessed both his theft and disposal of the property to the defendant. The prosecutor and the confessed thief were together for two days, but upon the latter's promise to testify against the receiver, he was not taken into custody. Some time afterwards the prosecutor and thief met by appointment, and although an attempt was then made to take the latter into custody, he was rescued by several companions and escaped. A majority of the judges upheld the conviction.[82]

---

against One and the Same Mischief, *viz. where the Principal abscondeth and is not amenable to Justice.* Which the Preambles of Both shew to have been the Mischief in the Contemplation of the Legislature at the Time they were made. . . .

"WHERE the Principal is Amenable the Prosecutor hath no Option whether to proceed against the Receiver as for Felony or Misdemeanour, He must proceed as for Felony. If He be not Amenable, and the Prosecutor chooseth to wait for his conviction He may do so, and then proceed against the Receiver as for Felony; or at his own Pleasure, as for a Misdemeanour without waiting 'till the Principal shall be Amenable. Under these Limitations and these Only, as I conceive, the Prosecutor hath an Option." Foster, Crown Law (1762) 373–4. East thought, also, that "where the principal is amenable to justice, the receiver ought still to be prosecuted as an accessory to the felony, and not for a misdemeanor only." 2 East, P. C. 745.

[80] O. B. May 1766; 2 East, P. C. 781.

[81] 168 Eng. Rep. 154 (1774), 1 Leach 103.

[82] "But seven of them were of opinion, That the word cannot in the statute means if he cannot be taken at the time of the prosecution for the misdemeanor, and as it did not appear from the finding of the Jury, that the principal felon was out of custody by collusion or could have been taken, so as to be prosecuted and convicted at the time the present indictment was found, the verdict was right: . . ." *Id.* 154–5.

Apparently the point was not considered entirely settled, for shortly thereafter 22 Geo. III, c. 58 (1782) was enacted, providing specifically that the receiver could be prosecuted for misdemeanor whether the principal felon could be apprehended or not. This statute made a further departure from the accessory theory by providing that, whether the theft was grand larceny, some greater offense or petty larceny (except where the person committing the felony had already been convicted), the receiver could be prosecuted for misdemeanor.[83]

Another vital point was settled by 22 Geo. III, c. 58 regarding the capacity of the thief to testify against the receiver. This was definitely adjudicated in The King v. William Haslam.[84] In that case the trial court permitted the thief to testify, and upon submission of the cause to the twelve judges they unanimously found "that a principal felon may be admitted as a witness against his accessory, under this Act of Parliament."[85]

Note—EARLY NINETEENTH CENTURY AMERICAN CASES
ON CRIMINAL RECEIVERS

Early nineteenth century American cases show conclusively not only that the English decisions were well known and followed, but also that the English statutes were copied with hardly a change.

In The State v. Harkness,[86] the defendant was charged with

---

[83] The statute was thus construed in the Baxter case (101 Eng. Rep. 48 (1792)) which also affirmed King v. Pollard and Taylor in holding that it was not necessary to allege in the indictment that the principal felon had not been convicted.

[84] 168 Eng. Rep. 311 (1786).

[85] "And at the Old Bailey in Jury Session 1786, on the trial of Hugh Price for stealing, and William Collins for knowingly receiving a quantity of paper, the property of Edward Cox, Mr. Justice Heath said, 'There is a determination lately made on the statute 22 Geo. III, c. 58, by the Twelve Judges, that ought to be publicly known, viz. That the principal may be admitted as a witness against the accessary under this statute.' And in Patram's case, Bridgewater Summer Assizes, 1787, before Mr. Justice Grose, the principal, on a prosecution under 22 Geo. III, c. 58, was admitted a witness against the receiver, and approved before all the Judges, 2 East, C. L. 782. See also Jonathan Wild's case, who was indicted as a receiver on 4 Geo. I, c. 11, and the principal felon was examined as a witness on the part of the Crown. 4 Bl. Comm. 132; 2 East, C. L. 770." 168 Eng. Rep. 311–2, n. (a)².

[86] 1 Brev. (S. C.) Law Rep. 276 (1803).

criminally receiving five quarters of beef. Two statutes were involved, the act of 1769 P. L. 273, 274 and the act of 1789 P. L. 468. The former was modelled after 5 Anne c. 31, while the act of 1789 repealed the common law as to cattle stealing and changed the offense from felony to misdemeanor. It was urged successfully that it could not have been the intention of the legislature to punish an accessory after the fact with greater severity than the original felon.[87] It was also argued that since the thief could have been taken, it was impossible to proceed against the defendant for misdemeanor. In argument by counsel and in the opinion of the court, reference was made to the English statutes, to Foster, Hawkins, and Blackstone, as well as to The King v. Wilkes.

The State v. Sanford and Robbins was also brought upon the statute of 1769.[88] Although the general enacting clause referred to goods "feloniously stolen," it was added in a proviso that "if any such principal felon who shall commit such burglary or felony cannot be taken . . . it shall be lawful to prosecute . . . for a misdemeanor." The court, apparently anxious to avoid the infliction of the death penalty, emphasized the word "burglary,"[89] and held that "receivers of goods, otherwise taken than by burglary or housebreaking are not embraced or punishable by the provisions of this Act of Assembly."[90]

---

[87] "WATIES, J., expressed the opinion of himself, and of GRIMKE, J., that the goods received criminally within the intent and meaning of the A. A. of 1769, must be such, the stealing whereof would be a capital felony, or they must be taken burglariously, inasmuch as the act subjects the receiver of such stolen goods, as accessory, to the pains of death, which the legislature never could have intended as the punishment of an accessary in any offense less than capital." Id. 277–8.

[88] 1 Nott and McC. 512 (S. C. 1819).
This statute also provided that a reward be paid from the public treasury for apprehending, prosecuting and convicting burglars, and that compensation be paid to persons disabled in this service, or to their families if they were killed.

[89] At 514.

[90] Idem.
Similarly the opinion in the State v. Counsil, Harper's (S. C.) Law Reports 53, (1823) shows close contact with the English law.
For further application of copies of the English statutes and cases in South Carolina in the early part of the nineteenth century, see Butler and Quin ads. The State, 3 McC. 383 (S. C. 1825); and State v. Coppenburg, (2 Strob.

In Swaggerty v. The State [91] it was held that the defendant was guilty of the felony of criminal receiving, and that he need not be tried as an accessory since the act of 1829, c. 23, 26, based upon the statute of 7 & 8 Geo. IV, c. 54, made receivers of stolen goods guilty of a felony as principals.[92]

In Commonwealth v. Andrews [93] the receiver was sentenced to pay treble the value of the stolen goods. The court held that the Massachusetts statute of 1785 was a revision of 4 W. and M. c. 6, and 10 Geo. II (1736) which provided for forfeiture of treble the value, and for fine or whipping. The Massachusetts law, however, provided for the conviction of the receiver as for a misdemeanor "before or without the prosecution of the principal," a rule, which as we have seen, became part of the English law in statutes enacted from 1706 to 1782.

In another prosecution against the same Andrews,[94] for receiving from another thief, it was held that the defendant could not be prosecuted for felony unless the principal had been previously convicted or outlawed, or unless both were charged in the same indictment or the accessory requested that he be tried before the principal, in which event judgment against him would be suspended until the principal had been convicted. It was held that the Massachusetts statute adopted the principle of 1 Anne c. 9, sec. 2 and judgment was arrested.

S. C.) L. R. 273. In the Coppenburg case, it was held that even though the receiver instigated and encouraged the commission of the theft, and was therefore an accessory before the fact, the misdemeanor of receiving stolen property was not merged in the offense of being accessory before the fact to the larceny because the two were distinct acts and crimes and the defendant might have been accessory and receiver of the goods. But if the defendant had been present at the commission of the larceny he would have been a principal and could not have been indicted for receiving (citing Dyer's Case, and Atwell's Case, 2 East, P. C. 768).

In this last case the thief was permitted to testify and it was held "there can be no doubt of his competency," citing Haslam's Case, 168 Eng. Rep. 311 (1786).

And see State v. Goode 8 N. C. 463 (1 Hawks 1821) regarding prosecution of the receiver of goods valued at six pence.

[91] 17 Tenn. (Yerger 9) 338 (1836).
[92] A similar statute was passed in Connecticut in May, 1830, c. 1, sec. 47, p. 261, discussed in State v. Weston et al. 9 Conn. (Day) 527 (1833).
[93] 2 Tyng 14 (Mass. 1806).
[94] 3 Tyng 126 (Mass. 1807).

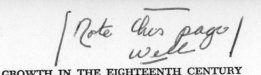

LEADING CASES AND STATUTES IN THE LAW OF THEFT

This table is presented as a summary and also in order that the salient points in the development of the law of theft may be kept in mind with reference to the following discussion of the economic history of the 18th century.

Larceny	*Embezzlement*	*Fraud*	*Receiving Stolen Property*
1857 — Lar. by bailee 20 & 21 Vict. 54.			
			1827 — made substantive felony; also misdemeanor if etc. 7 & 8 Geo. 4, c. 20.
	1812 — banker, broker, agent, etc. 52 Geo. 3, c. 63.		
		1805 — acts (without words) R. v. Story	
	1799 — servants and clerks 39 Geo. 3, c. 85		
		1789 — false pretenses R. v. Young	
		1789 — damages allowed. Pasley v. Freeman	1782 — thief may testify against receiver 22 Geo. 3, c. 58
1779 — Lar. by trick Pear's Case	1765 — Post Office 5 Geo. 3, c. 25.	1757 — false pretenses 30 Geo. 2, c. 24.	
	1751 — So. Sea Co. 24 Geo. 2. c. 11, s. 3.		
	1742 — Bank of England 15 Geo. 2, c. 13, s. 12.		
			1706 — 1702 — punishable as misdemeanor if, etc. 5 Anne c. 31. 1 Anne c. 92.
			1691 — accessory guilty of felony 3 & 4 W. & M. c. 9, s. 4.
1529 — Lar. by servant 21 Hen. 8, c. 7.		1541 — cheating by false token, etc. 33 Hen. 8, c. 1.	
1473 — breaking bulk Carrier's Case.			

American states in the post-revolutionary period and in the early nineteenth century were following the English statutes and decisions almost to the letter.[95]

II. The Economic and Social Conditions and Their Effect upon the Law

The era of discoveries and the Commercial Revolution whose advent substantially coincided with them poured into Europe specie in quantities sufficient to turn existing values topsy-turvy. This influx of specie, vastly increasing the supply of liquid capital, must be regarded as one potent factor in stimulating economic enterprise.

Moreover, by shifting trade routes from land to sea the discoveries made possible the carriage of merchandise in bulk theretofore unknown. A trade which had been limited largely to spices and other luxuries now became available to sugar, to-bacco, tea—and in quantities [96] sufficient to broaden the market enormously and to multiply transactions geometrically. At the same time, England, in particular, moved into the focus of trade, indeed, in time, into a position almost analogous to that the Italian cities had occupied in the days of the caravan.

Late-comer in the exploration, England's road ran over conquest. Her sailors, led by Drake, preyed on the Spanish fleets—while Elizabeth hanged petty thieves at home. Beginning in 1607, advancing rapidly with the emigration consequent on the civil disturbances, the colonial expansion followed, 1640–1664 presenting a peak.

Immediately the colonies served a double purpose. They supplied raw materials. They also furnished a market for the sale of goods manufactured at home; and the home manufacturers were

---

[95] In 1824 Nathan Dane's Abridgement and Digest appeared in Massachusetts. This work contained a thorough discussion of the criminal law, including the English statutes and cases and practically all of the authorities.

[96] As an example,—at the beginning of the eighteenth century England was importing 20,000,000 pounds of sugar annually, a great advance over previous periods. By 1782, she was importing 160,000,000 pounds. Hammond and Hammond, Rise of Modern Industry 22.

prompt to protect that market.[97] The tremendous change in the organization of industry is the first development of major importance which closely touches the law of the eighteenth century. Trade became increasingly impersonal and free from supervision. In this transformation of the economic organization of England, it will be recalled, four stages are usually distinguished. In the Middle Ages goods were produced by individuals, their families and neighbors, for local consumption. Next came regulation and close supervision by crafts and gilds in villages and small towns. This was still rather largely a primary group organization until the modern period set in. There followed a period of individual and group production, but with an increasing trend toward large-scale marketing. And, finally, with the Industrial Revolution, came large-scale production.[98]

All this was accompanied by changes in the economic organization of society. The growing wool industry aided by the recurrent enclosure movements had swept and continued to sweep away a vast number of tenant farmers. This movement was a symptom of the transition from an agricultural economy toward a dominantly manufacturing system. It permitted the introduction of more modern methods of raising sheep; it supplied labor for expanding industries; it led to the rise of cities.[99]

There was another eighteenth century development of the greatest importance, namely, the rise of credit and banking facilities and the use of modern instruments to facilitate trade.[1]

---

[97] In 1651 the Navigation Act was passed compelling her colonies to use English ships manned by English seamen; and ten years later it was required, also, that the ships be built and owned by Englishmen.

[98] Cf. "To these several stages it is difficult to give brief designations which shall not be misleading. It is common to speak of them as (1) the *family* or *household system*, (2) the *gild* or *handicraft system*, (3) the *domestic system* or *house industry*, and (4) the *factory system*." Ashley, The Economic Organization of England 36.

[99] By the latter part of the eighteenth century the government itself was advancing the enclosure movement vigorously. "No less than 700 Enclosure Acts were passed between 1760 and 1774." Gibbins, Industry In England 335.

[1] "Thus in the realm of finance there was more of novelty, of actually new development, during this period than in agriculture, manufacturing, or commerce." E. P. Cheyney, An Introduction to the Industrial and Social History of England (1916) 196.

Banking had been of slow growth in England.[2] Up to the end of the sixteenth century, financial affairs had remained largely in the control of foreigners. But the new possibilities of accumulation of large amounts of precious metals had effect. In 1545 it became legal to lend money at interest rates not exceeding ten per cent.[3] Overseas trade and expansion of business made financing essential. The goldsmiths, who had long functioned as depositories for precious metals, began to make loans.[4] Their rates were very high; the risk of defalcation was great. Thus, when Charles II in 1672 repudiated a debt of almost one and a half million pounds to the goldsmiths, they in turn were unable to meet their obligations to the merchants who had deposited these funds.[5]

In 1691 William Paterson made his famous proposal to establish a Bank of England which would loan money at reasonable rates, do a general banking business, and assure security. For political reasons, in reality, but avowedly because the govern-

---

[2] The lending of money at interest was condemned by the Church. A detailed statement of the rise of risk enterprise would necessarily include the theories of the effect of the Reformation upon commerce. Max Weber's famous theory relegates such factors as the accumulation of precious metals from America, the reaction of large markets upon industry, improvement in technology, etc., to a secondary place, as occasions, but not causes, of capitalism. The real cause of the construction of the rationalist economic system which characterized capitalism, was, according to Weber, the sixteenth century religious revolution. Calvinism, in particular, taught that the accumulation of wealth was a duty. This theology, it is urged, completely motivated the new bourgeoisie. "Thus the pursuit of riches, which once had been feared as the enemy of religion, was now welcomed as its ally." Tawney, Foreword to Max Weber's The Protestant Ethic and the Spirit of Capitalism (Parsons' transl.) 4. See also, Weber, General Economic History (Knight's transl.) c. 3, 354. For criticism of Weber's theory, see Tawney, op. cit. 7.

[3] This law was repealed in 1552, under Mary, but was reënacted in 1571.

[4] "A pamphlet of 1676, called The Mystery of the Newfashioned Goldsmiths or Bankers Discovered . . . gives the year 1645 as about the time when commercial men began regularly to put their cash in the hands of goldsmiths." Gibbins, op. cit. 299. Cf. Andréadès, History of the Bank of England 21-6.

[5] "This was the first State bankruptcy of England since 1339, and it was the last. . . . It was the Revolution of 1688 which brought about the decisive change."

"It was only after the revolution that the English State became what the Dutch Republic had long been—a real corporation of individuals firmly associated together, a permanent organism." R. Ehrenberg, Capital and Finance in the Age of the Renaissance 348, 354.

ment objected to the legalizing of paper money,[6] Paterson's scheme was rejected. However, it was taken up later and arrangements for loans to the government being made, the Bank was organized in 1694. The growth of provincial banks, however, was a very slow process. Burke stated in 1750, and his opinion is generally accepted, that there were not more than "twelve banker's shops out of London";[7] and the Clearing House was not established until 1775. From the middle of the century on, however, the careers of many prominent merchants gravitated from business to banking;[8] and by 1793 there were over four hundred county banks in England.[9] In 1759, the Bank of England, which had not issued notes for less than £20, began to issue £10 notes. Paper had, indeed, been used for several centuries by merchants, but ordinary traders were compelled in the eighteenth century to carry considerable amounts of coin with them. Payment by check apparently did not begin until the end of the eighteenth century.[10]

This growth in banking and the use of paper currency and instruments of credit affected the law of theft in several important respects. The effect upon the law of embezzlement was direct and sharply marked. We have met the Act of 1742, the first true embezzlement statute passed by a Whig parliament, anxious to protect the greatest Whig mercantile institution in the country;[11] but this, it will be recalled, applied only to officers and

---

[6] "The political enemies of the bank were supported by the goldsmiths and other financial men whose monopoly of money lending was assailed by the new institution." C. A. Conant, A History of Modern Banks of Issue (1927) 84. *Cf.* Andréadès, *op. cit.* 67–71.

[7] Quoted by Toynbee, Industrial Revolution of the 18th Century in England (4th ed. 1894) 55.

[8] C. S. Sutherland, *The Accounts of an Eighteenth Century Merchant,* 3 Econ. Hist. Rev. 368.

[9] Buer, Health, Wealth and Population in the Early Days of the Industrial Revolution (1926) 49, and Exelby, An Outline of British Economic History (1931) 110.

[10] Conant, *op. cit.* 94, and *cf.* H. T. Wood, Industrial England in the Middle of the Eighteenth Century (1910) 180n.

[11] The word embezzle or imbezzle was used in a number of early statutes as a synonym for larceny by a servant. *Viz.,* 21 Hen. 8, c. 7 (1529); 31 Eliz. c. 5 (1589); 13 and 14 Car. II, c. 15 (1662); 1 Anne c. 18 (1701); this applies also to the cases of embezzlement of materials by artisans, discussed by Ashley, *op. cit.* 145.

servants of the Bank of England. Just prior to the passage of this Act, one John Waite, a cashier of the Bank, had taken six East India bonds of the value of 13,300 pounds. He could not be convicted under the common law rule incorporated into 2 Geo. II, and was discharged.[12] The second embezzlement statute, enacted in 1751, applied to officers and employees of the South Sea Company; and the third (1763) extended only to employees of the Post Office. This last followed a large number of cases involving the theft of paper money and valuable instruments sent through the mail. These three statutes were enacted between the years 1742 and 1763. In 1799 Bazeley's Case, as we have seen, brought on the first general embezzlement statute.

Whig mercantile interests and the importance of the three corporations concerned account for the special acts. In all three statutes the offense was made a felony without benefit of clergy.[13] The appearance of the general act of 1799 followed shortly after the organization of some four hundred banks in the last decade of the century.

The pattern of conditions which gave rise to embezzlement may therefore be delineated as follows: (1) the expansion of mercantile and banking credit and the use of credit mechanisms, paper money, and securities; (2) the employment of clerks in important positions with reference to dealing with and, in particular, receiving valuables from third persons; (3) the interests of the commercial classes and their representation in Parliament; (4) a change in attitude regarding the public importance of what could formerly be dismissed as merely a private breach of trust; and (5) a series of sensational cases of very serious defalcation which set the pattern into motion and produced immediate action.[14]

---

[12] 168 E. R. 117; 1 Leach 28.

[13] See *infra* p. 110 for a discussion of this privilege.

[14] "Peculiarly interesting results are obtained by the intensive study of criminal statistics in particular countries. It appears that in nations whose modern economic development is recent or as yet incomplete the more involved forms of dishonesty increase rapidly from year to year. We therefore expect to find, and do find, that in Germany and Austria, frauds, embezzlements and forgeries are for the time being on the increase. On the other hand, a nation that is advancing very slowly in economic standing, such as Italy, or scarcely at all,

Fast upon the heels of the sixteenth and seventeenth century colonization and as a phase of the changing financial organization, came the joint-stock companies, promoted for the conduct of the new colonial commerce.[15] These companies required enormous investment of capital and led to the formation of a type of limited partnership and to popular investment which grew very rapidly and soon took on huge proportions.

The first true joint-stock company was the Russia Company, formed in 1553 with 240 shareholders who had paid £25 each.[16] The Hudson Bay Company was chartered in 1670. Between these dates the Levant, the East India, the Virginia, and other stock companies were formed. These companies paid enormous dividends. The stock of the East India Company, to pick an extreme case, paid 245 per cent in profits in 1676.[17] But extreme cases fire popular fancy. The South Sea venture is familiar to all; but there had been previous investment "phrensies" in 1694, 1695 and 1698.[18] "London, at this time [1698] abounded with many new projects and schemes promising mountains of gold, the Royal Exchange was crowded with projects, wagers, airy companies of new manufactures and inventions, and stock-jobbers, and the like."[19]

The South Sea Company itself was formed in 1711 with the encouragement of the government.[20] Its stock rose like a meteor

such as Spain, displays no increase in these more refined offenses of modern life, while retaining a conspicuously high average in the unpremeditated and savage crimes, such as homicide, rape, assault and battery." Raymond B. Fosdick, European Police Systems (1915) 12.

[15] Several reasons are assigned for the rise of regular stock exchange dealings. Macaulay states that during 1661–1688 large amounts of capital had accumulated; and that the high price of land and houses led to the formation of joint-stock companies to provide avenues for investment.

Houghton, the publisher of a contemporary weekly, attributed investment in stock companies to the desire to have capital available immediately in case of need.

Ehrenberg, with greater probability, states that the wish to make capital profits was more operative than the need for investment to get a return. Op. cit. 364–5.

[16] Ashley, op. cit. 84.
[17] 2 Craik, British Commerce 101.
[18] Id. 192.
[19] Quoted by H. R. Fox-Bourne, English Merchants (1886) 282.
[20] Andréadès, op cit. 128–45.

from £100 to over £1000. Brokerage offices were opened every-where. In coffee houses, bars, at milliners and dressmakers, men and women in all walks of life placed their orders for stock—and not only in the South Sea Company, but in dozens of others promoted upon most fantastic projects.[21]

In 1721 came the crash. The panic which ensued recalls the United States in 1930. Public indignation demanded strong re-pressive measures against the directors of the South Sea Com-pany.[22] Walpole, although he had himself made a neat fortune in this stock, was recalled into office as the one man who could exercise some control in the crisis. Even he could not prevent the passage of drastic legislation to satisfy the public clamor. The Chancellor of the Exchequer was impeached. A bill was carried to compensate the victims out of the private assets of the promoters. The grandfather of Gibbon, the historian, forfeited almost his entire fortune of £60,000; others suffered like treat-ment. "There is," writes Thorold Rogers, "I believe, no other in-stance in our history in which a fraud has been punished by an *ex post facto* law."[23] Prior to this financial panic the Bubble Act of 1719 had been passed, ironically enough at the instigation of directors of the South Sea Company in order to check competi-tion. It prohibited the formation of companies with transferable shares unless chartered by the Crown or Parliament. In 1734 an act was passed "to prevent the infamous Practice of Stock Job-bing." But although speculation stopped for a time, it began again and by 1769 had become common.[24] Still, the more flagrant practices of promoters were checked, and most people turned to safer investments.

So striking and far-reaching was this experience in the promo-

---

[21] Companies were organized for the purpose of making salt water fresh, planting mulberry trees and breeding silk-worms in Chelsea Park, importing jackasses from Spain, "as if, remarks a later writer with some severity, there were not already jackasses enough in London alone." Gibbins, *op. cit.* 303.

[22] *Cf.* the prosecution of bankers in the United States in the 1930's.

[23] The Industrial and Commercial History of England (1892) 79.

[24] "The East India Company is all faction and gambling. Such fortunes are made and lost every day as are past belief." Thus wrote Walpole to Horace Mann in 1767. Quoted by J. B. Botsford, English Society in the Eighteenth Century 120–1.

tion of stock that it must necessarily have formed an important factor in the change of social attitudes regarding false representations, which expressed itself later in the criminal law. Yet the connection was not avowed. Repression of fraudulent stock promotion did take specific form, but the thought did not transfer itself to ordinary commercial transactions for some time. Nevertheless, it is impossible to read the vivid accounts of wholesale ruin produced by reliance upon fraudulent representations without placing stock speculation high among the factors that changed attitudes regarding misrepresentations in general. And it will be recalled that the major emphasis in Young's Case was that protection must be afforded "the weaker part of mankind."

There were a number of other less dramatic developments which influenced the law of criminal fraud.[25] They were the disappearance of gild regulation, the concomitant rise of intercommunity transactions; and the development of vast, new types of business enterprise, particularly at the end of the eighteenth century.[26]

The decline of the gilds was accompanied by an increase in commercial frauds but, as we have seen, it was not until the end of the eighteenth century that the law was adjusted to meet the new conditions. The gilds were designed for a local trade economy. "What the public desired, above everything else," writes Ashley, "was that the wares should be of good or standard quality. This was the main purpose of the whole system of regulation by gild wardens and town authorities."[27] From the four-

---

[25] For several reasons it is necessary to identify larceny by trick with fraud in so far as economic conditions are responsible for changes in the substantive law concerning these crimes. Thus the most important feature of Pear's Case, from the point of view of the adoption of a new policy, is that it provided a formula for future cases.

[26] It may be well to recall that, with regard to the described changes in law, there were many other factors involved besides social and economic conditions, and that the existing body of law was one of the most important. Thus Pasley v. Freeman was, without doubt, one of the most important factors in the decision of R. v. Young et al. Yet Pasley v. Freeman must, itself, have been affected by social and economic conditions under the hypothesis employed above.

[27] The Economic Organization of England 40.

teenth to the sixteenth century the gild system was at its height. Then decay set in and it passed away completely in the eighteenth century.[28]

With the growth of large scale production and the marketing of goods on a wide national basis the personal, immediate relationship that existed between manufacturer, merchant and buyer in the manorial system and under the gilds gave way to an impersonal, distant relationship.[29] As a result, buyers of merchandise were without the first-hand protection they had previously enjoyed.

Instead, the rule *caveat emptor* was invoked, and buyers were required to safeguard their own interests, lest trade be smothered by claims raised after sale. Yet the combination of large-scale marketing and the purchase of goods at a distance in reliance on representations of the seller, produced conditions which in due course could be seen to make safeguards against fraud necessary. Again, the transition from a system of cash on delivery transactions to a credit economy made the sale of goods on time a vital factor. Accordingly it became necessary to safeguard merchants against an extension of credit upon misrepresentations. Finally, the breakdown of primary groups by a succession of enclosure movements concomitant with greatly increased mobility in population and the rise of cities produced new alignments of persons unknown to one another—a condition of affairs which lent itself to fraud quite apart from commercial transactions.

The most significant result of the commercial changes described above was the rise of large-scale dealing in stolen goods. This was dramatically exhibited in the case of Jonathan Wild. In the early part of the eighteenth century Jonathan Wild, the most remarkable receiver of stolen goods on record in the modern world, made his distinctive contribution to a commercial age. A case study of Wild would be most profitable, perhaps especially for those well-intentioned souls who imagine that by

---

[28] *Id.* 39.

[29] "In the course of the 18th century the wholesaler becomes finally separated from the retailer and comes to constitute a definite branch of the merchant class." Max Weber, *op. cit.* 292.

any simple device such as passing a new law or restoring capital punishment on a wholesale scale, anti-social behavior can be made to disappear. The study of crimes against property without violence and particularly of this offense of receiving stolen property shows that criminal behavior must be viewed in relation to the culture of which it forms a part.

Wild, notorious organizer of criminal bands on a scale that would make most gangs of today (except those involved in gambling, narcotics, and prostitution) seem ordinary, was an original thinker and a shrewd, capable executive. His career has captured the imagination and engaged the pens of Fielding and Defoe. His exploits have been recorded in numerous monographs.[30]

The following quotation from Gordon presents the salient facts:

"But he dealt extensively in stolen goods, so much so, that he bought a sloop (Captain Roger Johnson), to trade to Holland and Flanders, in which were carried over gold watches, rings, snuff-boxes, and articles of plate, and sometimes bank notes, the proceeds of some mail robbery. His chief-trading port was Ostend, whence Bruges, Ghent, Brussels, and other large towns were easily accessible, and a market existed for his wares. A lading of Hollands and other goods was then shipped, and on the return to England, the custom-house was never troubled.

"An epitome of his villanies is to be found in some sworn informations handed in at his trial.—1. That for many years he had been a confederate with great numbers of highwaymen, pickpockets, housebreakers, shoplifters, and other thieves. 2. That he had formed a kind of corporation of thieves, of which he was the head, or director; and that, notwithstanding his pretended services in detecting and prosecuting offenders, he procured such only to be hanged as concealed their booty, or refused to share

---

[30] See the various Newgate Calendars; Charles Gordon, The Old Bailey and Newgate 134 et seq.; 2 Pike, op. cit. 255 et seq.; A. L. Hayward (Ed.), Lives of the Most Remarkable Criminals (1927), collected from original papers published in 1735. For an account of his trial, see 2 Select Trials at the Session House at the Old Bailey (1742) 212–18 and 635.

it with him. 3. That he divided the town and country into so many districts, and appointed distinct gangs to each, who regularly accounted to him for their robberies. That he had also a particular set to steal at churches in time of divine services; and, likewise, other moving detachments to attend at court, on birthdays, balls, etc.; and at both Houses of Parliament, circuits, and county fairs. 4. That the persons employed by him were, for the most part, felons convict, who had returned from transportation before the time for which they were transported was expired; and that he made choice of them to be his agents, because they could not be legal evidence against him, and because he had it in his power to take from them what part of the stolen goods he thought fit, and otherwise use them ill, or hang them, as he pleased. 5. That he had from time to time supplied such convicted felons with money and clothes, and lodged them in his own house, the better to conceal them, particularly some, against whom there are now informations for counterfeiting and diminishing broad pieces and guineas. 6. That he had not only been a receiver of stolen goods, as well as of writings of all kinds, for nearly fifteen years past, but had frequently been a confederate, and robbed along with the abovementioned convicted felons. 7. That, in order to carry on these vile practices, to gain some credit with the ignorant multitude, he usually carried a short silver staff, as a badge of authority from the Government, which he used to produce, when he himself was concerned in robbery. 8. That he had under his care and protection several warehouses for receiving and concealing stolen goods; and also a ship for carrying off jewels, watches, and other valuable goods to Holland, where he had a superannuated thief for his factor. 9. That he kept in pay several artists to make alterations, and to transform watches, seals, snuff-boxes, rings, and other valuable things, that they might not be known, several of which he used to present to such persons as he thought might be of service to him. 10. That he seldom, or never, helped the owners to the notes and papers they had lost, unless he found them able exactly to specify and describe them, and then often insisted on more than half their value. 11. And lastly, it appears that he has often sold human blood, by procuring false evidence to swear persons into facts they were not guilty of; sometimes to prevent them from being evidence against himself, and, at other times, for the sake of the great reward given by the Government." [31]

Pike summarizes the situation thus:

"In the republic of the thieves' guild Jonathan Wild became as it were a dictator; but like many of the great men of the middle ages, he owed his greatness to double-dealing. From small beginnings he became in London at least, the receiver-in-chief of all stolen goods. He acquired and maintained this position by the persistent application of two simple principles; he did his best to aid the law in convicting all those misdoers who would not recognise his authority, and he did his best to repair the losses of all who had been plundered and who took him into their confidence. By degrees he set up an office for the recovery of missing property, at which the government must, for a time, have connived. Here the robbed sought an audience of the only man who could promise them restitution; here the robbers congregated like workmen at a workshop, to receive the pay for the work they had done.

"Wild was, in some respects, more autocratic than many kings, for he had the power of life and death. If he could reward the thief who submitted to him, he could hang the robber who omitted to seek his protection." [32]

We need to note one other phase of Wild's activities which was a tribute to the man's originality and a contribution to large-scale theft that has persisted to this day. After the enactment of 1 Anne c. 9, and 5 Anne c. 31 which superseded it, the risk of operating as a buyer of stolen goods was greatly increased. The techniques Wild had applied to protect himself, of concealing the thief or having him executed for another offense, were not helpful in this new situation. Wild, thereupon, refined his *modus operandi*. He became a self-nominated quasi-public police department. He would, for a "reward," and upon receipt

---

[31] The Old Bailey and Newgate (1923) 139–40.
[32] 2 Pike, *op. cit.* 256–8.

of a detailed description of stolen property, undertake to find and restore it to the owner.[33] The new venture flourished, until in 1718 the statute of 4 Geo. I, c. 11, sec. 4 was passed directed at this very activity.[34]

Wild's career ended on the gallows in 1725, but only after three trials. First, he "was indicted for a misdemeanor in receiving goods knowing, etc. But it appearing that the principal felons had been convicted and executed, it was objected that this indictment would not lie, being only given by the Stat. 5 Ann., where the principal felon cannot be taken and convicted. And Pratt C. J., being of that opinion, the defendant was acquitted." [35]

Wild was again indicted, this time for privately stealing in the shop of Catherine Stetham fifty yards of lace, value £40, on January 22, 1725. "But it appearing from the testimony of *Henry Kelly, the principal felon* who had actually stolen the lace, and *who was admitted an evidence for the Crown,* that

---

[33] "Among the *Egyptians* there was a remarkable Law, or rather custom, which had the sanction of Law, with regard to robbers and sharpers. Whoever entered himself of their gang, gave his name to the Chief, promising to deliver to him all the booty that he should from time to time purloin. On this account, it was customary for such as had anything stolen from them, to apply to the chief of the gang, and give a more particular account and description in writing of what they had lost; as also of the day, hour, and place, when and where they had lost it. This information being given, the stolen goods were easily found, and restored to the right owner, upon his paying a fourth part of the value.
"The institutors of this extraordinary Law, probably thought, that since it was impossible to prevent thieving entirely, it would be more tolerable for the injured party to lose a fourth, by way of redemption than the whole." Henry Dagge, Considerations on Criminal Law (Dublin 1772) 390–1.
[34] This statute is most interesting, and throws light upon a situation which has remained typical until the present day. It provided: "And whereas there are several persons who have secret acquaintance with felons, and who make it their business to help persons to their stolen goods, and by that means gain money from them, which is divided between them and the felons, whereby they greatly encourage such offenders: be it enacted by the authority aforesaid, That wherever any person taketh money or reward, directly or indirectly, under pretence or upon account of helping any person or persons to any stolen goods or chattels, every such person so taking money or reward, as aforesaid, (unless such person doth apprehend, or cause to be apprehended, such felon who stole the same, and cause such felon to be brought to his trial for the same, and give evidence against him) shall be guilty of felony. . . ."
We have here the remarkable instance of the passage of a law aimed directly at the activities of a particular criminal, and of his being indicted, convicted and executed for a violation of this law. See the text directly *infra.*
[35] 2 East, P. C. 746.

Wild was not in the shop at the time, but only waited at the corner of the street to receive the goods, he was acquitted on this indictment." [36] The Crown was not, however, deterred. Again Wild was immediately arraigned, tried and, this time, convicted of the offense of receiving a reward of ten guineas from Catherine Stetham for helping her to recover the box of lace stolen by Henry Kelly, who again testified against him. [37]

Wild's elimination in 1725 did not stop the business of dealing in stolen goods. [38] Other receivers continued and appeared; other thief-takers operated upon the same plan. It is a significant commentary that the reward became established as a principal method of recovering stolen property. It became customary to advertise publicly that a reward would be paid for the return of the property, that no inquiries would be made of the person who returned it, and that no attempt would be made to cause his arrest. [39] The inability of the police and other officials to cope adequately with the problem of theft perpetuated the system,

---

[36] 1 Leach 21, n. a; 168 E. R. 111.

[37] Pike informs us how Wild finally came to his end. "A highwayman was apprehended near Bow: Wild came to the rescue, and aided him to escape from his captor. For this offense Wild was committed to Newgate. When he was thus rendered powerless, the fear with which he had been regarded began to be diminished, and witnesses were less reluctant to give their evidence against him . . . information after information was sworn respecting his past deeds . . . He was hanged on May 24, 1725." 2 Pike, *op. cit.* 259.

And see N. 34 *supra.*

[38] The spread of the business is evidenced by the matter-of-fact confession of an offender about to be executed in 1732. He stated: "The sheets we sold to one *Irish Nell*, a fence, for 9s, the Petticoat for 7s 6d to the same person . . . other articles which we sold in *Crooked Lane* for 1d per Pound (lead) . . . at a *Ginn Shop* . . . where Thomas Edwards and I often sold him lead at several times about forescore hundred weight." Old Bailey Trials (1731–1732) 16.

One of the best descriptions of the operations of criminal receivers is given by Colquhoun, Police of the Metropolis (1796), Chap. 8.

[39] "But at present, instead of meeting with any such Discouragement, the Thief disposes of his Goods with almost as much Safety as the honest Tradesman; For first, if he hath made a Booty of any Value, he is almost sure of seeing it advertised within a Day or two, directing him *to bring the Goods to a certain Place where he is to receive a Reward* (sometimes the full value of the Booty) *and no Questions asked.*" Henry Fielding, An Enquiry Into The Causes of the Late Increase of Robbers, etc. 68–9. *Cf.* 2 East, P. C. 770; 4 Bl. Comm. 132.

Typical legislation forbidding this followed in the enactment of 25 Geo. II, c. 36, sec. 1. *Cf.* Larceny Act, sec. 102 (24 & 25 Vict. c. 96).

and encouraged the intervention of laymen who specialized in the recovery of stolen property.

The legal measures taken to control the criminal receiving of stolen property became prominent at the end of the seventeenth century, and in the first quarter of the eighteenth century they are accentuated in statutes aimed directly at the business of dealing in stolen goods. Thus, the correlation between Wild's elimination and 4 Geo. I. c. 11 sec. 4 (1718) is direct and positive. In general, it was necessary to deal with the problem under handicap of the traditional view of the receiver as an accessory after the fact. Various methods were employed to compensate for this perspective but it was not until 1782 when commerce, including that in stolen goods, had greatly expanded that a major objective was achieved—the use of the thief's testimony in prosecution of the receiver was established by statute.

We have met similar developments in other parts of the law of theft. The intimate interplay between commercial and non-commercial frauds has been pointed out. Whether sound distinctions, legally significant, can be drawn between them is problematic; in both, the conduct of the defendant is practically identical. Yet certain differences may be recognized in the types of offenders which appear to have had considerable effect. Thus in the ring-dropping cases and in R. v. Young et al.,[40] the offenders were professional sharpers; whereas in commercial frauds, like R. v. Wheatly [41] and Pasley v. Freeman,[42] ostensibly respectable business men were involved. The dominant social attitudes favored the encouragement of trade, and Pasley v. Freeman, which provided a civil remedy, satisfied both the judges' conscience and the needs of free commerce. These commercial requirements did not apply to R. v. Young et al.[43]

---

[40] See pp. 50–51 supra.
[41] See pp. 46–47 supra.
[42] See pp 49–50 supra.
[43] The net effect was that respectable business men were immune from prosecution and subject only to civil suit. It was not until after the middle of the nineteenth century that successful prosecutions were brought for commercial frauds; and the decisions show that the courts were reluctant to attach a criminal liability to commercial transactions.

See Reg. v. Bryan, 7 Cox C. C. 312 (1857); Reg. v. Goss and Reg. v. Ragg, 8 Cox C. C. 262 (1860).

We may summarize and conclude this discussion by noting that the last twenty years of the eighteenth century produced the most rapid and extensive growth of the entire law of theft. What conditions influenced this accelerated development? To the continuing and cumulative effects of the social and economic conditions described thus far, it is necessary to add that trade was increasing at enormous strides as the Commercial Revolution advanced to its peak. But most important were the effects of the Industrial Revolution. Both of these factors were aspects of the same movement.

As to the first, the point that must be stressed is the *rapidity* with which the volume of trade grew. It was expanding in geometric proportions. For example, the tonnage of the ships which left English ports increased from 289,000 tons in 1709 to 647,000 in 1760 to 2,130,000 in 1800: [44] over twice the tonnage in 1760 as in 1709; and over three times the tonnage in 1800 as in 1760.[45]

As to the second factor, it is important to distinguish the beginnings of the Industrial Revolution from its effects; and with regard to both, to note that economic history presents divergent views.[46] Until very recently Arnold Toynbee's classic exposition was generally accepted. According to him,[47] the Revolution be-

---

[44] "From 1700 to 1783 the annual value of the combined exports and imports increased gradually and fairly steadily from ten to twenty-eight millions of pounds. In the next seven years they jumped to thirty-nine millions, and during the decade from 1790 to 1800 they reached the huge total of seventy-three millions." W. E. Lunt, History of England 622.

Cf. Clive Day, A History of Commerce (1907) 205, and Mantoux, The Industrial Revolution in the 18th Century 103–4.

[45] From 1760 to 1775, 542 statutes were passed dealing with the construction and maintenance of roads. Redfield, *op. cit.* 9.

There was also a "canal mania," and between 1791 and 1794 eighty-one canal and navigation acts were passed. E. A. Pratt, A History of Inland Transportation in England 183. Between 1790 and 1800 over a thousand miles of canals were built. H. R. Exelby, *op. cit.* 81. ". . . during its short reign the canal had a revolutionary effect upon the economic development of the country." M. C. Buer, *op. cit.* 54. "The improved means of communication saw an extraordinary increase in commerce." A. Toynbee, *op. cit.* 91. *Cf.* the problem of the Carrier's Case.

[46] This problem must be constantly watched in utilizing data from a field in which one is not a specialist. For an excellent discussion of what is involved, see W. Sombart, *Economic Theory and Economic History*, 2 Econ. Hist. Rev. 1.

[47] A. Toynbee, *op. cit.* 32.

gan precisely in 1760 and ended a century later.[48] Later students, however, fix the date of the beginning of the Industrial Revolution at the very dawn of the eighteenth century and some of them go back to 1688.[49]

Likewise, it has now become rather clear that the *effects* of the Revolution were not evident until the end of the eighteenth century. Thus, Paul Mantoux states that "the modern factory system originated in England in the last third of the eighteenth century." [50] Mantoux presents detailed figures on exports and imports and shows that there was a steady upward rise with short, temporary drops coinciding with war periods until about 1780, when there was a tremendous rise which continued through the remainder of the century. "The most striking thing is the way they rise almost vertically towards the end. This corresponds precisely to the period when machinery first made itself felt and when the products of the factory system began to spread all over the world." [51]

Set against this the principal changes in the law: Pear's Case in 1779 marks the inception of a vastly accelerated growth of the entire law of theft. In 1782 the thief's testimony is admitted

---

[48] *Cf.* "The change, which has been briefly sketched in the previous chapter, from the domestic system of industry to the modern system of production by machinery and steam power was sudden and violent." Gibbins, *op. cit.* 341. But *cf.* "The Industrial Revolution was thus a revolution in every sense of the word, except that of suddenness of transition." A. P. Usher, Industrial History of England (1919) 271.

[49] "The abandonment of the idea that the Industrial Revolution was sudden involves a considerable readjustment of chronology for the entire movement. . . . There is a growing disposition to carry the beginnings of the movement back to 1700. . . . The date is wholly satisfactory except for the metal trades, in which the abortive experiments of Dudley (1619–1622) are pretty clearly the beginning of the story." Usher, *op. cit.* 271.

[50] The Industrial Revolution in the Eighteenth Century 25.

Quite clearly many of the earlier writers have been unduly influenced by the dates when important inventions made their appearance. These great inventions were perfected between 1733, when Kay invented the flying shuttle, and 1785, when steam power was substituted for water power in factories. Watt patented his steam engine in 1769, Hargreaves his spinning jenny in 1770, Arkwright the water frame in 1771, Crampton his "mule" in 1779 and Cartwright his power loom in 1785. But time elapsed before the inventions were generally utilized and new methods of production were organized around them.

[51] Mantoux, *op. cit.* 103–4.

against the receiver. 30 Geo. II expands in 1789, with Young's Case, to include false pretenses in a modern sense. That same year comes Pasley *v.* Freeman, and ten years later the first general embezzlement statute.

Whether regarded as the peak of the Commercial Revolution or regarded partly as the era which also ran well into the Industrial Revolution or as a transition, there is unanimity that with reference to the volume of business done, the nature of commerce, and the prevailing types of social and economic organization, the century, as a whole, stands out clearly against all preceding periods in English history. It would be extraordinary if this had left no mark on the growth of the law on crimes against property without violence.

In each development of the law, the particular step taken was a resultant of forces determined largely by social and economic conditions, the existing legal sanctions, the whole body of precedent, and the established judicial techniques. The interplay of law, case, and conditions can be understood only when the meaning of each factor is known.

CHAPTER THREE

THE CONSTRUCTION OF THE SUBSTANTIVE LAW AS SHOWN IN THE SUBJECT-MATTER OF LARCENY

Against the background of the history of the law of theft, presented in the preceding chapters, we shall explore a specific point—the subject-matter of larceny. Among the various "material" elements of the several offenses comprising theft, which might be selected for "depth analysis," the subject-matter of larceny, for reasons that will become evident as we proceed, is the most significant one.

Any person uninitiated into the intricate vagaries of Anglo-American criminal law must be struck by a number of peculiarities in that venerable discipline. If he should seek an answer to so apparently simple a question as, what can be stolen?, he would be introduced into a labyrinthian network of legal propositions woven into innumerable statutes and cases. A long list of specific objects, including such curiosa as *feræ naturæ*, appended to an enumeration of several types of property, winding up with a blanket clause which makes the prior specifications more mysterious than ever, purports to answer his inquiry.

If an explanation for this bizarre and apparently irrational state of affairs is sought, in what directions shall inquiry be pursued? An intimate relationship between the law of larceny and the things that men value is clear. The whole body of the substantive criminal law, in so far as it concerns the so-called crimes against property, has been designed for the protection of possessions. Its shape has been modified and directed to conform with the desire to protect the numerous forms of wealth which were produced as the economic organization of society changed.

In considering the question, *why* the Anglo-American law of theft has taken its particular form, I propose, first, to discuss briefly the economic conditions which influenced the formulation of the basic rules in this branch of the law and, second, to discuss more fully the operation of the legal institution itself as represented by (a) a group of trained officials who learned the same body of rules and were thus, to a considerable extent, uniformly conditioned to the use of a standardized technique in deciding cases, and (b) a group of untrained officials who attempted to solve each practical problem as it arose, and depended upon their trained brethren to make the remedial measures work.

I. MOVABLE POSSESSIONS AND THE PRIMARY RULES

The mere mention of Anglo-Saxon England conjures up a picture of a primitive, agricultural community. The land under cultivation was divided into strips; pasture was held in common. Beyond these lands were forests inhabited by wild animals, and there were streams and lakes abounding in fish. Farming, grazing, hunting and fishing supplied the needs of life. The implements used were few, crudely fashioned, and dearly cherished. The houses were of the simplest type imaginable.[1] Built in clusters near the cultivated land, they contained the most ordinary of utensils and furniture. The local lord had a few chattels of relatively rare value, perhaps some silver plate, several gold ornaments, his weapons, horses and dogs. "Till nearly the end of the fourteenth century," writes Ashley, "England was a purely agricultural country."[2] These were the conditions with reference to which there was formulated a number of distinctive rules regarding the subject-matter of larceny which have ever since characterized the basic conceptual structure of this branch of the criminal law.

Cattle were by far the most important of the possessions. Horses and oxen were the means of transportation and com-

---

[1] "A dwelling with an earthen floor, with no carpet, and in which there was hardly any furniture, where meat was served on spits for want of earthenware plates and there was no glass for drinking out of, would seem to imply the lowest depths of squalid poverty; but royal palaces were little better provided till after the time of John, and well-to-do burgesses lived in some such fashion at the end of the thirteenth century." 1 Cunningham, *op. cit.* 297.

[2] An Introduction to English Economic History and Theory (3rd ed. 1894) 5.

munication. Horses were essential for the conduct of war. Oxen drew the ploughs. Cattle, moreover, carried themselves, a matter of no small importance and, as we shall see, very significant for the law of larceny. Food, transportation and communication, war, tillage, all depended, therefore, upon these lesser creatures. It is not surprising, then, to find that cattle were used as the common medium of exchange and that they represented the commodity of greatest value.[3]

Accordingly, in the dooms of the Anglo-Saxon kings, as far back as the seventh century, there are not only edicts against the solitary cattle-thief, but also against bands of marauders. In Bracton, the "cattle-lifter," an early prototype of the "rustler" on our western prairies, is singled out for special condemnation.[4]

The paramount importance of movable property, and especially of cattle, as the foundation-image upon which the rules were constructed, is apparent. Thus one primary rule was the result of the distinction between *feræ naturæ* and goods *in possession* (cattle). One version of the rule is stated by Britton.[5]

---

[3] "Whatever might be the value of the forest for deer and other wild beasts, all other uses were subordinate to the feeding of the 'cattle upon a thousand hills', which formed at once the coinage and the food and the means of cultivation of the land.

"The king is paid both the money penalties of his courts and the terms due to him from the counties largely in cattle and other animals, and in fact in produce of all kinds."

"The chieftain rank was graded according to wealth in movables and cattle, and the privileges of each chief were according to his degree. According to his wealth and birth was the value of his oath, which was measured in cattle. . . ." Jeudwine, The Foundations of Society and the Land (1918) 188, 82. *Cf.* 1 Cunningham, *op. cit.* 121–2.

[4] 2 Twiss ed. 157.

[5] "As to pigeons, fish, bees or other wild animals, found in a wild condition, we ordain that no man have judgment of death on account of them; but otherwise, if they have been feloniously stolen out of houses, or if they are tame beasts, out of parks." 1 Camb. ed. 122. This is repeated in a note of a case decided in 1348 (Lib. Ass. 22, f. 106, pl. 95).

Cf. the *Mirror's* inclusion of *feræ naturæ* within the scope of theft. With regard to the statement found there that "into this sin fall thieves of others' deer, fish in a stew, conies, hares, pheasants and partridges in warrens, pigeons and swans, eyrie of all manner of birds" (at 27), Stephen writes, "This is directly opposed to some of the best ascertained and most ancient rules of the law." 3 H. C. L. 135.

But *cf.* 2 Pollock and Maitland, The History of English Law Before the Time of Edward I (2nd ed.) 498, where it is stated that *feræ naturæ* in possession are subject of larceny. Perhaps this represented the refinement of an earlier crude rule which wholly excluded *feræ naturæ* regardless of possession.

It was not until 1478, however, that we find a decision which clearly enunciated one phase of it.[6] An indictment for having "with force and arms broken into a dovecoat and feloniously taken twenty young pigeons" was sustained; but it was pointed out that it would have been otherwise if the pigeons were old, "for they go about the country and he cannot take them at his pleasure." In subsequent cases it was emphasized that things must be under someone's actual or constructive control, that is, in the "possession" of some individual, before they can be stolen. It is certain that the formulation of that rule, even in Britton, succeeded a long line of cases in which complaints were made for loss of chattels. The right to retain what one had must have been recognized long before any generalization was made regarding the nature of things which could be stolen. In any event, *feræ naturæ* and possession, though often confused as grounds for decision, become recognized as limitations on the subject-matter of larceny.

In 1527 it was argued at length before all the justices whether taking tame peacocks was felony or not.[7] The question turned upon whether peacocks were *feræ naturæ* like pheasants and partridges or domesticated like hens, capons, geese and ducks. The justices adopted the latter view. In addition to the *feræ naturæ* issue, it had been argued that peacocks being "things of pleasure rather than of a profit," could not be the subject of larceny. This suggestion was applied in a case occurring in the reign of Edward VI by Hales J., who apparently "thought it no felony to take a diamond, rubie or other such stone (not set in gold or otherwise) because they be not of price with all men, howsoever some do hold them both dear and precious."[8] This represented the beginning of the third exclusionary rule which determined the subject-matter of larceny, namely, that the chattel must have value.

The author of the *Mirror* (*circa* 1290) to whom we are indebted for the first clear formulation of a modern definition of larceny, emphasized that only *movables* could be the subject of

---

[6] Y. B. 18 Ed. IV, 8, pl. 7
[7] Y. B. 19 Hen. VIII, f. 2, pl. 11.
[8] Quoted in 3 Stephen, H. C. L. 143.

larceny;[9] and this principle was applied some years later in the case of a forester who felled and carried away trees owned by his lord.[10] The justices refused to arraign him because "the felling [and carrying away] of trees which are so annexed to the soil cannot be called a felony, even if a stranger had done it." Alleburgh J. simply stated, "We adjudge that it is no felony, because he was the keeper; and a tree is part of the freehold." [11] It will be seen that this rule rested upon the distinction between things *affixed to the soil* (trees and crops) and other property which was *movable* (cattle). The relatively minor initial importance of immovable property is further shown by the fact that, despite the reference in the *Mirror* to land, nowhere in the long list of illustrations of theft is any mention whatever made of trees or crops or other things attached to the land. Nor does Britton discuss them in connection with larceny. As stated by Pollock and Maitland: "Cattle lifting is our starting point. It is a theme to which the Anglo-Saxon dooms and the parallel 'folk laws' of the continental nations are ever recurring. If only cattle lifting could be suppressed, the legislators will have done all or almost all that they can hope to do for the protection of the owner of movables." [12] The rules reflect the situation.

It seems fair to assume that all that was decided in the earliest cases, during what may be called the pre-formula period, was that certain defendants were guilty of theft of certain property (which probably was movable). When cases arose involving the taking and carrying away of growing trees,

---

[9] The important portion of the *Mirror's* definition is the statement "A corporeal moveable, we say: for no larceny can be committed of an immoveable or incorporeal thing such as land or rent or advowsons of churches" (at 25). *Cf.* Stephen: "It [the definition in the *Mirror*] contains much which undoubtedly formed for centuries, and indeed still forms part of the law. . . . This is, as far as it goes, a perfect definition of the offense of theft, as it is still understood in this country." 3 H. C. L. 134, 135.

[10] Anon., Assizes 1338, Y. B. 11 & 12 Ed. III, 640.

[11] *Ibid.* The same question was argued the next year, "which would show how slowly the law was formed." 3 Stephen, H. C. L. 136. In 1389, the line of thought is refined: "If a man cut and carry away corn at the same time, it is *trespass* [a civil wrong] only and not *felony*, because it is but one act; but if he cut it and lay it by, and carry it away afterwards, it is felony." Emmerson, Executor of Fisher *v.* Annison, 86 Eng. Rep. 755.

[12] 2 H. E. L. 157.

corn or other cultivated products of the soil, they might logically have been decided either way, namely, that theft had or had not been committed. The decision that things viewed technically as immovables could *not* in law be stolen indicates that cases and instances involving movables (cattle, ordinary chattels, *feræ naturæ*) had been both prior to [13] and more numerous than other cases, until they provided a weighty reference for deciding cases involving things attached to the soil.[14]

The substantive criminal law is a very complex structure, and many agencies have directed, conditioned, and multiplied the primary rules whose emergence we have been watching. Our interest in the economic conditions centers on the formulation of the subject-matter of larceny. No attempt will be made to follow the persistent interaction of the legal institution with social and economic institutions. The problem here is rather to describe the growth of a typical phase of the legal institution itself, tracing the various factors which, *within itself,* contributed to its unique structure—sometimes in the teeth of such pressing economic influences as the last chapter showed to have been operative.

II. The Influence of Coke

During all the time the earliest rules were being developed, as is to be expected, nothing was said about choses in action.[15]

---

[13] In the raid, the "cattle-lifter" did not stay to reap crops, etc.

[14] This view regarding the greater frequency *and importance* of cases involving movables may receive support from the thesis advanced by Bacon, in his Abridgment, that the rules were based on the conditions found in military camps. "Hence we have the Reason of the Distinction between the Real and Personal Property, and why our Law does not punish the Stealing of Corn or Grass growing, or Apples on a Tree, or Lead on a Church or House with Death; because these never came under the Camp Discipline; and therefore it was not necessary to guard this Sort of Property with such Sanguinary Laws, where the Redress may be by a Civil Action." 2 Bacon's Abridgment (3rd ed.) 470.

While the opportunities for theft of movables and the resulting harm might well have been greater in camp, Bacon's attribution of the origin of the rule entirely to the conditions of military tenure is more than dubious. Long before there was military tenure, the cattle thief and bands of marauders preyed upon the population.

[15] "A right to receive or recover a debt, or money, or damages for breach of contract, or for a tort connected with a contract, but which cannot be enforced without action." Bouvier's Law Dict.

There was, to be sure, the statement in the *Mirror* excepting incorporeal things such as "rent or advowsons [16] of churches." [17] There were also earlier cases involving instruments, but they were disposed of without any analysis of the document as a thing-in-action and without using the term. As far back as 1429, a statute of Henry VI made it a felony to take documents filed in court where a judgment was reversed for that reason,[18] but this statute was designed to prevent interference with the king's courts; there is no indication that it developed from the existing law regarding the subject-matter of larceny. The first recorded case of importance concerning the theft of documents was Rex *v.* Wody, decided in 1470.[19] Wody was indicted for taking and carrying away "six boxes, with charters and muniments concerning the inheritance of" etc. Choke J., who was three years later to provide the theoretical basis for deciding Carrier's Case, held that the documents were "real in themselves; for if a man be attainted of felony, the king shall not have his charters concerning his land for they are real." As for the boxes, it was argued that "if sealed, [they] shall be deemed of the same nature as the charters contained in them." "This," says Stephen, "appears to me to be one of the most pedantic and unmeaning decisions in the whole law." [20]

The origin of the rule excepting choses in action from the subject-matter of larceny is attributed directly to Coke [21] by Stephen who stated that this "doctrine rests upon no foundation except a wholly unauthorized extension by Coke in treatment of a different subject, of a case in the Year-books" (Rex

---

[16] "A right of presentation to a church or benefice." *Id.*

[17] *Supra,* footnote 9.

[18] "If any record, . . . return, . . . process, or warrant of attorney in the King's courts of chancery, exchequer, . . . be willingly stolen, taken away, withdrawn, or avoided by any . . . person, because whereof any judgment shall be reversed; that such stealer . . . shall incur the pain of felony." 8 Hen. VI, c. 12, s. 3.

[19] Y. B. 49 Hen. VI, f. 14, pl. 9, 10.

[20] 3 H. C. L. 138–9. Curiously enough, and not without significance, is the fact that this identification of box with charters was acquiesced in by Choke J., who was later, in Carrier's Case, to differentiate sharply the mere wrappings on the bales from their contents.

[21] Cayle's Case, 8 Co. Rep. 32a (1584).

v. Wody).[22] Whatever might be said in justification of Coke's gratuitous remarks on choses in action in 1584, no support can be found in Rex *v.* Wody, upon which he relied. For it is clear that Rex *v.* Wody was the result of the extension of rules of property law which were conceived to require the conclusion that the particular instruments involved were realty.[23] Even as late as 1739 when similar facts arose in The King *v.* Westbeer, the decision that the defendant was not guilty of stealing a "parchment writing" was based solely on the ground that "they concerned the realty, and could not become the subjects of larceny, from their constructive adherence to and connection with, the freehold."[24] The omission of any reference in that case to choses in action shows that the courts distinguished deeds and other documents relating to realty from things in action. Furthermore, the jury fixed the value of the instrument at one penny. Therefore, it could not possibly have been thought that it was a chose in action since choses were, by a rationalization, declared to have no intrinsic pecuniary value whatever, being *mere* evidence of rights.[25]

The rule on choses in action, together with the others discussed above, by and large determined the subject-matter of larceny. These decisions, modeled on cattle-lifting, led to the formulation of the rule that movables could be stolen and that immovables could not be stolen. Early rules formulated in the

---

[22] "The Year-books do not refer to *choses* in action other than deeds. There is no decision that a bond, for instance, which did not affect land was incapable of being stolen. Coke, however, who accepted any sort of principle laid down in the Year-books as if it was a law of nature, accepted this principle and applied it to all *choses* in action whatever. In Cayle's case he gives an elaborate commentary on the writ in the Register which defines the liability of innkeepers for the goods of their guests. Some of its words, he says, 'extend to all moveable goods, although of them felony cannot be committed, as of charters, evidences, obligations, deeds, specialities, &c.'" 3 Stephen, H. C. L. 144.

[23] *Cf.* "A *gard* [a ward, guardian, a *judgment*—perhaps something guarded or kept] cannot be taken because it is a real thing. The law is the same with respect to a box of charters for the reason already stated and also because it is impossible to place a value on the charters as is shown in M. 10, E. 4, f. 15." Staunford, Pleas of the Crown, Book 1, cap. 16.

[24] 168 Eng. Rep. 108 (1 Leach 11) 109. For the effect of the existing sanction, see p. 119 *infra*.

[25] 2 East, P. C. 597.

law of real property declared that trees, growing grain and *fructus industriales,* in general, were part of the freehold. These rules were reasonable enough when applied to the transfer and descent of land. But the same judges decided both civil and criminal cases. Accordingly, when cases involving the felonious taking of such property arose, they were perhaps naturally, but utterly without regard to the purpose of the larceny rules, treated as being realty *and therefore "immovable."* [26] The application of the concepts of the law of real property relating to trees and growing grain lay technically close and had warrant in the relative infrequency of such thefts. Their application to documents in boxes in 1470 in Rex *v.* Wody was a logical extension of a formula which had become set. The appearance of the rule regarding choses in action several centuries after the other exceptions were formulated, seems to have been fortuitous. [27] This rule, because of the subject with which it dealt, necessarily originated very much later than the others.

III. Legislation

As the above formulas became fixed in the case-law, new conditions arose. The problems which resulted concerned the application of these formulas in a changed environment and required the modification of these rules by legislatures and by judges. In order to understand the immediate reasons for the volume and type of legislation which was enacted, it is necessary to recall the significance of the above common law rules in their negative aspects, namely, that no real property, no *feræ naturæ* or goods not possessed, no choses in action, and no goods without pecuniary value could be stolen.

The modifying legislation reveals an amazingly long list of

---

[26] Stephen suggests (3 H. C. L. 132–3) that the advantages arising from bringing trespass rather than an appeal of larceny (avoidance of trial by battle) is one reason "why so many different classes of things should have been held not to be the subject of larceny." For Professor Beale's rejection of this view see *The Borderland of Larceny,* 6 Harv. L. Rev. 245.

[27] Note the above remarkable decision by Coke in relation to the "great lawyer" interpretation of legal history. Note, also, that Coke decided Cayle's Case in *1584* and that not until 1729 was appropriate legislation passed bringing choses within the subject-matter of larceny. *Cf.* Pound, Interpretations of Legal History 128.

statutes which may be characterized as follows: First, they were designed to fill the gaps in the law constructed by the decisions. They were very specific enactments which made it criminal to take feloniously certain property which had been excluded from the subject-matter of larceny by the cases. Second, these statutes removed ambiguities in the case-law regarding certain types of property. Third, many of the statutes were designed to protect the interests of special classes, such as the nobles or business and industrial groups. Indeed, in some aspects, the subject-matters that swing into the light, from statute to statute, amount to a running commentary on the advance of agriculture, the arts, and finance. Fourth, numerous statutes, particularly those in the above, last class, provided for especially severe punishment in many cases. These statutes were, in turn, succeeded by other specific enactments designed to soften the rigor of the earlier laws. Fifth, more of the statutes by far were enacted in the eighteenth century than in any other.

The statutes follow quite definitely the rules of exclusion which had grown up in the decisions. Thus, a large number of statutes was passed to narrow the *feræ naturæ* rule. A few illustrations will suffice. Starting with Richard II numerous enactments were passed regarding hunting in forests and parks.[28] These were directed chiefly at hunting the king's deer.[29] In the reign of Edward III, it was made criminal to steal hawks.[30] The statute recited that taking reclaimed hawks and falcons should be felony "in respect of their generous nature and courage, serving *ob vitæ solatium* of princes and noble persons to make them fitted for great employment." Pheasants and partridges were added to the rapidly expanding subject-matter of larceny as were the eggs of falcons and other wild birds. In the latter part of the eighteenth century dogs were likewise included.[31]

---

[28] 13 Rich. II, st. 1, c. 11. For detailed discussion of the following legislation see Radzinowicz, *op. cit.*

[29] 9 Geo. I, c. 22, one of many statutes protecting the proprietorship of the king.

[30] 37 Ed. III, c. 19, made it equivalent to stealing a horse.

[31] 10 Geo. III, c. 18 (1770). The long omission of dogs is a curious chapter. The Conqueror's forest legislation had taken clear enough account of their value in hunting.

The same type of legislation was passed to limit the rule regarding real property. Again, specified property was brought within the scope of larceny. In 1601 taking corn, grain, or fruit was added but the statute, reflecting the inertia of the traditional view, did not make the offense a felony "as a man cannot steal any part of the freehold." Most of the legislation regarding *fructus industriales* came in the eighteenth century. Numerous statutes of George II and George III added madder roots, turnips, potatoes, carrots, cabbages, parsnips and a long list of other vegetables. In 1766 it was made a felony to cut and take trees or plants in the night time.[32]

A second group of statutes, passed with reference to property annexed to the land, related to fixtures. One of the first,[33] passed in 1731, made it a felony to steal lead and iron affixed to houses, the prevalence of such depredations being recited in the preamble. Later, copper, brass and bell metal were added.[34]

The third group of statutes dealing with property that had been classified as realty was concerned chiefly with the protection of the mines and collieries. These, too, appear in the eighteenth century and extend into the nineteenth, covering the period of the most important industrial developments. In 1752 it was made a felony to steal black lead from mines;[35] in 1798 a similar statute was passed with respect to coal.[36]

Lastly, the same type of narrow legislation was passed regarding choses in action. Specific choses in action were named and brought within the subject-matter of larceny. There was no legislation until 1729, but at that time "the legislature found it necessary to interfere upon this subject."[37]

---

[32] 6 Geo. III, c. 36.
[33] 4 Geo. II, c. 32.
[34] 21 Geo. III, c. 68 (1781).
[35] 25 Geo. II, c. 10.
[36] 39 Geo. III, c. 77, s. 5.
[37] 2 Russell on Crimes 143. *Cf.* the commercial developments described in Chapter Two. *Cf.* "The notes issued by private bankers were at first written on paper for any odd sums, like promissory notes. The practice was introduced by Child and Co. in 1729, of having the notes partly printed and partly written like a modern check." Conant, *op. cit.* 94.
The statute made it a felony to steal certain instruments "though the thing

Besides the need to fill lacunæ in the case-law, it was thought necessary or desirable to punish the theft of particular types of property more severely than other thefts.[38] Accordingly, the underlying philosophy of severe punishment, combined with the felt need to prevent the theft of particular types of property, resulted, also, in the passing of a long series of specific statutes similar in nature, though not in purpose to the ones described.[39] The property selected in England, the theft of which was specifically proscribed and punished severely, consisted chiefly of cattle, horses, deer from the king's park, mail from the post office, cloth and minerals. Such thefts were, for the most part, capital felonies without benefit of clergy until the beginning of the nineteenth century.[40] With the growth of

---

taken be a chose in action," and included "any exchequer orders or tallies, or other orders, intitling any other person or persons to any annuity or share in any parliamentary fund, or any exchequer bill, bank notes, South-Sea bonds, East-India bonds, dividend warrants of the bank, South-Sea company, East-India company or any other company, society or corporation, bills of exchange, navy bills or debentures, goldsmiths notes for payment of money or other bonds or warrants, bills or promissory notes for the payment of money, etc. . . ." 2 Geo. II, c. 25, sec. 3 (1729). This act provided that it was to be in force for five years. It was made perpetual in 9 Geo. II, c. 18 (1736).

3 Geo. IV, c. 24 (1822) provided that the buying or receiving shall be a felony or misdemeanor as if the securities were goods or chattels.

[38] The actual effect of these statutes, which was quite different from the legislative intent, is discussed in the next chapter.

[39] An anecdote related by Fowell Buxton in his debate on the mitigation of punishment bill, indicates the pressure of private interests in securing the enactment of such legislation. On one occasion Sir William Meredith is supposed to have gone into a room where he saw a gentleman, apparently asleep, to whom a clerk was reading a long series of proposed laws. Every few moments came the chorus "shall suffer death without benefit of clergy." On inquiring what the heinous offenses were the more fully awakened legislator replied, "Why sir, we country gentlemen have suffered much by depredations on our turnips—we have at length determined to put a period to the practice; and my good friend the minister has been so obliging as to allow me to make it death without benefit of clergy." Buxton asked: "Are laws thus extorted by private interest, and thus conceded to political subserviency—are these laws too sacred for revision?" Op. cit. 928. Cf. Radzinowicz, op. cit.

[40] Similarly severe laws were passed in the United States in the nineteenth century. In a number of southern states it was a capital felony to steal a slave. State v. Miles, 2 Nott and McCord 1 (So. Car. 1819). Perhaps the most typical and widespread legislation of this type dealt with the theft of cattle and horses. Not only in the South, but throughout the West, until comparatively recent times, loss of cattle or horses was a very serious matter; and in places in the West where doors were left unlocked and any wayfarer might

the humanitarian movement in the eighteenth century, however, the rigor of these statutes was mitigated. But this, also, when it was the work of Parliament, was done in the same manner as the originals were fashioned, namely, by specific, narrow enactments.

IV. THE CASES

The final factor to be discussed, which entered into the construction of the law of larceny, was provided by the activities of the judges who sharply modified the rules described above. The combination of primary formulas, narrow legislation, and judicial reconstruction of both produced an enormous number of highly refined concepts ("technicality"). The following cases illustrate two causes of the growth of technicality in the law of larceny: first, the great variety of facts dealt with, and the consequent logical necessity to draw fine distinctions in order to apply the specific, narrow legislation; and, second, the need to expand concepts and rules in order to attach criminal liability to the misappropriation of certain types of property not included within the existing definition of the subject-matter of larceny.[41]

In Carver v. Pierce [42] an action for slander was brought, based upon the words, "Thou art a thief, for thou hast stolen my dung." An elaborate discussion ensued with regard to whether dung was a chattel or part of the realty, and the decision turned upon whether the dung was piled up or spread upon the

---

enter at will and consume all the food he needed, the theft of live stock or horses was a capital offense. Texas, Act of Jan. 26, 1839, Laws of The Republic of Texas (2 Laws of Texas, 1838–1846). Similarly in Maryland, Act of 1793, c. 57, sec. 10, and that of 1799, c. 61, sec. 1, 3, with labor on the roads made optional later; North Carolina, Act of 1830 (6 Stat. 413) first offense, from 50 to 200 lashes, and also fine and imprisonment at the option of the court, and see State v. Mayor et al. (14 Rich. 76, 1866); in New Mexico stealing a horse or cattle, etc., punishable by from 30 to 60 lashes and imprisonment. Garcia v. Territory (1 N. M. 415, 1869). This act passed in 1865 was repealed in 1870, c. 26, Laws of 1870.

[41] A third use of technicality, to wit, as a device employed to mitigate the rigor of prescribed penalties, is discussed in the next chapter.

[42] 82 Eng. Rep. 534 (1648).

ground.[43] For centuries cases have accumulated on the question whether particular fixtures were within statutes designed to bring certain property within the subject-matter of larceny.[44] Such cases [45] illustrate the persistent problem of applying fixed concepts to a constantly changing subject-matter;[46] and sometimes, rather strange decisions are met. For example, an enterprising medical student was charged with stealing a corpse from a grave for the purpose of dissecting it. The court was in a difficult position because of the common law rule that there can be no property in a corpse; nevertheless, because the offense was "highly indecent and *contra bonos mores*," the conviction was upheld, though only a fine of five marks was imposed.[47]

But the maximum technicality was exhibited in prosecutions relating to choses in action. One of the first cases of major importance was that of Maria Theresa Phipoe,[48] who subsequently was landed in Newgate Prison for another offense.[49] A knife was held against the throat of the complainant and he was compelled to sign a promissory note for the sum of two thousand pounds. The defendant was held not guilty of larceny on the ground that the note was of no value to the prosecutor who did not even own the paper on which it was written.[50] The de-

[43] A similar problem was presented in Commonwealth v. Steimling and Steimling v. Bower, 156 Pa. 400 and 408 (1893) where large quantities of coal dust deposited along the shores of complainant's property were collected by defendant.

[44] In The King v. Hedges (1 Leach 201 (1779)) it concerned window sashes; in the King v. Hickman and Dyer (1 Leach 319 (1784), 168 Eng. Rep. 262) lead from a church; in The King v. Senior (1 Leach 496 (1788), 168 Eng. Rep. 350) a window casement; in Reg. v. Jones (169 Eng. Rep. 1118 (1858)) metal affixed to land; in Smith v. Commonwealth (14 Bush Rep. Ky. 31 (1878)) chandeliers attached to a house, etc. *ad infinitum*.

[45] Many of the relevant statutes are collected and discussed by Radzinowicz, *op. cit.*

[46] Plato's Statesman presents the first formulation of this problem.

[47] The King v. Lynn, 100 Eng. Rep. 394 (1788); and *cf.* 2 East, P. C. 652.

[48] 168 Eng. Rep. 438 (1795), 2 Leach 673.

[49] The Newgate Calendar gives an interesting account of her career.

[50] The decision was the result of logical application of numerous rules defining chose in action. The subsequent conviction of the defendant on another charge reveals the administrative application of various sanctions to secure the elimination of a notorious offender.

cision in Rex *v.* Hart [51] is typical of the lengthy involved discussions that became necessary because of technicalities in the
law of negotiable instruments. The defendant agreed to lend
the complainant five thousand pounds and produced ten instruments which were later stamped and upon which were written
"Payable at Messrs P., London," "Accepted," and the signature
of the complainant. At that time the instruments did not bear
the name of any drawer or any sum or date, but it had been
agreed that the sum of five hundred pounds was to be inserted.
The defendant, who did not advance any money for the instruments, immediately negotiated them. He was charged with larceny under a statute (7 & 8 Geo. IV, c. 29, s. 2) which penalized the theft of any "bill, note, warrant, order, or other security
whatsoever for money, or for payment of money," etc. Four
counts were placed in the indictment, but the defendant was
discharged because the instruments taken did not come within
the class of any of those described in the statute. The following
excerpt from Baron Bolland's opinion indicates the nature of
the problem:

"The first three counts are for stealing bills of exchange, securities for money, and orders for the payment of money. I
will, to simplify the argument, put it as if one only of these
papers was taken, instead of the ten. Is the paper a bill of exchange? No: it was at first a six-shilling stamp, with the words,
'Payable at Messrs, Praed & Co.'s, No. 189 Fleet Street, London,' written upon it. In its then state, no piece of paper could
be more useless. However, it is brought to Mr. Astley again,
and the word 'Accepted,' and his signature, are added; and it
is in that state when it is charged to have been taken away.
Can it, then, be called a bill of exchange? I should say, certainly not. In the next count it is called an order for payment
of money; and that it clearly is not, as by it no money is directed to be paid; and it certainly cannot be called a security
for money, as no money is even mentioned in it."

In the above case the fourth count charged the defendant

---

[51] Carr. & Payne 106 (1833).

with stealing ten pieces of paper, but this did not suffice for the same reason that it failed in the Phipoe case. However, by the middle of the nineteenth century, prosecutors had discovered the hazard resulting from the necessity of identifying the instrument in question with one of the classes described in the statute. In order to avoid complete acquittal, they resorted to the expedient of adding a count charging the theft of a piece of paper. This was done in Reg. v. Perry [52] where the defendant converted a check. Because it was unstamped it was held to be void as a note; but a verdict finding the defendant guilty of stealing a piece of paper was upheld. In Reg. v. Watts [53] where the defendant took a written but unstamped agreement, the judges disagreed as to whether the defendant could be held guilty of stealing a piece of paper. Lord Campbell, expressing the majority view, distinguished between instruments which were entirely void when unstamped (and hence subject to larceny as a piece of paper), and instruments which retained a degree of validity though they were unstamped. "If the agreement had been stamped," he said, "it seems to be allowed . . . that an indictment for stealing a piece of paper could not be supported; because then it would be a chose in action, and by the common law, larceny cannot be committed of a chose in action." He then went on to hold that the instrument taken was "evidence of a chose in action, and not the subject of larceny." The defendant who had made way with a valuable document was accordingly discharged.[54]

A recent American case which aroused considerable feeling in Missouri will illustrate the extent to which the tenuous fibres of legal history survive in contemporary law, demonstrating that when we study the past, we often study, also, much of what is present.[55] The defendant, a local politician, misappro-

---

[52] 1 Carr. & Kir. 725 (1848).

[53] 169 Eng. Rep. 747 (1854).

[54] In People v. Griffin, 38 How. Pr. 475 (N. Y. 1869), it was held that common receipts were not personal property within the statute defining larceny.

[55] The case, State v. McCulloch, is reported and commented upon at length by Professor Kenneth Sears (1921) 21 U. of Mo. Bull. (Law Series) 3, and 22 U. of Mo. Bull. 3.

priated a referendum petition containing over 10,000 names. The trial court directed an acquittal which was based upon the following propositions:

1. The petitions ceased to be mere paper when they were signed, and became written instruments.

2. "Under the common law written instruments were not the subject of larceny."

3. Only certain written instruments were included in the statute defining the subject-matter of larceny; and referendum petitions could not be identified with any of these.

The court was correct about the local statutes, but its interpretation of the common law rules was unwarranted. Stephen severely criticized Coke's extension of a rule concerning deeds to include choses in action, "which has for its consequence the absurd conclusion that a bank note cannot be stolen." [56] Here in the United States in a case of great importance, we find the common law rule interpreted to include not only choses in action but *all written instruments!* The fact that the Missouri decision aroused not only the indignation of laymen generally, but had a like effect on lawyers, indicates that there are serious defects in the law.[57]

Many courts have in recent years deliberately evaded the common law restrictions in order to extend the subject-matter of larceny.[58] Sometimes this has been facilitated by a blanket

---

[56] 3 H. C. L. 144.

[57] W. L. Sturdevant wrote as follows in the American Bar Association Journal: "It is not our purpose here to discuss the merits of the legal question involved in this prosecution; but we think it would not be out of the place to suggest that this is but one more example of a judicial proceeding that has caused people, not only by thousands, but by hundreds of thousands, to express, in their various ways, their utter contempt for the law and its administration. It is such judicial fiascos that shock the common sense of the masses of people and sow the seeds of anarchy; and this is equally true whether due to defects in the law itself or in its administration. The average man cannot, will not, understand how the perpetration of a great wrong, affecting a public or a private interest, can be accomplished without a violation of the law." 6 A. B. A. J. (1920) 113.

[58] *Cf.* State *v.* Wolf, (Gen. Sess.) 6 Penneville 324 (22 Del. 1907).

In Hoskins *v.* Tarrance, 35 Am. Dec. 129 (Ind. 1840), the court upheld a conviction for larceny of a key, rejecting the analogy provided by Rex *v.* Wody that title deeds descended to the heir, and were therefore not subject to larceny. The court said: "We see no necessary or reasonable connection

provision inserted in the statutory definition of theft.[59] Although it is very questionable whether the addition of a general clause in the same statute which first enumerates a number of specific things may properly be interpreted to include *all* other personal property,[60] some courts have not hesitated to modify established common law rules in reliance upon such a clause.[61] But most courts, adhering to traditional lines, have held that a penal clause must be strictly construed.[62]

---

between the rule that title papers shall pass with the estate, and the principle which has been made to exclude them from the possibility of being feloniously stolen."

[59] Sec. 1290 of the New York Penal Code includes ". . . any money, personal property, thing in action, evidence of debt or contract, or article of value of any kind."

[60] *Cf.* footnote 54, *supra* and see the discussion of incorporeal property, *infra.*

[61] Thus in Mullaly *v.* People, 86 N. Y. 365 (Ct. App., 1881), the defendant was convicted of stealing a dog. The court admitted that at common law a dog was not subject to larceny; it admitted, further, that there was no statute providing that a dog could be stolen. After rejecting the common law reason for the rule, namely, the "baseness of their nature", the court indulged in a eulogy of canines, calling to mind "the small spaniel that saved the life of William of Orange, and thus probably changed the current of modern history," and concluded that, "The artificial reasoning upon which these rules were based is wholly inapplicable to modern society. *Tempora mutantur et leges mutantur in illis.* Large amounts of money are now invested in dogs, and they are largely the subject of trade and traffic. In many ways they are put to useful service, and so far as pertains to their ownership as personal property, they possess all the attributes of other personal property" (at 868).

In U. S. *v.* Carlos, 21 Philipp. 553 (1911) the defendant was held guilty of stealing electric current under a statute containing a general provision— "another's personal property." Yet it has often been thought necessary to pass statutes specifically naming electricity. English Larceny Act 1916, sec. 10; Cal. Penal Code, sec. 499a.

[62] "Farther; an indictment on the act of 1790 lies only, where the offense is committed in respect to the 'personal goods' of another. To ascertain what is the meaning of these words we must resort to the common law, for that furnishes the proper rule of interpretation. Now, in the strict sense of the common law, personal goods are goods, which are moveable, belonging to, or the property of, some person, and which have an intrinsic value . . . [choses in action not subject of larceny]. It is true, that the words 'goods' or 'chattels', may, in the construction of wills, include bonds, notes . . . etc. . . . But in penal statutes a more strict construction is adopted; and the analogy of the common law in respect to larceny may well furnish the proper rule for decision." U. S. *v.* Davis, Fed. Cas. No. 14,930 at 783 (C. C. Mass. 1829).

Cf. Johnson v. State, 100 Ala. 55 (1893), where the court adheres to the rule that corn, while on the stalk, partakes of the realty and that only "if the stolen corn or cotton has been previously severed from the realty by a separate act, and is afterwards stolen by the defendant, he may be prosecuted for larceny . . ."

ADDENDUM

We have followed the traditional rules on the subject-matter of larceny into the present law in order to indicate the continuity of the legal history. With reference to both substantive law and legal method, we confront the same type of problems, with no great increment in legislative and judicial proficiency, which eighteenth century officials met.

Because of this close similarity in problems, we pause briefly before presenting the rest of our analysis of the eighteenth century substantive law (in the next chapter dealing with the actual operation of the rules), to consider certain legal problems which would need to be dealt with by a legislator desirous of drafting a modern statute on the subject-matter of larceny. In general, what problems would he encounter?

It seems reasonable to conclude from the foregoing survey (1) that the rules defining the subject-matter of larceny have become so highly involved, numerous, and technical that they are sometimes extremely difficult to apply; (2) that results are therefore reached which are irrational and unjust; (3) that the effect of this on the community and particularly on the public sense of justice is harmful; and (4) that even when desirable conclusions are reached, they are the result of an arbitrary refusal to apply well established precedents or of very questionable interpretation; and that these judicial devices increase the confusion in this branch of the law by introducing constructions at odds with canons which are more frequently used.

That the courts are now confronted with all the difficulties described above may be readily seen by reference to American statutes. For if we examine the criminal statutes of almost any state, we find that the ancient hands of the Anglo-Saxons and Normans stretch across the centuries and dominate large sections of our criminal law today. These statutes contain long lists of specifically described property harking back to the *feræ naturæ* concept, things affixed to the freehold, and choses in action.[63] Thus the modern American statutes, with rare exception,[64] are of a piece with the legislation that started as far back as the thirteenth century. They are not based upon an analysis of the entire problem but represent cumulative narrow amendments to the common law where gaps existed or developed. The present substantive criminal law is the result of historical accidents which gave rise to specific formulas, a particularistic method of legislation, and the spinning of tenuous, complicated technicalities from the plethora of case material which arose in the last two centuries.

How can the shortcomings in the existing law be corrected? In the following discussion of this problem we shall not be concerned with the drafting of any specific statute. The following analysis is designed, instead, to reveal the legal problems involved in any formulation of a more adequate definition of the subject-matter of larceny than now exists.

1. The Relationship between Subject-Matter of Larceny and Property

The chief defect in the particularistic legislative method described above is not that certain objects have been *included* within the scope of larceny which should not have been, but that many objects have been *excluded*. Given the method of specific inclusion, the defect was probably inevitable.

---

[63] The Revised Statutes of Illinois (1947) are typical. The following are some of the sections found there: c. 38, sec. 387—"Personal goods . . . money or other personal property, or those means or muniments by which the right and title to property, real or personal, may be ascertained . . . any bond, bill, note, receipt or any instrument of writing of value to the owner"; sec. 388—taking dog or bitch, larceny; sec. 388a—stealing a motor vehicle, a felony; sec. 397—horse stealing; sec. 398—lead pipe, faucet or stopcock; sec. 399—newspapers, periodicals; sec. 400—things attached to the realty; sec. 401—public records; sec. 396—domesticated wild animals.

See O. C. Snyder, *Word Magic and the Embezzlement of Real Property* (1937) 28 J. Cr. L. 166–168.

[64] *Cf.* Louisiana Code of Criminal Law and Procedure (1942) 740–67 and Wisconsin Bill No. 784, S. Ch. 343, line 102, Rep't. Wisc. Legis. Council, April, 1951. The draftsmen's commentaries reveal an intention to avoid the difficulties indicated above and discussed in the following text.

See Stumberg, *Criminal Appropriation of Movables—A Need for Legislative Reform* (1941) 19 Tex. L. Rev. 119, 300.

The constant addition has been of things which had become recognized as "property" within the civil law, but which had happened to remain excluded from the criminal law of theft. Such intimate relationship between the "subject-matter of larceny" and "property" as defined by the civil law, is evident. Both fields, whatever the technical categories may be, center on the question of whether a person's *right of property* has been violated.

Increase in the complexity of social and economic organization was accompanied by the transformation of free goods (those existing in nature independently of any human effort, *and* not appropriated by anyone) into economic goods. This transformation represented effort and acquisition. Goods so far as thus acquired and transformed become valuable and recognized as the "property" of the individuals who got them or had them. We know what goods existed in Anglo-Saxon England. The products of the soil, both cultivated and wild, and the lesser inhabitants of forests and waters formed the storehouse of supplies. Thus comes the distinction between *feræ naturæ* and domesticated animals. The former and other things beyond the cultivated lands may be acquired, subject to superior rights of king and nobles. Things in possession may not be taken.[65] Things in possession are defined with reference to such cases

---

[65] Undoubtedly, the need to maintain the peace was an important influence. Two other ideas also exercised a profound effect: (1) the notion that what a man had acquired or occupied, what he already had in his possession, he ought to retain (Ritchie, Natural Rights 266); and (2) that his efforts and his labor entitled him to protection, *i.e.*, gave him a "right." Thus in the Case of the Swans (34 Eliz. 76 Eng. Rep. 435) the judges said, "nor can felony be committed of them, but of those which are made tame, in which a man by his industry hath any property, felony may be committed." This idea recurs constantly. In an early American case, it was stated that "Their labour in killing the deer and bears, *feræ naturæ*, gave the Indians a property in the skins, meat and tallow of those animals." Pennsylvania v. Becomb *et al.*, Add. Rep. 386 (Pa. 1799).

Professor R. T. Ely discusses nine theories of property: (1) natural rights; (2) social contract (3) human nature; (4) occupancy; (5) labor; (6) theistic; (7) robbery and violence; (8) legal; and (9) general welfare. 2 Property and Contract in Their Relations to the Distribution of Wealth (1922) 531-2.

as arise. Rules are made in first instance to fit specific situations. Thus property becomes a legal relationship existing between persons with reference to economic goods.[66] Thus, the *feræ naturæ* rule represents not only an early link between the criminal and civil law but also the germ of an idea which, though it seems commonplace, raises difficult problems in the construction of statutes, namely that (with rare exceptions) only *property* can be the subject of larceny.

The relationship of the two sets of rules suggests the substitution of the concept of property for that of the subject-matter of larceny. This was the recommendation which Stephen made in 1865 when he attempted to formulate a more adequate definition of larceny which would include "any property whatever." [67] He was confident that his recommendation would "do away with all the technicalities about the kinds of property which are the subject of larceny, and with those which arise out of the obscure definition of possession." [68]

An analysis of Stephen's proposal shows that a number of important results would follow its adoption, namely:

1. Certain economic goods which are now within the scope

---

[66] *Cf.* 1 Bl., op. cit. 138.

Its essentials are (1) a purely factual situation based upon a person's actual (and later constructive) physical control of an object, and an intention to control the object (which join to constitute the fact of possession), and (2) the recognition and the protection by the state of this person's relationship to other persons with reference to the object. It will be seen that the above definition of property includes possession which is recognized by law. It may, therefore, be stated that possession differs from property merely in degree. It is the foundation-stone of thinking about "property." Wrongful dispossession and any type of transaction involving absentee-ownership force more refined thinking.

[67] The following is relevant: (to appropriate) "any property whatever, real or personal, in possession, or in action, so as to deprive any other person of the advantage of any beneficial interest at law, or in equity, which he may have therein." General View of the Criminal Law of England 129.

[68] *Cf. id.* 129–30. Again he wrote: "This [definition] would include all property whatever, real or personal, in possession or in action; and so do away with all the cases which show what is not the subject of larceny; and with the necessity for cumbrous statutory exceptions to a principle which, though admitted to be absurd, is left existing." *Id.* 132.

of larceny would be excluded because, for reasons of public policy, they are not property, as defined by the civil law.

2.   The distinction between movables and immovables would become non-essential.

3.   The distinction between corporeal and incorporeal property would become non-essential.

4.   All goods which come within the private law definition of property, whether or not they have been previously excluded from the subject-matter of larceny, would be included there.

2.   *Economic Goods Which Are Not Property*

The first factor noted above had its greatest application during prohibition with reference to alcoholic beverages. Legal rights in such goods were not recognized. Some courts applied this rule to criminal cases in which the defendants were charged with theft of liquor.[69] Although these narrowly conceived decisions will largely disappear, there are other possible

---

[69] *Cf.* Comw. *v.* Rourke, 10 Cush. 397 (64 Mass. 1852); People *v.* Wilson, 298 Ill. 257, 231 N. E. 609 (1921).

"As the Supreme Court of this state has said in Dixon *v.* People (1897) 168 Ill. 191, and again in Transcontinental Oil Co. *v.* Emmerson (1921) 298 Ill. 394, 'property' in its legal sense, is not the thing itself, but certain rights in and over the thing, to-wit, the unrestricted right of use, enjoyment, and disposal of the object in question. The National Prohibition Act, *supra,* has taken away from the holder of intoxicating liquors all those legal relations in respect to them which an 'owner' would necessarily have were they 'property' in the above sense. It is unlawful for him to possess, to use, or to dispose of them. If they are converted by another, the Statute expressly provides that he shall not have an action of replevin to recover the converted articles. It seems that the holder has no rights which can be violated by another. His aggregate of legal relations in respect to the liquors is no larger than that of a stranger. Surely then, in the absence of all the attributes of ownership in respect to them, these liquors held without permit cannot be 'property' in legal contemplation. This decision can be sustained only from a policy standpoint." Note (1922) 4 Ill. L. Q. 144.

Cf. also (1923) 8 Minn. L. Rev. 64, and Iowa *v.* May (1866) 20 Ia. 305. For a contrary case see People *v.* Spencer, 201 Pac. 130 (Cal. App. 1921), and (1922) 6 Minn. L. Rev. 165. In State *v.* Clementi, 272 N. W. 29 (Wis. 1937) a conviction for larceny of a slot-machine, a gambling device, was affirmed. "We can see no inconsistency in holding that contraband property may be the subject of larceny and in holding that a court will not lend its aid to a party to recover the value of contraband articles in a civil action."

applications of such a legal principle [70] which will need to be considered in the construction of a statute.[71]

3. *Land and Things Attached to It*

The problems which arise with reference to immovable property were discussed by Stephen in his *General View of the Criminal Law*. Concerning his proposed definition of larceny he stated, "There is no reason why real property should not be stolen as well as personal property." [72] He illustrated his point by supposing the removal of landmarks, the fraudulent building of a wall to enclose a strip of another's land, or the conversion of an estate by a trustee; and he asked, "Why should he not be indicted for stealing the land? . . . The existing rule proceeds on the ground that a principle cannot be true, because it is difficult, in fact, to apply it. It is perfectly true that real property is seldom the subject of larceny, but it is as capable of being stolen as anything else. It would be as wise to declare that a mass of iron, weighing a thousand tons, is not the subject of larceny, because no one could carry it away." [73] In his later work he, in effect, retracts these assertions regarding land. It is rather difficult to follow his discussion here. He first reasserts that "immovable property [is] obviously capable, in all cases, of being fraudulently misappropriated." He then limits this by adding "though not by removal from place to place." [74] He con-

---

[70] *E.g.*, it has been held that taking money from one to whom it had been paid as a gambling debt by the loser was not larceny. State *v.* Price, 219 Pac. 1095, 38 Idaho 149 (1923), and (1924) 72 U. of Pa. L. Rev. 330.

[71] It is possible, though not easy, to avoid this difficulty by formulating a statute in terms of economic goods rather than property as defined by the civil law. The subject-matter of larceny would include every "thing" which has been *appropriated* by some "person", has *value* and is *transferable* (briefly—transferable economic goods). As used in this definition, "thing" means not only any physical object but, also, any benefit, advantage, use or enjoyment. "Appropriated" means acquired or in the physical control of some person. "Value" means value measurable in money. "Transferability" means exchangeability, that is, that one person can, as a matter of fact, be substituted for another person with reference to the "thing.

[72] General View of the Criminal Law of England 132.

[73] *Id.* 132–3.

[74] 3 H. C. L. 126.

cludes by stating that "a distinction must always exist between offenses against moveable and immoveable property," and that "misappropriation, whether of moveable or immoveable property, is possible only where the property misappropriated can be concealed or made away with, which is not the case with land." [75] Stephen thus modified his views because (*a*) land cannot be removed from one place to another, and because (*b*) other criminal laws penalize the acts which he had designated as larceny of land. Yet he seems to have adhered to his former views regarding the irrationality and needless technicality of the subject-matter of larceny.

The fact that "downright robbery" of land is impossible and that the felonious removal of landmarks and the destruction of wills are made criminal offenses by other statutes are practical considerations which may make it expedient to limit the requirements of logical consistency with regard to the provisions of an inclusive statute. There is at least one practical reason, however, for the inclusion of such offenses within the provisions of a larceny statute. It is sometimes desirable to attach a common symbol to stigmatize particular types of criminal behavior, hence the dictates of intelligent policy may well require that such acts be called thefts, the purpose being to create sustaining social attitudes regarding these offenses. [76]

4. *Incorporeal Property*

Corporeality, like movability, was apt and sufficient as a limitation when theft of cattle was the primary hazard. But to-day intangible economic goods are among the most important forms of property. It is true that most of them, such as stocks and bonds, choses in action, and evidences of debt or contract have been the subject of special legislation. It is true also that in a few situations courts have deliberately departed from the common law rules without aid of any statute. [77] Yet there remain

---

[75] *Id.* 126–7.

[76] See the Louisiana and Wisconsin provisions cited *supra* n. 64.

[77] *Cf.* "It is true that electricity is no longer, as formerly, regarded by electricians as a fluid, but its manifestations and effects, like those of gas, may

many situations where it is unfortunate that existing categories in the law of larceny cannot be applied, resulting in failure to achieve sound principle and the escape of offenders who should have been convicted.

In People v. Ashworth, an important New York case,[78] one defendant was the mill superintendent and general manager of the A. O. Worsted Co. Inc. His brother, also a defendant, was the owner of a company which had a contract to comb twenty thousand pounds of raw wool and to spin this wool at twenty cents a pound. Having no facilities for spinning the wool, he arranged with the mill superintendent to have the spinning done at the Worsted Co. Without the knowledge of this company, its machinery, facilities and laborers were used. When the facts were discovered the brothers and three other persons were indicted for conspiracy and grand larceny. They were convicted, but on appeal the judgment was reversed by a unanimous court. The conspiracy counts were eliminated because of the defective pleading of overt acts.

With reference to the larceny, it should be noted, first, that the New York statute is very inclusive.[79] The court, however, pointed out that taking the "use" of anything is not specifically

---

be seen and felt. The true test of what is a proper subject of larceny seems to be not whether the subject is corporeal or incorporeal, but whether it is capable of appropriation by another than the owner." (Citing no authority) . . . "Electricity, the same as gas, is a valuable article of merchandise, bought and sold like other personal property and is capable of appropriation by another. So no error was committed by the trial court in holding that electricity is a subject of larceny." United States v. Carlos, 21 Phil. Rep. 560, 561 (1911). The decision of Regina v. White, 3 Carr. & Kir. 363 (1853) holding that gas was subject to larceny, provided an analogy (at least so thought the courts) for holding similarly with reference to electricity.

[78] 220 N. Y. App. Div. 498 (1927).

[79] The Penal Law, section 1290, reads in part as follows:

"A person who, with the intent to deprive or defraud the true owner of his property, or of the use and benefit thereof, or to appropriate the same to the use of the taker, or of any other person:

"1. Takes from the possession of the true owner, or of any other person; or obtains from such possession by color or aid of fraudulent or false representation or pretense, or of any false token or writing; or secretes, withholds, or appropriates to his own use, or that of any person other than the true owner, any money, personal property, thing in action, evidence of debt or contract, or article of value of any kind; . . ."

included in the statute, and interpreted the relevant words to mean the "physical taking or acquiring of some concrete article." Next, asportation was held essential, and this was defined in the usual way, as "any appreciable changing of the location of the property involved." The court conceded that "It may be conceivable that if these defendants stole the use of the spinning facilities of the A–O Company, they carried the 'use' away, or appreciably changed its location, although the work was all done on the premises of the A–O Company. But," it added, "to conceive this requires a certain intellectual flexibility which is probably not possessed by the average person."

Lastly, the court considered section 39 of the General Construction Act which defines personal property very broadly, describing several types and then adding "everything except real property which may be subject of ownership." This portion of the opinion is especially significant. After the quotation of section 39, the court said:

"There is a very comprehensive definition, for it includes intangible property as well as tangible. (*Matter of Bronson,* 150 N. Y. 1, 15.) Electricity and gas have been held to be the subject of larceny. (L. R. A. 1918C, 580.) Perhaps some court may soon hold that a property right, through a license in a radio wave length, may be stolen. It is reasonably clear, nevertheless, that all intangible personal property is not the subject of larceny, at least under section 1290 of the Penal Law as now worded. For instance, the right to produce oil is personal property. (*Wagner* v. *Mallory,* 169 N. Y. 501; Gen. Constr. Law, 39 ¶ 2.) But it seems that it would be impossible to steal such property. Good will is personal property. (*People ex rel. Johnson Co.* v. *Roberts,* 159 N. Y. 70.) But if an unscrupulous competitor steals the good will of a rival business is he guilty of larceny under section 1290 of the Penal Law? A leasehold interest in land is personal property. (*Matter of Althause,* 63 App. Div. 252; affd., 168 N. Y. 670.) But there can be no larceny of such an interest or right. A mere credit is not the subject of larceny at common law. (*Higbee* v. *State,* 74 Neb. 331.)

"Take the case of a franchise. This is an incorporeal hereditament, 'intangible, invisible, . . . unseen, without form or substance, and, as it were, the mere breath of the Legislature.' (*People ex rel. Met. St. R. Co.* v. *Tax Comrs.*, 174 N. Y. 417.) It is not easy to conceive of such a thing being the subject of larceny.

"Personal property has been variously defined. That which may be the subject of larceny is well comprehended in the following statement (36 C. J. 737): It 'should have corporeal existence, that is, be something the physical presence, quantity, or quality of which is detectable or measurable by the senses or by some mechanical contrivance; for a naked right existing merely in contemplation of law, although it may be very valuable to the person who is entitled to exercise it, is not a subject of larceny'" (501–2).

Here were twenty thousand pounds of wool to be spun at twenty cents per pound, four thousand dollars to be paid the defendant (of which more than half was actually paid) for labor and the use of machinery. This labor[80] and machinery were admittedly the property of the Worsted Company. Use of them cost money and had value, which was measurable in monetary terms. It could be and was transferred, bought and sold. Yet the above decision was reached because the thing taken had no "corporeal existence." The cases supported the decision. Larceny and concrete objects have been associated so many hundreds of years that we hardly have the words to describe adequately the intentional deprivation of the benefits which one secures from relationships, functions and uses which cannot be sensed or referred directly to physical objects.

Two major problems exist, therefore, in connection with adequate statutory definition of the subject-matter of larceny: (1) the classification of land and intangible economic goods, both of which are clearly property, but involve practical difficulties and serious questions of policy; and (2) difficulties in-

---

[80] The California statute includes theft of "labor or services of another." Cal. Penal Code (1949, Deering) Ch. V, sec. 484. *Cf. Stealing the Use of a Thing* (1923) Just. P. 198–200.

volved in determining whether or not certain goods are "property" in private law.

The current movement for attaching criminal liability to the willful infringement of trademarks, patents and copyrights accentuates the need for solution of the first problem.[81] Present penal statutes covering such infringements are of minor consequence and they are not based on an analysis of the nature of the behavior involved. The second problem provides the major difficulties, for "property" has changed so constantly and the concept is so vague and mobile that the application of any rule is beset with difficulty.[82] For example, in International News Service v. The Associated Press,[83] the Supreme Court divided sharply on the question whether the appropriation of news from bulletin boards was a violation of the complainant's property right. The majority concluded that there was a property right in news because "news matter, however little susceptible of ownership or dominion in the absolute sense, is stock in trade . . . to be distributed and sold to those who will pay money for it, as for any other merchandise." This argument was rejected by Justice Brandeis chiefly on grounds of public policy, but also because "an essential element of individual property is the legal right to exclude others from enjoying it." This decision indicates how difficult the problem may become in exceptional cases.[84] But the existence of rare cases which cannot be fitted

---

[81] *Cf.* Merchandise Marks Act. 1887, 50 & 51 Vict. c. 28.

[82] "Another common mistake is to speak of 'property' as if it were an institution having a fixed form, constantly remaining the same; whereas in reality it has assumed the most diverse forms, and is still susceptible of great and unforeseen modifications." Laveleye, Primitive Property (Marriott's transl. 1878) 338.

[83] 248 U.S. 239 (1918).

[84] In a strict sense all legal rights are property rights because damages will be awarded for violation of them. A man's right to his leg, his reputation, the services of a minor child, and the companionship of his wife are, in this sense, property rights. But how classify such rights with reference to larceny? Two suggestions are offered: first, that cognizance must always be taken of social attitudes regarding interference with such rights; and, second, that the criterion of *transferability* may serve as a useful characteristic to distinguish property rights from other legal rights. Property as a legal term would then be limited to legal rights which are transferable, whether they can be referred to physical objects or not.

into any accepted classification is the inevitable limitation of any law, as was first pointed out by Plato in the *Statesman*.

The method of construction which produced the subject-matter of larceny is characteristic of the entire Anglo-American criminal law. Hardly ever has penal legislation been based upon a thorough analysis of the problems involved. Practically nothing has been done to systematize the substantive criminal law; and upon those rare occasions when commissions of competent scholars have been appointed to revise the law, pressing demands of immediate problems have restricted the range of investigation and limited the significance of the results.[85]

I have emphasized some of the limitations of the existing law on the subject-matter of larceny. It is necessary to remember, however, that in the criminal law it is especially desirable, if not absolutely necessary, that legal sanctions find support in public attitudes. A very broad statute will probably include behavior which is not generally regarded as being sufficiently dangerous to be treated as criminal (*e.g.,* the case of "news," good will, etc.).

Thus the demands of logical consistency do not necessarily point in the same direction indicated by practical considerations. As a matter of fact, there is bound to be conflict between a logically constructed code and one which has developed spontaneously over a period of many centuries. In such matters the greatest desideratum is not always logical consistency.[86] When, however, legal rules become complex and unwieldly and, because of attenuated logical applications of these rules and inferences drawn from them, there result distinctions which are unjust, the reconstruction of the law along lines dictated by existing social needs becomes essential.[87]

---

[85] *Cf.* Hall, *The Proposal to Prepare a Model Penal Code, infra Appendix,* and *Science and Reform in Criminal Law* (1952) 100 U. of Pa. L. Rev.

[86] *Cf.* Freund, *Classification and Definition of Crimes* (1915) 5 J. Crim. L. & Criminol. 826.

[87] From the above analysis, the necessary approach appears to be the drafting of a general clause plus the exception of some objects or types of property (although they logically fall within the clause), conversion of which it is deemed wise to treat in some other manner.

CHAPTER FOUR

THE FUNCTION OF TECHNICALITY AND DISCRETION IN CRIMINAL LAW ADMINISTRATION

Between a legal structure and the social problems with reference to which it was designed, gaps open; lag sets in. The changes called for are too detailed, frequent, and varied for legislation. Accordingly, the need for administration is fundamental and constant. Only after thorough study of it can one appreciate how a fixed, disorganized body of law, such as that described in the preceding chapter, can survive and even function usefully.

I. Benefit of Clergy

Nowhere can significant data relevant to this basic problem be found in greater abundance than in the administration of the English penal law during the eighteenth century. One chief feature of this law was benefit of clergy and non-clergable felonies.

Benefit of clergy was originally a privilege which exempted ecclesiastics from criminal liability under the secular law, leaving them subject only to the jurisdiction of the church courts.[1]

---

[1] "Till 1487 any one who knew how to read might commit murder as often as he pleased, with no other result than that of being delivered to the ordinary to make his purgation, with the chance of being delivered to him, 'absque purgatione.' That this should have been the law for several centuries seems hardly credible, but there is no doubt that it was. Even after 1487 a man who could read could commit murder once with no other punishment than that of having M branded on the brawn of his left thumb, and if he was a clerk in orders he could till 1547 commit any number of murders apparently without being branded more than once." 1 Stephen, H. C. L. 463–4.

Cf. "Practice, however, reveals the canonical procedure in criminal cases to have been largely an empty form favorable to the accused; purgation was almost always granted and rarely failed." Gabel, *Benefit of Clergy in England in Later Middle Ages* (1928) 14 Smith College Studies in History, No. 1–4, 113. This book contains a lengthy bibliography, pp. 136–144.

At the end of the thirteenth century, it covered all crimes except very minor transgressions, which afterwards became misdemeanors, and a few offenses against the forest laws.[2] So important was this privilege that an analysis of it is essential to an understanding of contemporary criminal law administration. For benefit of clergy developed a number of practices which sharply accentuated what was and still remains *the* distinctive administrative problem, namely, the ways in which we depart from rules to arrive at entirely different results from those prescribed. The same type of problem has been studied with reference to civil proceedings, and the literature on judicial legislation and the use of fictions to arrive at desired results has been abundantly produced from Maine down to the present time.[3] Similar analyses have been rare in the field of criminal law.

The administrative practices surrounding clergy came into most frequent and important application in cases of larceny. They colored the whole meaning of the substantive law. Its history and effect would be as empty without consideration of clergy as it would be without consideration of the jury system or the machinery of prosecution.

The history of clergy has been excellently described by several writers,[4] which makes it necessary merely to outline its development in order to orient and fix the sphere of discussion. This history can be related generally to three periods. From the Conquest to the death of Becket marks the initial supremacy of secular over ecclesiastical courts. The royal courts asserted their authority by virtue of feudal fealty. Thus, when in 1084, Odo, Bishop of Bayeux, claimed exemption from the royal jurisdiction, William replied, "I do not condemn a clerk or a bishop, but I arrest my earl to whom I entrusted the government of my realm"; and the Bishop was imprisoned.[5]

The second period, which marks the height of the clerical

---

[2] 3 Holdsworth, H. E. L. 297.
[3] See *supra* ch. 1, n. 22.
[4] 3 Holdsworth, H. E. L. 293–302; L. Gabel, *op. cit. supra* n. 1; 1 P. and M. H. E. L. 441–457
[5] Gabel, *op. cit.* 16.

privilege, received its great impetus from the assassination of Becket, and extended to the middle of Henry III's reign, from which point on the royal courts began to reassert their claims regarding jurisdiction.

During this third period, which developed considerable momentum by the middle of the fourteenth century and extended into the nineteenth, two general movements are discernible. On the one hand there is the gradual extension of the benefit of clergy to increasingly large numbers of lay persons, a process which marked its transformation from an ecclesiastical to a general privilege. On the other hand, and concomitant with this movement, comes a series of legislative enactments which entirely exclude an increasingly large number of felonies from any operation of the privilege. It was between these two movements that the administrative practices were woven. The development of clergy, its progressive application to wider circles of persons concomitant with some narrowing of it with reference to the clerical class itself, and the synchronous exclusion of particular felonies from the operation of the privilege regardless of who the offender was—both of these movements are traceable in legislation.

II. TRANSPORTATION OF CONVICTS

But this legislation cannot be understood apart from a further factor: the transportation of convicts to the English colonies. Transportation, as a form of punishment, started in the latter part of the seventeenth century [6] in the reign of Charles II, and

---

[6] Earlier references to transporting convicts are generally regarded as having been acts of banishment somewhat similar to common law outlawry. But *cf.* Radzinowicz *op. cit.* 109, n. 10. Ives is one of the few students who regards 39 Eliz., c. 4 (1597) "as a measure sanctioning transportation." History of Penal Methods (1914) 107. He states that in 1611 Sir Thomas Dale took 300 disorderly persons overseas with him to Virginia; and that in 1618 the regular shipment of criminals began. (*id.* 108–9). An order of the Privy Council of 1617 provided for the reprieve of criminals guilty of lesser felonies "who for strength of bodye or other abilityes shall be thought fitt to be imployed in forreyne discoveryes or other Services beyond the seas." 1 Acts of P. C. (Col. Series) 10, quoted by J. E. Gillespie in *The Transportation of English Convicts After 1783* (1922) 13 J. Crim. L. and Criminol. 359ff. Henley, writing in the eighteenth century (Principles of Penal Law 31n.) and Stephen (1 H. C. L. 480) fix the time of transportation in the reign of Charles II. See 18 Car. 2, c. 3 (1666) in the Appendix *infra*.

the practice was sanctioned in the Habeas Corpus Act of 1679. Since 1660 represented the high mark of American colonization, the rise in importance of transportation after this date was quite natural. "The young colonies hungered for laborers,"[7] and the demands made upon the mother country to supply the need were met by substituting transportation in many cases of non-clergable felonies for the prescribed capital penalty. There is little if any evidence that transportation rested on other than economic motives,[8] although it is probable that it received an impetus from the development of the humanitarian movement organized in England at the end of the eighteenth century under the immediate stimulation of Beccaria's work. Transportation of criminals became highly profitable not only for colonists but also for shipowners and officials strategically situated in England and the colonies. By the time of the American Revolution, England had been transporting two thousand convicts to the colonies annually. After the Revolution, English prisons filled beyond capacity.[9] The colonization of Australia provided a new outlet: [10] from 1787 to 1857 more than one hundred thou-

---

[7] Ives, op. cit. 112.

" '. . . whereas in many of his majesty's Colonies and Plantations in America there is a great want of servants', [etc.] persons henceforth convicted of offences within Clergy were to be liable to seven years transportation, and those reprieved from the execution for graver crimes were to serve fourteen years or it might be longer, and the contractors for their transportation were to possess a property in their services, and this was considered to be sufficient reward though at one time the government had paid £5 a head passage money. (See Journal of the House of Commons, Vol. XL, p. 1161.)" Id. 109.

[8] "This short summary of the history of transportation tends to show, that its adoption does not rest upon any broad and deliberately sanctioned principle; that its origin was owing to that state of things in the American plantations which led to the illegal kidnapping of Europeans, and to the legalization of the slave trade; and that its continuance was forced upon Government against its wishes by the immediate pressure of events." D. D. Heath, in The Report from the Select Committee on Transportation Together with the Minutes of Evidence (1837) 259.

[9] Gillespie, op. cit. 360.

[10] "At length they got together 564 males and 192 female prisoners, or in all 756, and placed them on board six transports escorted by two vessels of war and accompanied by three store ships. Along with the human freight were sent a large number of farmyard animals, including horses and cattle, besides seed, implements and tools, and the expedition, which was to go down in Australian history as the First Fleet set forth in the month of May in the year 1787." Ives, op. cit. 128.

sand convicts were transported there.[11] Toward the end of this period, their descendants, having established themselves in profitable enterprises, objected strenuously to the continued influx of convicts, and transportation was finally abandoned.

III. THE PENAL LAW AS A PHASE OF THE ADMINISTRATIVE PROBLEM

Clergy, non-clergable felonies, and transportation were introduced into the law by a flood of legislation.[12] The dates 1350 and 1706 are particularly important with reference to the classes of persons affected by the privilege. The statute passed in 1350, though it extended the privilege only to secular clerks who assisted the clergy, was interpreted to apply to all persons who could read.[13] The important consideration is that the judges thus inserted a wedge for the use of discretion, and they constituted themselves the examiners.

In 1706 the most important development of all occurred—clergy was extended to include all persons, literate or not. This extension meant that thereafter *no* person was specially privileged. Yet it took more than a century to discard the traditional terminology of the outworn institution of clergy and to recast the penal code along more rational lines. During this period, to state that a felony was non-clergable meant that it was capitally punishable. To state that a crime was clergable or to provide transportation or some other penalty or, as will appear, simply to omit any reference to clergy meant that the offender was not capitally punishable.

---

[11] Gillespie, *op. cit.* 364.

[12] Note the table of statutes in the Appendix. Throughout the following discussion it will be helpful to refer to this table.

If the whole historical process represented by this legislation be visualized as a rectangular figure divided into two triangles by a line drawn from the upper left angle to the lower right angle, the triangle at the left represents the *persons* affected by clergy, and shows a spread (from the apex at the top with time advancing downward) from a small class of clerics to the whole population in 1706. The right triangle with its base upwards represents the movement towards the progressive concomitant narrowing of the *offenses* within the privilege regardless of who the offender was.

[13] As may be imagined, this ruling was a great stimulus to the education of the criminally disposed. Jailers were punished for permitting their prisoners to learn to read. 1 Pike, *op. cit.* 300.

Enactments dealing with theft were much more numerous than any others. This applies both to the exception of all aggravated [14] forms of theft from the privilege and also to the later statutory repeal of many of these provisions. There were so many types of property of special value and so many places where thefts could be committed, some of which were regarded as more serious than others, that numerous statutes seemed necessary.

It is clear, also, why theft was more quickly excluded from the list of non-clergable felonies, once the movement in that direction began. Larceny had been the last of the felonies to be created at common law, and criminal fraud had never been more than a misdemeanor. The first general embezzlement act, that of 1799, provided for punishment by transportation, although the special embezzlements concerning the Bank of England, the South Sea Company, and the Post Office had been made non-clergable. Thus, on the whole, simple theft was considered less serious than other major offenses, and it was therefore not unnatural that it should be the first to be punished more leniently. The records of the Old Bailey Trials during the eighteenth century show that most of the defendants found guilty of simple larceny were transported and, also, that most of those transported were thieves.[15] M. Cottu, an unusually acute observer, who visited England at the beginning of the nineteenth century, wrote in his report that "Grand larceny is punishable with death; but as the majority of those who are

---

[14] *E.g.*, larceny from the person, from a dwelling house, above a certain amount, etc. Simple larceny was the less serious offense which covered the small area which remained after almost every conceivable special act was excepted and made non-clergable.

[15] The Old Bailey Trials in the first part of the eighteenth century show transportation in full swing, and the dominant treatment for simple larceny. The following figures are typical:

Sentenced to death—8 (2 had been convicted of larceny from house, 4 of robbery, 1 of arson, and 1 of forgery); burnt in the hand—2; to be whipped —5; transportation—33. (First session—1730.)

Sentenced to death—6; burnt in hand—6; transportation—31. (Second session —1730.)

Sentenced to death—10; burnt in hand—6; whipped—3; transportation—32. (Third session—1730.)

Sentenced to death—11; transportation—51; burnt in hand—3; whipped—5; pillory and fine—1. (Seventh session.)

guilty of this description of crime, are, generally speaking, admitted to the benefit of clergy, it follows that grand larceny is no longer considered as a capital crime in itself." [16] Over a century before he wrote this, the statute of 4 Geo. I, c. 11, which gave special impetus to transportation, provided that persons guilty of clergable felonies were to be transported for seven years. This, however, was followed by a long series of statutes excepting almost every form of aggravated larceny from the privilege.

The enormous body of non-clergable felonies which conditioned the eighteenth century administrative problem had been enacted during the period of almost three centuries beginning with the reign of Henry VII. Under the Tudors, benefit of clergy was restricted both as to the persons who could avail themselves of it and with reference to the crimes included in its operation. Limitations were placed upon the rights of clerics who committed more than one felony, and most of the serious crimes were entirely excluded from the privilege. Moreover, it seems to be well established that this increased severity in punishment was not merely a matter of statutory threat. The actual administration of the law was, judged by both earlier and later standards, severe. Thus it is believed that Henry VIII executed 72,000 thieves and vagabonds during his reign. [17] During the same reign boiling to death was legalized by a statute passed in 1531. Apparently the hangings decreased under Elizabeth, due, according to Pike, to the greater security of the throne, the increase in wealth, relief laws for the poor, and the growth of maritime activities which provided an outlet for "restless spirits." [18]

---

[16] M. Cottu, On the Administration of the Criminal Code in England, and the Spirit of the English Government (1820) 37.

[17] John Laurence, A History of Capital Punishment 8.

[18] 2 *op. cit.* 110–11.

It may be noted, in passing, that except for occasional demur, punishments which are now regarded as barbarous aroused little criticism until late in the eighteenth century. The execution scenes, though perhaps not the best evidence of the temper of the people, are indicative of the prevailing attitudes. The following is descriptive of such events: "Frightful scenes were witnessed at executions in those days, the crowd standing awestruck as it watched the convulsions

The multiplication of non-clergable felonies continued from Tudor days and increased at an accelerated rate after 1688 until Blackstone observed that there were one hundred and sixty capital offenses on the books. With the third George, it reached a grand total of two hundred and twenty-two.[19] Yet it is certain that when Blackstone wrote only a relatively small number of persons tried for non-clergable felonies were actually executed. At the end of the period characterized by "non-clergable" legislation, few of those condemned were executed.[20]

It is apparent from the above summary that if one were to mark out the period of greatest severity in modern English law, the sixteenth and seventeenth centuries would undoubtedly form the central area. The non-clergable felonies had already piled up, while evasion of the statutes did not occur to any great extent until the eighteenth century. Non-clergable felonies continued to be created throughout the eighteenth century, and clergy was not abolished until 1827. Blackstone's substantive law looks formidable. But forces other than express legal enactment were now at work.[21]

The extension of clergy to all persons in 1706 by eliminating the literacy test, the beginning of transportation on a large scale in the latter part of the seventeenth century, the prominence of theft in the non clergable felonies, and the rela

---

of the strangling culprit. Every contortion of the limbs was hailed with a cheer or a groan, according as the sufferer was popular or not; appalling curses and execrations occasionally rent the air and rendered the last moments of the unfortunate criminal more odious; hawkers boldly sang the praises of their wares the while a fellow creature was being doomed to death. Rich and poor, thief and lord, gentle and simple, attended to see 'the hanging,' and cracked jokes at the sufferer's expense." Laurence, *op. cit.* 44. As late as 1789 an offender against the coinage laws was burned alive, although in the next year hanging was substituted. *Id.* 10. In 1818 women were hanged for passing one-pound forged notes. Andrews, Bygone Punishments (1899) 33; and as late as 1849 an execution scene which horrified Dickens delighted a crowd of over thirty thousand persons who paid exorbitant prices for the most improvised seats. Laurence, *op. cit.* 209–10.

[19] *Ives, op. cit.* 18n.; and *cf.* Laurence, *op. cit.* 13.

[20] ". . . from May 1827 to May 1830, four hundred and fifty-one persons were condemned to death and only fifty-five executed." Laurence, *op. cit.* 14. And *cf.* the table on p. 132 *infra*.

[21] *Cf.* Radzinowicz, *op. cit.* 139–142.

tively lesser gravity of this offense set up tensions with the rigorous penal legislation. Back of these more immediate legal phenomena lay the Reformation, cutting away many special clerical privileges, colonization, from which flowed not merely transportation itself but also changes in penal attitudes, the Revolution of 1688 and its movement to liberate the individual from oppressive government, and the emergent philosophy of individual rights. These forces transformed a formally barbaric criminal code into relatively moderate, actual law.

IV. Eighteenth Century Administrative Practices

What in fact happened was that, beginning in the early part of the eighteenth century, the persons, lay and official, who administered the criminal law, invented and indulged in practices which almost nullified the capital penalty in most nonclergable felonies. Juries, judges, prosecutors, and complainants collaborated. The juries returned verdicts which were palpably not findings of fact but such deliberate misstatements of facts as would have been punished by attaint a half century earlier. The judges developed many technicalities by which they effectively submerged statutory provisions of capital penalization. These practices have significance not only for eighteenth century criminal law administration but also for the legislative reforms which followed.

In The King *v.* Baynes and Others (1731), four defendants were indicted upon 8 Eliz. c. 4 [22] for privately stealing a hundred pound banknote. The note was taken in a scuffle and it was impossible to prove which of the defendants took it. The court said: "The statute upon which this indictment is founded, takes away the benefit of clergy from those who shall be found guilty of privately stealing from the person; and as it is totally silent respecting aiders and abettors, it must be construed to extend only to principals in the first degree. It follows, therefore, that the hand alone which takes the property can be guilty of the offence; and as it is uncertain which of the prisoners took

---

[22] See the Appendix for this and other statutes referred to in these cases.

the note, it is impossible to find any of them guilty of the capital charge." (168 E. R. 106–7)

In The King *v.* Westbeer (1739), which has been discussed above in connection with the subject-matter of larceny, judges and jury combined to avoid the operation of the statute. Upon a prosecution brought for stealing parchment papers, the trial judge expressed doubt as to whether the offense was felony. "The Jury therefore found a special verdict, 'That the prisoner was guilty of privately taking away a parchment writing, value one penny, from etc.'" (1 Leach 13) The judges who considered the case later "were unanimously of opinion that these parchment writings concerned the realty, and that therefore the prisoner was *Not Guilty* of the felony charged in the indictment." (15) Although there was a technical basis for supporting the decision, the conduct of both judges and jury leaves little doubt that avoidance of a severe penalty was the dominant factor. (168 E. R. 108)

In The King *v.* Comer (1744), an indictment was brought on 12 Anne c. 7 for burglary and theft of a necklace worth £ 150 from a dwelling house. The jury found the defendant "*Guilty* of felony only, in stealing goods and chattels to the value of one hundred and fifty pounds from the dwelling house. Not Guilty of the burglary." It was then debated whether the prisoner, under this finding, was not entitled to the benefit of clergy. Nine of the judges "unanimously agreed, that as the felony itself was made to constitute the burglary, and not the intention to commit a felony, the acquittal of the burglary did, by necessary consequence, include in it an acquittal of the felony also; and that the prisoner, by this mistake in the mode of entering the verdict, was intitled to the benefit of the statute." The judges pointed out that if the verdict had been "not guilty of breaking and entering but guilty of the rest," the defendant would have suffered judgment of death since the theft was committed in a dwelling house and the property taken was worth more than 40s. (168 E. R. 121)

In 1749 there was decided the important case of The King against Midwinter and Sims. Indictment was brought upon 9

Geo. I, c. 22, for feloniously killing a mare. The two defendants and one Taylor who testified for the Crown, sought to take revenge upon the complainant because he was prosecuting them for stealing rabbits, and they decided to kill one of his breeding mares. They got a mare, and Midwinter tied his girdle around her neck, and at the end of this girdle he fastened Sims'. Sims then held the girdles to prevent the mare from escaping or moving while Midwinter cut a deep gash in the mare's belly. Midwinter was sentenced to death, but the trial judge doubted "whether, as Sims did not give the stroke, his being present and aiding . . . will bring him within the penalty of this law, so as to oust him of clergy." The judges differed in their opinions about the case since the statute did not expressly include accessories. After a lengthy delay, he was finally sentenced to death but reprieved, while Midwinter had already been reprieved by the trial judge. (168 E. R. 90)

In a lengthy note following the above case the reporter questions whether the common law rule by virtue of which Sims was clearly a principal should be applied in cases of non-clergable felonies. He quotes Hale's statement that "where a statute ousts clergy, it is only so far ousted, and only in such cases, and to such persons, as are expressly comprized within the statute; for *in favorem vitæ et privilegii clericalis,* such statutes are construed literally and strictly." The reporter concluded that "Cases without number might have been cited to shew how extremely tender the judges in all times have been in the construction of the Acts, which take away clergy."

In 1755 Uriah Pearles was indicted for stealing a horse alleged to be worth 23s6d. On Mr. Justice Foster's recommendation, the jury found the defendant guilty of petty larceny, fixing the value of the property at 12d, and he was transported. (2 East, P. C. 741)

John Leigh was indicted in 1764 on 24 Geo. II, c. 45, for stealing wearing apparel worth 21 shillings, together with two guineas and two dollars, all taken from a vessel on the Thames. The theft was proved without doubt, but it was objected that the statute removing clergy included only goods, wares and merchandise, and that money did not come within this category. The court so held, and the defendant was found guilty of simple larceny. (168 E. R. 129)

In The King v. Cook (1774), the defendant was indicted under 14 Geo. II, c. 6 and 15 Geo. II, c. 34 for stealing a cow worth £5. The theft was clearly proved; but it was argued that the animal being only two and one-half years old, and never having had a calf, was not a cow but a heifer. The twelve judges decided that since the statute mentioned both cow and heifer "the one must have been used in contradistinction to the other, and therefore that the evidence did not support the indictment, and the prisoner was intitled to his acquittal." (168 E. R. 155)

In 1784 Moses Pike was tried on the statute 24 Geo. II, c. 45 for stealing merchandise from a boat on the Thames. At the time of the theft, the boat was docked, and the court held that the statute did not apply because it "was not committed on the navigable river Thames, but on the banks of one of its creeks." The statute, however, specifically included any port of entry or any creek, "but," held the court, "this being a different branch of the Act, the indictment should have charged the fact accordingly." This defendant was convicted of simple larceny, a clergable offense. (168 E. R. 261)

The case of The King v. Aickles decided in 1785, had an important bearing on the law imposing transportation. Several statutes made it a non-clergable felony to return from transportation prior to the expiration of the term of sentence. Similar provisions applied to persons sentenced to be transported who were found at large in England. This was the defendant's situation, having overstayed his leave of fourteen days after his conviction for simple larceny. The case was directly within the statutes. It appearing, however, that the defendant had intended to leave England but was prevented from doing so by poverty and ill-health, the trial court was of the opinion that "these impediments, if true, amounted to a lawful excuse." The jury found the defendant not guilty.[23] (168 E. R. 297)

The King v. Sterne (1787) was another case of theft from the person committed by two men, one of whom jostled the

---

[23] To the same effect was Thorpe's Case, 168 E. R. 300n. (1785).

complainant while the other took a gold decoration. Sterne was caught and indicted on 8 Eliz. c. 4. The other offender escaped. The court instructed the jury that the statute did not include persons aiding and abetting and that, although the stolen decoration was found in the possession of the defendant directly after the theft upon the complainant's raising an alarm and pursuit, nevertheless it might have been handed to him by the other man who escaped, and the presumption arising from recent possession could thus be refuted. The jury found the defendant guilty of simple larceny and he was transported. (168 E. R. 338)

One Margaret Kennedy (1797) induced an intoxicated coachman to accompany her to a house. While there he fell asleep, and upon his awakening he found that two and a half guineas, three shillings, and a silver plated button worth one penny had been taken from him. In the trial brought upon 8 Eliz. c. 4, the jury found the defendant guilty of the entire charge and judgment of death was imposed. On reference to the twelve judges, however, it was held that the defendant should have been acquitted as regards the capital charge because there had been "no fraud used by the prisoner in making the prosecutor drunk." The defendant was accordingly pardoned of the capital offense, fined one shilling, and imprisoned in the house of correction for twelve months. (168 E. R. 494)

Henry Beaney, indicted for horse stealing, (1820) was charged with feloniously taking two colts. The animals were described and the evidence was ample to secure a verdict of conviction; the case was then referred to the judges to determine if the conviction was proper. They unanimously held that the defendant could be guilty of simple larceny; but since "colts were not named, *eo nomine* in the statute the judges could not take notice that they were of the horse species, and consequently clergy was not taken away." (168 E. R. 874)

In R. *v.* Edwards and Walker (1823), it was held that an indictment for stealing live turkeys could not be supported by proof that dead turkeys were stolen. (168 E. R. 917)

"With regard to description of stolen property in an indictment, it is particularly necessary to be precise. Nothing is so common as for the clearest cases to fail from a misdescription of this kind. I need not mention the well known case of a man, indicted for stealing a pair of stockings, being acquitted, because the stockings were proved to be odd ones; or of the person acquitted of stealing a duck, because in proof it turned out to be a drake." Reporter's Note to Rex v. Halloway, 171 E. R. 1131n (1823).

The above summary of decisions rendered from 1731 to 1823, reveals the extremes to which the judges went to invent technicalities in order to avoid infliction of the capital penalty.[24] These cases have covered generally the range of the aggravated larceny offenses. Closer examination of a specific statute, the so-called "shop-lifting" act, 10 and 11 W. III, c. 23 (1699),[25] reveals the process even more sharply.

Almost every conceivable refinement was made by the courts to avoid application of this statute.[26] In 1711, in the case of Tims and Cecil, and again in 1726, in Rex v. Cartwright, it was actually held that the use of force to make entry excluded the cases from the scope of the statute.[27] In this regard, Jones' Case[28] is as curious a legal specimen as ever has been collected. A shop was left locked Saturday night, and on the Monday following it was discovered that the place had been entered by means of a key or pick-lock, and that goods valued at £700 had been taken. There was no evidence of force used to gain entry; but a desk had been broken into. The defendant was convicted

---

[24] See Radzinowicz, op. cit. 88.

[25] After stating that the crime of shop-lifting had considerably increased, this statute enacts, "that all and every person and persons that shall at any time or times, by night or in the day time, in any shop, warehouse, coachhouse, or stable, privately and feloniously steal any goods, wares, or merchandizes, being of the value of five shillings or more (although such shop, warehouse, coach-house or stable be not actually broke open by such offender or offenders, and although the owners of such goods, or any other person or persons be or be not in such shop, warehouse, coach-house or stable, to be put in fear) or shall assist, hire or command any person or persons to commit such offense . . . shall be excluded from the benefit of clergy."

[26] Romilly states that in the year 1731–1732, of 33 persons indicted on this statute, only one was convicted, twelve were acquitted, and twenty were found guilty of the theft of goods found by the jury to be worth less than five shillings. See 1 Wheeler Cr. Cas. 110.

[27] 2 East, P. C. 641.

[28] 2 East, P. C. 641 (1787).

under the statute "but it was objected on his behalf, that force having been used by breaking the lock and wrenching the desk open, the offense was not that of privately stealing." And "all the Judges held the conviction wrong as to the capital part of the charge, there having been force used."[29] A pardon was recommended and transportation followed.

The jury participated in the circumvention of this statute, also. William Sherrington, indicted in 1732, had actually sold the goods he stole for £1 5s. The jury fixed the value of the goods at 4s.10d. On the trial of Michael Allen in 1733, a witness testified that he purchased forty-three dozen pairs of stockings from him for a guinea and a half, and it was claimed that the merchandise was worth £3 10s. The jury which found him guilty fixed the value at just two pence below the 5 shilling mark set by the statute.[30]

Even more remarkable was the case of Dawson and Hitch, indicted in 1773. The defendants entered a shop together and stole merchandise at one time. Both were found guilty, but in the case of Hitch the value of the goods taken was put at 4s.10d. while in that of Dawson, the identical goods were valued by the jury at 5s. Dawson had been previously convicted at that same sessions, and in that case the jury had fixed the value of the goods he stole at 4s.10d. There was apparently a limit to which even an eighteenth century jury would go to avoid the capital penalty.[31]

In Howard's Case,[32] the defendant was indicted for stealing goods owned by F. and Co. in the warehouse of John Day, where they were stored prior to shipment. The court held that "by the word warehouses in the statute are meant not mere repositories of goods . . . but . . . shops . . . whither customers go to view them."[33]

---

[29] *Ibid.*
[30] 1 Wheeler Cr. Cas. 110.
[31] *Ibid.*
[32] 168 E. R. 39 (1751).
[33] To the same effect was The King *v.* Godfrey, 168 E. R. 246 (1783); so also in the case of The King *v.* Stone, 168 E. R. 270 (1784), which concerned theft of a watch from a watchmaker's shop.

In Sea's Case [34] the defendant stole a livery coat from a stable, a place specifically named in the statute. The court doubted whether a coachman's livery coat was "any part of the proper or usual furniture of a stable"; the defendant was acquitted of the capital charge, and found guilty of simple larceny. He was finally ordered to be whipped and confined six months in the house of correction with hard labor.

The shoplifting statute was modified in 1820 so that theft of goods worth less than fifteen pounds was no longer a capital offense. In that same year Elizabeth McKenzie and another were tried [35] for a theft committed on the 11th of July. Not until the 25th of July did the repeal of the old statute become effective, at which time the new law was signed by the king. The judges, after some debate, agreed that the new statute could not apply, which was, of course, good law. They then decided that the defendants must be punished for simple larceny "without reference to either statute"—poor law indeed, whatever else it had to recommend it. [36]

The technicalities described above concerned the most common class of cases to which this process was applied, namely, the aggravated larcenies. The judicial technique employed consisted principally of very strict interpretation of the statutes imposing capital penalties. Since every set of facts is unique in some respect, it is obvious that a *sufficiently* narrow interpreta-

---

[34] 168 E. R. 255 (1784).

[35] 168 E. R. 881.

[36] Massachusetts enacted that persons who had previously been convicted of two thefts of property valued at 40s., should upon a third conviction of theft of property valued at three pounds, be subject to capital punishment without benefit of clergy. Mass. Charter (1759) 283. Some of the American states adhered to the letter of non-clergable felonies much later than did the courts of England. Thus in 1819 Hardy Miles was convicted of stealing a slave (2 Nott & McC. So. Car. Rep. 1) under a statute which fixed the penalty at death without benefit of clergy. 2 Brev. Dig. 245 P. L. 236. The trial court instructed the jury that it might fix the value of the property taken at less than twelve pence, but a general verdict of guilty was brought in. The upper court held that judgment of death should have been rendered, and that the value of the property was immaterial.

Benefit of clergy was extended to slaves because of their economic value. Flogging was generally substituted for prescribed capital penalties. Wm. K. Boyd (1923) 8 J. of Negro History No. 4; Gabel, *op. cit.* 125, n. 39.

tion could exclude any case from the scope of a non-clergable offense. In a sense, this method is the opposite of that which employs legal fictions, for the usual effect of the latter is to include a case within the scope of a rule by expanding the meaning of words. Both methods are alike in that they result in judicial legislation, that is, in rules which were clearly outside the contemplation of the legislature, or even directly opposed to the known legislative intent.

Sometimes the courts went so far in their refinement of the law that it was practically impossible to apply the rule in any case. Occasionally, as in the McKenzie Case, noted above, they deliberately set aside a statute without even attempting to disguise the nullification. Again, the judges granted reprieves [37] even in cases where a fertile imagination could not conjure up a legal basis of any plausibility.[38] Finally, the courts made recommendations to juries; or they expressed doubts regarding the guilt of many defendants, and the juries were not loath to bring in the indicated verdicts.

As for the juries, themselves, the area within which they functioned limited the possibilities of their intervention. They could acquit, or return a verdict of guilty as charged or a verdict of guilty of a lesser offense. They acquitted very frequently. But the return of a verdict of guilty of a minor offense was the principal method of compromising statutory law. Here again the aggravated larcenies afforded a special opportunity. For it was possible to find a verdict of guilty of simple larceny or even of petty larceny [39] by the expedient of fixing the value of the property at less than one shilling. Again, in aggravated larcenies the jury could find that the theft was committed but

---

[37] 8 Geo. III, c. 15 (1768) enacted that Judges of Assize should have power to order transportation in cases of persons convicted of crimes without benefit of clergy. Prior to that, conditional pardons were provided for by the Habeas Corpus Act (31 Chas. II, c. 2) and were granted by the king upon recommendation of the Judge of Assize.

[38] *Cf.* Midwinter and Sims' Case, *supra* pp. 119–120.

On the power of the judges to grant a reprieve, see Radzinowicz, *op. cit.* 110–112.

[39] Petty larceny was excepted from the capital penalty at least as far back as the early Anglo-Saxons.

not in a dwelling or warehouse or boat on a river or privily, and so on. All this joined with increasing disapproval of an indiscriminate capital penalty and the very high frequency [40] of crimes against property without violence to segregate these crimes from others and to stimulate humane treatment of these offenders.

The influence of the jury upon the transformation of the penal law was perhaps even more effective than that of the judges. By the middle of the eighteenth century the practice of returning fictitious verdicts was so widespread that it was generally recognized as a typical feature of English administration of criminal justice. Blackstone's famous characterization of these verdicts as "a kind of pious perjury" [41] was only one of many similar observations regarding verdicts by twelve good men and true. Fielding,[42] Romilly,[43] and others [44] discussed it at

---

[40]

	1812	1813	1814	1815	1816	1817	1818
Persons tried for Simple Larceny	4,363	4,623	4,259	5,409	6,123	9,396	9,303
Persons tried for Various Forms of Larceny including Simple	5,022	5,481	5,136	6,184	7,154	10,880	10,864
Total no. persons tried for All Offenses	6,576	7,164	6,393	7,818	9,091	13,932	13,567

Source: Statement of the Number of Persons Committed to the Different Gaols in England and Wales, etc., Sec'y of States' Office, Whitehall (1818) 4.

The inclusion of other crimes against property, e.g., robbery, burglary, embezzlement, forgery, fraud, receiving stolen property, etc., would show that the offenses against property account for approximately 90% of all the cases. For 1812, the figure is 91.5+%.

[41] "It is true, that the mercy of juries will often make them strain a point, and bring in larceny to be under the value of twelve-pence, when it is really of much greater value: but this, though evidently justifiable and proper, when it only reduces the present nominal value of money to the ancient standard, is otherwise a kind of pious perjury, and does not at all excuse our common law in this respect from the imputation of severity, but rather strongly confesses the charge." 4 Bl. Comm. 237.

[42] "But since Juries have taken upon them to consider the Value of Goods as immaterial, and to find upon their Oaths, that what is proved to be worth several Shillings, and sometimes several Pounds, is of the Value of Tenpence, this is become a Matter of more Consequence." H. Fielding, An Enquiry Into the Causes of the Late Increase of Robbers, etc. (1751) 72.

[43] "The latitude which jurors allow themselves in estimating the value of property stolen, with a view to the punishment which is to be the consequence of their verdict, is an evil of very great magnitude. Nothing can be more

length; and the data marshalled by Fowell Buxton in his speech
to Parliament in 1821 [45] leave little doubt that by that time, at

pernicious, than that jurymen should think lightly of the important duties they
are called upon to discharge, or should acquire a habit of trifling with the
solemn oaths they take. And yet ever since the passing of the acts which punish with death the stealing in shops or houses, or on board ships, property of
different values which are there mentioned, juries have, from motives of
humanity, been in the habit of frequently finding, by their verdicts, that the
things stolen were worth much less than was clearly proved to be their value."
Quoted in 1 Wheeler Cr. Cas. 109–10.

[44] John Earl Russell, History of English Government and Constitution (1865)
140–1.

Henley, Principles of Penal Law (3rd ed. 1775) 293; Kenny, Outlines of
Criminal Law (15th ed. 1936) 208.

Such verdicts were frequent also in early American cases. *Cf.* 1 Wheeler
Cr. Cas. 111; and 1 City Hall Record (N. Y.) 52; 3 *id.* 158.

In State *v.* John Bennett the court stated: "However absurd it may appear,
that a jury who are sworn to determine a case according to evidence, should
be authorized to find goods stolen of less value than twelve pence, when all
the witnesses swear they are of much greater value, it is what Judge Blackstone calls a pious perjury, which they have indulged in, until it has become
the law of the land. The principle has been too long established, to be now
called in question, and, therefore, a new trial must be refused." Constitutional
Court, Charleston, 2–3 Brev. S. Car. Rep. 567 (1815).

[45] *Cf.* "And here, Sir, I must refer to the Sessions papers. My object is not
to demonstrate perjury in a few special and selected cases. I admit that I
prove nothing at all, if I do not prove it in tens, nay in hundreds of thousands
of instances. For the sake of clearness, I shall advert to but one species of
crime; namely, Larceny; and to one species of perjury; namely, a diminution,
by the jury, of the value of goods stolen, below the sum made capital by law.
The House are aware, that larceny from the person is, or has been to a late
period, capital, to the extent of twelve pence; from a shop, to the extent
of five shillings; from a dwelling-house, to the extent of forty shillings. Now,
I will read to the House a few cases, by which they will judge whether juries
do or do not perjure themselves, for the purpose of saving the life of the
prisoner. Mary Whiting was indicted for stealing 7 guineas and 34 shillings,
in the house of John Sun. Verdict, guilty 39*s.*—Jonathan Smith was indicted
for stealing 20*l.* in money in the house of J. Marsh. Guilty 39*s.*—Elizabeth
Parsons was indicted for stealing 23 guineas in the dwelling-house of Richard
Staples. Guilty 39*s.*—Joseph Court was indicted for stealing 8 pair of gold
earrings, value 3*l.* 16*s.*; 121 other pairs of ditto, value 74*l.* 10*s.* 6*d.*; 48 pairs
of ditto, value 12*l.* 12*s.*; 204 pairs of ditto, value 36*l.* 9*s.*; 24 pairs of ditto,
value 6*l.* 6*s.*; 2,488 gold beads, value 72*l.* 18*s.*; 864 coloured beads, value
18*l.*; 144 pairs of gold earrings, value 20*l.* 8*s.*; 3 pairs of gold enamelled
bracelets, value 9*l.*; 18 pairs of gold ditto, value 11*l.* 7*s.* 6*d.*; 3 small cases
for bracelets, value 6*s.*; 36 gold seals, value 33*l.* 12*s.*; 12 gold lockets, value
3*l.*; and a parcel of shoes, value 14*s.* 8*d.*; the property of Messrs. Mackenzie
and Grey, in a lighter belonging to them on the Thames navigable river.
Guilty 39*s.*—Stephen Blanrise and John Parker were indicted for stealing 68
lb. of beef, value 15*s.* and 12 lb. of pork, also a stock-lock, privately, in the
shop of Thomas Burdett. Guilty 4*s.* 10*d.*—William Parker was indicted for

stealing 4 cocks, 17 hens, 5 ducks, 15 drakes, 20 fowls, the property of E. Tilson. Guilty 10*d*.—Barbara Hensley was indicted for stealing a gold watch, and a gold chain, value 10*l*.; 2 cornelian seals, value 40*s*., privately, from the person of Edward George. The watch and chain found on the prisoner's person. Guilty 10*d*.—David Dickson was indicted for stealing 18½ guineas in the dwelling-house of Mr. Hall. Guilty 39*s*.—Edward Greenwood was indicted for stealing 240 gallons of vinegar, value 22*l*., a hogshead and 6 half hogsheads, value 4*l*, the property of Elizabeth White, on a wharf adjoining the Thames navigable river. Guilty 39*s*.—William Moore was indicted for stealing 10 gallons of wine, value 10*l*.; 42 bottles, 7*s*.; and a handkerchief, 2*s*., in the house of Peter Dennis. Guilty 39*s*. George Taylor and William Dove were indicted for stealing a bed, bedstead, and curtains, set of fire-irons, a stove, a looking-glass, 4 checked linen shirts, a chest containing a bill, value 4*l*. 8*s*.; another bill, value 4*l*. 4*s*., another bill, value 2*l*. 2*s*., two dollars, and 7 bills (Spanish money) in the house of Mary Glass. Taylor guilty 39*s*.; Dove guilty 10*d*.—Catherine Tracey was indicted for stealing 6 guineas, and 2 half guineas, from the person of George Bennington. Guilty 10*d*.—John Powell was indicted for stealing 34 wooden half-firkins, and 1,150 lb. of soap, value 20*l*. Guilty 10*d*.—John Martin was indicted for stealing 6 guineas, 2 crowns, 3 silver shoe-buckles, and 11 silver buttons, in a small trunk, in the dwelling-house of Thomas Smith. Guilty 39*s*.—Thomas Radford and Thomas Williams were indicted for stealing 7*s*.; a bank-note, value 10*l*.; 1 ditto, value 2*l*.; 3 others, each 1*l*.; and 2 others, each 5*l*., monies of John Hartshorne, in his dwelling-house. Guilty 39*s*.—Alexander Chalmers was indicted for stealing 333 yards of Holland linen, value 105*l*. 5*s*.; 24 yards of printed linen, value 4*l*. 4*s*.; 45 yards of damask, value 16*l*.; 26 yards of striped linen, value 3*l*. 5*s*., in the dwelling-house of Edward White. Guilty 39*s*.—Joseph Day was indicted for stealing a gold watch, value 20*l*.; a gold watch-string, value 2*l*.; a gold chain, value 10*l*.; a pair of diamond earrings, value 20*l*.; a silver snuff-box, value 3*l*.; 6 silk gowns, value 12*l*.; 2 pieces of gold and silver brocaded silk, containing 40 yards, value 60*l*.; 10 pieces of silk, containing 80 yards, and other things, in the dwelling-house of Thomas Cooke. Guilty 39*s*.—William Fox was indicted for stealing 50*l*. in money, numbered, in the house of Alexander Steele. Guilty 39*s*.—Philip Shovel was indicted for stealing 9 geese, value 40*s*. Guilty 10*d*.—Mark Woddin was indicted for stealing 12 guineas, and 4 shillings, in a dwelling-house. Guilty 10*d*.—Henry Todd was indicted for stealing 2 live pigs, value 10*s*., the property of John Dunn. Guilty 10*d*. . . .

"Here is another case to which I beg to call the particular attention of the House. William Earl, alias Day, was indicted for stealing 13¾ yards of lace, value 6*l*. in the dwelling-house of Arabella Morris. Guilty 39*s*. He was a second time indicted for stealing 4½ yards of lace, in the House of Henry Pearse. Guilty again 39*s*. Now, it is somewhat curious, that 4½ yards of lace, and 13¾ of lace, upon the oath of twelve jurymen, should be valued at precisely the same sum. But, what is still more extraordinary, he was a third time indicted for stealing 6½ yards of Mecklin lace, and 7 yards of English lace, in the shop of John Gubbins. Now, if 4½ yards were worth, valued upon oath, 39*s*., one would have thought that these 6½ yards of one description, and 7 yards of another, must have been worth something more. But it appears, they were worth a great deal less; for the jury brought in their verdict, guilty of stealing to the value of 4*s*. 10*d*. Is there any man who doubts the reason of these strange and sudden fluctuations in the value of the property? That their value was limited to 39*s*. in the two former instances, and to 4*s*. 10*d*. in the latter, because in the former, the larceny was from the dwelling-house; in the latter, from the shop?

any rate, the verdicts described above were a commonplace of English criminal law administration. When an occasional sentence of death was imposed in a case of theft, it greatly shocked the sensibilities of those who had participated in the trial.[46]

Much less noticed, though even more suggestive, was the participation of prosecuting counsel in avoidance of the capital penalty in cases of aggravated larceny. In The King v. Thompson [47] the defendant was convicted on 8 Eliz. c. 4 for privately stealing from the person while the victim was asleep. After a verdict of guilty of the charge brought, "the Counsel for the prosecution having very candidly produced a case decided at Durham some years ago, where it was ruled that the statute does not extend to protect persons asleep, the execution of the sentence was respited, and the case reserved for the opinion of the Twelve Judges." They, however, upheld the conviction.

In a later case the kind offices of the counsel for the prosecution were more effective. Dixon, Hodge and others [48] were convicted of stealing linen and sentence of death was imposed. Thereupon "a doubt was suggested by the counsel for the prosecution, whether it ought not to have been proved that the

---

"Again a bank-note of 50l. is taken from the pocket of the prosecutor, the jury swear it is worth but 10d.—from the shop of the prosecutor, the jury swear it is worth 4s. 10d.—from the dwelling-house of the prosecutor, the jury protest that it is worth but 39s. Now, Sir, if any man denies that this is palpable and rank perjury, he is bound to explain so curious a phenomenon. Here is a piece of paper worth 10d. in one spot, 4s. 10d. in another, 39s. in a third, and 50l. all over the world besides.

"These are some few of the cases of this nature which I have selected; *and I hold in my hand twelve hundred of a similar description*, with which, I need not trouble the House. I, in the little leisure that I enjoy, have only been able to select so limited a number; but, if any gentleman wishes to enlarge his collection, he will find no difficulty in making that twelve hundred, twelve thousand. Now, observe: each of these cases involves the perjury of twelve men. I have confined myself to one species of crime out of a multitude— to one species of evasion out of a multitude—and to one court, the Old Bailey, without touching upon the remainder of England, all Ireland, and all Scotland. And, thus, restricted, I prove my point. But, had I enlarged upon all crimes, tried in all courts, subject to every species of evasion, what would then have been the number of demonstrated perjuries?" Fowell Buxton, Debate in the House of Commons on the *Forgery Punishment Mitigation Bill,* 1821, 5 Hans. Deb. (N. S.) 942–5.

[46] See *infra* p. 136 for an instance of a complainant's efforts to secure a pardon for an offender in such a case.

[47] 168 E. R. 323 (1787).   [48] 168 E. R. 680 (1803).

building was made use of for the purpose of drying calico . . .
This doubt being communicated to the counsel for the prisoners, he wished it might be considered, and though the objec-
tion, if taken at the trial, would probably have led to evidence
that the building was frequently used for the purpose . . . the
case was thereafter submitted . . . to the consideration of the
judges." They held that the conviction on the capital charge
was error. The defendants were pardoned to this extent and
transported.

The participation of prosecuting counsel in mitigation of the
rigor of the law went far beyond recommendation after conviction, as may be seen from the remarks of M. Cottu in his critical
discussion of English criminal law administration in the early
nineteenth century:

"As, however, it often happens that these counterfeit notes
are found in the hands of forgers, or of those who have circulated forged notes, there are generally two bills of indictment
framed against the party; the first, accusing them of having
made or uttered forged notes, and the second, of having them
in their possession with the intention of uttering them. In this
situation, when the accused is standing at the bar, in order to
take his trial, the counsel for the bank asks the counsel for the
prisoner if his client be willing to plead guilty on the second
indictment, which only involves transportation; promising him
that in that case the bank will relinquish the prosecution on the
first which is a capital crime. If the accused acquiesce in this
proposition, he is immediately found guilty on the second indictment, on his own confession; and with regard to the first,
the counsel for the bank informs the jury that he does not
intend to bring forward his witnesses, and they consequently
return a verdict of *not guilty*, for want of evidence. Nor does
this sort of transaction take place secretly, or in a corner, but
incredible as it may appear, in open court, in the face of the
public, the jury, and the judge." [49]

---

[49] M. Cottu, On the Administration of the Criminal Code in England, and
the Spirit of the English Government (1820) 51–2.

This practice was all the more significant because prosecution was by private
counsel. See Howard, Criminal Justice in England (1931).

The official records reveal the widespread nullification of non-clergable felonies especially in the early nineteenth century.[50]

[50] Number of Persons Tried, Convicted and Executed for Crimes Against Property Without Violence (and Murder) in England and Wales (1812–1818).

Simple Larceny	1812	1813	1814	1815	1816	1817	1818
Tried	4,363	4,623	4,259	5,409	6,123	9,396	9,303
Convicted*	2,777	3,006	2,813	3,529	4,093	6,420	6,459
Executed	——	——	——	——	——	——	——**
Cattle Stealing							
Tried	17	16	14	11	20	30	43
Convicted	12	10	13	10	13	25	27
Executed	——	——	——	——	——	——	1
Horse Stealing							
Tried	68	107	92	91	90	114	168
Convicted	46	82	66	65	62	75	130
Executed	3	4	3	1	——	——	1
Lar. in Shop							
Tried	66	67	67	50	52	52	81
Convicted	33	34	35	34	36	27	41
Executed	——	——	——	——	——	——	——**
Lar. on Navigable Rivers							
Tried	15	5	11	10	7	9	4
Convicted	9	4	3	2	4	7	2
Executed	3	——	——	——	2	——	2
Lar. of Naval Stores							
Tried	2	3	3	1	5	2	8
Convicted	2	3	3	1	5	2	4
Executed	——	——	——	——	——	——	——**
Lar. from Person							
Tried	214	272	311	277	402	519	551
Convicted	98	135	167	151	224	257	282
Executed	——	——	——	——	——	——	——**
Sheep Stealing							
Tried	71	125	92	85	125	306	277
Convicted	41	82	51	48	79	169	177
Executed	1	2	3	3	——	5	14
Larceny in a Dwelling-house to 40s							
Tried	128	140	133	160	202	207	217
Convicted	69	84	86	86	122	143	142
Executed	——	——	2	——	3	1	4
Murder							
Tried	66	87	80	61	85	80	51
Convicted	19	29	25	15	30	25	13
Executed	16	25	23	15	21	25	13
Total for All Offenses							
Tried	6,576	7,164	6,390	7,818	9,091	13,932	13,567
Convicted	3,913	4,422	4,025	4,883	5,797	9,056	8,958
Convicted and Sentenced to Death	532	713	558	553	890	1,302	1,254
Executed	82	120	70	57	95	115	97

*The statistics do not show the convictions in relation to the charges.
**These offenses are not found in the statistical tables on executions, apparently because there were none.

Source:—Statements of the Number of Criminal Offenders Committed to the Different Gaols in England and Wales, etc., 1819, Secretary of State's Office, Whitehall (1819).

V. The Background of Public Opinion and
Reform of the Penal Law

The effect upon Parliament was inevitable, though slow. After much opposition and many interminable delays, various committees were appointed to consider the laws relating to capital punishment. Their reports reveal a background of public opinion against which the behavior of juries and officials becomes highly significant, and the whole problem of criminal law administration is clarified. The Report of the Select Committee of 1819 is particularly illuminating with reference to crimes against property without violence and public attitudes regarding capital punishment in these cases. It is a document of rare importance for anyone interested in the effect of public opinion upon the actual operation of legal rules.

The thoroughness of the Committee and the modernity of its approach are shown by the method and extent of its research, and especially by the investigation of cases which never reached the courts. The members believed that "the most accurate and satisfactory evidence of the effect of the Penal Law" could not be gotten from the judges.[51] Accordingly, the Committee secured its data from victims of theft, businessmen from

---

[51] "They only see the exterior of criminal proceedings after they are brought into a court of justice. Of the cases which never appear there, and of the causes which prevent their appearance, they can know nothing. Of the motives which influence the testimony of witnesses, they can form but a hasty and inadequate estimate. Even in the grounds of Verdicts, they may often be deceived. From any opportunity of observing the influence of punishment upon those Classes of men among whom malefactors are most commonly found, the Judges are, by their stations and duties, placed at a great distance." Report of the Select Committee of The House of Commons, Appointed to Consider Of So Much Of The Criminal Law as Relates To Capital Punishment in Felonies (1820) 357.

Cf. "The modern teacher of law . . . should know not only what the courts decide and the principles by which they decide, but quite as much the circumstances and conditions, social and economic, to which these principles are to be applied; he should know the state of popular thought and feeling which makes the environment in which the principles must operate in practice." Pound, *The Need of a Sociological Jurisprudence* (1907) The Green Bag 611–12.

A detailed, well-documented discussion of the report of the Committee of 1819 is provided by Dr. Radzinowicz, *op. cit.* 526–566.

London and Westminster, experienced magistrates and their clerks, officers who received information and prepared indictments, jailers, and others.

The findings, based upon reliable testimony, are highly significant concerning the function of the administrative machine in relation to group attitudes and values.[52] Mr. Shelton, for nearly forty years Clerk of Arraigns at the Old Bailey, stated that in aggravated larcenies, constructive burglaries, and forgeries, the juries were anxious to bring in verdicts which avoided the capital penalty. T. W. Carr, Solicitor of Excise, stated that severe punishment made the law ineffective. As evidence of this he reported that prior to 1806 counterfeiting a stamp was punishable only by a fine of £500, and that subsequently it became a transportable offense. During 1794 to 1806, under the old law, 19 convictions were secured in every 21 prosecutions; but from 1806 to 1818, under the severer law, there were only 3 convictions out of every 9 prosecutions. Mr. Newman, Solicitor for the city of London, testified that during his thirty years' experience he had frequently observed much reluctance to prosecute or to convict in capital offenses against property. The Reverend Mr. Cotton, Ordinary of Newgate, "described in strong terms, the repugnance of the Public to capital execution in offenses unattended with violence, and the acquiescence even of the most depraved classes in their infliction in atrocious crimes."

The Committee reported that Colquhoun, the well-known police magistrate, declared "his firm conviction that capital punishment in the minor offences operates powerfully in preventing convictions; and that there is a great reluctance to prosecute in forgery, shop-lifting, larceny in the dwelling-house, burglary without actual entry, horse stealing, sheep stealing, cattle stealing, frame-breaking, house-breaking in the day time, robbery without acts of violence, and other minor offences, now subject to the punishment of death. According

---

[52] Relevant theory is discussed in Hall, Living Law of Democratic Society (1949) ch. 3.

to the testimony of this intelligent observer, the public mind revolts at capital punishment in cases not atrocious."

Basil Montague informed the Committee that "From the year one thousand seven hundred and thirty-two, when embezzlement of property by a bankrupt was made a capital offence, there have been probably forty thousand bankruptcies; in that period there have not been more than ten prosecutions, and three executions for the capital offence, and yet fraudulent bankruptcies have become so common as almost to be supposed to have lost the nature of crime."

Mr. Hobler, a magistrate's clerk in London for thirty years, stated that grand juries had frequently refused to indict in cases where the judge had no doubts; and that many prosecutors, "especially females, say 'I hope it is not a hanging matter,' and 'cannot this be put under forty shillings.'" [53]

There was considerable evidence that tradesmen generally were very reluctant to prosecute for non-clergable larcenies; and one London merchant stated that he had refrained from prosecuting in a case where property worth a thousand pounds had been stolen from him. Richard Martin, a member of Parliament and a landowner in Ireland, told the Committee that the capital penalty for theft of horses, cattle and sheep and, in general, for all larcenies without violence, prevented his prosecuting for these offenses although his large estate was "almost laid waste by sheep stealing." He thought that his interests and the security of property generally in Ireland would be better protected if the penalties were reduced. Joseph Harmer, for twenty years a solicitor at the Old Bailey, reported that many persons evaded jury service because they were opposed to the capital penalty for crimes without violence, and

---

[53] Fowell Buxton, in his speech before Parliament on the Forgery Punishment Mitigation Bill related that: "Martha Walmsley was indicted for stealing 1 pair of silver shoe-buckles, 2 pair of leather shoes, 3 shirts, 3 other ditto, 3 aprons, a frock, a gown, a bed-gown, 2 pair of hose and 2 curtains, with many other things, value 3*l*. 10*s*., in the house of Henry Grinling. Court of prosecutor: 'If you can fix the value under 40*s*., you will save the prisoner's life.' Prosecutor: 'God forbid I should take her life! I will value them at 8*s*.' Guilty 8*s*." *Op. cit.* 944.

they frequently bribed the summoning officer not to serve them. Professional thieves were aware of these public sentiments. *They preferred to be prosecuted on capital indictments.* "Certainly," he concluded, "the general feeling does not go along with the infliction of death in the case of crimes unaccompanied by violence; there are very few advocates for the generality of the present punishments; these punishments rather tend to excite the public feeling against the Criminal Laws."

A large number of merchants supported the above views. They testified that public condemnation of the capital penalty in non-violent crimes was general; that the severity of the law discouraged prosecution by persons who would otherwise "have regarded it as highly criminal in themselves to have forborne prosecution"; that, accordingly, severity encouraged criminality because it went unpunished even though theft was very common. It was stated that these views prevailed among farmers, also, regarding the theft of cattle. Mr. Collins, a leading Westminster merchant, reported that, although many thefts had been committed by employees during the past twenty years, only one was prosecuted. In this case there was a conviction and sentence of death. "The pain and anxiety," added Mr. Collins, "occasioned by that event, until we obtained for him the Royal Mercy, none can describe but ourselves; which made us resolve never to prosecute again for a similar offense." [54]

In the eighteenth and nineteenth centuries there were, as now, numerous diverse and conflicting views regarding capital punishment. There were many advocates of rigorous treatment; there was the usual mass of indifferent or at least inarticulate

---

[54] *Cf.* "Penal Laws are sometimes called into activity after long disuse, and in cases where their very existence may be unknown to the best informed part of the community; malicious prosecutors set them in motion; a mistaken administration of the Law may apply them to purposes for which they were not intended . . . such seems to have been the case of the person who, in the year 1814, at the Assizes of Essex, was capitally convicted of the offense of cutting down trees, and who, in spite of earnest applications for mercy from the prosecutor, the committing magistrate, and the whole neighborhood, was executed, apparently because he was believed to be habitually engaged in other offenses, for none of which however he had been convicted or tried." Report of the Select Committee (1820) 354.

citizenry. Change was slow and piece-meal, spreading from individuals to particular groups until a pronounced attitude became sufficiently widespread to affect profoundly both the administration of the law and legislation. It is possible here merely to indicate the above, principal features of the dominant movement.[55]

One other parliamentary development was of great importance for reform of the criminal law, namely, a series of debates which took place in the House of Commons in 1821 on the Forgery Punishment Mitigation Bill.[56]

In the debates on the bill, the remarks of Fowell Buxton were the most informative. He replied to the Solicitor General who had argued for the capital penalty because "The object of punishment was the prevention of crime by terror . . . transportation was scarcely regarded in the light of a punishment . . . the criminals on being sentenced to it, often bowed to the judge and thanked him." [57] Buxton admitted that transportation was no deterrent and argued that imprisonment with hard labor should be substituted. He then discussed the history of the criminal law during the preceding century and pointed out that it had "increased to four-fold dimensions." Despite that, crime was a commonplace; and there were thousands of small children who were committing petty thefts of all sorts in an apprenticeship which would turn them into hardened criminals in the course of a few years. The chief reason for the ineffectiveness of the criminal law, he argued, was its crude classification of penalties, with the result that it bore down with inordinate severity upon many minor offenders.[58] This indiscriminate punishment had alienated the

---

[55] For full discussion of the 18th century literature on punishment, see Radzinowicz, *op. cit.*

[56] *Op. cit. supra* p. 130.

[57] *Op. cit.* 897–8. Some of the transported convicts had made fortunes in the colonies, and word of this and rosy exaggerations circulated widely in England, so that many persons violated the law for the purpose of being transported at public expense. Gillespie, *op. cit.* 367.

[58] "For example: kill your father, or catch a rabbit in a warren—the penalty is the same! Destroy three kingdoms, or destroy a hop-vine—the penalty is the same! Meet a gipsey on the high road, keep company with the said gipsey, or kill him, no matter which—the penalty by law is the same." Buxton, *op. cit.* 905.

public. He reiterated Samuel Romilly's plea that "the penalty was too severe for the feelings of your people"; and drew fully upon the report of the Select Committee with reference to the prevailing attitudes and their effect on prosecution and conviction. He recited a long list of the findings of juries in cases of aggravated larcenies, and concluded with the description of "the celebrated case at Pevensy." A man was charged with stealing a pair of breeches, and the evidence being clear, the jury brought in a verdict of guilty. Just before the magistrate was about to pronounce sentence of death, the clerk informed the jurors that the offense was capital. The jurors were dismayed, and sought immediately to modify their verdict. One suggested that the word *Not* be inserted before *Guilty;* another desired the discharge of the prisoner without any formality. This being impossible, it was decided to adjourn court and consult Mr. Willard, a local counsellor of eminence. It happened that the chief baron and another judge were dining with Mr. Willard when the deputation arrived. Upon hearing the case the chief baron recommended that the best way out was to insert after the word *Guilty,* the words *Of Manslaughter.* The jurors were delighted and returned in triumph to the courtroom, where the defendant, tried for stealing a pair of breeches, was convicted of manslaughter—a verdict which, of course, would have to be set aside.[59]

The debates in Parliament in 1821 indicate that by that time the humanitarian movement initiated by the classical school had gained considerable momentum. The reform of prison conditions was chiefly the work of Howard. He commenced his investigations into the deplorable state of imprisonment in 1773, when jailers were paid fees to cover both expenses and salary.[60] To this movement to reform penal institutions and to

[59] *Id.* 946–7. Buxton spoke also of a case in which a man charged with returning from transportation, was found guilty of petty larceny.

[60] "Thomas Allen, in his *History of London,* relates that in 1750 'the Lord Mayor, some of the aldermen, two of the judges, the under sheriff, many lawyers, and a number of onlookers, died of the gaol distemper.' The prison was afterwards cleansed! Howard asserts that in 1773–1774 more people died from the gaol fever than were executed in the kingdom. . . . He quotes

limit capital punishment, Elizabeth Fry and Samuel Romilly made important contributions. All were inspired by the epoch-making work of Beccaria, Voltaire [61] and other advocates of reform. The movement in England was thus a phase of a general eighteenth-century European development.

The process of legislative mitigation started with the offenses committed without violence. It continued until only four or five crimes remained subject to the supreme penalty. In 1820 the shop-lifting act was modified; in 1827 came the sweeping act of 7 & 8 Geo. IV, c. 29 which abolished most of the capital penalties and, as of course, that ancient hangover which only capital penalties had kept alive: the benefit of clergy. In 1832 the capital penalty was abolished for theft of horses and cattle.[62] In 1835 stealing from the mails was similarly treated. By 1860 over one hundred and ninety capital penalties had been eliminated.[63] The way was thus cleared for the use of various methods of treatment which transformed the criminal law from a heavy-handed, awkward weapon into a vastly more refined instrumentality. The above summary of the modernization of English penal law merely indicates the contours of the movement begun in practice and administration long before the legislature acted.[64]

Thus we have completed the cycle circumscribed by clergy. Originating as the privilege of a small group of ecclesiastics, it

---

Lord Bacon as saying that the most pernicious infection next to the plague is the smell of the jail." Ives, *op. cit.* 17–18.

As a result of the reform agitation, a series of laws improving prison conditions was passed, the most important of which were 22 Geo. III, c. 64 (1782) and 24 Geo. III, c. 54.

[61] "In countries where a trifling domestic theft or breach of trust, is punished with death, is not the disporportioned punishment dangerous to society? Is it not even an encouragement to larceny? If, in this case, a master prosecutes his servant and the unhappy wretch suffer death, the whole neighborhood hold the master in abhorrence: they perceive that the law is contrary to nature, and consequently that it is a bad law . . . so true it is, that rigorous laws are often productive of crimes." Voltaire's *Commentary,* in An Essay on Crimes and Punishments by Beccaria (1788) c. XVIII, 224.

[62] 2 & 3 W. IV, c. 62.

[63] Laurence, *op. cit.* 14.

[64] Dicey's aphorism that "the legislature tends to express the opinion of yesterday and the judges the opinion of the day before yesterday" should, in this instance, be reversed.

became a mechanism for applying similar rights to an ever widening class of persons until, in 1706, it was extended to all. During the span that covers the period of what might be termed the democratization of the criminal law, all the historical changes described in the second chapter of this book occurred. As part of this same legal development, it was inevitable, the legislative method being what it was, that with the levelling of political inequalities, non-clergable felonies should have appeared. For clergy originally covered all felonies. When the privilege was extended to all persons, a saner line of development opened: thinking in terms of the gravity of the offense and making some crimes exceptions to the rule. For almost three centuries the English criminal law grew in this manner. As we have seen in connection with the subject-matter of larceny, this method of specific, narrow legislation was typical and traditional. The characteristic rigid framework was subjected to the stress of new, urgent problems which the opening up of the Western world and the ensuing social and economic forces created. The power of the word and the imperious need to escape the power of the word constituted the problem of the men who, as jurors, judges, and prosecutors, were the chief administrators of the criminal law. But these functionaries were not about their own business. They were the representatives of an organized society. The parliamentary investigations and debates, especially at the beginning of the nineteenth century, reveal the transformation of public attitudes regarding the relative gravity of various crimes and the infliction of the capital penalty indiscriminately. What might have been surmised even in the absence of this evidence accordingly became quite probable, namely, that the administrative officials reflected the social attitudes of the community. Legislative reform of the criminal law in the early nineteenth century came then as the ratification of practices which had existed for a century.

The above discussion was intended less to reveal the conditions which gave rise to the devices used to counteract a body of law which lagged behind social needs than to present the most important permanent problem of administration and to discover the methods employed to solve it. The problem includes the selection of means to achieve certain ends where the rules fail to square with those ends, and it involves the invention of appropriate techniques. Thus, as to many non-clergable felonies, during the eighteenth and the early nineteenth century the end desired was to mete out punishment less severe than that prescribed.[65] The methods:

by judges— (1) narrow interpretation of statutes
(2) recommendations to jury and to counsel
(3) failure to apply statutes even when they clearly governed the cases
(4) grant of reprieves.

by juries— (1) placing a fictitious value upon the property stolen at an amount just below that set in the non-clergable statutes
(2) returning verdicts of simple larceny where the facts showed an aggravated larceny such as theft privately from the person, from a dwelling, from a warehouse, etc.
(3) returning verdicts which had no foundation in fact.

by prosecutors—(1) withdrawing the charge of non-clergable felony upon plea of guilty to a minor offense
(2) charging the commission of a clergable offense in the first instance where in fact a non-clergable offense had been committed
(3) calling to the attention of court and defense counsel certain decisions to show that verdicts of guilty as charged were defective.

And analogous practices were resorted to by complainants, witnesses, and grand juries.

---

[65] This, of course, is a simplification. In many cases, it was desired to acquit entirely, and in others to punish according to law. Neither of these present special problems, however, because both were in accord with the law as written.
See Radzinowicz, *op. cit.* 83-164.

VI. Contemporary Criminal Law Administration

The use of discretion in contemporary criminal law administration has three characteristics which distinguish it from that of the eighteenth century. First, the legally sanctioned area of discretion has increased considerably. Second, the use of discretion is now directed primarily toward individual cases and offenders rather than toward the statutes or rules in their general operation. Third, the discretion exercised by the eighteenth-century jury has shifted very largely to the modern prosecutor. In the eighteenth and the early nineteenth century, the efforts of the courts were necessarily directed toward "interpretation" of the statutes and a refinement of rules. Under such conditions, not only does a body of law become highly technical, the law also becomes directly and permanently altered—this in contrast with the verdicts of the jury, which, though effective, leave no permanent marks on the written law. Contemporary criminal law, in contrast with that of the eighteenth century, is characterized by a nicer classification of penalties, by probation, suspended and indeterminate sentences, juvenile and boys' courts. The incorporation of all these instrumentalities *within the law* has changed the lines of judicial discretion. Only occasionally do judges oppose and nullify contemporary penal laws in their entirety. The rules are, indeed, modified in the sense that different consequences are attached to substantially the same behavior, but the basis for departing from the rules is determined largely by individual considerations regarding the defendant and his particular situation.

With regard to the jury, the major questions concern the nature and extent of its exercise of discretion.[66] The salient general fact is that the use of the jury has very sharply dimin-

---

[66] In some states the jury fixes the sentence. Verdicts of guilty of manslaughter or of not guilty in cases where the plea has been the "unwritten law"; verdicts based upon evidence in mitigation introduced by psychiatrists under pleas of insanity; and verdicts of not guilty of violating certain unpopular laws are instances where the jury's verdict overrides rules of law.

ished.[67] The decline of this ancient institution in the United States during the present century, particularly after Patton *v. U.S.*,[68] has concentrated the administration of the criminal law in the courts and, even more, in the prosecuting attorneys. The petit jury is now important in exceptional cases where unusual circumstances cause either party to be unwilling to trust its fate to the judge. One determinant of the new allocation of functions is that conviction by a jury probably brings a severer sentence than a plea of guilty, especially one made on arraignment.[69] But nothing better illustrates the marked transformation of the jury than the recent insistence by the State upon a jury trial after waiver of it by the defendant, particularly in cases where it is apprehended that political influence may control a judge.[70]

The use of the jury in only five per cent of the *felony* cases means that ninety-five per cent of all such cases (and an even greater percentage of misdemeanors) are disposed of by officials. Other very important statistical findings are that: (*a*) a majority of all felony cases which appear in court are dis-

---

[67] "Eliminations. As a matter of fact in the State as a whole in only 4.45 per cent. of the arrests for felonies do the cases ever come before the juries for trial and the remaining 95.55 per cent. are disposed of on pleas of guilty or disappear on account of the failure of the state's attorney to prosecute before the magistrate on the preliminary hearing, the failure of proof before that magistrate sufficient to induce him to hold the defendant to the Grand Jury, a dismissal of the complaint by the state's attorney before the committing magistrate, the failure of the Grand Jury to indict even if the defendant is held over, and, even if an indictment is returned, the dismissal or nolle prosequi by the state's attorney." Bruce, *The Administration of Criminal Justice in Illinois* (1929) 19² J. Crim. L. and Criminol. no. 4 (A Summary of the Crime Survey of the Illinois Association for Criminal Justice) 27. And see Moley, *The Vanishing Jury* (1928) 2 So. Cal. L. Rev. 97.

[68] 281 U. S. 276 (1930). This case held that the defendant in any criminal case with the consent of the judge and prosecutor could "waive a trial by a constitutional jury and submit to trial by a jury of less than twelve persons, or by the court. . . ."

[69] Missouri Crime Survey 149.

[70] Hall, *Has the State a Right to Trial By Jury in Criminal Cases?* (1932) 18 A. B. A. J. 226; H. A. Roberts, *The Right in Colorado of One Accused of a Felony to Waive Jury Without the Consent of the State* (1951) 24 Rocky Mt. L. Rev. 106.

posed of *on preliminary hearings by magistrates*,[71] and (*b*) the vast majority of all persons who are punished for serious criminal offenses *have filed pleas of guilty*.[72]

As a consequence, the police magistrate and the prosecuting attorney loom up as by far the most powerful officials in our system of criminal justice. Examination of their work reveals a practice so frequent, typical, and significant, that it has become vastly important, namely, *waiver of the major felony charge* and acceptance of a plea of guilty to a lesser offense.[73] Frequently in the large cities, the magistrates take the initiative in waiving felony charges, and the prosecutor exercises very little influence. The city judges are really examining magistrates not only in preliminary hearings but in the cases which appear for trial before them. Formal requirements to the contrary notwithstanding, these judges frequently dispense with the prescribed rules of procedure.

In the county courts, on the other hand, the judge has a smaller calendar consisting of cases which appear before him because other officials have considered them to be serious. Moreover, these courts are accustomed to a formal procedure and they depend upon the prosecution to prove its cases. With the elimination of the jury in recent years, the procedure in many county courts has also become relatively informal and the function of the judge in these courts now approximates that of the city magistrate in many respects.

In the county courts, the prosecutor controls the cases disposed of on pleas of guilty. He has in all probability been consulted regarding these cases by counsel for the defense; generally, he is the only official who has an opportunity to study the files which give the past record of the defendant, the

---

[71] *Cf.* Bruce, *op. cit.* 40.

Cf. "Of all felony cases originating in arrest in New York City, about two percent are eliminated by the police, 57 percent in the preliminary hearings, 12 percent in the grand jury, 8 percent in the trial court, and 5 percent after guilt is established." Report of N. Y. Crime Commission 1925.

[72] Over 80 per cent of persons receiving any punishment, have pleaded guilty (liquor cases omitted). Missouri Crime Survey 149.

[73] Before a magistrate, the plea of guilty will necessarily be to a misdemeanor. In the county criminal court, the plea may be to a misdemeanor or to a less serious felony than the major charge in the indictment.

police report, and the facts in the case. As a result of the total situation as it is generally presented in the county courts, the prosecutor determines the charge upon which a plea of guilty will be accepted, and his decision is almost always ratified by the court.[74]

Despite the lack of detailed information about waiver of the felony, it may be hazarded that in the vast majority of cases in which defendants charged with felonies have pleaded guilty to misdemeanors, they have committed a more serious crime, if not, indeed, the major felony charged against them.[75] If that estimate is valid,[76] we have a remarkable parallel between this important practice in contemporary criminal law administration and the most important practices in such administration in the eighteenth century. For as a result of both, offenders who commit major crimes, for which the statutory law prescribes severe punishment, are found guilty of relatively minor crimes and receive relatively light punishment.

A brief examination of typical situations in Chicago presents the problem in a specific form.[77] During 1926, 78.81 per cent

---

[74] Missouri Crime Survey 149.

The prosecutor also (a) may ask indictment for a less serious offense than the one committed; and (b) he eliminates entirely a large number of cases by refusing to prosecute, by effecting a compromise prior to prosecution, and by dismissing cases on the trial calls of both magistrates and county judges. The last (nolle prosequi) requires the consent of the judge in most states. But this is rarely withheld.

[75] Cf. Bruce, op. cit. 33–36.

Obviously the administrators of the criminal law are not always concerned with mitigation of punishment. Frequently, the opposite is desired, especially in sensational cases and in the trials of notorious offenders. In such cases, officials seek to have maximum sentences imposed, and they will employ any statute or series of statutes in persistent attempts to secure a conviction. Again, they sometimes use all the techniques and skill at their disposal to stretch a statute to include conduct which was not previously criminal in order to eliminate a major offender.

[76] I am writing chiefly of the large metropolitan centers, and I am, also, generalizing somewhat in order to set the outlines for the problem of major interest, i.e., waiver of felony.

Cf. S. C. Wallace, *Nullification: A Process of Government* (1930) 45 Pol. Sci. Q. 347.

[77] The practice of waiving felonies is general throughout the country. Report on Prosecution of the Natl. Comm. on Law Obs. and Enf. 95–7; cf. also Survey of Admin. of Cr. Justice in Oregon, 17 A. B. A. J. 212, where it is stated that "There is a marked tendency to reduce many felony charges to lesser charges."

of all pleas of guilty in felony cases was entered to minor offenses.[78] Just as in England in the eighteenth century, so in Chicago in 1926, crimes against property were most frequently reduced. The order, beginning with the most frequent, was robbery, burglary and larceny; [79] while, on the other hand, in homicide, rape, and other sex crimes the convicted persons were most frequently punished for the major offense charged.[80]

The fact that the various crimes against property overlap allows a relatively wide choice to be made. Thus in the case of robbery with a gun, it is possible (1) to find the defendant guilty as charged, or (2) to eliminate the gun charge, or (3) to eliminate the robbery counts and charge grand larceny, or (4) to eliminate all the felony counts and find the defendant guilty of petty larceny. Since petty larceny is the minimum charge common to all of these offenses, it is inevitable that it should be most frequently used. Petty larceny, though not included in them, also has a functionally parallel relationship to burglary, fraud, and embezzlement as well. Accordingly, petty larceny is used in our legal system as a general catch-all (as simple larceny was used by the jury in the eighteenth cen-

---

[78] Bruce, *op. cit.* 34.

[79] Of all the offenses against property without violence charged in Chicago in 1926, the smallest number of convictions on the principal felony count occurred in embezzlement and fraud cases. Bruce, *op. cit.*

The Missouri Crime Survey shows that in embezzlement cases, the highest percentage, in comparison with that in other offenses, was eliminated in preliminary hearings, and also that a smaller percentage of embezzlers was sentenced than any other class of offenders. At 319, Table XIV.

[80] John J. Healy, a former State's Attorney of Cook County and a very competent observer, adds, "In these property crimes there are probably more interests involved in exerting influence and pressure for the lessening of the charge. There is, moreover, less moral stigma attached to these crimes and therefore less public danger of criticism if the prosecutor reduces the charge. In other words, an outraged public opinion is likely to be stirred by the reduction of a homicide charge, but after a burglary or robbery has been committed few people will feel themselves outraged, with the exception perhaps of the innocent victims, if petty larceny is substituted for robbery." Illinois Crime Survey 312–4; and see Bruce, *op. cit.* 33–5.

Cf. table of statistics from 1812–18 in England, footnote 50 *supra*.

For an interesting, indeed shocking, description of the present practice in Chicago, see Samuel Dash, *Cracks in the Foundation of Criminal Justice* (1951) 46 Ill. L. Rev. 392–405.

tury), a purely administrative device, when it is thought desirable to grant probation, suspended sentence, a minor imprisonment or to avoid a record of conviction of felony.

Almost as striking as the waiver of felonies is the fact that while criticism of the practice has been vehement there has been "no attempt to go deeply into the causes, or to discuss the effective remedies, or to present principles and procedures which should govern acceptances of pleas." [81] With the exception of one or two studies, the factors which have been emphasized in explanation of felony waivers have been political and corrupt influences. Undoubtedly such influences exist, especially in large cities, but while it is to be expected that abuses will be emphasized in surveys designed to formulate programs of reform, it is also obvious that such a particularistic explanation is superficial.[82] The problem received more critical treatment at the hands of Justin Miller,[83] who assigns relatively little importance to corrupt influences in his appraisal of the factors responsible for waiver of felonies. He emphasizes: (1) the great increase in the number of crimes, which makes prosecuting staffs inadequate; (2) the inability of the courts to handle the increased volume of cases; (3) the burden upon the public by way of jury and witness duties; and (4) the defendants' strong opposition to serious charges.

All of these factors are undoubtedly contributing causes, and they are particularly significant in an analysis of contemporary criminal law administration. It is at this point that the above study of eighteenth century administration supplements such analyses significantly by providing a substantial body of past experience from which it is possible to draw several probable

---

[81] Natl. Comm. on Law Obs. and Enf., Report on Prosecution 96–7.

[82] Questionnaires sent to 225 Bar Association committees in all states showed that, in great contrast with many evils in criminal law administration, "The policy of bargaining with the offender for a plea of guilty of a lesser offense is abused *in scarcely more than one community out of ten*" (Author's italics). Will Shafroth, *The Bar Reports On Some Phases Of Criminal Law* (1934) 20 A. B. A. Jour. 463.

Cf. 20 A. B. A. Jour. question 2 g. at 533.

[83] *The Compromise of Criminal Cases* (1927) 1 So. Cal. L. Rev. 1–31.

generalizations. Thus, it may be shown that felony waiver is the result of the following causes in addition to those already stated:

1. Occasionally, officials regard a law as too severe in any case. For example, the frequent nullification of the automobile felony law in Illinois must be ascribed primarily to the attitude of officials regarding its severity.[84]

2. More often, however, mitigating circumstances provided in the facts or the personality of the defendant, or both, lead officials to conclude that it is desirable to inflict a lighter penalty than that prescribed by statute for the offense actually committed.

3. Another common reason for the wide use of felony waivers is the weakness of the State's case due to factors beyond the control of the prosecution. The dependence of competent prosecution upon thorough investigation by police, the availability and quality of witnesses, the personality and record of the defendant, the ability of the prosecutor and many other factors comprise a highly complex situation. Frequently it is wiser to inflict some certain punishment than to hazard the escape of an offender after an expensive trial.

4. Finally, the desire to establish a record for numerous convictions, to be used in seeking reëlection, tends to encourage prosecutors to waive felonies and accept pleas of guilty to minor offenses.

To the extent that waiver of felonies has been influenced politically and corruptly, the remedy is obvious, if impracticable. The difficulty does not arise from lack of knowledge of existing evils, but from lack of ability to reform political conditions. For example, a much greater problem than that created by undisguised corruption is discussed by Judge James Pope of California.[85] It is not often the corrupt politician, he points out, but instead, interested members of the public who intercede with officials in behalf of known offenders. The public

---

[84] See Chapter Six on Automobile Theft.
[85] 1 So. Cal. L. Rev. 151ff.

has become aware of the power of officials to modify the prescribed law. Not differentiating use from abuse of discretion, ignoring the effect of their intercession upon the administration of the criminal law, upsetting standards of justice and sense of official responsibility, eminently respectable members of the public enlist businessmen, politicians, clergymen, and every available agency to persuade officials to grant special favors.

Nevertheless, the present concentration of discretion in the hands of judge and prosecutor has a number of advantages over the older system. Such discretion is now exercised more deliberately. It is exercised by public officials who can be held responsible. It is exercised by men who, by virtue of experience (attained, too often, at public expense in their first years of office), are qualified to function wisely. With its developed, refined and nicely differentiated system of penal and corrective sanctions, the criminal law has become so complex that, if it is to be soundly administered, there must be a greater use of qualified specialists.

When one casts a reflective eye over the course of human experience described in this book, he may observe that there is represented in the history of the criminal law from the seventeenth century to the present day a process roughly analogous to that described by Maine in his *Ancient Law*. There is first the formal body of rules which, with changes in conditions and passage of time, lag behind the needs of the community. There results in the civil law the growth of equity, a superior body of rules. In the criminal law the absence of a dual system of courts confines change in the case-law to the narrow limits of judicial redefinition of this law. Accordingly, practices analogous to equity in civil proceedings develop in the *trial* of criminal cases which, in effect, supercede and are superior to the rules of law. Finally, the legislature takes cognizance of what is being done and what has in fact been established, and enacts legislation which directs these practices into expressly legal avenues. Whereupon a new cycle sets in. This process is only very broadly applicable, however, because there are no definite temporal limits which can be placed around any of the three movements described above. Nor can each movement be sharply separated from the others. All three processes intermingle. The later do not supplant the earlier.

As we have seen in our survey of this legal history, one of the major questions concerns the differential functions of substantive law and administration. In our current legal system, it is clear that although the sanctioned area of discretion has increased considerably, there are certain legal limitations upon official behavior. Precise definitions of criminal conduct provide definite controls. So, too, the prescribed sentences, though they are called "indeterminate," are really minimum-maximum ones. Probation and suspended sentences are available for specified crimes. The prevailing rules of the criminal law of democratic countries for the most part require that, subject to various substantial discretionary powers, relatively certain consequences must follow certain behavior.[86]

The problem set for administrative officials by restrictions in the written law, though not as simple or as sharply marked as that of the eighteenth century, remains thus essentially the same. Waiver of felony is only one of many practices which have been designed to make the substantive law flexible. From complaint to parole, the process of applying the criminal law qualifies written enactments and adapts them to current needs. Suspended sentence, probation and parole, compromise, restitution, followed by modified or withdrawn complaints, dismissals, waivers, judicial interpretation, complete nullification by failure to apply laws, verdicts at odds with facts—these and a score of other practices of both laity and officials characterize the modern administration of the criminal law. Despite abuse, there is no doubt that this is the mark of an advanced system. The early law was a crude and heavy weapon which, once employed, operated with devastating effect. In advanced societies, the law is a more refined instrumentality. It functions with a nicer precision. It is more suited to particular, differ-

---

[86] For a detailed study of the principle of legality, see Hall, General Principles of Criminal Law (1947) ch. 2.

entiated needs. But no system, however advanced, has by its written law alone, proved sufficiently flexible to cover all cases, all types of offenders, all situations in a way which satisfies the sense of justice of the community and its officials or the special needs and new problems which arise. It is, indeed, inevitable that changing ideas and ideals combine with the infinite variety of facts and problems to push the limits of legal discretion beyond any existing area. Out of the lag between the written word and the variety and the novelty of the social problem is born the need for flexible, intelligent administration [87] with the double task of meting out justice and, at the same time, maintaining the continuity of the legal tradition.

The relationship between the legal path and the extent of discretion allowed to modify it is a perennial question of legal science. The only method by which technicalities and practices which secure desirable ends by indirection can be eliminated is to make the written law incorporate in advance the possible attainment of these objectives—specifically, for example, to increase the offenses for which probation [88] and suspended sentences can be granted. It follows that the task for legal reform lies not in the direction of eliminating either law or discretion, but rather in the direction of securing a wiser use of discretion under sound legal controls.

---

[87] *Cf.* Pound, Criminal Justice in America (1930) 36ff.

[88] *E.g.*, in Illinois, probation could not be granted in cases of larceny or embezzlement in excess of $200 or burglary of a dwelling house in the night time; but because of some quirk in the penal philosophy of the legislators, it was permissible to grant probation in cases of robbery while armed with a dangerous weapon. See comments by Judge McGoorty in 1 U. of Chi. L. Rev. (1933) 162. It frequently happened therefore that persons who committed aggravated burglaries were allowed to plead guilty to larceny of property valued at $195. Cases of embezzlement and grand larceny were similarly manipulated.

"The records in burglary, larceny and embezzlement cases, however, show a wholesale changing of charges, according to court attaches. These records disclose that practically every judge who has sat in the Criminal court during the last year has granted probation in cases of these classifications where the original charge did not permit such action." Chicago Daily Tribune, Aug. 15, 1932.

For the present Illinois law on probation, see Jones Ill. Stat. Ann. (1947 Cum. Supp.) 37. 772.

We have hardly begun to devote to this fundamental question the persistent, careful study required to attain precise knowledge of the sound allocation of law and discretion. In the following discussion of current socio-legal problems, further consideration will be given the above question, aided by insights derived from the history of the law of theft.

BOOK TWO

CURRENT PROBLEMS

CHAPTER FIVE

RECEIVING STOLEN PROPERTY

I. THE BUSINESS OF DEALING IN STOLEN COMMODITIES

THE only adequate approach to the criminal receiver is that which deals with him as an established participant in the economic life of society, whose behavior has been institutionalized over a span of more than two centuries in Anglo-American experience. The legal instrumentalities which grew out of ancient problems (when emphasis upon *receiving* was quite rational) do not fit the present-day type of criminal activity. First, they select as crucial one small segment of the socially significant behavior, namely, the receiving, which is not even the most important characteristic of this type of criminal behavior. Second, the traditional law does not differentiate between the behavior of non-professional offenders and that of the *dealer* in stolen goods. This distinction is, in fact, essential.

The behavior of the professional criminal receiver is persistent and complex. His activities are entirely different from those of the lay or the occasional receiver.[1] Nor do the laws directed at habitual offenders remedy the defects which result from the failure of the legal criterion to represent the actual pattern of behavior. The meaning of "habitual" in such laws is technical; that is, within the purview of existing statutes, an "habitual" offender is one who has been *convicted* of more than a specified number of crimes.[2]

---

[1] By the lay receiver is meant one who knowingly buys stolen goods for his own consumption. By the occasional receiver is meant one who buys for resale but very infrequently. The difference between the occasional and the professional receiver is partly one of degree. The professional, however, maintains an organization.

[2] The New York statute provides that a person is an habitual criminal who, being convicted of a felony, "has been before that conviction, convicted in this state of any other crime"; or "a person convicted of a misdemeanor, who has been already five times convicted in this state of a misdemeanor." McKinney's Consolidated Laws of New York (1944) Penal Law sec. 1020.

The professional receiver is "habitual" in a more thorough-going fashion. Even the criminological terms "repeater" and "recidivist" do not begin to describe him. "Institutionalized behavior," if this term may be applied to criminal conduct, is perhaps most fitting. Specifically, there is this distinctive feature (among several others to be discussed later): The professional receiver operates a business. He can no more stop his criminal activities for any length of time than a legitimate businessman or manufacturer can shut his doors for indefinite and irregular periods.

As indicated, the professional represents one of several types of receivers. Varieties shade off until they include the respectable lady who buys a fur coat or a ring once in a lifetime, knowing or suspecting that she is buying stolen merchandise. The essential defect in the traditional law on this problem is that *the ultimate consumer is lumped in the same category with the professional receiver.* For the professional receiver, however, buying or receiving is only one part of his activities, just as it is for any merchant. He buys for a different purpose, namely, to resell. Here we are at the core of the essential difference—purchase for resale, not for consumption. Add to that the stream of purchases, the complex auxiliary behavior and organization required—and the unique role of the professional receiver becomes understandable. For the prospective thief, he is a *reliable* market, known in advance to be available.

To establish a sound basis for criticism of existing legal categories and approaches and for the construction of new ones,[3] it becomes necessary to analyze the problem in detail.[4] The business of dealing in stolen goods requires a trained personnel. It requires most of the qualifications necessary to carry on any

---

[3] *Cf.* "A complete system of the relevant elements of guilt is . . . a prime desideratum of criminal law reform." Freund, *Classification And Definition Of Crimes* (1915) 5 J. Crim. L. and Criminol. 826.

[4] The following description of the behavior of criminal receivers is based upon (1) interviews with public officials, private investigators, representatives of insurance companies and other experienced persons, (2) materials found in the law reports, (3) biographies, (4) case studies and autobiographies of criminals and delinquents, and (5) newspaper reports.

business and a number of additional ones. Most professional receivers seem, indeed, to be offshoots from legitimate businesses. This is especially true of furs, silks, and automobiles. The fur industry generates considerable human energy which is finally devoted to carrying on illegal traffic. The jewelry receiver may have been an ex-jeweler; and he has frequently become a gambler and money-lender, whose contacts with thieves are numerous. The automobile receiver is apt to emerge from the garage business. In brief, the executives in this business of dealing in stolen goods are experienced men, frequently specialists in their chosen fields, able to evaluate merchandise expertly and to compete generally on the basis of their special skills. Indeed, many criminal receivers reënter legitimate business, despite the police phrase "once a fence—always a fence." Besides, a large number of receivers are engaged in legitimate business at the same time they are carrying on an illegal traffic in stolen goods. Their legitimate business masks the illegitimate.

The criminal receiver of today, unlike the redoubtable Wild, does not participate in the actual thefts. He is rarely the sort of person who commits burglaries or larcenies. He has too much canniness to participate, if he could. The association of Grizzard, the most notorious receiver of stolen jewelry in England in recent years, and Lockett, the experienced burglar, is typical.[5] It is an association of brains and brawn.

Successful association with thieves requires a number of exceptional qualifications. Here, as generally, a reputation for fair dealing and for loyalty, misplaced as it may seem, is particularly valuable. A receiver who will finance a thief over a period of inactivity, share equitably in the spoils and be not intimate with the police will be preferred over competitors whose standing is less secure. Thus we are told that Grizzard was loyal to all who served him. "His word was his bond . . . for this reason no one of his tools was ever persuaded to give their 'chief' away, though more than once considerable pressure

---

[5] *Cf.* C. Humphreys, The Great Pearl Robbery (1913).

was put upon men in custody to turn 'King's evidence' against the master criminal." [6] Fear plays as large a role as desire for gain in maintaining loyalty to the thief, who will take revenge upon a traitorous receiver in no uncertain manner.

The dealer in stolen goods must know the sources where the merchandise he wants can be had, and he must be able to get it. His special training in a particular business supplies the necessary knowledge in a general way. Detailed information is secured from contacts with businessmen, their salesmen, from employees whom he bribes, the reports of his scouts, from thieves to whom he represents a market, or by his own investigation through calls upon prospective victims as a pretended buyer. He frequently pursues his investigation until he knows the exact location of the desired merchandise. In jewelry thefts, for example, it frequently occurs that the particular drawer in which the jewels are kept is the only place entered.[7] In fur thefts this knowledge is apparent in many instances. Clever specialists have devised the technique of "crashing the door," dashing in with four or five men each of whom seizes a bundle of the most valuable furs and carries it to a waiting automobile—all of this occurring, according to police officials who, having received information, were present and timed one such burglary, within two minutes, and long before the representatives of the protective agency which had elaborately wired the store, were able to arrive. Experienced thieves invariably take only the most valuable furs, sometimes more than $100,000 worth, a performance impossible without advance, detailed information.

---

[6] *Id.* 9.

[7] "$25,000 GEMS GONE IN BROOKLYN HOME."

"Burglars Apparently Knew When Importer and Family Would Be Away. Police and Investigator for Insurance Company Unable to Identify Thieves' Work.

"Mr. De Picciotto had taken his family to a theatre. When he returned he found a side door of the one-family house had been broken open. The burglars had gone to the library on the ground floor, broken open a secretary and taken the gems from a strong box secreted in the secretary. Mr. De Picciotto told the police, whom he notified at once, that he could not understand how the location of the strong box could have become known to the intruders." The New York Times, May 25, 1933.

Among the largest sources of merchandise available to the receiver are the fraudulent bankrupt and the defrauder of insurance companies through deliberately arranged "thefts" and "fires." These offenders first dispose of their merchandise at prices far below the market, and they collect, in addition, the insured value of it. Their methods of operating are numerous, but they interest us here only as enormous sources from which receivers are regularly supplied with merchandise.[8] Dishonest bailees also sell much merchandise to receivers. There is a constant stream of such sales from dressers of furs who substitute cheap skins for valuable ones, and they escape detection because of the impossibility of identifying the furs. Dishonest employees of fur companies and drivers of trucks also participate. Thus, the criminal receiver acts as a bridge over which many millions of dollars' worth of illegally acquired goods pass annually from criminals to merchants and on to the consuming public.

The receiver must be supplied with cash to finance his purchases although, where very valuable jewelry is stolen, the thief may be compelled to wait until the receiver can raise the cash by securing a purchaser. But it is frequently necessary for the receiver to finance accomplices while a crime is being plotted; in jewelry thefts this may mean a period of several months. Other persons in the employ of the receiver must be financed. The costs may include entertainment of servants, bribing of employees such as shipping clerks or watchmen, and expenditures for protection by persons in strategic positions to interfere with plans under way.

---

[8] Mr. A. A. Clune, representing the Silk Association of America, testified before the House Judiciary Committee at its hearing on H. R. 10287 that ". . . in as high as 75 per cent of the bankruptcies, there is some merchandise missing that is never accounted for.

"The plan of operation . . . briefly is that the bankrupt before bankruptcy, engages in a scheme with a receiver of stolen goods, whereby the merchandise that he buys on credit, without having paid for it, is turned over for a fraction of its value to the receiver of the stolen goods.

"The merchandise is sold for cash, the proceeds going into the pockets of the bankrupt, and never being accounted for on his books." Serial 19 (Govt. Printing Off. April 3 and 4, 1928) 35.

Because identification of goods is the chief risk to be avoided, merchandise which for one reason or another cannot be identified or whose marks can readily be destroyed, is preferred. This factor together with the market value of the merchandise per unit determines the nature of the stock in trade. It is no accident that jewelry, furs, silk, securities, and automobile accessories are the principal commodities.

The amount of merchandise which a receiver buys is affected by a number of factors: the condition of the market in general; the amount of capital which he has; the difficulty of securing the merchandise, which is determined largely by the measures that the industry concerned has taken to protect itself, rather than by the activities of the police; and the receiver's contact with potential buyers. Of all these factors, fluctuations in the general market are the most important conditioning forces upon the receiver's purchases and consequently upon professional theft.

The receiver frequently engages in a limited manufacturing or production in the sense that he alters and reconstructs the goods that are delivered to him and markets them in their changed form. Stolen automobiles are dismantled and new ones are assembled from the parts. Identification marks must be removed from jewelry and gems are frequently reset. This requires the finest skill, and in New York some of the city's best artisans are said to be employed regularly by receivers and jewel thieves. A carefully reset stone can hardly ever be identified. The manufacturer's scratches on jewelry, the tags on silk and furs, and the numbers on automobiles are all skillfully removed.

Only jewelry is small enough to be concealed for a long period of time and reconstructed at leisure. The receiver accordingly keeps his stock in trade in motion constantly. He takes the goods from the place where the thief has delivered them and moves them about rapidly, all the while engaged in removing identification marks, reconstructing, and selling. This accounts for the fact that most receivers do not have permanent business locations. They have "drops" for merchandise which are little more than hiding places. They remove the merchandise immediately from the first "drop" where it was left by the thieves, partly because they distrust the thieves. They keep the property moving until it is finally sold. The exceptions to this *modus operandi* are the criminal auctioneers, pawnbrokers, junk dealers, and the pseudo-respectable merchants whose business consists, in part, of dealing in stolen goods.

The final phase of this business is the marketing of the merchandise. Most analyses of criminal receiving emphasize the fact that the thief depends upon the receiver, that without the latter, the former could not exist. What has not been appreciated is the fact that the receiver is in precisely the same position as the thief as regards his dependence upon a market for stolen goods, which is, in the last analysis, a phase of the market in general. Thus, it is reasonably certain that the depression in the thirties affected theft in two ways:

(1) It sharply decreased the number of large scale thefts, particularly of the most valuable furs, silks, and automobiles. Jewelry thefts were less affected because such merchandise could be concealed until market conditions improved.

(2) Petty thefts increased.

The explanation generally given to account for the changes noted above is that the depression limited the market for stolen property with the result that large scale thefts committed for the purpose of sale decreased whereas unemployment and poverty increased the number of thefts committed to secure goods for consumption. This is impossible to demonstrate but it represents the views of experienced observers and is supported by reasonably reliable, though fragmentary, data. The silk and fur industries report that the drop in turnover and price of their commodities was accompanied by a sharp decrease in the number of thefts committed.[9] Insurance companies state that automobile thefts not only decreased in number during the depression,[10] but also that they were confined almost exclusively to small, inexpensive vehicles. Police officials

---

[9] *Cf. infra* pp. 208–209.
[10] *Cf. infra* p. 248, footnote 54.

concur in these statements. A positive correlation seems to exist between the general market and large scale theft.[11]

Sometimes the receiver negotiates a sale before he buys the goods or, indeed, before they are stolen. Even though he may not have an order in advance, the receiver, like most business men, has definite leads. It is also alleged by competent observers that salesmen travel about the country soliciting orders. A large amount of stolen property is sold to small dealers through "in-between men" who make a livelihood by knowing to whom stolen property can be disposed. They operate like brokers rather than jobbers or salesmen. Sometimes a buyer must present credentials and be vouched for by a friend or a well-known criminal before the receiver will deal with him. This is frequently the case in the disposition of jewelry of considerable value, and of securities.

To reach markets for his merchandise, the receiver ships by rail and by truck. Wild owned a large vessel and did business in Holland and other foreign countries. His successors have all the modern carriers to accommodate them. They do an international trade; they use the railroads to carry merchandise to markets in every part of the country. They use trucks for shorter hauls and for quick movement of the goods. And the receiver employs many persons at every stage in his activities.

The business is closely interrelated with those of auctioneers,[12] pawnbrokers, and dealers in second-hand goods who provide large outlets for the sale of stolen goods. These busi-

---

[11] Professor J. P. Chamberlain writes:

"As thieves become organized with gangs and conduct their operations on an enlarged scale, the importance of the outlet through the fence becomes greater. Without a good sales organization, a producing organization on a large scale would be ineffective, and this is as true in illegitimate as in legitimate business. Men do not produce for the sake of producing, but produce to sell, and the rate of production must necessarily be limited by the rate at which the goods produced, legitimately or illegitimately, can be disposed of to the public." *Anti-Fence Legislation* (1928) 14 A. B. A. J. 517. *Cf.* The Panel (Feb. 1928) 3.

[12] "Auctions of jewelry in New York City are responsible for the most flagrant abuses. One jewelry auction place on the Bowery is on the floor above the stalls of 74 jewelry second-hand dealers. Precious stones and jewelry of all descriptions are bartered in large quantities at this address and adjoin-

nesses are "regulated," but in such a perfunctory manner that they continue to be active in both the receipt and the disposal of stolen property.[13] There is very little regulation of transient vendors of jewelry or of smelters and refiners of precious metals.[14] The street sale of jewelry in downtown New York is generally believed to involve much stolen property.[15]

Finally, it may be noted that criminal receivers, like other business men, engage in competition directly among themselves and more remotely with legitimate enterprises. There is no doubt whatever that competition among receivers is very

---

ing buildings, also occupied by auctioneers and jewelry second hand dealers. Some of the bartering of unset diamonds is done on the sidewalks.

"The auctioneer insists that the jewelry he sells represents unredeemed pledges of pawnbrokers. The police have attempted to compel him to show the pedigree of the jewelry he offers for sale, but without satisfactory results." Criminal Receivers in the United States (1928) 36.

Cf. "*Short Sentence Given Fence Under Old Law.* Judge points out Baumes Act would have brought long term.

"Convicted by the jury in General Sessions of having received 1,000 dozen pairs of stolen gloves worth $7.50 a dozen. Louis Smerling, 54, who conducts an auction house at 263 East Houston Street, was sentenced by Judge Nott to-day to from two to four years in Sing Sing. . . .

"Probation officers reported that Smerling had conducted his auction business for upward of thirty years, and that he had been arrested at least five times for having received stolen goods. But he always managed to win his freedom, they added." New York World, March 31, 1927.

[13] Cf. "The Criminal Record Office [in England] is responsible for three publications . . . the '*Pawnbrokers' List*', issued daily to all pawnbrokers, giving details of goods reported stolen." C. M. Craven in (1933) 24 J. Crim. L. and Criminol. 232.

[14] Illinois, New Jersey and a few other states purport to regulate the transient vendors and buyers. (Illinois Revised Statutes (1947) c. 121½ secs. 158–165.17.)

The United States government unfortunately encourages theft of jewelry by purchasing gold indiscriminately. The government buys gold in many forms from anybody. No questions are asked of the vendor, and there is little doubt in the minds of police officials, that considerable stolen jewelry finds its way into the government treasury which thus forms a convenient outlet for stolen merchandise which cannot be disposed of through more profitable avenues.

[15] "Held as Gem 'Fence' in $19,000 Robbery.

"Hyman Pearlman, 45 years old, who has a booth in the Jewelers Exchange at 82 Bowery, was held in $19,000 bail by Judge Mulqueen, in General Sessions, charged with having criminally received $10,000 in jewels which had been stolen from an automobile in Brooklyn on Aug. 5. . . .

"His arrest followed the investigation of Detective Harold J. Fay, and Richard C. Murphy, general Counsel for the Jewelers' National Crime Committee." New York Times, Oct. 16, 1927.

active. It is a business, moreover, which is likely to remain un-affected by national planning and control of industry. Al-though the writer, like others, entertained the thought that receivers were united in a few large associations, his investi-gation has not led to reliable evidence of any such organization. This is also the opinion of police officials, private investigators, and informed laymen who were consulted. There are several reasons why large combinations have not been formed: first, danger of detection increases with size; second, the need for constant mobility makes difficult the accumulation of stolen goods; and, third, the persons in this field are extremely indi-vidualistic and are by temperament disinclined to form lasting associations.

Occasionally, there are monopolistic forces in operation and relatively large organizations are formed to deal, *e.g.*, in stolen securities.[16] The chief executive is at the top of a pyramid which radiates down to the bribed employee, the "brief snatcher", the hold-up man, and up to forgers, contact men, and the per-sons who dispose of stolen securities.[17] Whether, at some future time, the economic forces which have produced large business combinations will have a similar effect on the business of deal-ing in stolen goods is problematic. At present it may be said with assurance that there are very few such combinations, and the indications are that students of private enterprise may depend upon the continued existence of superb specimens in this field.

II. The Operation of the Law

1. *The "Law-Process"*

One of the prime characteristics of a social problem is that people are actively engaged in efforts to solve it—by immediate

---

[16] *Cf. Bond-Stealing As Big Business* (Nov. 15, 1924) 83 Lit. Dig. 88–9.

[17] The above situation, represented by an actual nisi prius case (N. Y. *v.* Carr) discloses what might be termed a composite crime, *i.e.*, a number of crimes committed by a group of persons, *i.e.*, (1) larceny, (2) burglary, (3) robbery, (4) false pretenses, (5) forgery, (6) receiving stolen property, (7) possession and concealment of stolen securities.

reactions, by adjustments, by planning, and by long-range programs. In varying degrees, these efforts engage the energies of both laymen and experts. The tacit premise is that improvement is possible. This involves social values, legal norms which embody them, and legal instrumentalities which implement their preservation. For, while it is usual to think of solving social problems as a mere removal of undesirable situations, the end sought is positive—the greater enjoyment of value-experience, not in a superficial, but in a basic sense.

Accordingly, while the lawyer thinks of law and legal process in a technical, professional sense, the fact is that large segments of the population, indeed, with reference to some rules which everyone would grant are "legal," practically the entire normal adult population, participates in social problem-solving in ways that are significant when they are viewed from the perspective of the legal rules.

This is no new discovery although its relation to social science has been neglected. The relevant phenomena were at least noted by Aristotle and some of his contemporaries who spoke of the Greek constitution as "a way of life." In modern social science, Savigny represents the initial point of insight into the social aspects of law, viewed as the subject-matter of legal science; and the work of Ehrlich, Duguit, and many other scholars, particularly in this country during the present century, has explored the nature and functions of law in society. It is in this sense and from this perspective that the term "law-process" is used in this book. Our purpose here is not to engage in further analysis of that basic notion [18] but, instead, to present certain data in the context of efforts to deal with criminal receiving, which may be significant as manifestations of such a legal-social process. In the following sections of this chapter and elsewhere in the book the efforts of both professionals and laymen to solve serious social problems will be discussed. If the conduct of the experts is not to be regarded as narrowly pro-

---

[18] The writer's discussion of this problem is presented in Living Law of Democratic Society (1949) especially chapter 3.

fessional and the participation of the laymen, *e.g.* business organizations engaged in certain activities, is not to be written off as mere pursuit of property interests, we require a broader conception within which both professional conduct and lay activities may be more significantly located. It is the function of theories of law-process to provide such a fundamental conception.

In this regard the activities in early England designed to apprehend wrongdoers are especially suggestive. The most important fact about these activities is that they were every man's. This prompted the remark that in England police are persons who are paid for doing what is their duty to do without compensation. Not only was it the right of any person to apprehend offenders; there was also a positive duty to drop all work when the hue and cry was raised, and to join immediately in the pursuit.[19] To fail to do this or to withdraw from the pursuit too soon or without permission was punishable as a misdemeanor.[20] Early English law made no nice distinctions; the general imposition of police duties was based upon a division of all persons into two classes. It symbolized *de facto* war between felon, outlaw or marauding band and the rest of the community.[21]

This police duty, though it rested upon all freemen, was not discharged haphazardly. There was an elaborate network of individuals arrayed in small groups which, in their totality, comprised a national organization. The head borough or tithing man might be officially designated as policeman, but

---

[19] The duty was imposed upon all freemen except those who had bad reputations. Freemen were required by the Assize of Arms (1181) to have certain weapons and, in general, to be equipped for the pursuit of criminals when the hue and cry was raised.

[20] Lee, A History of Police in England (1901) 34.

[21] That such terms are relative to membership in a particular group is made clear by autobiographical data and statements by criminals. Thus, the following obituary of a notorious silk thief shows the other side of the picture—
Obituary: . . . beloved husband and son of. . . .
"A precious one from us has gone,
A voice we loved is stilled,
A place is vacant in our house
That never can be filled."

he could instantly enlist general assistance. Likewise the sheriff and his staff, the constable, and later, with the development of towns, the local watchman could, each, draft the laity into their posse comitatus. Long after frankpledge, the national organization of freemen, had disappeared, hue and cry and its concomitant duties persisted. This communal obligation to enforce the law was reflected in the financial liability of the hundred within which a crime was committed.[22]

The growth of commerce and industry had a double effect upon this police system. In the first place, the accumulation of valuables and the concentration of property required special protection. Secondly, the artisan and the merchant could not, like the farmer, drop their work, leave their places of business and pursue malefactors. Elected peace officers accordingly chose proxies to perform their duties in order that they might devote themselves to their business. The towns began to employ watchmen, though their efforts seem to have been rather ineffective.[23] Finally, at the end of the eighteenth century, due chiefly to the agitation of Sir John Fielding, a police magistrate, there was organized in London the Bow Street Runners: fifty picked men financed by property owners. The comparative success of the Runners contributed to the formation in 1829 of the London Metropolitan Police, the first definite representatives of the now familiar urban police forces.[24]

Frankpledge, the liability of local units for crimes committed there, hue and cry, and the traditional habits which centuries of such practices developed are but one side of the shield. The other and equally important fact is that at all times and particularly concomitant with the growth of an official

---

[22] Stat. of Winchester; and *cf.* Goldsborough's Reports 55–8, 86–7.

Cf. "In cases of theft (or indeed of any other crimes to which the principle of collective responsibility is applicable) it is not necessary to identify the thief; nor is it necessary that he should be produced or even known. It is sufficient if a case has been clearly established against a kraal." R. H. Dugmore, *Kafir Laws and Customs,* 1 Evolution of Law (Kocourek and Wigmore ed.) 319.

[23] Moylan, Scotland Yard 11.

[24] Hall, *Legal and Social Aspects of Arrest Without a Warrant* (1936) 49 Harv. L. Rev. 566.

class of functionaries there arose numerous and elaborate lay organizations which functioned much the same as did the officials. These lay organizations—the Bow Street Runners as an example—were privately financed. They were used especially for the protection of business and industrial property. Such organizations can be found as early as the eleventh century when numerous peace gilds were formed in London and other towns. These gilds were divided into several groups each under the leadership of one person. The members contributed to a common treasury, the dues depending to some extent upon the amount of property owned, while poor widows were apparently exempt.[25] Elaborate by-laws were adopted providing for coöperation in the apprehension of criminals, particularly cattle thieves, and the payment of sums of money to reimburse members who sustained losses as a result of such thefts.

Such organizations multiplied rapidly with the growth of towns and the concentration of valuable property in business establishments,[26] and it was possible for Lord Bowen to state that, "In the year 1839, there were upwards of five hundred voluntary associations for promoting the apprehension and prosecution of felons, for performing in fact, by individuals the first duty of a civilized government."[27] Thus these lay organizations continued to grow after official police forces had been organized.

---

[25] Attenborough, *op. cit.* 159ff.

[26] In 1696 a "Society for the reformation of manners in the cities of London and Westminster" was formed and in 1702 was instrumental in securing the conviction of 858 "Leud and Scandalous persons." Lee, *op. cit.* 143–4.

Cf. "WHEREAS idle, disorderly, and dangerous persons, of all descriptions are constantly wandering about, and the commission of crimes and offences hath increased to an alarming degree:

"IT IS RESOLVED . . . 1st. That it be earnestly recommended to the principal inhabitants of all places, to agree in uniting together under certain rules, and regulations for the better purpose of detecting felons, cheats, vagrants, nightwalkers, and night-proachers, pawnbrokers, who are often guilty of malepractices, and particularly in receiving stolen goods, knowing them to be such. Sellers by false weights, and measures, persons adulterating or improperly mixing meal, flower, &c. and in short all those who are in any way guilty of a breach of the law." H. Zouch, Hints Respecting the Public Police (1786) 20.

[27] Lord Bowen, *Progress in the Administration of Justice,* 1 Select Essays on Anglo-American Legal History 554.

The lay organizations described thus far fall into two classes: either they were composed of a representative cross section of the community, or they consisted of merchants and property owners who desired to safeguard their special interests.

There was a third type of lay organization engaged in police activities, and a most important one it was. This was composed of a large number of self-nominated "thief-catchers" who appeared at the end of the seventeenth and the beginning of the eighteenth century. The immediate impetus given to this development was a statute passed in 1692 offering rewards for the apprehension of highwaymen and thieves. Not only were rewards offered, but "the gracious pardon of their Majesties" was also held out to any robbers who "afterwards discover two or more persons who already hath or hereafter shall commit any robbery, so as two or more of the persons discovered shall be convicted of such robbery." The reasons for enacting this and similar statutes and the results produced by them may well be imagined. There grew up bands of unscrupulous criminals who divided their activities between the commission of crimes and the turning-up of other offenders. There were many of these thief-takers of whom, it will be recalled, Jonathan Wild was the most conspicuous. In 1749 the discharge of many soldiers and sailors from service in the war added numerous recruits. Parliament increased the rewards for capture and conviction. The thief-taking business flourished— frequently at the expense of the heads of many innocent persons.[28]

Thus far the discussion has been confined to the detection and apprehension of offenders in England, and we have seen that these activities were at no time confined to officials. Large numbers of laymen always participated in them. The officials

---

[28] The following seems to have been common. A gang of four men operated jointly: one would induce two persons to commit a highway robbery and would promise to assist in this; another would be the person "robbed"; a third would offer to buy the stolen goods; while the fourth would arrest the robbers, permitting his associate to escape. The two victims would be surrendered to the authorities, and the reward collected and divided. These operations went on for several years. Gordon, *op. cit.* 175–6.

were not even distinguished by the fact that they were trained and remunerated and devoted most of their time to police work, for all these characteristics applied also in varying degrees to lay persons.

A similar participation by laymen in even wider phases of the law-process occurred in the early history of our western states. Particularly significant is the history of the California Gold Rush in 1849.[29]

A few months after the discovery of gold in Sutton's Coloma Saw-Mill in January of 1848, Californians flocked to the foothills of the Sierras in large numbers. Not until 1849, however, did the influx of non-residents begin. By the middle of the year, immigration was mounting very rapidly. During 1848 and through the spring of 1849, practically no crimes had been committed. The miners were industrious and there were enough claims and supplies for all. In 1849 came the great rush, and with it convicts, gamblers and criminals from all parts of the world. At the same time the number of available claims diminished. There arose bitter conflicts for land and a wave of criminality consisting chiefly of murder and theft, the latter being particularly reprehensible because, whereas the claim of "self-defense" was popular, a thief, unless he was also a colorful highwayman, had no redeeming qualities whatever. Such officials as existed, like the military governor, were entirely unprepared to maintain order in the camps. The consequent situation—numerous men with past criminal records, a heterogeneous masculine population, the quest for gold, and the almost total absence of any official body or any legal machinery—set into motion a series of forces and activities of the utmost theoretical interest and practical importance. Especially significant were the popular tribunals, meetings, and councils, the formation and operation of vigilance committees,

---

[29] 36 and 37 Bancroft, Works (Popular Tribunals); Clelland, A History of California, 20 Studies in History, Economics and Public Law (Columbia Univ.) 206–358; The Diary of a Forty-Niner (Confield ed.); Gertrude Atherton, California, An Intimate History c. 8, 9, 10, 11.

the defense of claims against "jumpers," the publicly executed sentences—indeed, the general participation of the entire community in all aspects of the law-enforcement process. With the creation of adequate official instrumentalities came the regression of this popular participation in the administration of the law and its centralization in familiar agencies of government.

If we consider our present society in comparison, we are struck by the fact that political institutions, including those concerned with the criminal law, have become highly specialized.[30] As regards the work of police, however, especially detection and apprehension of criminals, it is easy to recognize many lay organizations that have precisely these functions, indeed, in a form more specialized still. Almost every large industry has its own protective association devoted to police work. There are literally hundreds of such organizations in each of the large metropolitan areas.[31]

The specialization of our political agencies restricts legislative and judicial functions, as technically defined, to particular officials. If, however, the question be asked, who and what, in fact, influence the behavior of legislators and judges, we need resort to no such vague datum as "public opinion" in order to demonstrate not only that the actual pattern of behavior which produces decisions and laws is highly complex and far-ranging, but also that the officials often play only nominally the most important part. The liaison between lobbyists for hundreds of special interests and legislators is a commonplace. That between newspapers, crime commissions, and the con-

---

[30] It is especially this fact which makes it necessary to study less developed societies in order to appreciate the relationship of officials to non-official functionaries.

[31] Cf. Nat'l. Com. on Law Obs. and Enf., Report on the Cost of Crime 349–369; Kuhlman, Guide to Materials on Crime and Criminal Justice, secs. 5598–5626; Wigmore, *Local Coöperation Against Organized Predatory Crime* (1933) 23 J. Crim. L. and Criminol. 909–12; J. P. Shalloo, *The Private Police of Pennsylvania* (1929) 146 Ann. Amer. Acad. Pol. and Soc. Sci. 55; and by the same author, Private Police (1934).

duct of judges and prosecutors is equally effective.[32] Some of these lay organizations directly participate in the detection and apprehension of criminals; others are intimately related to the courts and legislatures. It may therefore be concluded that if typical distinctive conduct provides the basis upon which a scientific theory of law is to be constructed, it is necesary to extend the area of observation far beyond that occupied by officials. It must here suffice to recognize that knowledge of the criminal law is considerably increased when persistent effort is made to relate the behavior of lay and professional groups to specific problems of law-enforcement.[33]

The concept "law-process"[34] may be employed to set the outermost limits of the field of observation which must be explained, if possible, by an adequate theory of law. The innermost boundaries confine the conduct of officials and offenders. Between these two extremes the line must be drawn as re-

---

[32] To give only one example of what is common—during the last nine months of 1928, the Chicago Crime Commission, supported by the newspapers of that city, was able to stop almost entirely the practice of felony waiver. Cf. "A study of the columns in the tabulations devoted to felony waivers discloses how effective the protest against this practice voiced in April, 1928, by the Chicago Crime Commission actually was. It will be noted, for instance, that during 1928 Judge Emanuel Eller permitted the waiving of 121 felonies. Records show that of this total 112 had been granted during the first three months of 1928, or prior to the Chicago Crime Commission's protest. The following tabulation (of which the totals are given) tells the story of the rise and fall of felony waivers clearly": Felonies waived, 1928 (1st 3 mos.) 568; 1928, 766; 1929, 176. Criminal Justice, pub. by the Chicago Crime Commission.

[33] Cf. K. N. Llewellyn, Law Observance Versus Law Enforcement, in Proc. Nat'l. Conf. of Soc. Work (1918) 133–5.

[34] Cooley's Social Process is suggestive but not very critical. Von Wiese's Systematic Sociology adapted by Howard Becker (1932) is probably the most detailed study of social process, but to the writer at least, the book was of little value. The Papers on Social Process published by the American Sociological Society in 1932 contain three suggestive discussions, those by Read Bain, E. H. Sutherland, and Florian Znaniecki. Finally, perhaps most important in several respects is A. F. Bentley's The Processes of Government (1908), and his chapter on Law (XI) provides a helpful starting point for those interested in pushing the concept "process" farther than it has usually been carried, especially as applied to law. E.g., "Law is activity, just as government is. It is a group process just as government is." Id. 272. Bentley, however, seems to have been committed to a behavioristic interpretation. For the writer's view, see Living Law of Democratic Society (1949) ch. 3, and Integrative Jurisprudence, in Interpretations of Modern Legal Philosophies (Sayre ed., 1947) 313.

quired by the particular problems investigated. The operation of legal sanctions related to the business of dealing in stolen property will illustrate this thesis.

2. *Procedure as an Instrument of Social Policy*

As long ago as the beginning of the eighteenth century, *i.e.* since Jonathan Wild, the professional receiver was recognized for what he was—a criminal businessman, a dealer in stolen goods. The consequent problem was to provide adequate controls consistent with established law and recognized values. We have followed the halting steps taken to achieve that end, which culminated in the statute of 1827, namely, the slow breaking-away from the fixation that the receiver was merely an accessory to the thief, provision for the independent trial of the receiver, first, if the thief could not be apprehended and, later, in any case, but only for a misdemeanor; then, the admission of the thief's testimony against the receiver, and finally, in 1827, the felony of receiving, regardless of the arrest of the thief. For a full century following the peak of English achievement in 1827 and on into the present, courts have been struggling to compensate for an inadequate substantive law (which does not come to grips with dealers in stolen goods) by adapting rules of procedure, especially evidence, to overcome the unusual obstacles in the way of convicting these astute offenders.

This phase of the problem requires an examination of procedure from a social viewpoint. Typical analysis implies that the rules of procedure are strictly logical or are the resultants of the purely logical requirements of forensic controversy, limited only by accidents of history or similar non-rational influences. Even the allowance made for certain conflicting ends, *e.g.*, to convict the guilty and acquit the innocent, has been regarded as an aspect of logical inquiry.

Our concern lies in the relation of criminal procedure to certain social problems. We have studied such relations between substantive law and social actualities as well as the responsiveness of administration to social change, including its ideal elements. Here, in the context of the problem of receiving stolen property, we must raise similar questions regarding procedure: Is criminal procedure a purely logical affair designed to determine contested issues of fact? Or, is criminal procedure also influenced by social needs?

There are, of course, important general rules, *e.g.* the presumption of innocence, which presumably exert influence in all criminal trials. We must omit all such general rules and consider only certain rules of evidence bearing directly on receiving stolen property. Procedure will thus be viewed both as logically related to substantive law and the requirements of controversy, and as causally or teleologically related to certain social problems, including relevant ideals. Stated otherwise, the theory underlying the following discussion is that procedure functions not only as the logical instrument of substantive law but also, like the substantive law itself, as a social instrument, responsive to the needs of social problems, interpreted to include various ideals.

In the following discussion, only a limited, tentative inquiry will be attempted. Specifically, the discussion will for the most part be confined to (1) recent possession, (2) corroboration of the thief's testimony, and (3) possession of other stolen goods to prove criminal intent; and it will also be largely restricted to New York, where the problem is most serious and the legal adaptations are particularly significant.

3. *Guilty Knowledge and the Recent Possession of Stolen Goods*

The first New York development, which was also the one presenting no technical difficulties, was the adaptation of the traditional "recent possession" rule to criminal receiving. This represented an effort to utilize circumstantial evidence in a situation where direct testimony is usually non-existent. Judge Cardozo stated the rule as follows: "It is the law that recent and exclusive possession of the fruits of crime, if unexplained or falsely explained, will justify the inference that the possessor is the criminal. That rule has most frequently been applied in

cases of burglary, and larceny, and receiving stolen goods." [35]
In New York it was applied to criminal receiving in 1880. [36]

Recent acquisition of stolen goods has for centuries been
considered relevant to the question of *animus furandi* and
admitted into evidence. [37] In the Anglo-Saxon period no questions were asked of a "hand-having" thief; he was assumed to
be guilty and was punished immediately. [38] At present, "recent possession" is admitted as evidence of guilt rather than
for the purpose of raising a presumption of guilt in the strict
sense. [39]

The rule originated in connection with larceny, but in
England [40] and in most American states [41] it is also applied to
criminal receiving, depending upon the surrounding circumstances. Some jurisdictions, however, hold that the rule does
not apply to receiving, [42] which seems to be a mechanical application of *stare decisis*. As noted, the majority rule has considerable precedent to support it. [43] No defect in its logic is
indicated. And on social grounds, it is obviously the sounder
rule. For criminal receivers can rarely be detected in the act
of receiving; certainly the professional bides his time or utilizes
safe "drops" so that direct evidence, other than the thief's, is
practically never available.

---

[35] People v. Galbo, 218 N. Y. 283, 290 (1916).

[36] Goldstein et al. v. People, 82 N. Y. 201 (1880); P. v. Friedman, 134 N. Y.
Supp. (Sup. Ct.) 153 (1912); P. v. Berger, 260 App. Div. 687, 23 N. Y. Supp.
2d 730 (1940).

[37] 1 Wigmore, Evidence, sec. 152.

[38] 2 P. and M., H. E. L. 496–7.

[39] 9 Wigmore, Evidence, sec. 2513. See also, Underhill, Criminal Evidence,
(4th ed. 1935) secs. 514–517 and 628.

Cf. J. H. Grimm, Missouri Crime Survey 228.

In Rosen v. United States, 271 F. 651 at 655 (1920) the court said: "The
possession of stolen property, standing alone, does not establish guilt. But the
possession of property recently stolen raises a presumption of guilt which in
the absence of explanation may authorize a jury to infer a criminal connection with its acquisition", citing Wilson v. United States, 162 U. S. 613, 620
and People v. Weldon, 111 N. Y. 569, 576.

[40] R. v. Langmead, L. & C. 427; 168 E. R. 1459 (1864), and see Archbold,
Criminal Pleading, Evidence & Practice (30th ed.) 745–6.

[41] 53 C. J. sec. 67.

[42] Id. sec. 70.

[43] ". . . it is generally conceded to apply also on a charge of *knowing receipt*
of stolen goods . . ." 9 Wigmore (3rd ed.) 422.

4. *Corroboration of the Thief's Testimony*

The next adaptation of procedure to social exigency in New York—the elimination of the necessity of corroboration of the thief's testimony—was much more difficult to achieve, and it is much more significant. The problem cut to the heart of legal control of criminal receiving.

Although the necessity of reliance upon the thief's testimony was long recognized, there were serious objections leveled against verdicts resting solely on such evidence. As early as 1680 Hale wrote:

"The credibility of his testimony is to be left to the jury, and truly it would be hard to take away the life of any person upon such a witness that swears to save his own and yet confesseth himself guilty of so great a crime, unless there be very considerable circumstances which may give the greater credit to what he swears." [44]

Dean Wigmore, however, advocating a flexible, more resourceful approach, rejects the view that the testimony of a confessed criminal is invariably false. "We have passed beyond the stage of thought," he writes, "in which his commission of crime, self-confessed, is deemed to render him radically a liar." [45] Nevertheless, this attitude toward the testimony of a confessed criminal, especially against a man who appears to be respectable, is deeply ingrained. [46]

Another reason for distrusting the testimony of such a witness is that it is often motivated by the desire to secure immunity from prosecution for his own detected crime. Dean Wigmore maintains that, since the promise of immunity is not invariably made, requirement of corroboration should not be invariable. He believes, also, that where a rule of invariable corroboration has been adopted, it has introduced refinements

---

[44] 1 Hale, P. C. 305.

[45] 7 Wigmore, Evidence (3rd ed.) sec. 2057.

[46] *Cf.* Lord Reading, C. J.: "The rule of practice as to corroborative evidence has arisen in consequence of the danger of convicting a person upon the unconfirmed testimony of one who is admittedly a criminal." The King *v.* Baskerville, 2 K. B. 658, 665 (1916).

which confuse juries and increase the risk of error and new trial.[47]

The justification for a rule requiring corroboration must rest upon a policy of safeguarding persons accused of crime from unfair tactics on the part of the prosecution and from malicious or revengeful conduct on the part of confessed criminals. Like many guarantees of fair trial, the rule has a basis in experience, sentiment and fear, against which reason is often an inadequate contender.[48] We find, therefore, cross purposes in operation: on the one hand the urgent need to utilize the evidence of the only person who can give first-hand testimony; on the other side, the confessed character of that person.

A brief glance at the history of the rule of corroboration will aid appraisal of the American law on the subject. Dean Wigmore summarizes the development of the "practice" in England as follows:

"As time went on, and the modern conception of testimony developed, the possibility of admitting a witness and yet discriminating as to the qualitative sufficiency of his testimony became more apparent; and the way was open for the consideration of this question. In a few instances, as the 1700s wore on, and even before then, judicial suggestions are found as to the feasibility of such a discrimination. But not until the end of that century does any Court seem to have acted upon such a suggestion in its directions to the jury. About that time there comes into acceptance a general practice to discourage a conviction founded solely upon the testimony of an accomplice uncorroborated.

"But was this practice found on a *rule of Law?* Never, in England,—until very modern times. It was recognized constantly that the judge's instruction upon this point was a mere exercise of his common-law function of advising the jury upon

---

[47] Some statutes restrict the rule to felonies or bribery. 7 Wigmore, Evidence sec. 2058, and citations.

See the discussion by Chief Baron Joy, Evidence of Accomplices, quoted in 7 Wigmore, Evidence sec. 2057.

[48] For further discussion and numerous citations, see 7 Wigmore, Evidence sec. 2056 *et seq.*

the weight of the evidence, and was not a statement of a rule of law binding upon the jury." [49]

This practice at common law, of the judge's cautioning the jury regarding the sufficiency of the testimony of an accomplice was enacted and extended in the statutory law of a number of states at the end of the nineteenth century.[50]

It may be questioned, however, whether the English practice has remained as flexible as it apparently was in 1848. *First,* under the Criminal Law Amendment Act, 1885, ss. 2 and 3, it is provided that regarding certain sexual offenses no person shall be convicted upon the evidence of one witness unless there is corroboration. *Second,* whether it be termed a practice or a rule, the fact is that unless the trial court cautions the jury regarding the danger of accepting the accomplice's testimony without corroboration, the conviction will be quashed. *Third,* under the Court of Criminal Appeal Act, 1907, sec. 4, sub. 1, wide jurisdiction has been given to the appellate court to set aside verdicts, and the Court of Appeal has decided in no uncertain terms that even though the trial judge has given the required warning, it will set aside a verdict not supported by the evidence.[51] Whether corroboration of an accomplice's testimony is essential to the reasonableness of the verdict is the crucial question.

In The King *v.* Baskerville,[52] the leading case on the subject,[53] the Court of Criminal Appeal, by Lord Reading, C.J., stated:

---

[49] 7 Wigmore, Evidence sec. 2056. But *cf.* "But when, by means of his information you are made acquainted with the whole Gang, and have, with great Trouble, and often with great Danger, apprehended them, how are you to bring them to Justice? for though the Evidence of the Accomplice be ever so positive and explicite, nay ever so connected and probable, still, unless it be corroborated by some other Evidence, it is not sufficient." Fielding, An Enquiry Into the Causes of the Late Increase of Robbers (1751) 111.

[50] 7 Wigmore, *id.* 2056, n. 10 for reference to these statutes.

[51] King *v.* Baskerville, (1916) 2 K. B. 663–4.

[52] *Id.* 658.

[53] The charge was a sexual perversion. The leading prior decision involving receipt of stolen property was Reg. *v.* Stubbs and others, 7 Cox C. C. 48 (1855).

"There is no doubt that the uncorroborated evidence of an accomplice is admissible in law: See *Rex* v. *Atwood* (1787) 1 Leach, 464. But it has long been a rule of practice at common law for the judge to warn the jury of the danger of convicting a prisoner on the uncorroborated testimony of an accomplice or accomplices, and, in the discretion of the judge, to advise them not to convict upon such evidence; but the judge should point out to the jury that it is within their legal province to convict upon such unconfirmed evidence: *Reg.* v. *Stubbs* (Dears. 555); *In re Meunier* (1894) 2 Q. B. 415.

"This rule of practice has become virtually equivalent to a rule of law, and since the Court of Criminal Appeal Act came into operation this Court has held that, in the absence of such a warning by the judge, the conviction must be quashed."[54]

In sum, judicial caution is mandatory, and corroboration is not explicitly required. But the inference from the above emphasis on corroboration and the enlarged jurisdiction of the court under the act of 1907 is clear; for the reasonableness of the verdict, "or that it cannot be supported having regard to the evidence" is almost inevitably dependent upon the existence of substantial corroboration. This inference is strengthened when we find that three or four months later the Court of Criminal Appeal, consisting of Reading, C. J., Darling, and Avon, J. J., quashed a conviction for criminal receiving in *Rex v. Norris*[55] on the ground that "the corroboration of the accomplice was most essential . . . there was no corroboration of the evidence given by the accomplice which would justify the answer given by the jury to the fifth question."[56]

It therefore appears that despite theoretical differences, the English procedure is very similar to that of American states which hold that an accomplice's testimony must be corroborated. In practice, indeed, the English procedure safeguards

---

[54] *Id. supra* n. 51, 663–4.
[55] 25 Cox C. C. 601 (1916).
[56] Where the jury answered specifically that the evidence of the accomplice had been corroborated.

the defendant more effectively than does American law in the large majority of the states. For, it is widely held in the states that (*a*) either the thief is not an accomplice, in which event neither judicial warning nor corroboration is necessary;[57] or (*b*) where the thief is held to be an accomplice, it is provided by statute that corroboration is not required.[58]

Against the above background of the English law and Dean Wigmore's thesis, the development of the law in New York is particularly significant. In People *v*. Willard,[59] the conviction of the defendant for having criminally received stolen property was set aside because, "Under our Criminal Law the jury is not allowed to convict a defendant upon the testimony of an accomplice alone. The story must be corroborated, and corroborated *in each essential detail*" (italics added). The court simply assumed that the thief was an accomplice.

In People *v*. Markus,[60] a conviction for receiving was reversed upon the same ground that "the only direct testimony . . . was given by witnesses who were held by the trial court to be accomplices. No conviction could be based on their testimony unless 'corroborated by such other evidence as tends to connect the defendant with the commission of the crime.' Code of Criminal Procedure §399."

In People *v*. Kudon,[61] the defendant appealed from a judgment convicting him of having criminally received stolen goods. At the trial the thieves swore that they stole brass from a launch and sold it to the defendant, telling him at the time of the sale that it was stolen property. The court said, "If the defendant was guilty of the crime charged the thieves were ac-

---

[57] 111 A. L. R. 1398.

[58] In People *v*. Baskin (254 Ill. 509 (1912)) it was held that the thief is the receiver's accomplice, but "that the judgment of conviction for a crime may be properly based upon the uncorroborated evidence of an accomplice."

In People *v*. Covitz (262 Ill. 514 (1914)), an arson case, it was held that "while the testimony of an accomplice is subject to suspicion and should be received with caution, yet it may be sufficient, uncorroborated, to sustain a conviction."

[59] 143 N. Y. Supp. 1032, Sup. Ct. App. Div. 3rd Dept. (1913).

[60] 153 N. Y. Supp. 237, Sup. Ct. App. Div. 4th Dept. (1915).

[61] 158 N. Y. Supp. 817, Sup. Ct., 173 App. Div. 342, 3rd Dept. N. Y. (1916).

complices. A conviction cannot be based upon the uncorroborated evidence of an accomplice. (Code Crim. Proc. sec. 399.) This was the law before the Code; it has been the law for generations. The courts regard the evidence of a *particeps criminis* as spurious and worthless unless corroborated by the words of honest men." [62] The court assumed that the confessed thief was the defendant's accomplice without any discussion on the point. Thus far, New York law was well in accord with English law and practice.

We find, next, an interesting situation developing in the courts of New York. The above decisions were reached in the Appellate Departments of the Supreme Court located in upper New York. Shortly thereafter a number of contrary decisions were rendered in the First Department of the Supreme Court, located in New York City. They were decided by judges who may have been more familiar with the problem of large-scale theft in a metropolitan center, where the necessity of using the thief's testimony was thoroughly appreciated. In any event, in 1921 in the Kupperschmidt Case,[63] the First Department considered the Third and Fourth Department cases, discussed above, and concluded that the thief was *not* the receiver's accomplice—which was the best possible way of supporting the conviction.[64] Both for its summarization of the law of various states and for its analysis of the view that the thief is the receiver's accomplice, which had been previously assumed, the decision is important.[65]

---

[62] This case was remanded for a new trial not because the testimony of the accomplices in this instance was uncorroborated, but because of newly discovered evidence that would discredit the corroborating witness, and, as the court put it, "it is quite possible that another jury may not believe her" (the corroborating witness).

[63] 189 N. Y. Supp. 858.

[64] In view of Sec. 399 Code Crim. Proc.

[65] Smith J.: "In other states we find authority divided. In Arizona, Colorado, Georgia, Indiana, Iowa, Minnesota, Missouri, New Jersey, Oklahoma, Oregon, Tennessee, and Utah the law seems to be established that the thief is not an accomplice of the receiver of stolen goods, so as to require corroboration of his testimony as against the receiver. The contrary rule seems to have been held in Arkansas, California, Illinois, Kansas, Pennsylvania, and Texas. . . .

"It is difficult, if not impossible, to lay down any guiding principle which

The Kupperschmidt Case was carried to the Court of Appeals [66] where an unfortunate decision, reversing the judgment of the First Department, was rendered by a unanimous court through Judge Pound, who wrote:

"The question is whether the thief who delivers stolen goods to a receiver, who takes with guilty knowledge, is an accomplice of the receiver. The fact that the receiver is not in the absence of prior accessorial acts an accomplice of the thief in the larceny is irrelevant. The crimes of larceny and receiving are separate, distinct offenses. (Penal Law, 1308; *People* v. *Zimmer*, 174 App. Div. 471, 473; affd., 220 N. Y. 597.)

"The test is whether the alleged accomplice can be indicted for the offense. Sometimes as in prosecutions for abortion, the co-participant is regarded as the victim rather than the perpetrator of the crime (*Dunn* v. *People*, 29 N. Y. 523, 527), or as in the illegal sale of intoxicating liquors, it is said that the person making the sale is the only one declared by the law to be criminal. (*People* v. *Smith*, 28 Hun 626; affd., 92 N. Y. 665.) But under the Penal Law, section 2, one who aids or abets another in the commission of a crime is a principal, whether he has been previously guilty of an independent crime

---

will apply to all cases in determining what is an accomplice within this provision of section 399 of the Code of Criminal Procedure. In this case, however, the conclusion is simplified by the nature of the crime. The thief may sell the goods to an innocent purchaser, and the purchaser is guilty of no crime. If the sale be made to a party who has knowledge of the fact that the goods are stolen, the purchaser is guilty of a crime. To hold that the thief is an accomplice in the crime of criminally receiving, if the purchaser has knowledge of the theft, and that no such crime is committed, either by the purchaser or the thief, in the sale of such goods, if the thief does not know that the purchaser had knowledge of the theft, makes the criminality of the thief in such crime dependent solely *upon his knowledge of the knowledge* of the purchaser that the goods have been stolen. I know of no principle of the common law and of no statute which makes the test of criminality the knowledge of facts by a third party. If the thief is not guilty of a crime in making a sale to an innocent third party, he cannot be guilty of a crime in making the sale to a third party with notice of the fact that the goods were stolen. One act is morally as culpable as the other. Where the act is one that is made criminal solely by the knowledge of the receiver of the goods, I cannot see by any reasonable rule of law how the thief can become an accomplice in the crime which depends upon such knowledge."

[66] 237 N. Y. 463 (1924).

or not. The receiver cannot take with guilty knowledge unless aided therein by the act of the thief in delivering.

"If the proper test is not whether the alleged accomplice is indictable for the same offense, but whether he has taken a guilty part in the commission of the crime (McLaughlin, J., in *People* v. *Hyde,* 156 App. Div. 618, 624), the same result is reached. Is the act of the thief in delivering the stolen goods to the receiver under such circumstances as convey the knowledge that they were stolen, an innocent act? It is said that one cannot receive goods which he has himself stolen. Literally, but not in a legal sense, this may be true, but he is none the less "concerned in the commission of the crime" of receiving, and therefore, a principal. (Penal Law, 2.) We are dealing with the legislative definition of guilty participation, not with the common meaning of words. . . . In this case the court said in charging the jury that corroboration was not required because the crimes were different. *Non sequitur.* The charge was erroneous.

"The judgment should be reversed and a new trial ordered."[67]

This decision challenges and, indeed, renders impossible any easy correlation of judicial process and concomitant social needs. It introduces elements which reveal the complexities of judicial decision and the limitations of available knowledge regarding the judicial process. The fact that this decision was reached by the New York Court of Appeals, including Cardozo, Pound, Andrews, and Lehman, renders it impossible to indulge in any adverse criticism on either social or technical grounds. Nevertheless, the decision was unfortunate in view of the "interstitial spaces" available to the Court.

The Court said, "The test is whether the alleged accomplice can be indicted for the offense." [68] But it cited no New York or other decision holding that the thief can be indicted for the receiving. It simply held that under Penal Law Section 2,

---

[67] The effect of the decision was immediate, *e.g.*, People *v.* Enlind, 214 App. Div. 277, 212 N. Y. S. 77 (1925).

[68] So stated also in 2 Wharton, Evidence in Criminal Cases (11th ed. 1935) 1231.

the thief is a principal in the receiving—again without citation.[69] The fact that "In perhaps a majority of the jurisdictions
. . . the rule is that the thief is not an accomplice of the receiver within the rule requiring corroboration . . ." did not influence the distinguished jurists of the Court of Appeals of
New York—where the problem of large scale theft is most
acute. Even more significant is the fact that the Court also
granted that "no controlling case in this court is found," whereupon it adopted the assumption of the Appellate Division which
"baldly said:'If the defendant was guilty of the crime charged
the thieves were accomplices.'" Thus it is impossible to account
for the Kupperschmidt decision on the ground that the Court
of Appeals felt impelled to adhere to established precedent.
Perhaps the English decisions, noted above, influenced the New
York Court of Appeals; the opinion, however, contains no
English citation.

But our story is not ended. For, shortly after the Kupperschmidt decision was rendered in 1924, influential business
groups, intent on controlling criminal receiving, concentrated
their efforts on the remaining official agency of legal change—
the legislature.

The issue was agitated by numerous business associations.
They organized an intensive campaign to bring pressure upon
the legislature. The activities of these business organizations
and their agents illustrate the influence which groups of interested laymen exert upon legislation.[70] The law was amended

---

[69] For consequent difficulty caused by this language, see P. v. Bigley, 36
N. Y. S. 2d 133 (1942) where, after holding that a thief cannot be convicted
of receiving the same property, the court said: "In the latter case [Kupper-
schmidt] the court held that in a literal sense a larcenist could not also
criminally receive the same property, but he could do it in a legal sense . . .
the court there was dealing with the legalistic definition of guilty participation, not with the common meaning of words." But the recognized legal test
of participation is liability for the same offense, which is not a matter of
"common meaning."

[70]   "*Association Supports Fence Legislation*
Representatives appear at hearings in Albany and Washington to advocate
passing of 'fence' legislation" etc. *The Silkworm* 26 (1928), published by the
Silk Association of America.

in 1928, four years after the Kupperschmidt decision, to establish the rule of the decisions of the First Department as law.[71] Henceforth, in New York, as in a majority of the states, the thief's testimony against the receiver need not be corroborated.

5. Possession of Other Stolen Goods

The third major adaptation of New York criminal procedure is no less significant than the elimination of the necessity to corroborate the thief's testimony. It concerned the admissibility of the fact of the defendant's possession of stolen goods, other than those involved in the trial, as relevant to his knowledge that the goods in issue were stolen.

Many American jurisdictions make very little use of evidence of the defendant's possession of other stolen property to prove his guilty knowledge with regard to the particular goods in question.[72] But it is precisely the *professional* receiver who is likely to be in possession of a large *quantity* of stolen goods. The exclusion of such evidence is typical of our common failure to see criminal law problems against the background of modern fact and need.

Assistant District Attorney Harold Hastings of New York County, who tried many cases of criminal receiving, found this the most serious handicap to effective prosecution. He summarized the limitations of the New York law:

"But, let us assume that William Jones is a warehouseman and at the time of his arrest in possession of the stolen chairs the police find hundreds of *other stolen articles in his posses-*

---

[71] "ACCOMPLICES AND RECEIVERS. Upon the trial of a person charged with criminally receiving stolen goods under the preceding chapter the person selling, offering or delivering such goods shall not be deemed an accomplice of the person charged with receiving them, and it shall be competent for the jury to consider the testimony of the person selling, offering, or delivering such goods, notwithstanding the fact that such person may have been charged with their theft, and may have been convicted of their theft or may have previously been convicted of any crime." New York, Cahill's Consolidated Laws, 1930, Chap. 41, sec. 1308 a. (Added by L. 1928, ch. 170, July 1.)

[72] 45 Amer. Juris. 408–409.

sion which have not been delivered to him by the thief in the instant case.[73]

"The law says, or rather the cases in New York say, that *unless those other stolen articles found in the possession of Wm. Jones were all delivered to him, Jones, by the same thief, the fact that Jones had them in his possession is not admissible* on the People's case *to show knowledge on behalf of Jones,* that the chairs, the subject of the instant charge, were stolen.

"In other words, evidence that the accused had frequently received similar articles of property *from the same thief* is admissible upon the question of guilty knowledge, but the *fact that other stolen property not delivered by the same thief* was found in the possession of the receiver *is not admissible* unless, of course, it is developed by cross examination of the defendant or his witnesses."[74]

Certainly the possession of a number of stolen chattels, even without proof of guilty knowledge, is some persuasive evidence of the defendant's intent when he took possession of the property in issue.[75] Such evidence has been admissible in England since 1871.[76] If the description of the professional receiver's

---

[73] "William Feuer, 37 years old, and his brother, Leo, 26 of 107 Clinton Street, were arraigned for sentence yesterday before Judge Allen in General Sessions as fences for fur burglars . . . The Feuers were convicted of having received part of $25,000 worth of furs stolen from Green Bros., furriers at 135 West 26th St., on March 22, last. The police traced the loot to their fur shop at 33 Ave. C. They found also they said, other furs that had been stolen from the Stanley Fur Company, 123 West 28th St., and ninety six ermine skins stolen from D. R. Paskey, 39 West 32nd St. Subsequently the police raided the establishment of B. Gangel and Joseph Rothenburg at 43 West 27th St., in which they said, more loot from the Green Brothers robbery was found, in addition to furs stolen from other stores." The New York Times, May 7, 1927.

[74] The Panel (Nov.-Dec., 1932) 52.

[75] Wigmore distinguishes these two situations as involving "the Knowledge principle" and "the Intent theory." 2 Evidence (3rd ed. 1940) secs. 324, 325.

[76] This act is set forth and annotated in Chitty, Criminal Acts (1894) 144-5.
The English Act was modified in 1916 as follows:
"Whenever any person is being proceeded against for receiving any property, knowing it to have been stolen, or for having in his posssssion stolen property, for the purpose of proving guilty knowledge there may be given in evidence at any stage of the proceedings—
(a) the fact that other property stolen within the period of twelve months preceding the date of the offence charged was found or had been in his possession.

behavior, presented above, is accurate, and classification of him as a criminal dealer is valid, utilization of such evidence would seem quite proper. Indeed, the larger the business done, the greater are the probabilities that different thieves have been dealt with, that the property was stolen from different places and persons, and hence, that the receiving in question was with criminal knowledge. Nevertheless, as District Attorney Hastings stated in 1932, the law of New York did not admit evidence of possession of stolen property unless it had been delivered to the defendant by the same thief from whom the property in issue was received.[77]

But in 1936, in People v. Marino,[78] the Court of Appeals abandoned the long-standing limitation that the same thief must be involved, reversing the decision of the Appellate Division.

Three of the seven judges dissented, and their opinion reveals the significance of the Marino Case. The dissenting judges held themselves bound by the Doty Case[79] and others which, while admitting evidence of possession of goods stolen from various owners, emphasized that the same thief was involved throughout, including the case in issue. "The district attorney frankly asks us to overrule those cases . . . When a court of last resort violates the rule *stare decisis*, nothing except obscurity can result. Members of the bar will be unable to advise clients, trial judges will be without guide in charging juries, intermediate courts of review must be filled with confusion." The change in law should be effected "by statute." Thus spoke the minority.

(b) the fact that within the five years preceding the date of the offence charged he was convicted of any offence involving fraud or dishonesty.

This last-mentioned fact may not be proved unless—

(i) seven days' notice in writing has been given to the offender that proof of such previous conviction is intended to be given.

(ii) evidence has been given that the property in respect of which the offender is being tried was found or had been in his possession." 6 & 7 Geo. V, c. 50, The Treasury Act of 1916, sec. 43, sub-sec. 1. And see Archbold, *op. cit.* sec. 43, pp. 514–5, and pp. 732–4.

[77] P. v. Doty, 175 N. Y. 164 (1903).

[78] 271 N. Y. 317, 3 N. E. 2d. 439.

[79] Cited *supra* n. 77.

The majority opinion reveals an awareness of the social facts of professional receiving.[80] On the technical side, the majority opinion noted that the Doty Case was not directly in point since there the same thief was involved, the material question being confined to the fact that the other stolen property was acquired in various larcenies from different owners. What the majority derived from the Doty Case was that, "The court expanded the rule, as we must do, to meet new circumstances . . ." Nextly, the majority quoted from Funk v. United States,[81] an obvious, indeed, a deliberate, instance of undisguised judicial legislation, the statement that "a rule of evidence at one time thought necessary to the ascertainment of truth should yield to the experience of a succeeding generation . . ."—with which the minority also agreed, pointing, however, to the legislature as the proper organ to initiate such legal changes.

The majority, unlike the Court of 1924 which decided the Kupperschmidt Case, was impressed by the fact that its view found "ample support in the authorities" in other jurisdictions (citing numerous cases). And so, it expanded the rule of evidence, as stated above, bringing the New York law into closer conformity with the social facts of professional receiving of stolen goods.

Whatever one's interpretation of the Doty Case may be and even if the dissenting judges' view of that decision is sharply discounted, it remains certain that so far as the weight of precedent is concerned, the court which decided the Kupperschmidt Case in 1924 was much freer than the Court was in 1936 when it decided the Marino Case. Yet, legislation was needed to eliminate the rule of corroboration. In the Marino Case, the desired result was achieved by judicial decision in the face of substantial New York authority to the contrary.

Even a very able court (and the New York Court of Appeals

---

[80] "A reasonable person of ordinary intelligence would rightly conclude that a dealer in cars who had sold three or four stolen cars knew them to have been stolen if he had sold other stolen cars about the same time and referred to them as 'hot' or stolen cars, and cautioned his customers about them." 3 N. E. 2d 441.

[81] 290 U. S. 371.

in 1924 was among the ablest benches ever to sit in any state) may not always be cognizant of the social aspects of the cases heard on appeal.[82] To be sure, much happened in New York between 1924 and 1936 to enlighten the later bench. We have noted the legislation of 1928 removing the need to corroborate the thief's testimony. In that same legislation a new provision (to be discussed later) was inserted concerning "a dealer in . . . any merchandise . . ." The majority opinion in the Marino Case noted that "The defendant was proved to be a dealer in secondhand automobiles" and that he had violated the duty imposed upon him. Thus, recognition of the distinctive facts of the business of certain dealers, registered in the law of 1928, together with the implications that may reasonably be attributed to the judicial attitude of 1936, helps account for the Marino decision even if it leaves unanswered some pertinent inquiries regarding the Kupperschmidt Case of 1924.

In sum, we find that in New York the principal rules of evidence especially relevant to receiving stolen property, i.e., recent possession, corroboration of the thief's testimony, and the presence of other stolen goods, have all been adapted to meet the needs of the social problem.

6. *The Inadequacy of the Legal Sanctions*

Despite substantial progress in adapting rules of evidence to conform to sound policy regarding the social facts of criminal receiving, especially in New York, the conviction of these offenders continues to be exceptionally difficult. The reasons may be readily surmised.

First, before recent possession may raise the so-called presumption against the defendant, "the possession must be *unexplained* by any innocent origin . . ."[83] In the case of such shrewd offenders as those found among professional receivers, plausible explanations are always forthcoming. Invariably, in the case of dealers in stolen goods, a bill of sale, duly executed

---

[82] None of the facts of the Kupperschmidt Case were reported.
[83] 9 Wigmore (3rd ed.) 422.

to the smallest detail, is exhibited to investigating officials. The bill of sale is executed in anticipation of, or in response to, investigation. It contains the name and address of a supposed vendor and a consideration below the market value, which accounts for the payment by cash and the large "discount." This subterfuge is easy. There is no law licensing vendors generally, nor any requirement that purchases be made from established concerns, nor any sanctioned,[84] standardized way of doing business. Furthermore, it is known that the most reputable persons buy stolen goods. In fact, it must be assumed that most stolen goods find their way ultimately into the hands of consumers who buy innocently. What, then, is more natural and effective than for receivers to claim that they bought the stolen goods without criminal knowledge?

The fabrication of false explanations to refute the presumption of recent possession is facilitated by the usually defensible rule, consistent with the general requirements of the *mens rea* doctrine, that the knowledge of the particular defendant on trial controls rather than that of "an ordinary, reasonable, and prudent person" in the situation of the defendant and under the circumstances in the case.[85]

Other factors aid the persuasiveness of the explanations: defendants in these cases, though they may have dealt in stolen goods for many years, rarely have a criminal record. Where receiving is a misdemeanor, then, despite previous convictions, evidence of the past record may not be introduced. Finally, the prosecution is not permitted to introduce evidence of the defendant's bad reputation unless the latter has, himself, raised

---

[84] In a number of states there is a standardized automobile manufacturer's bill of sale and the automobile certificate of title which must be registered. *Cf. infra* p. 282 *ff.*

[85] State *v.* Ebeller, 222 S. W. 396, 283 Mo. 57 (1920). *Cf.* (1920) 30 Yale L. J. 194. And for a discussion of numerous cases, see note in 21 U. of Mo. Law Series (March, 1921) 37–40. See Com. *v.* Boris and Marcus, 317 Mass. 309, 58 N. E. 2d 8 (1944). But *cf.* Farzley *v.* State, 231 Ala. 60, 163 So. 394 (1935).

Even though an individual purchases property which he believes is stolen, he is not guilty of receiving if the property was not in fact stolen. Le Fanti *v.* U. S. (259 F. 460 (1919)); and *cf.* People *v.* Jaffe, 185 N. Y. 497, 78 N. E. 169, 9 L. R. A. (N. S.) 263 (Ct. of App. N. Y. 1906), discussed in Hall, General Principles of Criminal Law (1947) 127.

the issue.[86] This combination of rules of law and circumstances weighs heavily toward the acceptance of explanations given by apparently respectable business men.

The so-called presumption of guilt, arising from proof of the possession of stolen goods shortly after the commission of the theft, was undoubtedly a helpful rule several centuries ago. The society was simple; concealment and disposal of stolen property were difficult. But it may be questioned whether the rule remains very helpful at the present time. Certain types of property like jewelry and securities can be easily concealed for an indefinite period of time. Compact stolen goods can be transferred many times, which increases the interval between the theft and the acquisition of the property by more remote receivers. Tracing stolen property under modern conditions is frequently a slow process, and it may be several months before it is finally located.[87] Some of the above difficulties limit the utility of the rule regarding corroboration. In any event, the confessed criminal is bound to be regarded with suspicion regardless of what the rules provide. And such testimony is rarely available.[88]

Another limitation, which makes the prosecution of receivers

---

[86] Cf. State v. Creson, 38 Mo. 372 (1866); People v. Hinksman, 192 N. Y. 421 (1908); Anthony v. Com., 142 Va. 577 (1925).

[87] Cf. R. v. Hall, 1 Cox C. C. 231 (1845). Martin v. State, 151 Ark. 365 (1922).

To meet this difficulty, New Jersey passed a statute in 1928 which, after defining criminal receiving, provides:

"If such person is shown to have or to have had possession of such goods, chattels, choses in action, or other valuable thing within one year from the date of such stealing, robbery, or unlawful or fraudulent obtaining, such possession shall be deemed sufficient evidence to authorize conviction."

Provision is made for exceptions when:

". . . (1) the relations of the parties concerned and the circumstances would suggest that the transfer of the goods was a gift; (2) that the price paid for the goods represented their fair and reasonable value; (3) that the person buying such goods made inquiries sufficient to satisfy a reasonable man that the seller was in a regular and established business for dealing in such goods, and (4) that the person receiving or buying such goods reported the transaction to the police." New Jersey Compiled Statutes (1925-1930 Supplement) 52-166e (1). Cf. Nev. Laws (1929) c. 173. And see discussion in The Panel (May, 1928).

[88] This difficulty is not due to guarantees of the law—directed at protection of the citizen from arbitrary exectuive power—but abused to protect habitual criminals.

unusually difficult, is inability to identify the merchandise.
Thus Harold W. Hastings, formerly Assistant District Attorney
of New York County, wrote:

"The peculiar difficulty in the prosecution of receiving cases
is of two kinds:

"First, it is *absolutely necessary to prove the identity of the
goods received.* That is to say, it is necessary for the district
attorney to prove that the goods which have been received
are the very goods stolen. In many cases an owner is well able
to state that the goods viewed are goods manufactured or at
one time owned by him, but very often he is not able to state
beyond a reasonable doubt that the goods were stolen from
him.

"In other words most articles stolen are similiar to articles
lawfully sold, so that when it comes to a question of whether
these particular articles which are the subject of the controversy are the articles stolen, or are articles lawfully in the
market, the owner is unable honestly to state one way or the
other." [39]

Here we have a vicious circle in full operation. One of the
chief reasons (along with high value for small bulk) why
jewelry,[90] furs, automobile accessories, and silks form principal
commodities in the market of stolen goods is the fact that it
is possible to make identification very difficult. The industries
affected have struggled with this problem for a long time.[91] The

---

[39] The Panel (Nov.-Dec. 1932) 51.

[90] It has been recognized for centuries that jewelry can be disposed of with
ease, and we find that jewelry was, therefore, the subject of special legislation, which permitted a receiver of such property to be prosecuted for a substantive felony long before this procedure was generally applied. *Cf.* 10 Geo.
III, c. 48 entitled "An act for making the receiving of stolen jewels, and gold
and silver plate, in the cases of burglary and highway robbery, more penal."

[91] "A useful device to prove ownership of stolen goods is the serial number
which is being commonly stamped on manufactured articles. To protect this
evidence, it is becoming usual to punish altering or removing the number.
Automobile and pistol legislation embodying the principle is usual, and it is
being extended to other articles. California, by chapter 324, applied it to
a long list, including radios, pianos, and vacuum cleaners . . . It is interesting to notice that the articles enumerated are those commonly sold on installment payments. It will evidently be important to the vendor that the number
be not altered so that he can easily prove his ownership of a particular article
on which installments are due, if he finds it in the possession of another person
than the vendee . . ." The Panel, May, 1928.
    Cf. 39 & 40 Geo. III, c. 89, s. 4.

fur trade is reported to have retained chemists and expended thousands of dollars in an ineffective attempt to place permanent marks on furs. The silk industry has suffered similar failure in its efforts to identify silk by drawing special threads through the entire fabric, and by other means. Manufacturer's marks are placed on jewlery, but these can be effaced. Gems are reset, and it is impossible to identify them except in the case of rare stones which can be recognized by experts, and these can be recut at a sacrifice.

Not only must the stolen goods found in the receiver's possession be identified, but other essential elements of the original theft must be proved. The prosecution must virtually prove beyond a reasonable doubt the commission of two crimes before a conviction against a receiver can be secured. The defenses may, with very few exceptions, include any and all that would be available in a prosecution for the original crime.[92]

Finally, in addition to the special difficulties encountered in the prosecution of criminal receivers, the latter, until they are convicted, quite properly enjoy the usual advantages extended to innocent persons. Moreover, they have the money to employ competent counsel so that constitutional privileges become realities for them. One illustration of the actual functioning of the general privileges in such cases must suffice to conclude our survey of the inadequacies of existing legal controls.

The police know that certain persons are criminal receivers, and yet are often unable to secure evidence sufficient to estab-

---

[92] But cf. People v. Pollack (154 N. Y. App. Div. 716 (1913)), where the defense was that the goods were purchased from boys under sixteen years of age and since they were not guilty of larceny (because of the Juvenile Act), the defendant could not be guilty of receiving. But held contra. Cf. Note (1913) 13 Col. L. Rev. 350.

A recent English case, Walters v. Lunt (1951) 2 All E. R. 645, held that the defendant was not guilty of criminal receiving on the ground that the child who delivered the property, being under the age of eight years, could not be convicted of larceny.

And cf. Montana v. Sim, 92 Mont. 541 (1932) upholding a statute which provided that purchase of certain specified property from a minor at a place other than a fixed place of business carried on by the minor or his employer created a presumption that the defendant knew that the property had been stolen.

lish their guilt beyond a reasonable doubt. To this end, a rogues' gallery has been established by many police departments. The photographs are not indiscriminately exhibited. They are shown only to individuals who may be aided thereby to identify suspects. In Schulman v. Whitaker,[93] to cite an apt case, the complainant had kept a pawn shop in the same place for eleven years. He had been arrested several times for receiving, but never convicted. The defendant, an inspector of police, ordered his photograph taken and placed in the rogues' gallery. The complainant, employing competent counsel, succeeded in securing an injunction restraining this contemplated action.

In Itskovitch v. Whitaker [94] the facts and decision are the same as in Schulman v. Whitaker, except that in this case the right of privacy was invoked. Again, the complainant had been arrested several times; again, he had never been convicted. The court held that he must be considered innocent; therefore the intended publication of his picture in the rogues' gallery would be enjoined. "Every one who does not violate the law can insist on being let alone (the right of privacy). In such a case the right of privacy is absolute." [95]

The business of the complainants in the above cases, their many arrests, and the knowledge of the police regarding their activities all point toward the probability of the violation of penal laws. The court, however, viewing the facts or rather the admissible facts through a lens which must conform to existing legal presumptions, must treat the persons involved as innocent.[96] The above situation not only illustrates a phase of the police problem but reveals also the nature of the problem of enforcement in general. It emphasizes what most commentators on "efficiency" ignore when they assume that the operation of a machine governed by purely physical laws is

---

[93] 117 La. 704, 42 So. 227 (1906).
[94] 115 La. 479, 39 So. 499 (1905); 117 La. 708 (1906).
[95] Id. 481.
[96] "The plaintiff, for the said hearing, must be considered an honest man." Id. 480.

an apt analogy to apply to the functioning of officials: namely, that there are forces within the administrative "machine" which operate in opposing directions. The difficulties met in the prosecution of criminal receivers are not new ones, however aggravated they have become. It has always been difficult to convict professional receivers. From Wild on, they have been shrewd enough to devise methods of operation which escaped public notice. They dress their illegal traffic in all the paraphernalia of lawful enterprise; they conduct their businesses secretly; they are equipped both mentally and financially to take full advantage of the weaknesses in the administrative machine, should prosecution be initiated.

Indeed, the history of receiving stolen property might be written in terms of the difficulties of convicting these offenders. In 1740 Henry Fielding protested against the impotence of legal controls. "The thief," wrote Fielding, "returns immediately to his Trade of picking Pockets, and the Accessory is of course discharged, and of course returns to his Trade of receiving the Booty . . . And thus Stands the Law at this day; which, notwithstanding the repeated Endeavors of the Legislature, Experience shows us, is incapable of removing this deplorable Evil from the Society." [97]

Over a hundred years later we find similar complaints being made.[98] We still do. Fielding made several suggestions for the improvement of the law.[99] Some of them have since been

---

[97] *Op. cit.* 72–3.

[98] ". . . the receiver of stolen goods, who during many years has been deriving a profit from his nefarious occupation, corrupting all those with whom he has brought himself in contact, . . . has by his skill and talent eluded the law so as to escape detection." On the Principles of Criminal Law (Wm. Pickering pub., London 1856) 78.

[99] "What then is to be done, to extirpate this stubborn Mischief? to prove the pernicious consequences of which, I need, I think, only appeal to the Sense of Parliament, testified in so many repeated Acts, and very strongly expressed in their preambles.

"First, Might it not be proper to put an effectual Stop to the present scandalous Method of compounding Felony, by public Advertisements in the News Papers?

"2dly, Is it impossible to find any Means of regulating Brokers and Pawnbrokers?

adopted. Yet the gap between the social problem and the substantive law is almost as great as it was in Fielding's day. The consequent defects of law-enforcement remain unchanged.

The receiver has not only obstructed the operation of the law when it was aimed directly at him; he has also been the traditional protector of the criminals associated with him.[1] Thieves, robbers, and burglars found in their receivers powerful allies equipped with money, experience and influence, all of which were placed at their service. This alliance is an historic one.[2] Being mutually advantageous, it has persisted. The receiver is the natural rallying point for professional criminals. It is still good business and sound judgment for him to prevent their detection and conviction. An apprehended thief of ability represents a loss in business. He represents a potential state's witness.

"*3dly*, Why should not the receiving stolen Goods, knowing them to be stolen, be made an original Offence?

"*4thly*, Why may not the bare buying or taking to Pawn stolen Goods, above a certain Value, be made Evidence of receiving with Knowledge, &c. unless the Goods were bought in Market overt, (no Broker's or Pawnbroker's Shop to be reputed such Market overt) or unless the Defendant could prove, by a credible Witness to the Transaction, that he had good Cause to regard the Seller or Pawner of the Goods to be the real Owner.

"If none of these Methods be thought possible or proper, I hope better will be found out. Something ought to be done, to put an End to the present Practice, of which I see daily the most pernicious Consequences; many of the younger Thieves appearing plainly to be taught, encouraged and employed by the Receivers." *Op. cit.* 74–5.

[1] "Says Gang Started Big Bribery Fund.

"Defendant in Brooklyn Aspirin 'Fence' Trials Tells of Plan to Fix Whole Court. Proposed to Raise $9,000.

"One of the three defendants on trial in the Kings County Court on charges of receiving stolen goods in connection with the theft of $92,000 worth of aspirin from the Bayer Chemical Company, Manhattan, testified yesterday that the gang had started a bribery fund while some of its members were in the Raymond Street Jail for the purpose of blocking justice." New York Times, Dec. 25, 1927.

[2] Pike, writing of the administration of the criminal law in the fourteenth century, remarks: "Among other facilities for escape was the ease with which a law breaker could find shelter for himself and storage for his spoil. The Common Receiver is by no means a creation of our great modern cities, but has descended to us from the days when Europe was in a state of brigandage, and when the guilds assisted an accused brother to obtain an acquittal. Men and women are thus described in numerous cases recorded in the rolls, and were the fitting associates of the classes, described as common breakers of the peace, common thieves or robbers, and common malefactors." 1 *op. cit.* 285–6.

Judicial statistics from 1926 to 1932 for New York City [3] emphasize the inadequacy of existing legal controls. They show (a) that a very small number of criminal receivers are prosecuted, (b) that when action is brought, they usually escape conviction, and (c) that the probability of conviction for criminal receiving (in relation to arrests) is less than one-third of what it is in larceny, and that the ratio is even more extreme with reference to convictions in relation to disposition of cases.[4]

That relatively few professional receivers are prosecuted results from the fact that most of them escape detection entirely or they are permitted to operate without interference. It is impossible to determine the number of these offenses with any degree of precision, but the known facts indicate that they are far more numerous than the statistics on arrests and prosecutions suggest.

Later statistics (1935–1949) for New York City are equally significant. They show the following with regard to Receiving Stolen Goods and Larceny: [5]

	Larceny	Receiving Stolen Goods
Total Dispositions	41,656	4,585
Total Convictions	25,435	1,510
Total Imprisoned	15,215	734
Percent of Cases Disposed of which Terminated in Conviction:	62%	33%

[3] Cf. "Since 1926, there have been more receivers of stolen jewelry convicted in New York City than in all of the rest of the United States." The Jewelers' Security Alliance, 1931 Year Book 11.

[4] Judicial Statistics On Receiving Stolen Goods And Larceny (Except Auto) New York City 1926–1932.
Total No. Arrests for Receiving—1743
Total No. Convictions for Receiving—305
Ratio of Convictions to Arrests for Receiving—17.5%
Total No. Arrests for Larceny—8889
Total No. Convictions for Larceny—5012
Ratio of Convictions to Arrests for Larceny—56.4%
Total No. Receiving Cases Disposed of—1509
Percent Receiving Cases Disposed of which Terminated in Conviction—20.2%
Total No. Larceny Cases Disposed of—7739
Percent Larceny Cases Disposed of which Terminated in Conviction—64.7%
Source: Annual Reports of the Police Department of New York City, 1926–1932.

[5] Source: Annual Reports of the Police Department of New York City, 1935–1949.

Percent of Cases Disposed of which Terminated in Imprisonment:

	Larceny	Receiving Stolen Goods
	36%	16%

Percent of Persons Convicted Who were Imprisoned:

	60%	49%

The following data [6] are even more significant with reference to the administration of the law in cases of criminal receiving because they reveal the advantages of criminal receivers who are dealers in certain businesses over "general" receivers, specifically, the former emerge as the most favored members of a favored class.

	General Receiving	Receiving by Licensed Dealers	Total
Number of Arrests & Summons	5846	378 (6.1%)	6224
Total Dispositions	4300	285 (6.2%)	4585
Imprisoned	705	29 (4.0%)	734
Total Convictions	1453	57 (3.8%)	1510

Percent of cases disposed of which terminated in conviction:

	34%	20%

Percent of cases disposed of which terminated in sentences of imprisonment:

	16%	10%

Percent of persons convicted who were imprisoned:

	48%	51%

It is clear that at every crucial stage in the administration of the criminal law prior to the imposition of the sentence, the licensed dealers fare much more favorably than do general receivers. They have almost twice as many chances of escaping conviction and therefore, also, imprisonment as do the gen-

---

A few of the many larceny sub-classes shown in the Annual Reports have been omitted because they seemed to be cases of Embezzlement and in order to avoid some cumbersome details which would not alter the results.

[6] Source: Annual Reports of the Police Department of New York City, 1935–1949.

eral receivers. Only after conviction, when sentence is imposed, does the dealer fare less favorably than the general receivers and the difference is far slighter than expected. Accordingly, what we had previously hazarded as a guess regarding the advantages of experienced, crafty businessmen, who are also able to employ competent counsel, is verified by the statistical data. The most serious aspect of the situation is that the worst offenders, those who probably engage in professional receiving, are only rarely brought to trial, and when they are tried, under laws which indiscriminately provide the same penalties for all criminal receivers, their chances of escaping entirely unscathed are excellent.

The ineffectiveness of the official agencies in coping with criminal receivers thus appears on every hand. Accordingly, the activities of groups of laymen pursuing their respective interests, become of major importance—theoretical as well as practical.

III. Lay Participation in the Law-Process

1. *The Insurance Company, the Private Investigator, and the Criminal Receiver*

If one were to single out the most characteristic feature in the complex pattern of "solving" the problem of criminal receiving, it would undoubtedly be the payment of rewards for the return of the stolen property. Most of these rewards are paid by insurance companies to private investigators, informers, and police. In New York City the commissioner applies twenty-five per cent of the police rewards to pension funds and pays the balance to the officer who secured the return of the property.[7] A well-informed individual, whom the writer interviewed, suspected that the police officers distributed part of their seventy-five per cent to informers who helped them recover the property. But the police are not always driven to such an

---

[7] At the request of the Mayor of Chicago, the automobile insurance companies agreed to discontinue payment of rewards to policemen. 1932 Annual Rept. of the Gov. Bd. of the Nat'l. Auto. Theft Bur.

extremity. They have other effective methods of securing information.

The reward system operates to perpetuate itself. It operates also to stimulate criminal conduct. Thus one of the superior police officials in a large city informed the writer that many large thefts, particularly of jewelry, were prearranged by persons in a strategic position to secure rewards for the return of the property "after investigation." An investigator of unusual ability and many years of experience contributed the further thought that employees of insurance companies were sometimes involved in these corrupt rewards, and that they participated in the proceeds. The exceptional cases in which such conspiracies occur are extremely suggestive in revealing developments at the periphery of professional large-scale theft. The complexity of the problem is thrown into sharp relief when employees of insurance companies and private investigators conspire as "putters-up," taking advantage of confidential information in their files, arranging thefts of valuable insured property, causing rewards to be advertised and paid for the "recovery" of the property, and subsequently sharing in the spoils.

The insurance companies exercise an important influence upon large-scale theft and the receiving of stolen property. Since a large portion of stolen property comes into the possession of professional receivers, it is natural that efforts to recover such property should be centered upon these individuals. The insurance companies and their representatives are informed by paid spies of the activities of both thieves and receivers. The professional receivers most likely to be interested in particular merchandise are known. When a large theft is reported the company takes immediate steps. It summons its adjusters, private detectives, informers, and the police. Its own employees are used in preliminary investigation and to assist the private investigators. These latter form in many respects the most effective agencies for the recovery of stolen property. Whatever one may think about the methods employed, whatever suspicions one may have about the integrity of some of these individuals, there is no question that they are efficient. They recover the property. They excel principally because they are supplied with funds to pay informers [8] and to distribute as rewards to police and other persons. Their value to the insurance companies results from their contacts with criminals and informers. One investigator sent out advertisements soliciting employment in which he announced that he had "many influential points of contact with valuable channels of information." To such sophisticated investigators, scientific detection is a myth. Most large thefts are committed by experts who leave no traces and immediately divest themselves of possession of the loot. The efficient detective, according to a leading private investigator, is the one who has most informers.[9] Certainly the informer looms up very large in crime detection.[10]

The private investigator as a rule secures little help from professional receivers because when a receiver turns informer, his motive, generally, is not immediate cash but the elimination of a rival from business. Accordingly, the receiver is apt to give his information directly to the police. Some receivers have more capital than others; some underbuy, others undersell. Still others bear good reputations in the underworld.[11] A defeated, resentful receiver may supply information to the police.[12]

A number of criminal receivers in large cities manage to be

---

[8] A successful "investigator" must have a reputation among informers for being absolutely trustworthy. In a sensational case involving several hundred thousand dollars' worth of stolen jewelry, an investigator was himself indicted for criminal receiving, and he refused to divulge the name of the person from whom he secured the property.

[9] Cf. Waite, Criminal Law In Action (1934) 102–26.

[10] Not the least reason for the existence of informers is the failure of society to reëstablish released convicts in legitimate occupations. Cf. Glueck, 500 Criminal Careers (1930) 211–15. On informers, see Plato, Laws 745a.

[11] Thus was Nelson, the notorious New York receiver of stolen jewelry, described to the writer: "His word was as good as his bond; he treated the gang O.K.; he was a 'right guy'. i.e., he never gave information to the police", and so forth. See infra, pp. 214–215 for a discussion of his case in the courts.

[12] The writer was informed on good authority that Nelson was convicted on evidence supplied by other receivers who resented his constant underbuying them. This was almost too vigorously denied by police officials who had charge of this case.

regular informers not only for the police but occasionally, also, for insurance companies. The consideration for these services takes three forms: cash payments, protection from prosecution for past offences, and permission to operate as receivers without interference. Here is a phase of modern large-scale theft which makes elimination of criminal behavior seem a Utopian dream—police shutting their eyes at the commission of serious crimes, protecting their informers from imprisonment and obtaining the coöperation of the prosecuting authorities in this regard in order that they may secure information about other criminals. When receivers who inform are discovered, the swift retribution of criminal society follows.[13]

The insurance companies through their private investigators occasionally make special use of a known receiver. A recent New York case will serve as an illustration. Information received from spies resulted in the tracing of a quarter of a million dollars' worth of jewelry to a certain receiver whom we may call B. B was extremely cautious in his efforts to dispose of the jewels. The company's investigator employed another well known receiver, A, to act as a decoy and lure B into a trap by posing as a prospective purchaser. Apparently A became conscious of the possibility of grave danger if he proceeded in that role, or perhaps he was troubled by scruples in exposing a member of the fraternity. In any event, he insisted upon an "honest" transaction being entered into, that is, that the company "buy" the jewels from B at a price, of course, far below their insured valuation. The facts regarding the final arrangement may never be revealed; but within a short time thereafter the insurance investigator and police forced their way into a room in a hotel and arrested both A and B and the two thieves who had stolen the jewelry. How much money was spent and to whom it was paid is not known.

---

[13] Thus, in May, 1933, Joe Trop, a well-known New York receiver who had gained repute as the purchaser of the jewelry acquired by the notorious Whittemore gang, was tossed from an automobile, beaten and riddled with bullets from machine guns. The murder was generally recognized as indisputable evidence of his relationship to the police.

What is known is that the company recovered the jewels and saved many thousands of dollars.

The aftermath of the interrupted transaction in the hotel room is significant. *A* was indicted. So was *B*. Both were acquitted. There is reason to suspect that *A's* indictment was a merely formal affair to maintain his standing with *B* and other receivers, and that police and prosecutors were prepared to recognize the services rendered by *A* and to protect him if his conviction seemed likely. At the time *A* was employed to help recover the jewelry, there was an indictment pending against him in connection with the theft of a large amount of bonds. *A* was not brought to trial upon it.

The same methods employed in the above case were utilized by the English police to entrap the notorious receiver, Grizzard, several years ago. The case is significant for several other reasons. A pearl necklace worth £150,000 was stolen, and suspicion was directed toward Grizzard.[14] The Grizzard Case discloses the same pattern of behavior which characterizes this type of criminal activity in the United States. The central figure is a clever businessman, diamond merchant by trade. He plans many thefts himself; he uses other criminals to execute his plans to secure the property. Other typical characteristics appear: the employment of investigators by the insurance com-

---

[14] The case is discussed in an interesting book by C. Humphreys, The Great Pearl Robbery (London, 1913).

"Grizzard was much more than a famous 'fence' . . . In the words of Superintendent Leach, he was 'essentially a putter-up', that is an organizer of crimes which he carried out through carefully trained subordinates." *Id.* 4.

From a police report, which is quoted, we learn that:

"The prisoner, Grizzard is a well-known receiver . . . He is a diamond merchant by trade, but has no established business premises. He does undoubtedly do a little business, but the greater portion of his time is taken up by organizing crimes, and buying and disposing of stolen property. . . . A large number of statements made by prisoners are in our possession showing that they have disposed of their property to him, but unfortunately we have been unable to prosecute him because of lack of corroborative evidence. I have no hesitation whatever in saying that for a number of years past he has been the most notorious receiver of stolen property in this country. . . .

"There was hardly a robbery of any size in London in which he did not handle at least a portion of the goods obtained, and he knew and was trusted by the biggest continental dealers in stolen property." *Id.* 10.

panies; the offer of a reward of £10,000; and the use of pretended purchasers as decoys. By posing as prospective purchasers, two jewelers who knew one of Grizzard's confederates were able to secure evidence of guilt which resulted in the conviction of the entire gang.

The striking feature of the English case was the participation of the judges in all of the proceedings in a manner designed to expedite conviction.[15] The trial judge commented at length upon the evidence, indicating in no uncertain terms that he believed the defendants were guilty. The case was carried to the Court of Appeal where, despite the fact that there was error in the verdict because the defendants were found guilty of both stealing and receiving, the court upheld the conviction on the ground that the punishment was identical and the defendants were not therefore injured.[16]

Elsewhere in this book[17] certain unfortunate and harmful aspects of insurance and insurance companies' activities in relation to law-enforcement are discussed. With regard to professional dealing in stolen property, the insurance companies' interest is concentrated on "salvage"—reduction of financial loss through recovery of the insured property. This interest is held superior to that of elimination of dangerous offenders. Thus, it is the common complaint of police officials and representatives of protective associations that the insurance companies fail to cooperate in the apprehension and prosecution of professional thieves and receivers.[18]

2. Protective Associations

The most effective of the many lay organizations which supplement and influence the work of officials are the protective associations formed by industries which suffer the greatest

---

[15] "Some slight attempt at obtaining bail was made, but curtly refused by the magistrate who probably considered the request as bordering on the impudent." *Id.* 168.

[16] The King *v.* Lockett, Grizzard, Gutwirth and Silverman, (1914) 2 K. B. 720.

[17] *Infra* p. 311 *ff.*

[18] Proceedings of Governor's Conference on Crime, the Criminal and Society (N. Y. 1935) 356, 429–431, 435–436. Relevant excerpts are found in *Note* (1939) 39 Col. L. R. 1200–1202.

losses because of theft. These associations are generally directed by men who have had experience in police work. They collaborate with public officials, employ their own detectives, prepare the factual side of the cases for the prosecutors and are, by and large, the most persistent and active group in our society for the repression of professional theft and criminal receiving. They are most efficient because most specialized. In partial contrast to the agencies just considered, their objective tends to be the elimination of the offender rather than the recovery of the property alone.

Among the most effective are the agencies representing the silk and jewelry businesses. The Silk Association of America was a central bureau of the industry in this country. In 1918, after an unusually large number of silk robberies had occurred, this Association organized the Missing Property Bureau.

Most of the raw silk sold in this country is brought by ship to the western coast, and is then sent by fast freight to New York, where it is transferred by trucks to warehouses or is sent by rail to mills for manufacture. After manufacture, the silk is delivered in trucks to dyers in New Jersey, and from there it is sent to New York for sale. The hazards from theft arise at all of the points mentioned.

In 1923 an official of the post office, experienced in police work and especially in the protection of the parcel post, was retained as manager of the Missing Property Bureau. The following measures were then adopted:

1. All drivers of silk trucks were finger-printed. A number who had police records were discovered and eliminated. The men were also photographed, investigated, and bonded. They were then registered and given cards of identification to be presented to consignors of merchandise and to police, if occasion arose.

2. Definite routes were laid out, from which there was to be no deviation.

3. Recording devices were installed in the trucks which showed the stopping and running time of each vehicle. Insignia were placed on the trucks so that they might be readily recognized by police. Bullet-proof cabs were installed.

4. A road patrol was organized which covered the designated routes.

5. Strict supervision was maintained over drivers and other employees. They were given definite instructions regarding the operation of their trucks, stops to be made, suspicious circumstances, and behavior in case of robbery.

6. A definite program was adopted to educate the members of the Association so that merchandise might be carefully packed and marked, and that other precautions might be taken regarding shipment, checks on missing merchandise, and on employees. Bimonthly bulletins were mailed to members, advising them of any thefts which occurred, and suggesting additional preventive measures.

Contact was maintained with the police [19] and prosecutors, and active assistance was rendered by the Bureau in the arrest and trial of silk thieves. An individual businessman or concern is inclined to rest content as soon as the merchandise is recovered or the insurance collected. *The Bureau, however, retained interest in the cases* until some ultimate disposition of them was made. It secured the attendance of witnesses located outside the state. It secured and prepared evidence for trial. It watched the court calendars [20] and gave information to judges regarding the persons on trial.[21]

---

[19] "The coöperative support of state and local police agencies with the Missing Property Bureau has brought about a very material reduction in mill hold-ups in isolated sections during the past year. In accordance with a suggestion made by the bureau, watchmen in lonely districts telephone, hourly and half hourly, to the nearest police headquarters. Losses in certain districts, following the installation of this plan, have dropped fifty percent. As a result of New York police coöperation, not one bale of silk was lost during the year between railroad terminals and piers while enroute to warehouses." The Silk Association of America, Inc., Annual Report for 1930–1931, 38.

[20] "The Bureau watches the court calendars and if a receiver or thief who has escaped conviction in a silk case through some technicality, is up on a woolen or liquor case, the data we have against him is turned over to the district attorney handling the latter case and in this way, by showing that he is a habitual thief, many an offender has been sentenced who might otherwise have gone free." Report of the Missing Property Bureau, 1922.

[21] "In one case, where a letter outlining a prisoner's record was sent to the presiding justice, it was reported that the details thus presented were

Silk thefts decreased considerably after the formation of the Road Patrol in 1923 and the special activities directed against receivers of stolen silks.[22] But many factors were involved, hence, it is difficult to determine the precise effect of the activities of the Missing Property Bureau, isolated from the other factors. Thus, the weakness of the market due to the sharp drop in silk prices,[23] the advent of bootlegging which provided a more lucrative enterprise for thousands of offenders,[24] and the storing of silk in a few large, well-protected warehouses

---

a valuable supplement to an eloquent plea from the thief on the score of his innocence, with the result that he was sentenced to a substantial term." Report of the Missing Property Bureau, 1925.

The opportunities opened by such devices for venting grudges and the like are clear. Here, the circumstances militate strongly against much abuse of such opportunities.

[22] "It has, however, been the chief aim of the Bureau to seek out those who make the stealing of silk an attractive livelihood, to destroy the business of these 'fences' by communicating to their patrons the correct identity of their wares, and to see that punishment to the fullest measure of the law is meted out to them. It has been shown that thefts of large shipments are invariably instigated by 'fences' who have previously bribed employees of the freight carriers. . . ." Report of the Missing Property Bureau, 1919.

[23] The reports of the Missing Property Bureau constantly refer to the effect of the price of silk on theft. Thus in the 1920 report, it was stated that "the rising cost of silk, the demand for the product, and the ease with which it can be disposed has caused it to suffer heavy losses by pilferage and theft during the last year." And again, on October 27, 1932, the Association wrote its members, "with the upward price tendency in raw silk, we began receiving reports of increasing thefts."

[24] The striking similarities between the *modus operandi* of silk thieves who seize trucks and the "hi-jacking" by criminals engaged in organized bootlegging are not accidental. The following headlines from the *New York Times* of February 12, 1933, are suggestive: "Abduct Truckman, Steal $10,000 in Silk, Thugs Force Driver to Curb Here", etc. This robbery took place at Ninth Avenue and Thirty-fifth Street, Manhattan; the company whose truck was taken was not a member of the Silk Association, nor was the truck on the route recommended by the Missing Property Bureau.

Many of the offenders have been engaged in both types of criminality. Thus, the notorious "Legs" Diamond began his career as a package "snatcher." Later he became a silk thief. Only with the advent of prohibition did he turn to the more fruitful fields. The *New York Times*, April 9, 1933, reports the case of eight or nine defendants who were convicted of the murder of a police officer in Union City, New Jersey, who tried to prevent their escaping with a truckload of stolen silks. These defendants had previously been in the liquor traffic. One of them was reputed to be the Brooklyn representative of Capone.

Recent developments in hijacking are described by R. M. Yoder, *Softest Touch in Crime* (Aug. 18, 1951) Sat. Eve. Post 20.

have all been potent forces in sharply diminishing silk thefts.

Yet a fairly reliable quantitative basis for evaluating the similar influence of the Missing Property Bureau may be adduced:[25]

	1923	1930
Insurance rates [26]	7¢ per hundred	4¢ per hundred
Number of thefts and robberies [27]	50	21
Dollar value in thefts and robberies	$1,469,454	$175,361
Recoveries	6 involving $94,500	5 involving $106,000
Raw silk prices—annual average for the year (New York market quotations)[28]	$8.23	$2.71

After seven years of activity by the Missing Property Bureau insurance rates had become almost half of what they were in 1923; thefts dropped in number to forty per cent; the value of the merchandise stolen diminished to one-eighth of the earlier amount; and the ratio of value of the merchandise recovered to that of merchandise stolen increased almost ten-fold.

The loss from silk thefts was so greatly diminished that the Missing Property Bureau found it impossible to survive. Insur-

---

[25] From the Annual Reports of the Missing Property Bureau of the Silk Association of America.

[26] In 1918, prior to the formation of the Missing Property Bureau, it was practically impossible to secure insurance covering the theft of silk. Only one company wrote such insurance and the cost was from seven and one-half cents to fifteen cents per one hundred dollars. In 1932, the rate dropped to one and one-half cents to two cents, and every company is now willing to write such insurance. I. L. Blunt, Insurance Activities of the Silk Association of America, Inc. (1932) Insurance Series, American Management Association.

[27] The year 1923 was selected because the Road Patrol was started at that time.

[28] The peak in silk prices (New York Exchange) occurred in 1920, from which point there has been a strong decline. The years of general business prosperity and depression, 1926–1929 and 1930–1933, are not especially significant as regards silk prices. 1930 represents a point near the bottom in price; it also marked a seven year period of Road Patrol and other special methods discussed.

ance companies which formerly shared the cost of operation withdrew their support. Members of the Association who gave willingly and in large amounts when the Bureau commenced its work, lost interest. Indeed, the Bureau had been too effective for its own good! It was discontinued in 1933.[29]

Another important protective association is the Jewelers' Security Alliance, organized in 1883 and since then the model for many similar agencies. The activities of the Alliance directed against thieves have been adapted to cope with changing methods of theft. During the first ten or fifteen years of its existence, the safe burglar was the chief problem. This crime required considerable mechanical ability. After the most skillful cracksmen had been eliminated and improvements in safes had been made, there was a sharp decrease in these crimes. The sneak thief, the window crasher, and the shoplifter then succeeded the safe burglar. After 1918 robberies became prevalent, too, the war, the gun, and the automobile providing the stimuli. The constantly changing methods of theft have been met by appropriate measures.

The activities of the Alliance—in general similar to those of the Missing Property Bureau—consist of:

1. Education of jewelers by supplying detailed information regarding preventive measures,[30] the operation of thieves, and the protection of traveling salesmen.

---

[29] "The Missing Property Bureau of the Silk Association of America, which was discontinued in 1933, had for its primary objective the reduction of thefts and holdups in the delivery of raw silk and silk fabrics. Both these commodities had a high intrinsic value during the years of the Bureau's greatest activity, 1917–1930. The Bureau really worked itself out of a job, to use the vernacular. The precautions taken on the routing of trucks, the screening of drivers and helpers, the supervision of the entire shipping operation of raw silk and silk goods combined to make the stealing of these materials decreasingly attractive to the underworld.

"Then, too, after 1930, there was a shift to the use of man-made fibers in place of silk. The intrinsic value of this yarn compared to silk is much less so that this was an added reason for lack of interest by thieves." (signed) Irene Blunt, Secretary, The National Federation of Textiles, Inc. Letter to the writer, August 31, 1951.

[30] The Jewelers' Security Alliance Handbook No. 30.

2. Detection and apprehension of jewel thieves. The Pinkerton Detective Agency has been employed throughout the existence of the Alliance; contacts with local police and the F.B.I. are maintained; flash bulletins giving descriptions of wanted thieves are sent out and rewards are offered for information leading to their arrest and conviction.[31] Reward signs are distributed for display by members of the Alliance.

3. Assistance rendered in the prosecution of jewel thieves by preparing evidence, securing the appearance of witnesses, employing special counsel, and submitting past records of the offenders. The Alliance insists upon long prison sentences and brings pressure upon parole boards to prevent the early release of jewel thieves. It has used its influence to "strengthen" various criminal laws.

4. In recent years the Alliance has fostered national, systematic compilation of the scratch marks used by all retail jewelers.[32]

The Alliance and similar lay organizations represent highly specialized agencies which, within their particular fields, appear to be considerably more effective than the official police [33]—

---

[31] During 37 years, 1905–1942, "The JSA has paid out more than $250,000 which went direct to informers instrumental in the arrests and convictions of more than 2,500 criminals.

"Although the advertised reward is $100, through flexible authority of the board of directors, it may be increased to any amount depending upon the severity of the crime and the desire to apprehend the criminals." JSA, The Detector, Vol. 1, No. 6, 16 (1943).

In a case of murder of a jeweler by robbers, the Alliance offered a reward of $25,000. *id.* 8.

"The JSA has spent more than $1,100,000 in its campaign against crime." *id.* 20.

[32] It has mailed thousands of questionnaires to retail jewelers throughout the country. The compilation is available to the police, the F.B.I., and insurance companies. Insurance companies aid the compilation by sending questionnaires to persons insured by them, to be returned to the Alliance. So, too, does the International Ass'n for Identification. JSA, 68th Annual Report 1950.

The objective is "ultimately, to have a card-index file containing the scratch marks of *every* jeweler in the United States, whether or not they are actually members of the JSA." The Detector, Vol. 9 (Nov.–Dec. 1950) 2.

[33] "WHAT IF THEY CHOSE YOU AS THEIR NEXT VICTIM?

"*Could the Police Help You?*

"Could you reasonably expect that your entire police department would drop all of its other work—would stop protecting the other merchants of

except where the police have undertaken similar specialization *on particular phases* of crime. The continuing activity of the Jewelers' Security Alliance, when contrasted with the demise of the Missing Property Bureau of the Silk Association, raises interesting questions regarding the participation of lay groups in the law-process.

IV. INITIAL EFFORTS TO PROVIDE ADEQUATE LEGAL CONTROLS

In an effort to cope with the professional receiver more adequately, legislation requiring "diligent inquiry" by certain businessmen was finally adopted in New York. This legislation applied only to junk dealers in 1903, and later to second-hand dealers.[34] A presumption of guilty knowledge was added in

---

your city or town—would throw aside its duties of regulating traffic, and helping children and old people across busy arteries, and all the other routine tasks with which the force is faced—just to devote their entire attention to your one particular case, particularly when they have a new case almost every day? Could you expect them to seek every possible clue and trace it down to its ultimate conclusion? You could not expect it—and they could not do it.

"Could They Chase a Crook Who Left the State?"

"Do you realize that the bandits could put a complete stop to your policemen's efforts by speeding out of town in a high-powered car? Do you realize that the jurisdiction of your police force ends at the city line—and that they would have to call in the Sheriff to go to the county line or the State Police to carry on farther? But even that body cannot go across the State border. Beyond the State Line lies safety for any crook—that is, so far as police pursuit is concerned.

"Could They Offer a Reward?"

"But your local police have another hope—perhaps! If they would just post a cash reward for information leading to the arrest and conviction of those crooks, there might be a chance of getting valuable aid from witnesses or informers. Can they offer that reward? Have funds been appropriated for this purpose? Surely not in most communities where the police cannot even finance the return of criminals caught elsewhere. Will the reward be large enough to prove interesting? Or if they can't post the reward, can you?" From an advertisement issued by the Jewelers' Security Alliance.

[34] There was also a special clause on library books. See the Appendix, *infra.* Mr. Maxwell S. Mattuck, counsel for the National Association of Credit Men, in testifying before the House Judiciary Committee in the hearing on the proposed federal anti-fence law, stated: "He (the librarian of the Public Library of New York) told me that within a short space of time after that bill was passed, the second-hand books that had been stolen from the public library just came back by the thousands. The problem was solved right then and there by that very statute." Hearing on H. R. 10287 (April 3 and 4, 1928) 47. And *cf.* California Penal Code (Deering, 1949) sec. 496b.

1928,[35] at the same time the statute dispensing with the need for corroboration of an accomplice's testimony was adopted.

The constitutionality of one section of the New York statute was tested in People v. Rosenthal.[36] The defendant, a junk dealer, was indicted under the 1903 amendment for buying stolen copper wire belonging to a telephone company without ascertaining by diligent inquiry that the vendors had the legal right to sell the property. The defendant submitted that the amended portion of the act did not constitute any criminal offense, and that it was unconstitutional because (1) it applied only to junk dealers; (2) it protected only the property of certain corporations; (3) it was impossible in his business to make inquiries; and (4) it subjected junk dealers to prosecution even though the property purchased was not acquired by theft.

The Court of Appeals (by Vann J.) pointed out that the law in question followed a series of enactments regulating the business of junk dealers;[37] that under these laws the dealer was not only required to take out a license but also to secure a written statement from the seller "as to when, where and from whom he obtained" the property and file it with the sheriff or chief of police;[38] and that the next chapter in the penal code, adopted at the same time, prohibited purchases from "any child under the age of sixteen years."[39] The court found that

---

[35] "A person who being a dealer in or collector of any merchandise or property, or the agent, employee or representative of such dealer or collector, fails to make reasonable inquiry that the person selling or delivering any stolen or misappropriated property to him has a legal right to do so, shall be presumed to have bought or received such property knowing it to have been stolen or misappropriated. This presumption may however be rebutted by proof.

"Sec. 2. This act shall take effect July first, nineteen hundred and twenty-eight." Laws of New York, 151st Session 1928, c. 354, at 870.

All of the present Sec. 1308 is printed in the Appendix, *infra*.

[36] 197 N. Y. 394 (1910).

[37] Junk dealers and dealers in second-hand merchandise have been generally subjected to special regulation. *Cf.* Pa. Stat. Ann. (Purdon, 1938) tit. 53, sec. 10234. *Cf.* Cal. Pen. Code (Deering, 1949) sec. 496a; and see Commonwealth v. Mintz, 19 Pa. Super. Ct. 283 (1902), and Levi v. Anniston, 155 Ala. 149 (1908)

[38] Laws of 1903, c. 308.

[39] *Id.* c. 309.

the legislature had the power to confine the amendment to junk dealers "because they are way-wise and furnish the chief if not the exclusive market for stolen property" (*sic!*); that the property of telephone, gas, railroad, and other public utility companies was of such a character that it needed special protection; [40] that making an affirmative duty a "test of criminality" was "no more than is required by the common law in some cases especially in the purchase of commercial paper under certain circumstances"; and that "the legislature had the right to declare a junk dealer . . . guilty of a crime, whether he actually knew it had been stolen or not, provided he did not try to find out by making diligent inquiry." [41]

On appeal to the United States Supreme Court,[42] Rosenthal submitted that the 1903 amendment "abridged the privileges and immunities of the plaintiff-in-error, deprived him of his liberty and property without due process of law and denied him the equal protection of the laws." In affirming the conviction, the Supreme Court also emphasized the fact that junk dealers might reasonably be considered a special class.

The 1928 amendment attaches a specific consequence to purchases by certain dealers and collectors who do not make a "reasonable inquiry," namely, lack of "reasonable inquiry" is made not part of the substantive offense but, instead, raises a presumption that the dealer bought with guilty knowledge. Public officials and representatives of various businesses who have had considerable experience in these matters agree that the rule requiring inquiry and the 1928 amendment facilitate the conviction of professional receivers.[43]

---

[40] Railroad property has very generally received special protection. E.g. Cal. Pen. Code (Deering, 1949) sec. 496a.

[41] At 400.

[42] 226 U. S. 260, 33 Sup. Ct. 27 (1912).

[43] Thus, former Assistant District Attorney Harold Hastings of New York County wrote:
"This sentence in the statute has been an aid in the prosecution particularly of receivers of stolen securities, because dishonest stockbrokers had been for a long time able to say that they bought securities which were in the nature of negotiable instruments in the due course, without inquiry, and therefore had escaped liability." The Panel (Nov.-Dec. 1932) 52.

The opinion of the Appellate Division, First Department, in the case of People v. Nelson,[44] interpreted the 1928 amendment in one of the most significant decisions ever written on receiving stolen property; for the facts are presented much more completely than is customary.

The defendant was charged, among other offenses (six or seven indictments had been voted), with criminally receiving two ladies' bracelets of the value of $2,000 and $1,000 respectively. At the trial, Captain Oliver of the detective division testified that he arrested the defendant outside his residence, entered his apartment with him, told him he had a search warrant to examine his vault, and that the defendant and his wife admitted they had five vaults, three of them in the defendant's name, one in the wife's name, and one which had been held in the wife's maiden name some three years past. The contents of these boxes consisted of 3,000 pieces of jewelry, which the defendant said were worth $150,000. In response to advertisements inserted in newspapers by the police, the complaining witness in the case came from Margate, New Jersey,[45] identified the bracelets, and testified to that effect and to their theft from her apartment.

The defendant testified that he had obtained the 3,000 pieces of jewelry at race tracks, where he operated as a book-maker, from "suckers" in consideration of loans made to them; that he had at that time jewelry valued at many thousands of dollars in the hands of dealers in Chicago, Hot Springs, Arkansas, New York and elsewhere; that he never kept any books of account or any record of his transactions, but "carried them all in his head."

One of the principal objections raised against the conviction was that, although the defendant had been indicted for common-law receiving of stolen property, the jury had found

---

[44] 234 App. Div. 481, 255 N. Y. S. 558 (1932), aff'd. 260 N. Y. 559 (1932).

[45] Police officials informed the writer that there was great difficulty in getting cooperation from persons whose jewelry had been stolen and recovered; they had recovered their insurance and were not interested. Cf. Ch. 7 for a parallel situation concerning restitution by embezzlers.

him guilty under the 1928 amendment. It was conceded that the case was submitted to the jury "upon the theory that the defendant was a dealer, and that it was his duty to overcome the presumption enacted by the statute." The court then referred to the testimony of Captain Oliver, from which it appeared that the defendant had been buying jewelry for thirty years both in Chicago and New York, chiefly at the race tracks from men who "go broke"; that the jewelry he had on hand in the deposit boxes was worth a couple of hundred thousand dollars; that he might buy $20,000 worth a year, and that he sold it "but at the present time the selling is very poor"; and finally that it had occurred to him that the jewelry he bought "might be hot", but that he made no investigation whatever. The court said:

"We thus have clear evidence that the defendant was a dealer in merchandise and that when he received property which he admitted was quite possibly stolen, he failed to make any inquiry whatever as to whether the person who delivered the property to him had any legal right to do so. . . . The proven facts and admissions of defendant bring the case directly within the rule of evidence prescribed by the Legislature and give rise to the presumption that defendant received the jewelry in question knowing it to have been stolen, and rendered the defendant guilty of a violation of section 1308 of the Penal Law. There was no evidence given by the defendant sufficient to rebut such presumption." [46]

The 1928 amendment was also relied upon in People v. Silinsky,[47] in which the Appellate Division, First Department, reversed the holding of the trial justice dismissing an indictment against defendants for criminally receiving stolen securities. Among other grounds for its decision, the court pointed out that while the defendants claimed to be dealers in securities,

---

[46] 234 App. Div. 487, 488.

Nelson carried his case to the Court of Appeals, which affirmed his conviction. 260 N. Y. 559 (1932). No opinion was written. Justices Crane and Lehman dissented on the ground that the evidence of guilt was insufficient.

[47] 257 N. Y. Supp. 58 (1932).

they "made no inquiry whatever as to the true owner of the certificates of stock." [48] But the defendants alleged that they did interrogate the persons who delivered the stock and were informed that "they got the stock on a deal" with the owner "in consideration of mortgage bonds." The court held, nevertheless, that "The defendants made no inquiry whatever from Bruen [who delivered the stock] as to where Dumig or Deming [the owner] could be located and as to what was his business, or anything regarding the whereabouts of the true owner . . . We think the grand jury was justified in concluding that the defendants had made no reasonable inquiry as to whether the securities which they had received had not been stolen or misappropriated . . . The recent case of People v. Nelson . . . decided by this court is decisive authority as to the necessity of making reasonable inquiry with reference to the history of the securities which the defendants received." [49] Thus, the 1928 amendment has been used effectively.

But the advance in the New York law made by the 1928 amendment was confined to the problem of knowledge that the goods received were stolen. The New York statute did not impose severer punishment upon dealers in stolen property. And the segment of the behavior selected for definition of the offense remained the act of criminally *buying* or *receiving*. The primary need to segregate the professional receiver from the lay offenders[50] and to provide different modes of treatment was not met. That is the central thesis derived from the above empirical investigation of criminal receiving. It should guide appraisal of present laws and their reform.

We have seen that receiving stolen goods has long been "an original offense" in the sense that the receiver is no longer prosecuted as an accessory after the fact. Progress has been made along other procedural lines, mostly evidentiary. But with very few exceptions the theory applied two hundred years ago is still found in the treatment-content of the substantive law. Criminal receiving is still treated like larceny. The punish-

---

[48] At 62.
[49] At 63.
[50] See footnote 1, *supra* for a definition of these types of receivers.

ment of thieves on the basis of the value of the property stolen is applied automatically to the receiver.[51] Judged both from the standard that punishment should be proportionate to the magnitude of the harm and from that of social dangerousness, there is evident need for a radical modification of the scale of penalties now applied in almost all the states.

Going to the other extreme, in 1926 New York abolished degrees of receiving[52] and made the crime a felony, punishable much more severely than grand larceny, regardless of the value of the property received. The difficulty with that law was that it lumped professional dealers into the same category, felony, with the lay receiver. Not only is this unjust; [53] it is self-defeating. The effect of using such a blunt, indiscriminate tool is historic: juries acquit persons who are not notorious offenders.[54] At the same time, it is clear that differentiation solely on the basis of the value of the property received is also unsound. It is not based upon a criterion which differentiates the behavior of criminal dealers as a class.[55]

---

[51] Wisconsin Statutes (1947) sec. 343.19, and *cf.* sec. 343.17; Jones Ill. Stat. Ann. (1936) secs. 37.451 and 37.330. In Pennsylvania, 5 years' imprisonment may be imposed on thief and receiver alike but, while a fine of $2000 may be imposed on the thief, only one-half of that may be imposed on the receiver. See Pa. Stat. Ann. (Purdon 1945) tit. 18, secs. 4807 and 4817.

[52] In 1916 an amendment to the penal code had provided two degrees of criminal receiving—one where the property received was of the value of $50 or less, the other where the value was above $50.

[53] *Cf.* "Thomas Angley was convicted this week of receiving stolen goods, witnesses testifying that he had received $2 for disposing of plumbing supplies stolen from a vacant house. . . . Judge Downs remarked, 'I am ashamed to have to pronounce this sentence (twenty years imprisonment); it is absolutely unjust and unfair.' " *New York Times,* May 19, 1934.

The statute provided for the alternative punishment, "or by a fine of not more than one thousand dollars."

[54] Harold W. Hastings, Esq., Assistant District Attorney of New York County criticized this change as follows: "It would seem much better to have retained the degrees in the crime of receiving so that in the case of a petty receiver he could be prosecuted as a misdemeanant by information. It would without doubt lead to many more convictions. Is it not obvious that most juries will hesitate to convict a man and make him liable to tremendous punishment for receiving such small items as a crate of tomatoes or a package of cigarettes or a ten dollar ring?" The Panel (Nov.-Dec. 1932) 51.

[55] I do not maintain that severer punishment would be beneficial. What I do submit is that a *discriminate* classification and treatment, guided by the social problem, are required.

Within the past decade several states have sought to deal more adequately with professional receivers through the media of habitual offender laws.[56] Without going into the question of the efficacy of these laws in general,[57] it may be pointed out that although they may be of some assistance, they do not fit the problem in hand because:

1. Receivers are not habitual offenders *in the sense of the phrase as used in these acts.*[58]

2. It is so difficult to secure a conviction against a professional receiver that as to him a law based upon the assumption that a past *criminal record* is available, can rarely operate effectively.

3. Since receiving is often a misdemeanor under most statutes, it is necessary to introduce several records of convictions.

4. Even if it be conceded that these laws might otherwise operate with efficiency, they would not accomplish the necessary end because they do not differentiate between receivers who buy for consumption and those who buy for resale. A woman who knowingly bought a stolen fur coat, then a stolen diamond ring or a dress, could be treated exactly in the same manner as a professional receiver. Accordingly, although skillfull administration of the habitual criminal laws would go some distance toward meeting the problem of professional receiving, they do not provide an adequate solution.

Returning to the specific problem of differentiation of professional from other receivers,[59] we recall the following unique characteristics:

1. The professional receiver *buys for the purpose of resale,* whereas the lay receiver buys for consumption.

---

[56] Fla. Stat. sec. 811.18 (1949); Ill. Stat. c. 38, sec. 493 (1943), Ann. (Jones 1936) sec. 37.452; Maine Stat. c. 119, sec. 11 (1944); Mass. Ann. Laws c. 266, sec. 62 (1933); Mich. Comp. Laws, sec. 750.535 (1948).

[57] It is generally recognized that these acts cause prosecutors to waive felony charges in order to avoid the infliction of the maximum term of imprisonment.

[58] *Supra* pp. 155–156.

[59] There are intermediate groups of persons who buy occasionally for resale. These are omitted for the present in order to simplify the problem. Even if it were true that receivers cannot in fact be sharply divided, this would not affect the problem of treating the extremes differently, *i.e.,* of the need to construct at least two broad classes.

2. Hence the professional receiver *sells* stolen merchandise whereas the lay receiver *consumes* the goods.

3. The professional receiver *operates a business;* he *deals in* stolen commodities and is apt to be *in possession of a relatively large amount of such commodities, derived from different thefts and thieves,* as a stock in trade; the lay receiver does not operate a business nor does he deal in or possess a large quantity of stolen commodities.

Since it is factually and socially valid to place dealers in stolen property in a special class, greater punishment may be imposed for receiving by such a dealer than for other criminal receiving. This would not violate the Anglo-American principle that criminal liability is based upon conduct.[60] There is conduct —the act of receiving (or selling). It would merely recognize that single acts of receiving have differential social significance. Just as in the case of habitual offenders, so here—the same criminal conduct, receiving, is more serious when it is committed by a dealer in stolen goods. The "social definition" of a professional's receiving is that a graver harm has been committed. This is surely supported by sufficient facts to render such a legislative judgment "reasonable." In the penal codes of a number of foreign countries professional receivers have long been segregated. They are distinguished from persons who knowingly buy stolen goods for their own consumption and the former are subjected to much severer punishment.[61]

---

[60] Hall, General Principles of Criminal Law (1947) 11, 252.

[61] The following instances may be cited:

The Criminal Code of the German Empire. Receiving stolen goods knowingly (sec. 259)—Liable to confinement—same punishment as for theft (sec. 242). Sec. 260—Anyone who makes a business or practice of receiving shall be liable to imprisonment not to exceed 10 years.

Penal Code of the Union of Soviet Republics (sec. 181). The purchasing of goods known as stolen is punished by forced labor or "deprivation of liberty" for not more than one year.

The same crime, if committed as a business or for the purpose of sale, is punished by "deprivation of liberty" for not less than one year and by confiscation of the chattels.

The Swiss Federal Criminal Code of 1937, Art. 144, provides for three classes of criminal receivers with penalties ranging from a fine in "minor cases" to not over ten years' imprisonment "if the offender makes a business," etc. See 30 J. Cr. L. Supp. 52 (1939).

Although social research and foreign penal law establish the validity of separating the dealer in stolen goods from non-professional receivers for both definitional and treatment purposes and, at the same time, no principle of Anglo-American criminal law opposes that, the legislative problem is not simple. New York has had the widest experience in such legislation, hence its law merits further examination. The New York law is far from settled on this subject, but we can determine the principal issues and consider such partial solutions as have been reached.

It will be recalled [62] that in the Rosenthal Case, the United States Supreme Court upheld the constitutionality of the 1903 amendment which made it criminal for a "dealer in . . . junk, metals, or secondhand materials" to receive certain stolen property "without ascertaining by diligent inquiry that the person selling or delivering the same has a legal right to do so." Two points should now be added to our previous discussion of this case: (1) Neither the Supreme Court nor the Court of Appeals defined "dealer" and, indeed, the defendant did not raise any issue as to that. (2) Both courts implied that the 1903 amendment did not depart from the existing New York requirement as to *mens rea* in criminal receiving. That requirement was assumed to be the "objective test" ("circumstances such as would have put an honest or prudent man upon inquiry"); and "diligent inquiry" was held to be only a "further requirement." Moreover, "if the goods have in fact been stolen, a diligent inquiry into the right of the present possessor to make sale or delivery of them *will very surely tend to disclose* the larcenous origin of his title." [63] The objective test, however unsound it may be, is upheld in some states; and at least as to dealers in junk and secondhand materials the amendment is factually defensible. [64] In sum, the 1903 amendment advanced solution of the problem in a particular acute area.

---

[62] *Supra* p. 213.

[63] 33 S. Ct. 29. Italics added.

[64] Despite dicta in the Rosenthal Case by both the Court of Appeals and the Supreme Court, there seems to be no New York case, and none was cited, which holds the objective test sufficient in receiving stolen property. P. *v.* Gold, 267 N. Y. S. 582 (1933) contains dicta enunciating both rules.

It should be well noted, however, that the amendment speaks of a "dealer in junk," *not* of a dealer in stolen goods. The like is true of all the subsequent amendments and, thus, of the New York law today. Moreover neither the 1903 nor the 1928 amendment provided any other punishment for the dealer than for a person who criminally received goods for his own consumption. Thus it appears that the central thrust of the New York law, as of 1928, was (1) to treat certain dealers' conduct (dealers in secondhand books were also included and in 1938 persons engaged in the business of supplying "clean laundered articles of property" were added) as criminal receiving, and (2) to raise a rebuttable presumption of criminal knowledge in "a dealer in or collector of *any* merchandise or property" who "fails to make reasonable inquiry," etc.[65] Insofar as this was control of dealing in stolen property, which was surely intended, it was an oblique attack. It did not grapple directly with the *dealer in stolen goods*. It still held his conduct equivalent, as regards penal treatment, with that of "Aunt Emma" who, arriving from Pleasantville on her first trip to Metropolis, believed the tear-wringing story of the sidewalk seller of a stolen thimble and bought it. Both "Aunt Emma" and the professional dealer in stolen goods were guilty of a felony, and both were felons regardless of the value of the property received. Both might have been sentenced to imprisonment for as long as twenty years.[66]

In 1943 several important changes were made in the New York law. The former traditional classification was re-adopted and the crime became a misdemeanor if the value of the property received was not more than one hundred dollars.[67] Much more significant is the provision that the crime is a felony "regardless of the value of such property, *if it was purchased for resale or by a dealer, or* if the defendant has been previously convicted of the crime of buying, receiving, concealing or withholding stolen property as herein defined. . . ." (italics added).

---

[65] Italics added.

[66] In 1940 the maximum imprisonment was reduced to ten years. Session Laws 1940, ch. 443

[67] Session Laws 1943, ch. 180.

Here, for the first time in this country, was a statute directly addressed to some of the distinctive social facts of professional receiving.[68] It remains true, however, that the "dealer" designated in the statute is not (by legal provision) a dealer *in stolen goods*. Apart from the fact that an otherwise legitimate businessman who made one purchase of stolen goods, might fall within the statutory definition, the plain indication is that the central character of professional receiving still eludes the New York legislature. Other serious questions remain unsolved because of uncertainty regarding the relevant *mens rea*.[69] Fi-

---

[68] Certain serious problems remain unsolved. The term "dealer" in the above quoted clause of the present New York statute (1308, 1, d.) *follows* three specified types of dealers, namely, those dealing in junk, secondhand books, and laundry supplies. See Appendix, *infra*. This indicates that "dealer" in the quoted clause designates those types of dealer and no others. But a subsequent provision (the 1928 amendment) raises a presumption of criminal knowledge in "a dealer in . . . junk, metals, or *any other* merchandise or property." The italicized words may have been intended to include only dealers in secondhand books (a separate paragraph concerns laundry supplies) or junk dealers who buy property other than junk or metals (an earlier clause provides "junk, metals or secondhand materials"). An additional possibility, *i.e.*, that all other dealers are included is hardly tenable because the provision has been held to constitute a rule of evidence, not one of substantive law. See P. *v.* Estreich, 75 N. Y. S. 2d at 271, (1947), aff'd. 297 N. Y. 910, 79 N. E. 2d 742 (1948), which declared unconstitutional section 1.b of 1308, which held a junk dealer strictly liable since it lacked the qualification of "reasonable inquiry" included in the former statute. This qualification was restored by amendment in 1949. Similar laws are Cal. Deering Penal Code, sec. 496a (1949), and Mich. Comp. Laws, sec. 750.535 (1948).

[69] In 1910, in the Rosenthal Case, the Court of Appeals noted a loophole in the law preceding the 1903 amendment, namely, "it would be difficult if not impossible, owing to the nature of the [junk] business and the way it is carried on, to prove knowledge or circumstances imputing knowledge." Under the 1903 amendment, a junk dealer is "guilty of a crime, whether he actually knew it had been stolen or not, provided he did not try to find out by making diligent inquiry." 197 N. Y. 399, 400 (1910). *Cf.* the remarks of the United States Supreme Court, quoted above.
In 1920, P. *v.* Brown, 182 N. Y. S. 115, held that sec. 1308 prescribed two offenses, common law receiving which required knowledge that the goods were stolen, and another "unknown to the common law," which required diligent inquiry, but not knowledge that the property was stolen.
In 1932, P. *v.* Nelson, 255 N. Y. S. 558, discussed above, held that 1308 created only one crime, not two, as the defendant contended on the basis of the Brown Case. The one crime, just as did common law receiving, required criminal knowledge. The court rested this decision on the 1928 amendment which raised a presumption of such knowledge in the case of a dealer; but it entirely overlooked the 1903 amendment which imposed the duty of diligent inquiry.

nally, and most important, there is no differentiation of punishment to be applied to the very different types of felons who fall within the wide range of the legal definition.

All the more significant, therefore, is the proposed Bill of the Wisconsin Legislative Council [70] which speaks directly in terms of "a dealer in stolen property," defines such a dealer, utilizes his possession of other stolen property to establish that he is a dealer, and fixes a much more severe punishment for such offenders.

To summarize: reform of the criminal law should proceed along the following lines:

1. Receiving or selling stolen property knowingly, together with possession of other stolen goods, places the defendant in the category of a dealer in stolen goods. The possession of a quantity of stolen goods would be evidence, also (if not a presumption), that the particular property in question was known to be stolen.[71]

2. Receiving and selling knowingly but without possession of other stolen goods would raise a presumption that the defendant was a dealer in stolen goods. If this presumption were

---

The very next year in P. v. Gold, 267 N. Y. S. 582 (1933) the same judge who wrote the Nelson opinion held, without reference to the Nelson Case, that 1308 included two crimes. Under the statutory crime of receiving stolen property, knowledge is immaterial where no diligent inquiry was made by defendant as to the right of the person from whom he received the book to dispose of the same." Id. 586. This still leaves unsolved the effect of paragraph 3 which raises a rebuttable presumption of criminal knowledge in the case of a dealer.

Finally, in 1947, in P. v. Estreich, 75 N. Y. S. 2d 267, it was again held that 1308 includes two crimes: "that defined in the second was unknown at common law and was purely statutory." Id. 269, citing the Brown and Gold cases, and the Rosenthal Case, as sustaining the constitutionality of the statutory crime.

Subdivision 3 of 1308 "merely prescribes a rule of evidence, and is not part of the definition of the substantive crime." Id. 271. The difficulty here however is that "dealer" is not referred to in the first part of 1308, that restating common law receiving; and the second category, which does specify dealer, is now definitely held not to require criminal knowledge.

[70] The Wisconsin Bill, sec. 343.22 of No. 784 S. is reprinted in the Appendix.

[71] Provision might be made for giving the defendant notice that evidence will be introduced of his being in possession of stolen goods not shown in the indictment. With reference to the use of presumptions, see P. v. Terra et al., 102 N. E. 2d 576 (N. Y. Ct. of Appeals, 1951).

overcome, the defendant would then be within the category of a non-professional receiver.

3. Receiving or selling knowingly, with no evidence of possession of other stolen merchandise, would raise the presumption that the defendant was a dealer in stolen goods if he was engaged in one of certain businesses, e.g. jewelry, automobile, furs, junk, secondhand books or laundry supplies.

4. Penalties for receiving or selling by a dealer in stolen property, without regard to value, should be much more severe than for receiving by one not such a dealer.

5. Intermediate offenses would relate (a) to persons who, though not dealers in stolen goods, had been previously convicted of criminal receiving, and (b) to persons in certain businesses who buy stolen property without criminal knowledge and without making a diligent inquiry.

6. The least offense would be lay or simple receiving of stolen goods knowingly.

Finally, it may be suggested that there is much need for a better method than those now employed to refute explanations of recent possession. Certainly something better than spontaneous instructions regarding the irregularities of conducting the defendant's business can be provided to aid the jury in correct fact-finding and to raise a presumption of criminal knowledge. For, in addition to the pattern described above, it is clear that, characteristic of this type of criminal transaction is the fact that *the property in question was not purchased in the usual course of trade.* Almost invariably, for example, cash is paid for stolen merchandise despite the fact that such transactions, when legal, are on credit. The sellers rarely have any established place of business. They are not listed in trade reports. The merchandise is sold for much less than its market price.

It may, perhaps, be impossible to formulate a definition of "usual course of trade" which will fit all businesses.[72] However,

---

[72] The Association of Grand Jurors of New York County has summarized these characteristics as follows:

"When a commodity is offered for sale to a business-wise merchant, firm in each of the businesses chiefly involved, there are established, standardized ways of operating legitimately, which could be described and made the basis for a presumption of guilt. Furthermore, no reason appears *a priori* why a minimum definition could not be formulated which would apply generally.

V. FEDERAL LEGISLATION

Several attempts were made to secure passage of federal legislation designed to cope with the problem of interstate

---

or corporation it is reasonable to presume that he or it knows or will ascertain, before buying, certain things. These are:

1. The market value of the commodity.
2. The cause for its price being disproportionately low.
3. That certain identification marks usually appearing on the article or its container have not been removed or altered.
4. That the seller has the legal right to sell and conforms to the customs of the trade in so doing.
5. That the seller represents a firm known to the trade or is personally known to the buyer.
6. That the seller has a permanent address.
7. If the seller is a stranger to the buyer that he can furnish trade and other reliable references as to his good standing.
8. That nothing connected with the seller or his goods indicates fraud." Prison Committee of the Association of Grand Jurors of New York County, Criminal Receivers in the United States (1928) 69–70.

And they have added the recommendations of experts in this field:

"Mr. Leon Hoage, of the New York office of the Holmes Electric Protection Company, already mentioned, holds that an alleged Fence should be required to explain to the jury acts or omissions, such as the following:

1. Failure to keep bona fide books of account in connection with a business enterprise.
2. Neglect of dealer to keep bills received with goods delivered to him, for a reasonable period, such as two years.
3. Omission of the dealer to demand and keep as bills the receipts given in his commercial transactions.
4. Lack of itemized bills of job lots of standard goods purchased, apart from the balance of the items.
5. Inability or unwillingness of the possessor of goods ostensibly covered by a bill of sale from a reputable firm, to communicate with the firm, at the time the purchase is made, to corroborate the sale.
6. Presentation of a bill of sale, the billhead of which gives the name and address of a non-existent firm.
7. Purchase of valuable merchandise from a push cart, or similarly unreliable vendor." *Id.* 70–1.

Competent prosecutors, of course, make use of the irregular features of such transactions. My suggestion runs to giving necessary and proper judicial support.

theft,[73] which culminated in the enactment of the law approved
May 22, 1934.[74] The bill [75] which was most discussed was that
introduced on January 31, 1929 by Representative LaGuardia.[76]
Its proponents emphasized the following points:

1. "With the growth of transportation in this country there
has come into existence the interstate fence; so that goods
which are stolen from railroad cars, transportation companies,
or are stolen in great cities and gotten into railroads and sent
over State lines are received and with relative safety disposed

---

[73] U. S. Stats. 37: 670, c. 50, Feb. 13, 1913; *cf.* Sutherland and Gehlke, in
Recent Social Trends at 1119; Hall, *Federal Anti-Theft Legislation* (1934)
1 Law and Contemporary Problems 424.

[74] Public Act—No. 246—73rd Congress, S. 2845, An Act to extend the provisions of the National Motor Vehicle Theft Act to other stolen property.

[75] A similar bill was the Yates-Cummings (H. R. 7472) introduced January
12, 1926. Next came H. R. 96, introduced on December 5, 1927. This bill was
opposed by the Department of Justice and other government officials. Attorney-
General Sargent and H. W. Lord of the Treasury Department opposed it because it was "in conflict with the financial program of the President." Letters
in the Cong. Rec. Feb. 5, 1930, 3228, published in connection with the debate
on H. R. 10287. J. Edgar Hoover opposed the passage of the bill because it
"would make a veritable police force of Federal investigating agents throughout the country"; it would "require a large number of special agents to
properly enforce it"; substantially increased appropriations would be required
to enforce the law; and that, in any event, a minimum of $1,000 should be
involved before Federal jurisdiction should attach. *Id.* 3229–3230.

[76] H. R. 10287, "A Bill to prohibit the sending and receipt of the stolen
property through interstate and foreign commerce." The LaGuardia bill was
referred to the House Committee on the Judiciary, which held hearings on
April 3 and 4, 1928.
As preliminary persuasive information, the Committee was told that the
National Crime Commission was "earnestly in favor of the bill" (21); that it
was the only bill before Congress which the Commission thus actively favored; that it was in strict analogy to the interstate automobile law (Dyer
Act); that it probably had the "widest publicity and the most favorable reception of any piece of proposed legislation for a long time of anything like the
same character." (8) Two hundred and fifty editorials appearing in newspapers
in all the states were filed along with letters from prosecuting attorneys, attor-
neys-general and numerous representatives of business interests. (14) William
Green, President of the American Federation of Labor, stated that in supporting
the proposed bill he was "but reflecting the sentiment and the feelings of millions of working men and women in this country." (15) He said that labor was
injured by the sale of stolen goods in competition with merchandise manufactured and sold legitimately. Justin Miller reported that the members of the
American Bar Association committee were unanimously in favor of the bill, and
he filed letters from a number of judges and leading attorneys. (56) Hearing
before the Committee on the Judiciary, House of Representatives, on H. R.
10287, Serial 19, Govt. Pr. Off. (1928).

ot by criminals in other places than the scene of the crime . . . the use of an interstate transportation agency practically puts these stolen goods into interstate commerce." [77]

2. The chief virtue of the bill would be "*in terrorem,*" that is, "it serves notice on the maintainers of interstate fences that they have the Federal Government to deal with and can no longer count upon the difficulties with which States are embarrassed." [78]

3. Related to the above, was the suggestion that there was little local interest in prosecuting a receiver in cases where the theft was committed outside of the state because in such cases there was no injured complainant on hand to press the case.

4. Considerable advantage, it was said, would result from the ability of the national government to subpœna witnesses from all parts of the country. At present, if the receiver is located in New York and the thief in California, it is impossible for New York to compel attendance of the latter; yet proof of the theft is indispensable to conviction of the receiver in New York. Similarly, California cannot extradite witnesses from New York or any other state, to testify in a prosecution for the theft. [79]

5. Frequently receivers and thieves who participate in one transaction are located in several states. Under the present laws, a number of prosecutions are required because each state can proceed only against those individuals who have committed a crime within its jurisdiction. Accordingly, a multiplicity of prosecutions would be avoided by the adoption of a federal law.

6. Related to the above point was the recommendation stressed especially by several prosecutors, that the conspiracy law could be utilized to great advantage in the prosecution of receivers and thieves. [80] Not only could all the receivers who had

---

[77] Newton D. Baker's statement, *id.* 3.

[78] *Ibid.*

[79] *Cf.* J. P. Chamberlain, *Anti-Fence Legislation* (1928) 14 A. B. A. J. 520.

[80] "Assistant District Attorney Carstarphen expresses the opinion that 'Fences' could be convicted for the crime of conspiracy more readily than that of receiving stolen goods, but conspiracy is a misdemeanor and not a felony under existing [N. Y.] law." (Apr. 1927) 5 The Panel 1.

collaborated in one transaction be tried together, but all the thieves, agents, and other participants could also be joined in the prosecution. The conspiracy law would provide the necessary substantive law for joining the offenders and the recommended jurisdictional reforms would eliminate existing procedural difficulties.[81] It was urged that the presentation of a complete picture of this type of crime would result in more certain conviction than is now secured when the transaction must be split up, and only a part of the criminal behavior is presented.[82]

The chief concern of some of the Committee members was the opposition anticipated to the placing of additional burdens upon the federal government. It was suggested that it might be preferable to have the individual states extradite witnesses, even if it were necessary to amend the Constitution to do this.[83]

Another difficulty, which Mr. Baker conceded, was the possibility that the right to initiate prosecution might be abused, e.g., a merchant domiciled in California who received stolen goods from a thief who was in New York might be tried in any district through which the merchandise had been carried. The Committee was divided on this point; underlying this conflict in viewpoint were the usual diverse *assumptions* regarding the guilt or innocence of the persons who might be accused of the crime.

The problem that aroused the greatest discussion arose from the omission to make guilty knowledge an essential element of the crime.[84] Justin Miller suggested that "the bill might well be

---

[81] Hearing before the Committee on the Judiciary on H. R. 10287, at 10, 44.

[82] It was apparently assumed by all parties throughout the hearings and debates on the proposed bill that there were no difficulties in the substantive law to complicate prosecution by states. But *cf.* Part V of the Rep. Special Com. etc. (1925) 11 A. B. A. J. 738, 739–40.

[83] Hearing before the Committee on the Judiciary on H. R. 10287, at 29. *Cf.* The American Law Institute, Code of Criminal Procedure (Official Draft, June 15, 1930) secs. 56–8; and *id.* (Proposed Final Draft, April 1, 1930) secs. 320–1. And see the Uniform Criminal Extradition Act.

[84] Thus, Mr. Lewis Hahn, Manager-Director of the National Retail Dry Goods Association, had serious apprehensions regarding the possibility of honest tradesmen being brought within the terms of the bill as proposed. He pointed out that a large department store might have 750,000 separate items of mer-

amended to provide that . . . the defendant so received or
came into possession of the same under such circumstances as
to put a reasonable man upon inquiry; and then a failure on
his part to inquire." [85] The proposed bill already contained the
words "notwithstanding good reason to believe" and so forth,
but these words were deemed too broad. Mr. J. Weston Allen,
representing the American Bar Association, first pointed out
that the rule would "require the establishment of the fact that
the defendant believed that there was necessity for inquiry." [86]
Mr. Allen then made the suggestion, which was subsequently
adopted,[87] that the knowledge of the particular defendant and
not that of a "reasonable man" should be the standard employed.[88]

Representatives of the railroads and other carriers and of
the banking interests urged two amendments to the bill. They

---

chandise, some of which were purchased in small quantities. Said he: "I should
like to see this bill so worded that it would be impossible for a man who, amid
all those thousands or hundreds of thousands of transactions might happen to
buy something, not knowing that there was anything the matter with it, to be
put in an embarrassing situation.

"If we are going to put the burden of making diligent or reasonable inquiry
upon every buyer in every large store, I think it would result in being a well-
nigh intolerable burden."

[85] Hearing before the Committee on the Judiciary on H. R. 10287, at 58.

[86] *Id.* 70.

[87] "Whoever shall buy, receive, possess, conceal, sell or dispose of any property or thing of value, which is moving as, or which is part of, or which con-
stitutes, interstate or foreign commerce, or commerce between the District of
Columbia and some State or foreign nation, and which theretofore or while
so moving or constituting such part, had been stolen or taken feloniously by
fraud or with intent to steal or purloin, knowing the same to have been stolen
or taken, or whoever shall buy, receive, possess, conceal, sell, or dispose of any
such property or thing of value under such circumstances as should put him
upon inquiry whether the same had been so stolen or taken, without making
reasonable inquiry in good faith to ascertain the fact, shall be punished by a
fine of not more than $10,000 or by imprisonment for not more than ten
years, or both." H. R. 119, sec. 3.

[88] "I think there is very sound reason for saying that the test should not be
whether an ordinary man would have been put on inquiry." Hearing on H. R.
10287 at 75.

Cf. Justin Miller: "Personally I do not agree with General Allen on that
point. I believe the bill should put this man on inquiry, under such circumstances that an ordinary man would be put on inquiry, regardless of whether
or not you could prove that he knew or believed that he should make inquiry.
Of course that is a matter of policy for you to determine." *Id.* 82.

desired to except common carriers from the operation of the bill; and they requested a special provision regarding negotiable instruments acquired in due course. Both of these suggested amendments were subsequently adopted.[89] The other change made in the proposed bill was to increase the punishment from not more than a fine of $5,000 or imprisonment for not more than two years, or both, to a fine of not more than $10,000, or imprisonment for not more than ten years or both.

The proposed bill, with the changes noted above, was introduced into the House at various times. The proponents of the bill marshalled their forces. With its Judiciary Committee strongly supporting it, debate took place in the House on February 5, 1930.[90] The bill was adopted by the House and sent to the Senate where it was referred to the Committee on the Judiciary. The federal administration took active steps to defeat the measure. Attorney General Mitchell vigorously opposed the bill,[91] and it was defeated in the Senate Judiciary Committee.

---

[89] See the revised bill, secs. 2 and 5.

[90] The objections raised by the opponents of this bill were as follows: (1) that conferring jurisdiction upon the federal courts in petty larceny cases was an invasion of the States' powers; (2) that the passage of the bill would cause further congestion in the already too crowded federal courts and, in addition, cause crowded conditions in the federal jails; (3) that the bill was too inclusive in its scope (a) in that the punishment for the theft of a nickel was the same as that for the theft of a million dollars (the bill was later amended by making it apply only to property of a value in excess of $300), (b) that the bill, as drawn, was not limited to the fence, that is those making it a business to buy stolen property; (4) that the punishment was too severe; and finally (5) that the bill had not been submitted by the Judiciary Committee to the Department of Justice in order that the latter's opinion might be obtained.

[91] Attorney General Mitchell stated:

"There are two serious objections to this measure: In the first place, I am opposed on principle to extending the activities of the Federal Government into fields heretofore occupied by the States unless there are very cogent reasons for so doing, and I am not satisfied that there is any urgent reason at the present time why the Federal Government should take on this additional function and increase its activities accordingly.

"In the next place, even though this measure may ultimately be found to be justified, this is not a proper time for its enactment. The machinery now provided by the Federal Government for the prosecution and punishment of crime is overtaxed.

"Earnest efforts are being made to devise methods for the relief of those

Thus, even the powerful interests which supported this bill were unable to secure its passage in the face of opposition by the national administration. It should be said, however, that in the opinion of competent observers, the bill would have passed had its advocates been more skillfully organized. Beneath much of the expressed opposition from representatives of rural districts was the thought that the bill was a "big city" interest, and that the country at large should not pay for the solution of what was deemed to be a metropolitan problem.[92]

There were, indeed, data to support the claim that the passage of the bill in 1930 would have placed too great a burden upon the federal government. During the preceding twenty-five years there had been an enormous increase in federal criminal litigation. Thus we are told by Sutherland and Gehlke in *Recent Social Trends* that:

"Four federal laws enacted since 1910 have added immensely to the work of the federal agencies and also of some local agencies. These are the laws in regard to white slavery, narcotic drugs, national prohibition and interstate transportation of stolen automobiles. In 1910 the federal courts had no prosecutions for the offenses above mentioned. In 1920 these four contributed 27.3 per cent of all federal prosecutions and in 1930 72.2 percent. In 1910 they accounted for none of the commitments to federal prisons, in 1920 for 15.2 per cent of such commitments and in 1930 for 82.9 per cent."

In 1933, the repeal of the prohibition amendment was fol-

Federal courts which are congested, and to increase the capacity of our prisons to satisfy present requirements.

"Until we have dealt adequately with the troubles which now confront us we ought not to be adding to the burden of the law enforcement machinery by enacting legislation of this kind.

"Experience has shown that when Congress enacts criminal legislation of this type the tendency is for the State authorities to cease their efforts towards punishing the offenders and to leave it to the Federal authorities and the Federal courts. That has been the experience under the Dyer Act." The United States Daily, April 1, 1930, p. 2.

Cf. Pres. Hoover's remarks, 57 Ann. Rep. A. B. A. (1932) 287-8.

[92] Thus one representative stated: "We cannot consider this bill from the point of view of New York or a few other large centers that are troubled by this particular evil." Congressional Record (Feb. 5, 1930) 3233.

lowed by a series of kidnaping and other sensational crimes which aroused the country. The elimination of prohibition cases removed a great burden from federal officials. Several laws were enacted enlarging the boundaries of the federal criminal law. Among them was the law extending the provisions of the National Motor Vehicle Theft Act to other stolen property.[93]

The federal statute on interstate traffic in stolen goods follows the traditional lines of criminal legislation. No attempt was made to distinguish among various businesses. Nor was the statute drafted with reference to social facts which differentiate the business of dealing in stolen goods from non-professional receiving. It is evident that the federal government lags behind New York, Wisconsin, and other states with regard to important criminal legislation.

---

[93] The law provided that:

"SEC. 3. Whoever shall transport or cause to be transported in interstate of foreign commerce any goods, wares, or merchandise, securities, or money, of the value of $5,000 or more theretofore stolen or taken feloniously by fraud or with intent to steal or purloin, knowing the same to have been so stolen or taken, shall be punished by a fine of not more than $10,000 or by imprisonment for not more than ten years, or both.

"SEC. 4. Whoever shall receive, conceal, store, barter, sell or dispose of any goods, wares, or merchandise, securities, or money, of the value of $5,000 or more, or whoever shall pledge or accept as security for a loan any goods, wares, or merchandise, or securities of the value of $500 or more which, while moving in or constituting a part of interstate or foreign commerce, has been stolen or taken feloniously by fraud or with intent to steal or purloin, knowing the same to have been stolen or taken, shall be punished by a fine of not more than $10,000 or by imprisonment of not more than ten years, or both."

The present law is stated in U. S. Code Ann. Tit. 18, secs. 2314 and 2315.

CHAPTER SIX

AUTOMOBILE THEFT

After careful research on various crimes, Professor R. M. Perkins concluded that automobile theft "presents the most acute problem of unsolved crimes to be found in this study. . . . [In] auto theft, a subject is uncovered which seems to demand special study." [1] Beyond the particular significance of this subject, the larceny of automobiles involves other types of theft and reveals important characteristics of legal institutions. We have, moreover, reached the point in this book where explicit indications of the methods and conceptual plan employed may be more definitely illustrated, e.g. in the divisions of this chapter and the subjects discussed. A study of auto theft lends itself readily to that purpose.

I. The Social Problem

The social problem of automobile theft depends upon the following factors:

1. The frequency of the offense.

2. The pecuniary loss sustained by persons whose property is stolen, and by persons who innocently purchase stolen property (automobiles).

3. The cost of theft insurance.

4. The ecology of this crime, that is, the location and spatial limits of the criminal behavior.

5. The existence and size of a market for stolen property (automobiles and accessories), and the effect of this upon the business of legitimate dealers and other interests.

6. The use to which stolen goods not resold, are put, especially the use of stolen automobiles in the commission of serious offenses, and the effect, in general, upon the range, speed, and detection of crime.

---

[1] Perkins, Iowa Criminal Justice (1932) Sup. to No. 4, 17 Iowa L. Rev. 66.

233

7. To which should be added: various subtle, injurious effects of this type of criminal behavior, not capable of exact determination but susceptible of common sense appreciation.

1. *Special Features of the Motor Vehicle as a Factor in Its Theft*

Theft of automobiles is a problem which was born within the memory of most persons alive today. The abruptness and magnitude of the technological change is the most striking fact about the automobile. In 1895 there were four automobiles in the United States; in 1900 there were 8,000; in 1905 there were 77,400 and by 1910 almost half a million. In 1929, there were over 23,000,000 passenger cars and almost three and one-half million trucks registered in the United States. In 1941 there were 29,524,101 passenger cars. The number declined during the War, then rose to 30,718,852 in 1947. In 1948 there were 33,261,454 passenger cars in the United States[2] and in 1950, there were over 40,000,000. Sheer quantity is the first factor that makes possible their large-scale theft.

Another factor is the relatively high value of this chattel per unit.[3] Steel, foundry, machinery, and petroleum are too bulky or heavy to be stolen to any great extent. Such products as meat are perishable. Motor cars not only last; they not only have considerable value per unit. They roll on their own wheels. Is it strange that they should loom up in our theft-

---

[2] Facts and Figures of the Automobile Industry (1949).

[3] The 1929 census of manufacture places the value of the products of the automobile industry first in the nation, the estimate being almost four billions of dollars. Motor vehicle bodies and parts are valued at an additional billion and a half dollars. *Id.* (1932) 55.

Value of Property Stolen, by Type of Crime, 1949.

(Based on the reports of 346 cities over 25,000 in population, total population 37,480,886. All figures are stated in proximate even dollars.)

Classification	Average value per offense
Robbery	$172
Burglary	$116
Larceny-theft	$ 56
Auto-theft	$835

Source: 20 Unif. Cr. Rep. (No. 2, 1949) 110, Table 43.

problem as cattle did in that of the early English? Add that the car is left exposed on the streets—like range cattle, once, in the West. The automobile becomes the perfect chattel for modern large-scale theft.

Nor is this all. The chattel taken provides the means of the thief's escape. He who steals from a residence or breaks into a warehouse or place of business must supply his own means of escaping with the loot. Moreover, automobiles are driven by all classes of persons. Carrying fur coats or pictures arouses attention; driving an automobile or truckful of merchandise arouses no more than carrying a packet of jewels.

Related to these data is the fact that automobile theft is of unique importance as a standard part of the equipment for commission of serious crimes.[4] Major Goddard, a ballistics expert, believes that the automobile is much more important than the gun in the commission of crimes.[5] The reasons are clear: the automobile accelerates criminal activities; the possibility of effective surprise rises tenfold; the time required to

---

[4] That this development is not confined to the United States appears from an article by L. W. Lockhart, writing in the *New York Times* (Feb. 15, 1933). He states:

"For a long time we in England have read of the doings of the American gangster with happy detachment. Now we find ourselves threatened by a similar menace . . . As for the younger criminals, they belong to a mechanically minded generation which understands the mysteries of internal-combustion engines. To such as these the motor car becomes as essential a part of the thief's equipment as the jimmy. . . . It is reported that of 5,086 motor cars stolen in the London area in a year 4,869 were recovered shortly after, having been used for the commission of some illegal act."

Cf. "Even where it does not appear, the use of the automobile is often implied, as for example in murder, robbery, burglary, kidnapping, bootlegging and gang warfare. Along with good roads, it has made the small town and the open country accessible to the criminal. The motorization of criminals has done much to compel the motorization of the police as well as the adoption of radio and teletype communication by police departments. It may yet force a centralization of police administration over larger areas than have ever been under unified control." Sutherland and Gehlke, *Crime and Punishment,* 2 Recent Social Trends 1135.

See Bruce Smith, A Regional Police Plan for Cincinnati and its Environs; and in the Criminal Statistics for England and Wales (1928) pp. xiii, xiv is an interesting discussion of the significance of motor vehicles for crime in the suburban area around London.

[5] *The Motor Car and Crime* (1932) 22 J. Crim. L. and Criminol. 650.

commit the crime is reduced to seconds; armament is concealed; escape is instantaneous and inconspicuous; the locus
of the crime may be hundreds of miles from the starting-point
of the offenders. By necessity, the process of detection and of
apprehension must be vastly accelerated over that of the pre-
automobile era, and the area of search is greatly expanded.[6]
Thus, the unique characteristics of the automobile undoubtedly
contribute to the gravity of automobile theft as a social problem.

2. The Frequency of Auto Theft

Attempts to explain social problems by the use of quantitative methods alone are almost always unsatisfactory. Not only
are the available data incomplete, but concealed and untenable assumptions are too often made. But there are a number
of important purposes which such data can serve. For example,
though we know that large numbers of automobiles are stolen
and that the number of these thefts exceeds most other types,
we still have no *clear* appreciation of the relative magnitude of
the offense. Again, we may know that a large number of stolen
automobiles are recovered, but our knowledge becomes peculiarly significant if we know that ninety-five per cent of such
vehicles are recovered rather than forty or fifty per cent.

It is difficult, if not impossible, to determine the exact number of automobiles stolen in the United States each year.
Adequate national data do not exist; the best that can be done
is to utilize fragmentary materials as a probable index. There

---

[6] A number of states have fixed especially severe penalties in cases where
an automobile has been used in the commission of a crime, *viz.*, Penal Law of
New York, sec. 1944. Consol. Laws (McKinney, 1944).
   Cf. "Indiana, Chap. 32, 1921 [Burns, 4 Ann. Ind. Stats. 10–4710.] sets up
the crime of automobile banditry, a felony committed by two or more persons
who have an automobile, airplane or other self-moving appliance in which they
attempt or intend to escape, or who use such a conveyance in attempting to
escape after committing a felony. The seriousness of the crime is shown by
the penalty which is ten to twenty-five years in prison. The legislature of
Missouri, 1921, p. 280, punishes the person who uses a motor vehicle either
to assist in or escape from a robbery, no matter of what degree, as guilty of
robbery in the first degree." J. P. Chamberlain, *Automobiles and Crime* (1925)
11 A. B. A. J. 374.

are at present two relatively reliable sources: the National
Automobile Underwriters Association, whose members cover
approximately two-thirds of the insured automobiles in the
United States, and the Uniform Crime Reports issued by the
Bureau of Investigation of the Department of Justice in Washington, first published in 1930. I shall precede the examination
of these reports by a summarization of prior data compiled
by the National Automobile Underwriters Association.

The National Commission on Law Observance and Enforcement in its Report on the Cost of Crime, utilizing statistics
supplied by this organization, presents "total" figures on insured losses for a five year period ending in 1929.[7] According
to its tabulation, an average of 52,098 insured automobiles were
reported stolen annually during this five year period.[8] This
was approximately fifteen per cent of the total number of insured automobiles in the country. However, as pointed out by
the Commission, since "many uninsured automobiles are old
or cheap cars" that "are least often stolen" it is impossible to
determine the precise number of automobile thefts on the
basis of these figures. Other data issued by the National Automobile Theft Bureau,[9] a subsidiary of the National Automobile Underwriters Association, for two years, starting September 1, 1930, show that of the automobiles insured by its members, 43,146 were stolen in 1930–1931 and 34,199 in 1931–1932.
Officials of this organization estimate that one-third of all the
automobiles stolen during that period were insured. This, together with the fact that the National Automobile Underwriters Association carried approximately two-thirds of the
automobile insurance of the country, leads to the estimate that
as many as 190,000 automobiles may have been stolen in 1930–
1931 and 150,000 in 1931–1932.[10]

---

[7] At 389–90.

[8] Nat'l. Comm. on Law Obs. and Enf., The Report on The Cost of Crime
(1931) 390, table 7.

[9] Annual Report of the Governing Board (1932).

[10] These are obviously very rough estimates. The above estimate is also based
upon the assumption that the chances of non-insured automobiles being stolen
are as great as those of insured automobiles—which does not seem probable
in view of the greater value of insured automobiles.

More adequate data for 1931 are collected in the Uniform Crime Reports.[11] It appears that during 1931, 54,637 known auto thefts occurred in 511 miscellaneous cities with a total population of 16,458,401.[12] The number of automobile thefts was second only to the larceny-theft offenses for that year, which accounted for 48.8 per cent of the entire Part I class.[13] The proportion of automobile thefts to the total number of these offenses was 21.7; burglary was 20.5; robbery 5.2; while homicides of all types were 0.6 per cent.[14]

For 1932 data are presented in the Uniform Crime Reports from 1206 cities with a total population of 46,337,353. We learn from this compilation [15] that 171,103 automobile thefts were reported [16] as occurring in the above population. The rate per 100,000 was 369.1, this time slightly less than burglary which was 387.5; while, at the other extreme, the rate for combined homicide cases was 11.3. On the basis of the above data it has been estimated by the American Automobile Association [17] that (since 160,391 of the above automobile thefts occurred in 671 municipalities of over 10,000 population) grouping cities according to size and prorating accordingly, about 230,000 automobiles were stolen in 1932 in communities of over 10,000 in population. Since over fifty per cent of the automobiles are registered in towns under 10,000 in population,[18] this estimate would, for the country, be conservative. The Uniform Crime Reports for 1933 show that in 1264 cities with a population of

---

[11] 3 Unif. Cr. Rep. (No. 2, 1932) 9.

[12] *Ibid.* As will appear shortly, the rate drops considerably in smaller communities.

[13] This includes murder, manslaughter, rape, robbery, aggravated assault, burglary (and breaking or entering), larceny-theft and auto theft.

[14] Note that crimes against property amounted to over 96% of all of the Part I offenses. 3 Unif. Cr. Rep. (No. 2, 1932) 9, table 7. In 1940 the percentage was 95.9. See 11 Unif. Cr. Rep. 160.

[15] 3 Unif. Cr. Rep. (No. 4, 1932) 4, table 1.

[16] *Reported* thefts need not, of course, be actual thefts any more than (or even as much as) all actual thefts need be reported.

[17] 1932 Report by Burton W. Marsh, Director of Safety and Traffic Engineering.

[18] "55% of Cars in Towns Under 10,000. (Figures as of January 1, 1928. . . .)" Facts and Figures of the Automobile Industry.

49,470,686 there were 158,508 automobiles reported stolen,[19] a rate of 320.4 per 100,000 persons,[20] which represented a fairly substantial drop from that of the preceding year.[21] In 1945 the number of known auto thefts was 163,269 in 2267 cities with a total population of 67,608,610.[22] And in 1950 there were 106,816 known auto thefts in 2297 cities with a total population of 69,643,614,[23] and an estimated total of 170,780 for the United States.[24] While in 1931, the number of automobile thefts was second only to the larceny-theft offenses for that year, from 1933 on through 1950 auto theft continuously ranks third, competing unsuccessfully with burglary for second place.

It would appear reasonable to conclude that automobile theft is one of the most serious crimes committed, not only because of the large number of offenders who are involved, but

---

[19] *Cf.* "Automobile thefts are much more prevalent in America than in Great Britain, as is shown by the following table:

Thefts of automobiles reported in 1919*

New York	5527
Chicago	4316
Detroit	3482
St. Louis	1244
Cleveland	2327
Buffalo	986
London	290
Liverpool	10

(* Figures in all cases obtained from the police records.)" Raymond B. Fosdick, American Police Systems (1920) 18–19.

[20] 4 Unif. Cr. Rep. (No. 4, 1933) 4, table 1.

[21] The rates per 100,000 for various years, starting in 1935 were:

Year	Rate per 100,000
1935	241.8
1937	215.6
1939	178.0
1940	174.6
1941	188.5
1944	203.0
1947	182.1
1948	165.5
1950	153.4

Source: Uniform Crime Reports.

[22] 16 Unif. Cr. Rep. 78.

[23] 21 Unif. Cr. Rep. 89.

[24] 21 Unif. Cr. Rep. 74.

because of the apparently tremendous loss of property sustained. Representatives of insurance companies and advocates of strong repressive measures are prone to stop with the figures set forth above; their propaganda is based upon the largest figures shown. Indeed, there has been a curiously naïve general acceptance of the estimate of losses based upon these figures.[25] Proceeding in similarly dubious fashion, the Chicago Crime Commission estimated that the relevant loss sustained in Chicago each year was approximately $10,000,000.[26]

3. *The Recovery of Stolen Automobiles*

Two factors are neglected in appraisals of auto theft based upon the number of automobiles stolen, and the problem takes on an entirely different meaning if they are considered. *The first factor is the definition of automobile theft* as shown by the following instruction of the United States Bureau of Investigation to the police:

"The attention of contributors is invited to the fact that the term auto theft as used in the Uniform Classification of Offenses includes all cases where a motor vehicle is stolen, *or driven away and abandoned, or such a taking is attempted.* It does not include the taking of vehicle without the owner's consent by any one having lawful access thereto for temporary use, when the car or vehicle is actually returned to the owner or the place from which it was taken. There should be excluded from this group, therefore, all those cases where a vehicle is taken by chauffeurs, garage employees, and individuals in a similar status who had no intention of stealing the vehicle. *There should be included, however, in the monthly return, all cases where vehicles are taken and later abandoned by persons not lawfully entitled thereto.*" [27]

The second factor is that a very large percentage of all auto-

---

[25] *Cf.* National Conference on Street and Highway Safety, Uniform Traffic Laws 14.

[26] Chicago Crime Commission, Report of Operating Director, Jan. 19, 1933. Very substantial decreases in later years are discussed *infra* p. 287.

[27] 2 Unif. Cr. Rep. (No. 2, 1931) 4. Italics added.

mobiles "stolen" is recovered. For several years the insurance companies provided the principal source of national quantitative data[28] regarding this fact. The National Commission on Law Observance and Enforcement presents data supplied by the National Automobile Underwriters Association which show that during the five year period from 1925 to 1929 an average of 74.7 per cent of stolen automobiles was recovered and that an average of $15,831,425 was paid annually by insurance companies for losses to owners sustained from theft of their automobiles.[29] Data covering a longer period of time are presented by the National Automobile Chamber of Commerce. This information shows that the percentage of stolen automobiles recovered has increased progressively since 1920, *that the range in percentage recovered was from 71 per cent in 1920 to 94.4 per cent in 1930.*[30]

The report of the American Automobile Association for 1931 for 62 cities shows that 49,404 automobiles were stolen in

---

[28] Such information is not regularly compiled in the Uniform Crime Reports, although it is essential to an accurate description of this type of criminal activity. Furthermore, it would also provide a check upon the figures compiled by insurance companies—which would be particularly valuable in view of the fact that the companies collect only data on insured automobiles.

[29] Nat'l. Com. on Law Obs. and Enf., The Report on the Cost of Crime (1931) 390 1.

[30] 94% of Stolen Cars are Recovered. *Reports for 28 Cities, Compiled by National Automobile Dealers Association, 1928, 1929 and 1930 Figures from American Automobile Association.*

Years	% Recovered	Years	% Recovered
1918	79%	1924	83%
1919	74%	1925	86%
1920	71%	1926	89%
1921	71%	1927	91.7%
1922	77%	1928**	92.8%
1923	82%	1929**	92.6%
		1930**	94.4%

"** 1928 figures cover 26 cities; 1929 and 1930 cover 43 cities." Facts and Figures of the Automobile Industry (1931) 73.

Cf. "Berlin Police Recover 99 P. C. of Stolen Cars. Berlin (A.P.)"

"Of the 420 cars purloined last year 408 were retrieved, although the hunt in many cases extended to all parts of the country. The number stolen was nearly 2 per cent. of all the cars in the city. Sales and resales tax provisions are said to assist the police immensely, and, in addition, there is a heavy fine for dealers buying used cars of unknown pedigree." New York Sun, April 13, 1927.

these cities, valued at $12,283,652.10, and that 45,843 of the automobiles stolen, representing 90 per cent of this number and valued at $11,241,827, were recovered. The 1932 report of this association shows that in 78 cities, 35,074 automobiles were stolen, valued at $6,913,353.97, and that 33,798, representing 96.3 per cent of the total number stolen and valued at $6,659,066.97, were recovered. On the basis of these data the recovery of automobiles appears to have mounted steadily from 71 per cent in 1920 to over 96 per cent in 1932. In 1941, in 232 cities representing a total population of 28,496,861, 94.7 per cent of automobiles stolen was recovered.[31]

Some check on the above statistics and further light on the problem may be had by reference to the reports for various cities. The Missouri Crime Survey contains such information for St. Louis and Kansas City for a six year period from 1920 to 1925. In St. Louis almost 85 per cent of the stolen automobiles was recovered throughout this entire period. In Kansas City the percentage was very low for 1920 (38.1) and was 70.5 for 1921. From 1922 to 1925, however, the automobiles recovered averaged over 85 per cent of those stolen.[32] The 1929 report of the Police Bureau for Rochester shows that the value of automobiles stolen in that year was $169,382 and that automobiles valued at $162,771 were recovered.[33] Available data for Chicago, which was generally recognized as presenting the most serious problem in the entire country regarding theft of automobiles, show that in the seven year period from 1926 to 1932 an average of 79.5 per cent of automobiles stolen was recovered.[34] But for seventeen years, from 1932 through 1948,

---

[31] 12 Unif. Cr. Rep. 196, Table 85.
[32] Bruce Smith, Missouri Crime Survey 47–8.
[33] City of Rochester, Annual Report of the Police Bureau (1929) 24.
[34] Auto Thefts and Recoveries:

	1932	1931	1930	1929	1928	1927	1926
Automobiles Stolen in City	33,282	29,158	11,279	9,924	10,638	11,434	12,793
Total Recovered	29,170	23,416	8,425	7,905	8,388	8,798	9,093
Percentage of Stolen Cars Recovered	87.64%	80%	75%	80%	79%	84%	71%
Recovered for Other Jurisdiction	706	592	365	538	558	698	523

Source: Annual Reports of the Chicago Police Department.

almost 95 per cent (94.335) *of the automobiles stolen in Chicago was recovered.*[35] In Cincinnati 1,882 automobiles valued at $536,982 were stolen in 1931, of which number 89 per cent valued at $497,314 was recovered; and in 1932, 1,010 automobiles valued at $221,368 were stolen, of which number 89 per cent valued at $205,659 was recovered.[36] Los Angeles provides more complete information regarding the recovery of stolen automobiles than do other cities. The police reports for the fiscal years 1929–1930 and 1930–1931 show that a majority of the recovered automobiles are found within two days after the theft and that over 88 per cent of the automobiles recovered are found within one week after the theft.[37] The Los Angeles reports show, furthermore, that a small percentage of the automobiles recovered is damaged or stripped.[38]

A large part of the pecuniary losses due to theft is covered by insurance; and the cost of this insurance is an index of the loss sustained. Internal company policies undoubtedly affect

---

[35] Annual Reports of the Chicago Police Department.

[36] Letter from R. M. Hoisington, Executive-Secretary, Cincinnati Regional Crime Commission, March 28, 1933.

[37] The New York Crime Commission points out that the reason for the high rate of recoveries shown there is that "about half of the cars reported as stolen are abandoned by the takers within a few hours and later discovered by patrolmen." Report of the New York Crime Commission (Feb. 28, 1927) 224–5.

[38] AUTOMOBILES RECOVERED

Time Outstanding			*Condition of Cars*		
	1930	1931		1930	1931
Less Than One Day..	1349	1375	Good	4031	4459
One Day	3153	2751	Partly Stripped.......	391	355
Two Days	1314	1215	Mechanically Defective.	318	376
Three Days..........	682	692	Entirely Stripped	247	240
One Week...........	979	876	Wrecked	100	112
One Month	850	688	Not Stated*...........	3387	2264
Two Months	75	108			
Three Months.......	34	50	TOTAL	8474	7806
Four Months........	13	28	Percentage of		
Five Months........	13	12	Recovery	83.3%	82.3%
Six Months and Over..	12	12			
TOTAL	8474	7806			

Source:—Annual Report of the Police Department, City of Los Angeles, California, for the Fiscal Years 1929–30, 1930–31, pp. 19, 22.

* It seems likely that these automobiles were not stripped. Certainly any great damage would be generally reported.

rates in ways that may not seem equitable if risks are considered merely as such. Nevertheless, it is certain that the amount paid because of theft influences the rate charged for insurance against this risk.

In Chicago rates for automobile theft insurance were higher than in any other city. The rate in some cases used to be about 900 per cent higher than in Milwaukee which is located less than one hundred miles away. It cost $9.18 per $100 to insure a Ford or Chrysler automobile in Chicago while in Milwaukee, the rate for Fords was 95 cents per $100, and 65 cents per $100 for Chryslers.[39] The National Automobile Underwriters Association because of the situation in Chicago "established an extremely high level of rate, and provided for the elimination of equipment with the privilege to buy it at a graded scale of additional premium. . . ."[40]

The above data lead to the following conclusions:

1. automobile thefts are very numerous; of all the offenses listed in Part I of the Uniform Classification, they usually rank third in point of greatest frequency;

2. this relatively very high frequency is largely due to the classification of almost every kind of technical legal trespass as an auto theft;

3. (a) most of the estimates of losses sustained as a result of automobile thefts are grossly exaggerated;

(b) they fail to take into account the enormously large percentage of stolen automobiles which is recovered very soon after their theft, and in good condition.[41]

---

[39] Chicago Herald-Examiner, July 27, 1933. But see the following footnote.

[40] Annual Report of the Governing Board of the National Automobile Theft Bureau (1932).

V. W. Peterson, Director of the Chicago Crime Commission, reports that insurance rates dropped sharply in Chicago in 1934 to $3.10 for Fords, and later to $1.70. He accounts for this by the sharp decline in auto theft due to the creation of the Auto Theft Court and the adoption of the Certificate of Title Law. Peterson, The Automobile Thief, pub. in Criminal Justice, May 1947.

[41] Although I have presented only the Los Angeles data in support of this, it may be added that the opinions of police officials and various experts consulted confirm this conclusion.

In general, more than 90 per cent of the automobiles stolen is now being recovered.[42] Does the ten per cent which is not recovered represent the same type of criminal behavior found among the majority? What do we know about the ninety per cent which is recovered?

4. *The Offender and the Urban Community*

Considerable illumination is had with regard to both inquiries when it is discovered that most automobile thieves are young boys. That is the common observation of police officials and other informed persons. Their opinion is amply supported. Thus statistics on reported arrests in the United States, by age groups, from February 1 through December 31, 1932 [43] show that 28.52 per cent of the persons arrested for auto theft were from sixteen to eighteen years old inclusive; 39.47 per cent from sixteen to nineteen, inclusive; and 46.90 per cent were from sixteen to twenty, inclusive.[44] In 1943, 65.1 percent, and in 1950, 46.7 percent were under twenty-one.[45] In 1943 and 1945 over 80 percent of those arrested for auto theft were less than twenty-five years old.[46]

Boys of seventeen, eighteen and nineteen loom up not only as regards the number of automobile thefts committed by them, as compared with other age groups, but also as compared with the same age groups which commit other offenses. Thus, the percentage of offenders arrested for auto theft in this age group, from February 1 through December 31, 1932, was very much

---

[42] ". . . the reports received from police departments for several years have consistently reflected that more than 90 per cent of all stolen automobiles have been recovered by the police." 11 Unif. Cr. Rep. 19, 1940. "During 1950 the police recovered 92 per cent of all stolen automobiles." 21 Unif. Cr. Rep. 71, 1950.

[43] 3 Unif. Cr. Rep. (No. 4, 1932) 15, table 17.

[44] Similar data from February 1, 1932, to January 31, 1933, inclusive, show that over 50% of those arrested for this offense were from sixteen to twenty years old, inclusive. Report of the U. S. Bureau of Investigation, Feb. 17, 1933.

For 1933 the figures are 25.12%—16 to 18, inclusive; 35.23%—16 to 19, inclusive; and 42.9%—16 to 20 inclusive. 4 Unif. Cr. Rep. (No. 4, 1933) 17, table 11.

[45] 14 Unif. Cr. Rep. Table 39; 21 Unif. Cr. Rep. Table 42.

[46] *Id.*

higher than the percentage of offenders of the same age group arrested for any other crime. Whereas 46.90 per cent of the persons arrested for auto theft in 1932 were from sixteen to twenty years of age, inclusive, the corresponding figures for this age group for other crimes against property are 36.45 per cent for burglary; 27.42 for robbery; and 26.43 per cent for (other) larceny-theft. In 1946, the corresponding figures were: auto theft 50.5; burglary 41.2; robbery 28.3; theft 27.3; and in 1950 they were: auto theft 46.7; burglary 40.7; robbery 28.4; theft 27.2.[47]

Police statistics for Chicago over a period of twelve years show that boys between sixteen and twenty, inclusive, compose over fifty-four per cent of all the persons arrested for larceny of automobiles. These data become even more significant when it is noted that the 16 to 21 year group is numerically almost equal to the 31 to 36 year group, and that the latter, during the same period of years, accounted for less than five per cent of the arrests for larceny of automobiles.[48]

Much more significant are data which demonstrate that *the rate for automobile theft varies directly with the size of the city: the larger the city, the higher is the rate*. Thus in 1931, the rate per 100,000 population decreased progressively from 418.8

---

[47] Unif. Cr. Rep. 17, Table 45; 21, Table 42.

[48] FREQUENCY AND RATE OF ARRESTS PER 100,000 POPULATION BY AGE GROUPS FOR LARCENY OF AUTOMOBILES, CHICAGO, 1919–1931

Ages	Felony Larceny of Automobile (frequency)	Rate per 100,000 Population
Under 16 years	12	1.4
16–20.9	6462	2564.5
21–25.9	3223	994.5
26–30.9	1224	442.3
31–35.9	559	225.2
36–40.9	249	114.9
41–45.9	114	52.9
46–50.9	57	32.5
51–55.9	16	10.5
56–60.9	8	6.6
Over 60	15	7.9

Source: Chicago Police Department, Annual Reports, 1919–1931.

in cities over 250,000 to 126.5 in cities under 10,000.[49] In 1932 there was a similar steady decrease in rate from 497 in cities over 250,000 to 117.1 in cities under 10,000;[50] and for 1933, we find, again, a progressive increase from 93.8 for cities under 10,000 to 423.7 for cities over 250,000.[51]

The above italicized generalization was valid without qualification when it was written in 1934. The data available since that time permit a further testing of the generalization. On the basis of statistical data for the twenty-year period, 1931 to 1950, the following appears:

In 1931, 1932, 1933, 1934, 1937, 1938, and 1950 the rate per 100,000 population decreased continuously in direct proportion to decrease in the size of population of the cities. Throughout the entire period of 20 years (1931–1950) we find a similar unbroken decrease in rate from cities under 250,000 to cities under 10,000 with but one slight exception.[52] For the years 1935, and 1940 to 1948, inclusive, however, cities over 250,000 had from a 5.4% (1940) to a 65.9% (1943) lower rate than cities from 100,000 to 250,000.[53] And in 1936 the rate in the largest cities (over 250,000) was 1.2 percent lower than in the next largest cities; in 1939 the same irregularity between those cities was one-tenth of one percent; and in 1949 it was two percent.[54] In sum, with regard to the 20-year period, 1931–1950:

(a) for 7 years there was a continuous rate trend from the largest cities to the smallest, fully supporting the above 1934 generalization;

(b) for the entire 20 years there was such an unbroken trend in rate from the next largest cities (Group II, 100,000–250,000) to the smallest cities (Group VI, under 10,000);

---

[49] 3 Unif. Cr. Rep. (No. 2, 1932) 8, table 6.

[50] *Id.* (No. 4, 1932) 4, table 1.

[51] 4 *Id.* (No. 4, 1933) 4, table 1. *Cf.* For crime in general, G. B. Vold, *Crime in City and Country Areas.* (1941) 217 The Annals 38. *Cf.* the writer's text *infra* p. 248–249.

[52] In 1939, the rate increases from 164.8 in Group III cities (50,000–100,000) to 166.5 in Group IV cities (25,000–50,000).

[53] There was also a considerable drop in rate differences between cities over 250,000 and cities under 10,000. In 1932 this rate difference was over 380 while in 1947 it was only 81.

(c) thus the divergence from the 1934 generalization, found in 13 years, is only between the largest cities' rate (Group I, over 250,000) and that of the next largest cities (Group II, 100,000–250,000).

In three of these years, the divergence was a minor one; in ten years it was substantial. Accordingly, the generalization discovered in 1934 must be qualified in the indicated direction: For some reason, the largest cities sometimes have a lower rate than the next largest. Except for that, the 1934 generalization remains valid.

There was no such trend for other crimes, with one exception. Thus, in 1931 and 1933 the rate for murder was higher in cities under 10,000 than it was for any other cities except those over 100,000 where the rates were very slightly higher, while from 1934 to 1948 murder had its highest rate in Group II cities with but two exceptions (1936 and 1950). The rate for rape was higher in 1931 and 1933 in cities under 10,000 than in any other cities however large. From 1932 through 1947 the rate for aggravated assault was higher in cities between 50,000 and 100,000 (Group III) than in any other cities

[54] Rate of Auto Thefts per 100,000 by Population Groups

Year	Group I (over 250,000)	II (100–250)	III (50–100)	IV (25–50)	V (10–25)	VI (under 10,000)
1931	418.8	404.4	311.6	291.6	185.7	126.5
1932	497.0	401.4	313.0	264.6	170.6	117.1
1933	423.7	363.7	274.2	201.3	148.0	93.8
1934	355.8	353.5	265.4	220.5	149.5	101.8
1935	290.2	303.7	234.0	197.3	143.0	96.6
1936	255.8	257.0	218.6	180.4	135.3	89.6
1937	263.4	248.8	213.1	193.9	138.3	93.6
1938	233.7	213.2	183.8	168.8	121.5	87.3
1939	218.2	218.3	164.8	166.5	116.1	87.4
1940	203.5	208.9	168.1	158.2	111.0	94.7
1941	215.6	222.4	193.5	174.0	132.7	100.3
1942	187.8	213.6	172.8	150.8	119.0	90.1
1943	199.8	265.7	188.1	169.1	142.9	112.5
1944	218.6	275.0	208.8	176.9	158.9	123.3
1945	266.6	317.4	247.3	205.1	185.2	148.1
1946	251.4	300.6	234.7	201.2	176.6	148.6
1947	197.1	241.9	186.8	163.2	144.3	116.1
1948	184.0	212.8	172.6	152.3	119.7	100.0
1949	200.4	202.4	166.3	141.6	118.6	99.5
1950	195.1	186.4	149.7	120.1	95.9	76.3

Source: Uniform Crime Reports.

But in 1936 and 1937 the rate was higher in Group II cities and in 1948 and 1950 the rates were higher in cities over 250,000 (Group I) than in any other cities. The only other offense among those reported in the Uniform Crime Reports which shows a uniform trend like that for auto theft is robbery, which has an even more regular trend.

One other factor should be noted before synthesizing the results of the above analysis, namely, throughout the entire 20-year period there was very little change in the daily average number of automobiles stolen each month except for occasional slight increases in spring and toward the end of the year. It is well known that there is considerable seasonal fluctuation in the sale of automobiles. The lack of any marked seasonal fluctuation in the number of automobiles stolen throughout the country indicates that the disposal of this property in the market for stolen goods plays only a minor part in the commission of this offense. The data described above showed that less than ten per cent of the automobiles stolen is not recovered; this fixes the maximum limits upon the availed-of market for stolen automobiles. On the other hand, the number of boys in a given community does not vary to any great extent within short periods of time. Youth with its desire to ride in an automobile is the constant and the most important single factor in large-scale automobile theft.

Illegal taking of automobiles by boys is so common in the large cities that it has become part of the typical pattern of delinquent behavior. The small boys in a delinquency area are apt to pilfer the stock of the local fruit merchant or pedlar; the chase and the element of danger are exciting. Next, these boys in company with older ones go downtown and visit those carnivals and show places of the modern city, the department stores. It is thrilling to steal things in one of these great stores, then to go to another store where the articles stolen in the first are sometimes "exchanged" for others, without the help of a clerk. Like almost all delinquent offenses, these thefts in the department stores are committed by groups of boys and not by individuals. Unfortunately, at this stage, some of the boys discover that a merchant in the neighborhood will buy goods from them without asking embarrassing questions about their acquisition. In some such inconspicuous fashion, boys in delinquency areas bridge the gap between pilfering for fun or use and stealing for sale. There are, of course, a whole series of variants in the individual cases. The parents of some children compel them to steal coal, wood, and other goods for home consumption. The complex forces that grow from an inferior social and economic status influence these children more than others. The exact point where automobile theft fits into the picture cannot be stated with certainty; but the progress from neighborhood pilfering to shoplifting to auto theft is apparently a typical order of development. Most of the automobiles are taken by older boys, a year or two above the age fixed for technical juvenile delinquency in most jurisdictions; they are taken for excitement, to "show off", and for "joy-rides." And, as we found, they are quickly abandoned, recovered, and returned to their owners.[55]

5. *The Modus Operandi of Automobile Thieves*

A fuller study of automobile theft requires some knowledge of the offenders' *modus operandi* and of the measures stimulated to cope with it. *Modus operandi* can also be correlated with technological advance. But our inquiry in this regard concerns only the activities of private organizations in active law-participating roles, as these have developed to meet the techniques of 20th-century larceny. Only enough of *modus operandi* necessary to understand these lay activities will be detailed.

The most frequent *modus operandi* is the use of simple mechanical methods to enter the automobile and start the motor. A check-up by police squads in large cities has shown that very many automobiles are left unprotected. Accommodating owners leave doors unlocked, windows open, key in the

---

[55] This statement of the development of delinquency and criminality is based principally upon the two studies by Clifford Shaw, The Jack-Roller, and The History of a Delinquent Career.

switch, and sometimes even leave the motor running, all conveniently arranged for thieves who specialize in these easy pickings.[56] Where the automobile is locked, entry is effected by duplicate keys, breaking the handle, prying open a window, or by removing a foot-board and making an opening through which a small boy can enter.

Once within the automobile, the thief starts the motor with a duplicate ignition key or by applying wires to the motor. The "Elektrospark," like many other inventions, is a boon not only to the owner who has lost his switch key, but even more to the thief. According to one advertisement, this device "hooks-up in ten seconds—starts in two seconds" and "fits any battery ignition system, from Ford to Rolls-Royce." But a skillful thief need not invest ten dollars for this device. Ordinary wires can be manipulated to the same purpose and are generally used. The wires and two clasps "jump" the motor.

Another common device is a strip of thin metal—the blade of an ordinary pocket knife or a piece of aluminum—which is inserted into the motor lock and acts as an improvised key. In Chicago a boy of eighteen became so skillful in opening automobile switches that he was employed by a gang of automobile thieves to teach other boys the technique. Representatives of automobile companies learned about this boy and persuaded him to participate in a very interesting experiment. The president of a lock manufacturing company which had just invented an absolutely "thief-proof" lock went to Chicago, and the boy was summoned. With the use of an ordinary metal strip he opened the lock within three minutes. The manufacturer insisted that something must have been "wrong." The boy then opened the lock in less than two minutes. Aside from illustra-

---

[56] Note the statutes making this criminal (n. 71 *infra*), together with the apparent total absence of efforts to enforce these statutes. It has been estimated "that 70% of all automobile thefts could be prevented by the individual motorist using reasonable care and caution in removing keys, locking doors . . ." Letter to writer from W. J. Davis, Sec'y. and Mgr. National Automobile Theft Bureau, Western Div. Nov. 23, 1951.

For a study of this problem, including non-enforcement of relevant statutes, see the monograph of the Milwaukee Metropolitan Crime Prevention Commission, *Here Kid, Take My Car!!* (Sept. 1946).

ting the skill acquired by the professional, the case also shows
the impossibility of relying only upon mechanical devices for
protection. Lock manufacturers and automobile laboratories
have been working on this problem for years. Yet their representatives are least optimistic of all about the possibilities of in-
venting an absolutely thief-proof lock. Here, as in war, progress
in invention also aids the enemy; indeed, the skillful thief is
more up-to-date than his victim for he utilizes the advances
made in technology. The history of methods used to break into
safes would parallel that of inventions in several other fields;[57]
the methods devised to overcome the operation of electrical
wiring in stores provide a further illustration.

Occasionally, a bold thief will use a "wrecker" to tow a car
away; or he will use another car and ropes. Some of the thieves
who use such direct methods operate in theatre districts and
around ball parks. The congestion in these localities compels
the owner to leave his automobile several blocks away. Thieves
know just how much time will elapse before the owner returns,
and they use the circumstances to their advantage. One scheme
is placing an automobile of common type next to a vehicle of
similar appearance, then returning shortly and entering the
wrong car by "mistake."

It is difficult to differentiate the methods employed by the
"joy-riders" from those employed by the professional thieves.
But certain broad differences do exist. The use of keys indicates
planning and organization. Again, towing an automobile away
or using a vehicle of similar appearance is professional technique. The head of the police automobile squad in a large city
states that many experienced chauffeurs and former automobile
mechanics are to be found among the professionals.

There are a number of indirect and more intelligent ways of
getting possession of automobiles, which are employed by
professional thieves exclusively. One requires the collaboration
of garage or repair-shop employees who have possession of
the owner's keys or note the numbers and secure duplicates or

---

[57] *The New York Times* Sept. 17, 1933, reports that in New Mexico cattle
thieves use tear bombs and machine guns to escape capture by the posse,
which is still organized along primitive lines.

give the necessary information to their accomplices. Sometimes the same results are accomplished by simply copying the door and lock numbers, for automobile keys are apparently furnished to anyone who orders them.[58] Occasionally, a professional gang obtains possession of a garage which is not doing well, and automobiles begin to disappear on a large scale.

Many professional thieves specialize in acquiring automobiles through fraud. The means are numerous. One common method, known as the "mace," is started by the insertion of newspaper advertisements offering to buy an automobile. Possession is secured by payment of a few dollars and giving a note, supported by subtle representations of opulence. Other advertisements inserted under another name lead to the disposal of the automobile, and the perpetrator of the fraud flees, leaving two innocent victims to adjust the loss.

Finally, reference must be made to the larceny of automobiles by persons who have made a small down payment. This type of theft is very frequent.[59] Although a large number of professional thieves instigate and engage in these thefts, there are also many first offenders to be found here.

Thus far discussion has been confined to the criminal acquisition of the entire automobile. Increasingly prevalent is the stripping of automobiles of all salable accessories. This type of theft is clearly differentiated from "joy-riding." It is always caused by mercenary motives. Organized thieves have concentrated more and more upon it until, at present, this is the most serious phase of the problem.

This type of theft is intimately related to organized groups of offenders, receivers, and the market for stolen automobiles in general. In the early days the entire machine was taken and

---

[58] In June of 1933 the Chicago Motor Club took steps to secure passage of a law making it a crime to possess a master key with intent to commit larceny of a motor vehicle.

[59] "Neither the National Motor Vehicle Theft Act nor the laws of six or more of the states make the wrongful conversion of a motor vehicle a crime. The amount in losses suffered because of wrongfully converted cars has not been compiled but this fraud together with the fraud practiced upon innocent purchasers of stolen cars presents a problem similar to and second only to that of the theft of motor vehicles." Report of the National Crime Commission, May 25, 1931 at 6.

sold directly or to a receiver who disposed of it. Motor numbers were changed, new plates were substituted. But recent improvements have made it possible to discover that the numbers had been changed, no matter how skillfully it has been done, and to reproduce the old numbers by chemical processing. This ability to identify the automobile as a unit made its possession and transfer dangerous. But the parts of automobiles are neither numbered nor marked. Stripping of automobiles and stealing accessories represented a logical and a necessary improvement in methods of theft. The accessories are sold to dealers, to repair shops and garages, usually to persons who are criminal receivers.

When whole automobiles are stolen, they are dismantled, and the parts are used to construct other vehicles. Frequently the rebuilt automobile will then be exported to a market where the chances of detection are small.[60] Again, old car wrecks and old chassis are purchased; the parts needed to equip the automobile are stolen. This aspect of auto theft takes on many of the features discussed in connection with receivers and the market for stolen property.[61] There are similar types of organization with well planned methods of acquiring automobiles and accessories, with machine shops and factories to dismantle, re-

---

[60] "Federal investigators gave an insight into the manner in which the car thieves operated when they reported finding in Trenton a plant replete with special machines for disassembling automobiles and crating the parts preparatory to shipment in China, Persia, Siam, Norway and other countries. The ring employed specialized workers for the expensive process of removing the motor and serial numbers from the car and substituting new ones. It also used counterfeiters to forge bills of sale and lading. The cars were then disposed of through the gang's representatives in foreign countries, or, more often, forwarded through an unsuspecting bank abroad." *New York Times,* May 21, 1933.

It has been suggested by police officials that the exportation of stolen automobiles could be prevented if transportation companies notified the police of all automobile shipments, except those made by manufacturers, several days in advance of sailing.

[61] "The racketeers who reap the real profits, run few of the risks and remain in the background are the crooked second hand parts dealers and the crooked garage owners. These men are directly responsible for the automobile thefts because they create a market for automobiles and parts which otherwise would be of almost no value to thieves." Statement of Lieut. John M. Kelley, head of the stolen auto section of the detective department, in the *Chicago Tribune,* July 17, 1933.

construct and repaint automobiles, and with numerous channels through which the property can be distributed until it is
disposed of to ultimate users. This relatively small minority of
automobile thefts, motivated by gain, perpetrated by organizations of gangs, involving association with criminal receivers
and the market for stolen property, must be dealt with differently from the "joy-ride" cases.

All the data described above, cutting in from different angles,
demonstrate that automobile theft is mostly—though not entirely—a problem of juvenile or near juvenile delinquency. The
high rate of auto theft in large cities parallels a similar trend for
juvenile delinquency in general.[62] The conditions and characteristics of criminal behavior are dependent upon existing
culture media just as definitely as is any other human behavior.
Technological advances affect whole strata of culture; and of
all inventions, the automobile has been perhaps the greatest
single factor in modifying the structure of contemporary American society.[63]

Especially during the past century our cities have been
constantly forced into new adaptations to the demands and
facilities of improved technology. The metropolitan community
now comprises not only the central city but adjoining suburbs
and surrounding towns. These larger communities required
connecting roads and highways. The greater area made policing more difficult, and made it more difficult, also, to check
juvenile delinquency.[64] At the same time speed facilitated inter-
city communication, opened up travel, and transformed a sed-

---

[62] *Cf.* Elliott and Merrill, Social Disorganization (1934) 89 and Reckless
and Smith, Juvenile Delinquency (1932) 45–7.

[63] Ogburn and Gilfillan, *The Influence of Invention and Discovery* in 1
Recent Social Trends in the United States 141.
"It is probable that no invention of such far reaching importance was
ever diffused with such rapidity or so quickly exerted influences that rami-
fied through the national culture, transforming even habits of thought and
language." Wiley and Rice, *The Agencies of Communication* in 1 *id.* 172.

[64] "The rapidly changing conditions of American life, such as are emphasized by students of the causes of business instability, introduce factors
which play an immense part in the production of delinquency. Since 1910
we have had the vast growth in the number of automobiles which are such
great incentives to delinquency." Healy, *The Prevention of Delinquency and
Criminality* (1933) 24 J. Crim. L. and Criminol. 78.

entary population into a mobile one.[65] Habits of pleasure were likewise changed. "Joy-ride" expresses the attitude of the young, especially those who feel deprived of a common pleasure. Thus the new technology has not been an unmixed boon.

II. The Legal Problem

Thus far we have been concerned with automobile theft as a social problem. It is now proposed to consider the same phenomena as elements in the relevant legal problem. Analysis will run in legal terms. It will therefore be determined by, and formulated with reference to, a technical body of rules and principles. We shall, moreover, limit the inquiry to the criminal law, indeed, to a special classification within that law, namely, larceny. Traffic legislation, such statutes as that cited [66] on commission of a crime from an automobile and those penalizing the carrying of particular weapons in such a vehicle—these belong in the total picture. We focus, however, on the larceny phase—larceny *of the car*.

We have seen that the principal method employed to construct the substantive criminal law consists of recognizing and defining various types of behavior conceived as socially harmful, and of prohibiting any instance of their commission under pain of suffering penalties. Within the field of larceny, after the broad type of socially harmful behavior had been prohibited, certain acts falling within this general type have been penalized more severely than others. We found that chattels in which certain industries were interested, e.g. ore and coal from mines and wool, became subjects of such special legislation. We found similar legislation regarding governmentally owned property and, again, with reference to cattle.

The production of the automobile on a large scale has also been accompanied by considerable penal legislation regarding it:[67]

---

[65] See, generally, The Automobile: Its Province and Its Problems, The Annals, cxvi (1924).

[66] See *supra*, footnote 6.

[67] Most of the statutes cited in the following notes were selected from states where auto thefts are numerous. These states were chosen from the

1. There are statutes dealing with the theft of automobiles in the same manner that theft of other chattels is dealt with, that is, within the general grand larceny provision. Sometimes automobiles are specifically listed along with cattle and other chattels; in other statutes it is simply a question of whether the automobile is worth more than the amount fixed to mark off grand larceny from petty larceny.[68]

2. But a number of states have special statutes dealing with the theft of automobiles; and the penalty is then usually greater than that provided in these states for grand larceny in general.[69]

3. Some states have progressed to statutes differentiating the taking for temporary use from larceny of an automobile. Taking for temporary use is made a misdemeanor.[70]

4. Other statutes make it an offense to leave an automobile unlocked on the streets; and they require owners to take other precautionary measures against theft.[71]

5. There are many laws dealing with the registration of automobiles. In the states which have adopted the Uniform Motor Vehicle Anti-Theft Act or similar statutes, certificates of title are issued, and numerous statutory provisions regulate the keeping of records, the application for and issuance of certificates of title and the transfer of these certificates.

6. Most states have statutes regulating the transfer of mort-

---

1932 Annual Report of the Governing Board of the National Automobile Theft Bureau, where the number of insured automobiles stolen and recovered in each state during 1930–31 and 1931–32 is set forth. The statutes of eleven states where the number of insured automobiles stolen exceeded 1000, were examined. Significant statutes in a few other states are also noted.

[68] Ariz. Code Ann. (1939) Sec. 43–5503; Cal. Pen. Code (Deering 1941) Sec. 487; Mo. Rev. Stat. (1939) Sec. 4456; Vernon's Tex. Stat. (1948) Penal Code Art. 1421.

[69] Jones Ill. Stat. Ann. (1936) Ch. 37, Sec. 37.335; Mass. Gen. Laws (1932) Ch. 266, Sec. 28; Comp. Laws, Mich. (1948) Sec. 750.413; Mo. Rev. Stat. (1939) Sec. 8404; Page's Ohio Gen. Code (1939) Sec. 12619; Okla. Stat. (1949 supp.) Tit. 21, Sec. 1720; and Pa. Stat. Ann. (Purdon, 1931) Tit. 18, Sec. 2774 (Repealed 1939, June 24, P.L. 872, Sec. 1201).

[70] Cal. Pen. Code (Deering 1941) Sec. 499.b; Mich. Comp. Laws (1948) Sec. 750.414; Okla. Stat. (1941) Tit. 21, Sec. 1787; Pa. Stat. Ann. (Purdon 1939) Tit. 75, Sec. 231.

[71] Md. Ann. Code (Flack 1947) Art. 66½, Sec. 192; Ann. Laws of Mass. (1946) Vol. 3, Ch. 90, Sec. 13; Rev. Stat. Mo. (1939) Sec. 8401.

gaged automobiles and prohibiting their concealment or fraudulent transfer.[72]

7. There are numerous statutes penalizing the changing of serial and motor numbers, being in possession of an automobile which has such numbers changed[73] or transferring such an automobile. Other statutes require sheriffs to seize automobiles with altered numbers and to make reports of these vehicles.

8. A number of states have adopted special statutes with regard to criminal receiving of stolen automobiles. Generally these statutes are found in states which provide a greater penalty for the theft of an automobile than for other grand larceny; and a corresponding, higher penalty is provided for the receiving of stolen automobiles than for the receiving of other stolen property.[74]

9. Lastly, a number of states have statutes regulating owners of garages and repair shops and dealers in automobile accessories.[75]

---

[72] Arkansas (McClaskey v. State, 168 Ark. 339 (1925), Louisiana (Melson v. Calhoun, 120 So. 115 (1929), New Jersey (State v. Moldenhauer, 136 Atl. 412 (1927), New York, N. Y. Pen. Law (McKinney, 1944) Sec. 940; (People, Complaint of Perman Bros., Inc. v. Francia, 142 Misc. Rep. 143 (N. Y., 1931).)

State v. Bates (194 N. W. 107 (Minn., 1923)) holds that an intent to defraud is not a material part of the crime charged. *Cf.* sec. 31 of the Third Draft of a Uniform Chattel Mortgage Act (1925).

[73] In People v. Billardello, 319 Ill. 124 (1925), defendant was convicted of unlawfully possessing a motor vehicle, the original engine number of which had been destroyed, altered, etc. He appealed on the ground that he bought the automobile in good faith with no knowledge of the defacement of the engine number. The Supreme Court of Illinois sustained the conviction on the ground that "the statute was enacted in the exercise of the police power in the interest of the general welfare" in protection of the whole public against the commission of crimes and the escape of criminals whose identification is made difficult by the destruction of identifying marks. The absence of knowledge or criminal intent was held to be immaterial; the defendant could have discovered that the numbers had been changed by the use of reasonable care.

That the buyer of an automobile with a defaced number can rescind and recover the purchase price was held in Stein v. Scarpa, 96 N. J. L. 86; 114 Atl. 245, (1921).

[74] Jones Ill. Stat. Ann. (1936) Sec. 37.336; Ann. Laws of Mass. (1933) C. 266, Sec. 28; Ohio Ann. Code (Page 1939) Sec. 12619; and Pa. Stat. Ann. (Purdon 1931) Tit. 18, Sec. 2774 (Repealed 1939, June 24, P. L. 872, Sec. 1201).

[75] Uniform Motor Vehicle Anti-Theft Act, art. IV, secs. 14, 15, 16.

These criminal statutes on automobiles are, of course, embedded in many other laws concerning theft in general. Thus, the automobile has taken the place of the horse not only technologically but also as the subject of considerable special legislation. But, as with all legislation, only so much of it as the courts will uphold is valid. How, then, has the primary phase of the law been interpreted by the courts?

The analogy of the "horseless carriage" has apparently been sufficient to preclude any issue as to whether a general statute on larceny included larceny of an automobile. The definition of larceny is stated in terms of a felonious *taking and asportation* of personal property. As was pointed out by Holmes [76] larceny thus differs from other crimes, for the proscribed conduct is not very injurious. It is the continued deprivation of the owner's possession of the chattel which is really the harm. The criminal law, in selecting an important segment of this criminal behavior, has combined a minimum characteristic with the probability that the stolen article will be permanently lost. Thus, there must be an intention to deprive the possessor of his property "permanently," [77] but the meaning of *animus furandi* is not free from uncertainty. [78]

With reference to the "asportation" of the property, it has been held that removal to the distance of a "hair's breadth" is sufficient. [79] Hence, it is frequently difficult to see where taking ends and asportation begins. In any case, the offender's motive makes no difference whatever. He may have taken the property

---

[76] "Under this name [larceny] acts are punished which of themselves would not be sufficient to accomplish the evil which the law seeks to prevent, and which are treated as equally criminal, whether the evil has been accomplished or not. Murder, manslaughter, and arson, on the other hand, are not committed unless the evil is accomplished, and they all consist of acts the tendency of which under the surrounding circumstances is to hurt or destroy person or property by the mere working of natural laws." Holmes, The Common Law 70.

[77] 2 Bishop, Cr. L. (9th ed.) sec. 841ff.

[78] 8 Holdsworth, H. E. L. 438; Pollock and Wright, Possession in the Common Law 225. *Cf.* "If the thief once take possession of the thing, the offense is complete, though he afterwards return it." 2 East, P. C. 557.

[79] For citations, see Clark and Marshall, Law of Crimes (4th ed., 1940) sec. 322, n. 191.

lucri causa or for revenge or spite or to enjoy it or for no reason at all.

Thus, the method of the criminal law includes the selection of certain facts and the classification of these legally significant phenomena under a system which has been logically extended from a framework mainly historical and traditional. This does not mean that emotional drives as well as the needs of a changing culture have not motivated the courts in their work.[80] What is stated is that in law, as in other disciplines, system must be distinguished from history and the psychology of adjudication. Obviously the propositions selected to describe certain factual elements in a social situation must be formulated in terms of characteristics which are *legally* significant. Thus *legal* propositions about *larceny* must still run in terms of a taking which is felonious, an asportation, and so forth, and not in terms of keeping or of economic need.

If we bring this to bear upon the theft of automobiles as a legal problem, we find that legal analysis runs as follows: (a) an automobile is a chattel which is within the subject-matter of larceny; (b) "taking" and "asportation" include any removal of it from the possession of the owner (or other possessor even though he may be a thief); (c) *animus furandi* symbolizes an intent to deprive the possessor of the chattel indefinitely; and (d) the offender is or is not "responsible" depending on whether the defendant is an infant under seven, a child between seven and fourteen, or a person over fourteen years of age; [81] and relevant rules of mental competency apply.

Around each of these apparently simple propositions there has grown up an enormous number of decisions, discriminating, refining, and adjudging facts and cases. Distinctions have accumulated mountain-high and slippery as water-covered ice, to the dismay of even such redoubtable spirits as the law profes-

---

[80] *Cf.* Alexander and Staub, The Criminal, The Judge, and the Public (1931); Cardozo, The Nature of the Judicial Process (1921); Hutcheson, *The Judgment Intuitive: The Function of the "Hunch" in Judicial Decision* (1929) 14 Corn. L. Q. 274; and chapters 1 and 4 *supra*.

[81] Recent Juvenile Court Acts, Boys' Courts and various modern administrative practices modify the common law rules.

sor and his students. Some teachers "solve" the problem by simply omitting these technical matters from their courses. The problems persist. They plague lawyer, judge, and jury in the most frequent type of criminal case.

"Taking" and "carrying away" property seem to be easy everyday terms. But consider the following cases: (1) D puts his hand on X's watch-chain, lifts the watch out of X's pocket, and is about to dash off with it when the chain is caught in X's buttonhole; (2) D diverts some of the gas from the company's pipes into his own so that it does not pass through the meter; (3) D turns over a heavy package, which is in a wagon, so that it is end-up, his intent being to steal it; or (4) he picks it up and places it down near the rear of the wagon; (5) D drops corn in front of his neighbor's hog, which follows him eagerly. Have there been a taking and asportation in these cases? Not the most complex situations have been selected, for the purpose is to illustrate the nature of the legal problem rather than to explore its difficulty.[82]

If the two lines of inquiry which have been pursued in the analysis of automobile theft—as a social and a legal problem—are now compared, a number of conclusions can be drawn. With reference to the social problem we were able to arrive at certain conclusions regarding the extent and quality of social harm effected, the types of offender involved, the rate of such theft in relation to size of city, and so on. And, from an analysis of automobile larceny as a legal problem, it appears that the only answer possible without reconstruction of the traditional system is that any case in hand is or is not *"sufficiently like"* preceding cases,[83] i.e., that it can or cannot be identified with recognized legal categories.

---

[82] It is noteworthy that "theft" may have a different meaning in an insurance policy when the word is interpreted in a case by the insured against the company from that assigned to the word in criminal cases. See Felgar v. Home Ins. Co., 207 Ill. App. 492 (1917); Michigan Commercial Ins. Co. v. Wills, 57 Ind. App. 256 (1914). *Cf.* Note (1922) 94 Cent. L. J. 177. And *cf.* Note (1929) 13 Minn. L. Rev. 153.

[83] I am here confining my remarks about automobile theft as a legal problem to the substantive law; the function of the administration of the law in this connection will be considered shortly.

Where legal categories correspond to actual social situations,
the location of criminal behavior within the relevant substantive law provides a valid index of the extent of social harm
done. But it is apparent that existing legal categories in the law
of larceny do not always soundly differentiate lines of social
harm in the conditions which have grown up since those categories became tradition,[84] e.g., the classification of "joy-ride"
asportations as larceny of an automobile. Reconstruction of
existing legal categories is required. In the meantime cases
which arise call insistently for intelligent and fair adjudication.
In large measure, the need is met today, as it was in the
eighteenth century, by administrative discretion.

III. ADMINISTRATION OF THE CRIMINAL LAW IN RELATION TO THE SOCIAL AND LEGAL PROBLEMS

A significant fact about automobile theft is that relatively
few arrests are made in proportion to thefts committed. In
1931 the American Automobile Association compiled data for
sixty-two miscellaneous cities[85] and found that for 49,909 automobile thefts only 3,098 (slightly more than 6 per cent) arrests
were made. Data compiled by the Federal Bureau of Investigation[86] show that the percentage of automobile thefts "cleared"
by arrest[87] in 511 miscellaneous cities in 1931 with a total
population of 16,458,401 was 14.2, which was about half as
large as the percentage of other offenses against property
"cleared by arrest".[88]

There is almost nation-wide complaint with regard to the

---

[84] The above analysis of the substantive criminal law has been simplified
for purposes of emphasis. For fuller treatment of the system of the criminal
law, see Hall, General Principles of Criminal Law (1949) and Cases and
Readings on Criminal Law and Procedure (1949).

[85] By B. W. Marsh, Director of Safety and Traffic Engineering, the
American Automobile Association.

[86] 3 Unif. Cr. Rep. (No. 2, 1932) 10, table 8.

[87] "An offense is considered 'cleared by arrest' when one or more persons
have been taken into custody, charged with having committed it and are
held or turned over for prosecution." *Id.* 9.

[88] Percentage of known offenses cleared by arrest: murder, non-negligent
manslaughter, 77.9; manslaughter by negligence, 90.4; rape, 87.9; robbery,
37.0; aggravated assault, 73.5; burglary—breaking or entering, 28.1; larceny-
theft, 25.8; auto theft, 14.2. (*Id.* 10, table 8.)

small number of automobile thieves arrested. Thus, it is reported in the Missouri Crime Survey that, "During the period from October 1, 1923, to October 1, 1924, warrants were issued in Kansas City in less than one-half of 1 per cent of auto-theft cases, and the record of St. Louis is not materially better." [89] As to 1882 automobiles stolen in Cleveland from January 1 to September 30, 1924, 294 arrests were made, amounting to 15.5 per cent of the automobiles stolen.[90] The Cleveland Association for Criminal Justice concludes that "the facts indicate that of those who steal automobiles only one in seven is apprehended." [91]

Most striking is the fact that the percentage of automobile thefts "cleared by arrest" in 1931 decreased, with one exception, inversely in proportion to the size of the city. The range was from 10.9 per cent in cities over 250,000 to 27.8 per cent in cities under 10,000.[92] After combining these data with those examined above, the following generalizations may be made:

Not only is the rate for automobile theft very much higher in the larger cities than it is in the smaller ones, but the opposite

---

The data for 1932 are equally significant. Thus the report of the American Automobile Association shows that an average of 13.7 automobiles were stolen for each arrest made in 78 miscellaneous cities where 35,074 thefts occurred. Data for 1932 compiled by the Federal Bureau of Investigation (4 Unif. Cr. Rep. (No. 1, 1933) 19) for 506 cities with a total population of 21,001,300 show that 15.8 percent of automobile thefts was cleared by arrest. (As against 25.5 for larceny-theft, 26.9 for burglary, etc., 78.6 for aggravated assault, 34.6 for robbery, 82 for rape, 89.4 for manslaughter by negligence and 80.5 for murder, non-negligent manslaughter.)

[89] At 48.

[90] From Bull. No. 13, Cleveland Assn., Sept. 30, 1924.

Similarly, *the number of prosecutions and convictions is relatively small.* Thus the survey of Iowa Criminal Justice reports that only 238 prosecutions were instituted out of 2578 known cases. "Of the known auto thefts only about 8 percent result in *prosecution* and 5 percent in *conviction*."

The Cleveland Association points out that in Cleveland in the first six months of 1924, "of those apprehended only one in five is punished." The authors of this report concluded that the statistics "warrant the conclusion that the limited number of offenders punished, namely one for every 26 automobiles stolen, lends encouragement to the commission of this crime." Cleveland Association for Criminal Justice, Bull. No. 12, June 30, 1924. *Cf.* also a typical mortality table in Bull. 13, Sept. 30, 1924, 8. The familiar practices of waiver of felonies, dismissals, nolles, and probations augment the findings of not guilty, and altogether account for the very small percentage of persons punished.

[91] 2nd Quar. Bull. No. 12, June 30, 1924.

[92] 3 Unif. Cr. Rep. (No. 2, 1932) 11, table 10.

prevails with reference to the offenses cleared by arrest of the offenders. More specifically, *the rate of auto theft (per 100,000) increases directly in proportion to increase in population by cities, whereas the percentage of auto thefts cleared by arrests decreases directly in proportion to increase in population by cities.*

The trend in the percentage of automobile offenses cleared was even more marked the following year than in 1931, for in 1932 there was, without a single exception, a steady increase from the largest cities to the smallest cities in the percentage of these offenses cleared by arrest.[93] The range was from 13 per cent for cities over 250,000 in population to 27.1 for cities under 10,000 in population.

The above italicized generalization regarding arrests was thus verified in 1934, when it was formulated. The data now available, while they do not require drastic revision of the generalization concerning the percentage of arrests, do indicate a number of irregularities in the trend.[94] The statistics for the twenty years, 1931–1950, show:

[93] 4 *Id.* (No. 1, 1933) 12, table 8.
[94] Percentage of Offenses Cleared by Arrest

	Group I (over 250,000)	Group II (100–250)	Group III (50 to 100)	IV (25–50)	V (10–25)	VI (under 10)
Year						
1931	10.9	11.9	20.1	21.0	18.0	27.8
1932	13.0	15.7	16.8	20.7	20.8	27.1
1933	12.1	17.0	16.6	15.6	17.7	25.4
1934	11.1	14.9	16.3	18.6	21.7	27.9
1935	12.8	20.3	17.4	17.6	21.9	31.1
1936	23.3	16.9	18.8	18.2	26.8	35.9
1937	17.8	19.8	20.3	21.6	28.8	35.4
1938	19.2	23.2	20.6	22.6	30.0	39.4
1939	22.9	23.4	21.4	24.3	30.7	37.6
1940	20.6	24.9	22.6	21.6	34.2	39.3
1941	20.1	26.2	23.8	27.3	29.7	37.7
1942	21.7	25.3	22.7	25.3	30.1	38.2
1943	25.7	25.9	26.0	23.2	29.0	36.4
1944	23.2	22.4	23.4	24.7	29.5	31.6
1945	25.9	25.2	24.8	28.2	28.4	32.0
1946	30.3	24.8	23.7	28.6	31.8	35.4
1947	30.4	24.8	24.9	26.9	33.2	39.7
1948	25.9	26.4	24.3	26.8	32.4	39.0
1949	24.1	27.5	25.3	27.5	35.5	40.9
1950	21.0	25.8	25.8	30.5	37.5	44.9

Source: Uniform Crime Reports

The italicized generalization in the text above is discussed by G. A. Lundberg in his Foundations of Sociology (1939) 142.

1. In 1932, 1934, 1937, and 1950, and with only slight irregularity in 1944, 1945, and 1948, the percentage of auto thefts cleared by arrest had a uniform increase from Group I cities (over 250,000) to Group VI cities (under 10,000). That is, for seven years of this period the percentage of arrests decreased directly in proportion to increase in population by cities.

2. For two additional years, 1936 and 1947, the same trend prevailed from Group II cities (100,000–250,000) through Group VI cities.

3. For six additional years, 1935, 1938, 1939, 1941, 1942, and 1946, the uniform trend extended from Group III cities (50,-000–100,000) through Group VI cities.

4. For nineteen of the above years the trend was uniform from Group IV cities (25,000–50,000) through Group VI cities.

5. This indicates that the irregularities occur in relation to the largest cities, and as to these it may be noted that in only three instances (1936, 1946, and 1947) was the percentage of arrests somewhat higher in Group I cities than it was in Group II cities.

A number of explanations of the small percentage of arrests in relation to thefts are suggested by the previous analysis. First, the enormously large recovery of stolen automobiles results from the abandonment of the vehicle and not from the arrest of the offender. Second, the mobility of the automobile and the fact that it serves the offender as a means of escape enhance the difficulty of capture. Third, the conditions in metropolitan centers, notably in congested neighborhoods, near theatres, ball parks, bathing beaches and other places where large numbers of automobiles and crowds are found make it extremely difficult to detect automobile thieves. With regard to the described trends in theft and arrest, the following data concerning Chicago may suggest a tenable explanation.

A particularly acute problem of automobile theft in Chicago makes the situation in that city especially significant. Large delinquency areas and the consequently greater appeal of the joy-ride multiply offenses to the point where the police cannot cope with them. Officials consulted by the writer, in accounting for the relatively few arrests made, emphasized the following special factors: (*a*) Chicago has fewer police in proportion to population than other cities; (*b*) a sufficient quantity of necessary equipment such as automobiles and radios is lacking; (*c*) the large area covered by the city facilitates escape since speedy shift of location from the congested areas around ball parks and bathing beaches provides immediate access to non-congested streets and highways; (*d*) the proximity of Chicago to the state lines of Indiana, Wisconsin and Michigan enables the thieves to escape from the jurisdiction; (*e*) a weakened police morale, which is alleged to be the result of irregular payment of salaries, the fact that most of the persons arrested for auto theft receive little or no punishment, and other aggravating conditions.[95]

The work of the Chicago courts provides data which are unusually interesting and significant with reference to the relationship of administration to substantive law and the relevant social problems.[96]

As background:

(*a*) Illinois has a special automobile larceny statute which provides for a penalty of from one to twenty years in the state penitentiary; whereas the punishment for other grand larceny is one to ten years.[97]

(*b*) Illinois had another statute, not part of the penal code proper, which contained the provision that any chauffeur or other person having charge of a motor vehicle, who uses it

---

[95] For example, factors of a political nature which condition the activities of police generally. *Cf.* C. E. Merriam, *The Police, Crime and Politics* (1929) Annals Am. Acad. of Pol. and Soc. Sci. 115 and Nat. Com. on Law Obs. and Enf., Report on Police.

[96] The only existing studies of judicial administration in auto theft cases are, apparently, the two issued by the Chicago Crime Commission, May 10, 1933 and Nov. 21, 1933, both by H. B. Chamberlin, Operating Director, 24 pp. and 31 pp. respectively. Although the first report covers three months while the second report covers one year (including the three months previously reported) the former is more detailed and is generally more significant. Moreover, the disposition of cases in the three months first reported on is representative of the entire year. It is to the earlier report, therefore, that particular attention will be paid.

[97] Jones Ill. Stat. Ann. (1936) 37.335 and 37.330.

without the owner's consent, is guilty of a misdemeanor and punishable by a fine of not more than two hundred dollars or imprisonment of not more than six months, or both.[98]

(c) The maximum age of juvenile delinquents in Illinois is seventeen years. There is, however, one branch of the Municipal Court of Chicago, known as the Boys' Court, which has jurisdiction over boys from seventeen to twenty-one years of age. Although no distinctions are made in the substantive law between these boys and adults, it is the practice of judges sitting in the Boys' Court to waive felony counts and thereby assume jurisdiction in perhaps a majority of the cases. Social workers and representatives of various religious affiliations are present in court; the procedure is very informal; and the Court, in its actual practice, resembles the Juvenile Court more nearly than it does the County Criminal Court.

With this preliminary outline before us we can understand and evaluate an important report of the Chicago Crime Commission. The Commission found that during the three months from January to March, 1933, inclusive:

(a) 203 cases involving auto theft were disposed of in the Criminal Court; of these "in one instance only was a defendant sentenced to the Illinois State Penitentiary, and but seventeen to the reformatory, for the full term provided by statute in such cases."[99]

(b) In 47 of these 203 cases, the Criminal Court found that the value of the automobile stolen was less than fifteen dollars (and therefore petty larceny) "despite the fact that statistics show the average value per stolen car to be $485."[1]

(c) In 34 of these cases, the accused persons "were given punishment because they failed to obtain the consent of the

---

[98] *Id.* sec. 85.036.
This statute was repealed in 1938 when a typical "joy-riding" statute was adopted. Jones, Ill. Stat. Ann. 85.037 (1) No. 31a.
[99] H. B. Chamberlin (Operating Director), The Report of the Chicago Crime Commission (May 10, 1933) 1.
[1] *Ibid.* And *cf.* the analogous eighteenth century English practice, *supra,* Chap. 4.

owner to drive away his automobile" (that is, they were punished for the misdemeanor described above).[2]

(d) 49 defendants were released on probation.

(e) 17 of the 85 defendants who appeared in the Criminal Court in January, 1933, were found not guilty. We are informed that similar dispositions were made in February and March so that we may conclude that (of all the cases) a total of 55 defendants were found not guilty or discharged in one manner or another during this period in the criminal courts.

To summarize the disposition of cases by the county criminal courts during this period:

Number found guilty of felony (1 to 20 years)	18
Number found guilty of misdemeanor	81
Number found guilty and granted probation	49
Number found not guilty or dismissed	55 [3]
Total	203

The disposition of the 515 cases in the Boys' Court during the same period was even more striking.

(a) 193 defendants were held to the grand jury. (These cases appear later in the county criminal courts if the grand jury votes true bills.)

(b) 264 did not receive any punishment; of these 167 were discharged in one manner or another; 59 were placed on probation; and 38 were placed under supervision.

---

[2] In its later report for the year August 1, 1932, to July 31, 1933, the Commission writes: "The criminal court record of felony waivers is astounding. Felonies were waived in forty per cent of the disposed cases." *Id.* 18.

[3] *Cf.* During 1932, in 469 cases of automobile theft which appeared in the Criminal Court of Cook County, 377 or over 80 per cent were discharged or placed upon probation, and 63 or 13.5 per cent were sent to the reformatory. Chicago Police Department Annual Report (1932) 15.

Percentage of Auto Theft Cases Placed on
Probation, Discharged, Acquitted or Nolled
for Years 1932 through 1947

1932—81.6%	1940—67.8%
1933—77.4	1941—56.1
1934—58.8	1942—29.7
1935—59.2	1943—65.2
1936—58.2	1944—66.4
1937—62.3	1945—47.9
1938—56.9	1946—41.2
1939—65.7	1947—40.7

Source: Chicago Police Dept. Annual Reports

(c) 58 were given some sort of punishment ranging from a fine to from five days to one year's imprisonment; of those imprisoned, 6 received 30 days, 14—60 days, 8—6 months, and 6—one year. The other sentences were scattered within the limits stated above.

To summarize the record of the Boys' Court during this period: [4]

Number found guilty of misdemeanor	58
Number found guilty and placed on probation or under supervision	97
Number found not guilty or discharged	167
Number held to the grand jury	193
Total	515

The Commission emphasized the fact that in only 58 cases out of 515 which appeared before the Boys' Court was any sort of punishment given; and that in a large number of cases in which the defendant was discharged, he claimed to have purchased the automobile, but neither he nor the police produced any vendor in court. In addition to criticizing the courts for general laxity in the enforcement of the laws, the Commission arrived at the following conclusions:

1. That the Criminal Courts waived felonies and found defendants guilty of misdemeanors in cases which the Boys' Court considered too serious to be thus disposed of; that is, these were cases in which the latter court refused to waive the

---

In 1938 Illinois adopted a "joy-riding" statute (*supra* N. 98) and in 1934 a Certificate of Title Law went into effect. Although these changes are not clearly reflected in the above Table of figures, it should be added that the number of prosecutions for larceny of automobile dropped very sharply beginning in 1935. The generally lower percentage of probations, etc., shown in the above Table, starting in 1934, may have been due to the fact that the fewer prosecutions brought (because of the operation of the two laws noted above) involved serious, perhaps professional, offenders. Thus, in 1933 and 1934, there were, respectively, 608 and 616 cases disposed of in the county criminal courts. In 1938 there were 72, in 1942, 148. But in 1946 and 1947, the figures had climbed to 205 and 386, respectively.

[4] The following is a comparison of the disposition of cases by the Boys' Court during the three-month period and the entire year. Jan. through Mar. 1933—Guilty—11%; Prob.—18%; N. G. or Dis.—32%; Gr. Jur.—39%; Aug. 1, 1932 to July 31, 1933—Guilty—17%; Prob.—22%; N. G. or Dis.—28%; Gr. Jur.—33%.

felony count and held the defendants to the grand jury instead.

2. That too large a number of defendants were placed on probation "probably on the theory that every person should be given the right to steal at least one motor vehicle before punishment is administered." [5]

3. "That the judges consider the law too severe, and, in good conscience and with a desire to be merciful, refrain from inflicting the penalty prescribed by the statute, and in a large percentage of cases inflict no punishment at all, the defendants escaping through the medium of probation." [6]

4. That the judges and prosecutors are reluctant to "administer the law as the statute provides" because of

(a) the youth of the defendants (during the last five months of 1932 "of 1245 defendants charged with automobile larceny and related offenses appearing in the municipal court . . . 703 (56.4%) were of ages seventeen, eighteen, nineteen and twenty");[7]

(b) "sobbing parents (most of them probably upright citizens)";

(c) "the defense attorney speaks of the boy who merely took a pleasure ride";

(d) *"the owner has recovered his car . . . and has suffered only a monetary loss . . ."* (writer's italics);

(e) the intervention of social workers, church members and other persons who "procure the assignment of young defendants to them for purposes of supervision."

The Commission's recommendations are, in general, based upon the assumption that the infliction of more and severer penalties is desirable.[8] Thus the Commission believes that more

---

[5] Chicago Cr. Com. (May 10, 1933) Report 2.

[6] *Id.* 5.

[7] *Id.* 2. In 1932, over 60 per cent of the persons charged with auto theft in Chicago were from 16 to 20 years old inclusive; over 82 per cent of the persons so charged were from 16 to 25 years old. Chi. Pol. Dept. Rept. (1932) 14. And *cf.* table, footnote 48 *supra*, covering the years 1919–1931.

[8] Notable achievements of the Commission are found in the adoption in Illinois of the Uniform Motor Vehicle Anti-Theft Law, and of a special auto theft court in Chicago.

thought should be given "to the feelings of the citizen who suffered at the hands of the *accused*." [9] The efforts of "well meaning groups . . . consistently opposed to severe sentences for boys" which result in many grants of probation are unsound. "Punishment is a better teacher . . . than sentimental pampering." [10] "The practice of releasing defendants on probation was at one time considered to be the best way to reform" [11] but "its purpose has been virtually nullified." [12] Recognition of the fact that the youth of automobile thieves is an important factor which influences the administration of the law, did not affect the Commission. "The need for more drastic measures than have heretofore prevailed is apparent.[13] Age must be forgotten and the matter treated as a menacing situation." [14]

The Chicago Crime Commission therefore insisted that automobile thieves be sentenced under the special automobile larceny law which provides for a penalty of from one to twenty years' imprisonment. This statute was passed in 1927 as a result of considerable agitation and pressure upon the Illinois legislature; and it modified the general law which provides for a penalty of from one to ten years for grand larceny. When the Commission complained that "judges and prosecutors are reluctant to administer the law as the statute provides," [15] it referred to the 1927 statute.[16] In any of the large number of the states that have statutes which make it a misdemeanor to use an automobile temporarily without the owner's consent, such complaint would be obviously fallacious. In Illinois, however, there was no "joy-riding" statute until 1938.[17] There was the

---

[9] Chicago Cr. Com. (May 10, 1933) Report 6.
[10] *Id.* 8.
[11] *Id.* 14.
[12] *Id.* 15.
[13] *Id.* 18.
[14] *Id.* 17.
[15] *Id.* 2.
[16] "The Illinois General Assembly has recognized that automobile stealing has reached threatening proportions and a special statute was adopted dealing with automobile thieves exclusively. This statute has been almost totally ignored by most of the courts." Chicago Crime Comm. *op. cit.* 13.
[17] Jones, Ill. Stat. Ann. (1936) sec. 85.037(1) No. 31a.

above noted statute designed primarily to prevent chauffeurs from using their employers' automobiles without permission. This statute[18] penalized such driving; it prohibited chauffeurs or other persons having the care of a motor vehicle from accepting any gratuity in connection with work or supplies furnished; and it forbade anyone who furnished such work or materials to give a bonus to any chauffeur or other person. The provision, "no chauffeur *or other person* shall drive" and so on was available to courts which wanted to hold other offenders, who took an automobile, guilty only of a misdemeanor.

It clearly appears from the foregoing report that the Criminal Court imprisons a much larger percentage of persons than does the Boys' Court.[19] This difference in treatment is to be expected since the most serious cases are transferred from the Boys' Court to the criminal courts by way of the grand jury. But that is not a complete explanation. For example, it is interesting to note that one of the judges who had presided in the Boys' Court for several years, when he later served in the Criminal Court, placed seven of the nine defendants who appeared before him on probation.[20] This was a disproportionately large percentage for the criminal courts, but conformed roughly to the standards of the Boys' Court.

The maximum age for juvenile delinquency in Illinois is seventeen years,[21] whereas in other states persons up to eighteen and in some states persons up to twenty-one years[22] of age are treated as juvenile delinquents. The Boys' Court in Chicago

---

[18] Jones, Ill. Stat. Ann. (1936) sec. 85.036.

[19] 99 out of 203 defendants were punished in the Criminal Courts; whereas only 58 out of 515 defendants were punished in the Boys' Court.

[20] "Judge Allegretti disposed of 9 defendants. 1 he sentenced to the reformatory for a term of one to five years, 1 to the House of Correction, and 7 he released on probation." H. B. Chamberlin, Report of the Chicago Crime Commission (May 10, 1933) 4. During the year from August 1, 1932, to July 31, 1933, Judge Allegretti tried 26 automobile larceny cases. He placed 16 defendants on probation, *nolled* 5 cases and imposed sentences in 4 cases ranging from 1–10 years to 8 months imprisonment. Report of the Chicago Crime Commission (Nov. 21, 1933).

[21] Jones, Ill. Stat. Ann. (1936) sec. 37.089.

[22] See Dorothy W. Burke, Youth and Crime (U. S. Dept. of Labor, Children's Bureau, 1930). (Publ. No. 196.)

often functions as a necessary supplement to the juvenile court. The recovery of the vehicles in good condition shortly after they have been abandoned is evidence of their having been taken merely for "joy-rides." But, while most of these offenses are not very serious,[23] the only relevant statute in Illinois pro-vided a very severe penalty. Hence the courts selected the stat-ute directed at chauffeurs, and applied it generally. Or, they waived the felony charge and found the defendant guilty of stealing only a tire, or they otherwise arbitrarily fixed the value of the property taken at less than fifteen dollars, reducing the offense to petty larceny. Thus, we find criminal courts in Chi-cago—as we found English courts, juries and prosecuting wit-nesses in the eighteenth and early nineteenth centuries— invent-ing fictions to nullify a very severe law and attain just results.

It is noteworthy, also, that the great majority of the persons arrested were charged by the police with larceny and only a very small number were charged with using a motor vehicle without consent.[24] This might have been due to literal interpre-tation of the statutes along the lines suggested by the Crime

---

[23] Thus in Oklahoma larceny of an automobile is punishable by three to twenty years imprisonment, but joy-riding is punishable only by a fine of from five to one hundred dollars. Okla. Stat. Supp. 1949, secs. 1720, 1787, 1788.

[24] The following table shows also the steady rise in the number of persons arrested for auto theft throughout the period covered.

TRENDS IN ARRESTS FOR LARCENY OF AUTO AND USE OF MOTOR VEHICLE WITHOUT CONSENT, CHICAGO, 1919–1931.

Years	Larceny of Auto	Use of Motor Vehicle without Consent
1919	122	162
1920	409	149
1921	417	128
1922	345	140
1923	361	179
1924	612	234
1925	785	190
1926	1170	248
1927	1519	165
1928	1219	172
1929	1134	172
1930	1511	180
1931	2335	176

Source: Chicago Police Department, Annual Reports, 1919–1931.

Commission or, to some extent, at least, to anticipation of what the courts would do. The statistics on arrest, when compared with the preceding analysis of judicial administration, reveal an enormous difference in viewpoint between police and judges. The major unanswered question is how far the known judicial tendencies were discounted in advance in the work of the police.

Although the administration of the criminal law by the courts in these cases is quite different from what one would be led to expect from an examination of the statutory law, the decisions are consistent with the analysis of the social problem involved in auto theft. The judicial function is to interpret and apply the substantive criminal law to certain segments of important social problems. The judges, however, are sharply limited regarding the methods they can use and the ends they can reach. But so far as they are able, they attempt today, as in the past, to apply the law justly. Their performance of this function is conditioned by professional techniques and traditions, and is sometimes disguised because of the necessity to make the decisions appear both plausible and consistent with precedent. Finally, we see the fallacy of limiting research to the substantive criminal law, and the need in any sound critique to consider the administration of the law.[25]

Yet there remains this important question: What is the effect of such disparity between the substantive law and the administration of the law? Where different courts deal with the same problem, as in Chicago, lack of uniformity raises other problems. The Boys' Court approaches the problem of auto theft with a different body of experience and a different point of view

---

[25] An excellent illustration of this point is the situation in Illinois regarding the use of psychiatry in the state courts in 1930 and following years. An examination of the Illinois statutes showed no provision for the regular employment of psychiatrists. Yet for several years two psychiatrists and a staff of assistants had been attached to the Cook County Criminal Courts. They were employed at the request of Judge John McGoorty when he was Chief Justice of the criminal courts. The Cook County Board of Commissioners was persuaded to make the necessary appropriation, and this arrangement continued for several years. The same situation existed in Cook County with reference to the Public Defender.

from that of the Criminal Court. But what determines whether
a boy is held to the grand jury by the Boys' Court or whether
this court waives the felony and even grants probation?[26] There
are no carefully established standards.

Another difficulty resulting from the wide use of legal fictions
is the impossibility of comparing cases on any common basis.
Finally, great divergence between substantive law and judicial
administration creates friction with other officials, notably the
police, who feel aggrieved if the substantive law is not enforced
as it is written—when they call upon it.[27] Abuse of discretion,
lack of uniformity in treatment accorded similar offenders in
similar cases,[28] the inability to check and compare results, and
the disharmony created among officials—this is the price paid for
decent administration of unjust rules.

IV. Lay Participation in the Law-Process

1. The Activities of Insurance Companies and Other Groups

Just as in the case of silk, furs, jewelry, and securities, the
theft of automobiles and accessories for the purpose of sale has

---

[26] The writer was for several days in the summer of 1930 assigned as
an assistant state's attorney to the Boys' Court. Shortly thereafter he spent
several weeks in the County criminal courts. He was impressed by the
lack of uniformity of treatment given to offenders in the two courts. Exactly
the same type of boy who received probation or a sentence of from 30
days to 6 months in the Boys' Court was sometimes sentenced to one to
twenty years in the criminal courts. Occasionally there was a previous
record or a major difference in fact to account for this. Usually it seemed
to depend upon chance or the services of a competent attorney who could
have the case disposed of in the Boys' Court. Numerous fortuitous factors
of the most diverse sort seemed to determine whether the boy would be
dealt with in the Boys' Court or held over to the grand jury.

[27] "Then there is the policeman who is being harangued everlastingly by
his superiors and various organizations for not reducing automobile thefts.
He stands in court after risking his life chasing the thieves in the stolen
automobiles for miles and sees probation given a youth whom he knows
to be a menace to society. He knows that he will have this same defendant
on his hands sooner or later. He is impressed with the futility of arresting
youthful automobile thieves." The Report of the Chicago Crime Commission at 7.

[28] "A very natural result of such lack of uniformity is that the defendants
or their attorneys make a strong effort to locate their cases in the courtrooms
where the presiding jurist has not made his severity evident." Chicago Crime
Commission Report, Nov. 21, 1933.

stimulated activities by lay organizations. Although this phase of the problem is not as serious as the auto theft statistics indicate, it is yet of major importance, as appears from the very substantial sums paid by insurance companies to owners.

The insurance companies are, without doubt, the most potent of all groups, lay or official, in dealing with auto theft. Their representatives maintain cordial relations with police officials and legislators. Through contact with crime commissions and by propaganda in the newspapers, they undoubtedly influence the courts as well as many other groups.[29] Skillful propaganda is not the least technique conceived to be a help toward solution of this problem. "250,000 automobiles stolen annually" and "loss of $75,000,000" are effective stimuli. For these slogans cause automobile owners to be more careful; they work on police and judges; they helped secure the passage of the Uniform Anti-Theft Law. Last, not least, more insurance is written. Unfortunately, the propaganda may also stimulate criminal conduct, for many persons wish to secure a portion of this alleged $75,-000,000 annual sum. On the other hand, it is not justifiable to regard this propaganda as motivated purely by a desire for more profits: the insurance companies can earn as much or more with lower rates if theft diminishes sufficiently.

The insurance companies have taken the lead in urging preventive measures. They encourage inventions. Some of them subsidize laboratories which specialize in the improvement of locks and other mechanical devices. Thus technology is advanced by efforts to eliminate theft; thus, too, criminals unintentionally confer a boon by stimulating invention.

---

[29] About the middle of July, 1933, a very active campaign was started to repress auto theft in Chicago in which the insurance companies took the leading rôle, although it was made to appear that the Crime Commission and the motor clubs were the parties chiefly concerned. The City Council appointed a special committee to investigate, the mayor participated, and all of the newspapers carried full columns daily about auto theft. Shortly thereafter police killed several boys and seriously wounded others who were attempting to take automobiles. See *Chicago Herald-Examiner*, Aug. 15, 1933, and newspapers for two weeks prior to that date. In light of the discussion regarding the disposition of auto theft cases by the courts, the probabilities are great that these boys would have been found guilty of misdemeanors.

The fixing of insurance rates is employed to influence public officials to exert themselves in the reduction of auto thefts.[30] Representatives of the companies make contacts with local chambers of commerce. They inform them why relatively high rates are charged. The chambers of commerce and other business groups lose little time in exerting pressure upon the authorities. In a number of instances specific agreements have been made for reduced rates, conditioned upon the formation of police automobile units. The insurance companies occasionally engage in police activities on their own account. Thus the National Automobile Underwriters Association has employed agents to secure evidence regarding the operations of gangs of thieves and criminal receivers.[31]

The automobile finance companies participate actively in the detection of thefts. They employ investigators to trace owners who have "skipped" and to seize the mortgaged automobiles. In 1931, together with other groups in the installment and finance business, they organized a "skip" tracing system on a national scale. The plan is based upon the wide coöperation of finance dealers and other interested parties, the recording of data in a central office, and the free utilization of this information by all finance companies.

The insurance companies now delay payment of loss until

---

[30] "A reduction in the cost of automobile theft insurance is promised by the companies in the National Automobile Underwriters' Association if their newly established central salvage bureau is indorsed by Mayor Kelly and the police give their coöperation." *The Chicago Daily News*, July 25, 1933.

[31] A recent venture of this sort in Chicago ended disastrously. Of six informers who were employed to secure evidence in Chicago, one had his skull fractured in a garage, one disappeared entirely, and the remaining four quit. The Governing Board of the National Auto Theft Bureau stated (1932 Annual Report): "Very careful consideration was given by our Theft Committee to the operations of the Special Cook County Department and it was decided that the work of maintaining a corps of under-cover men did not justify the expense involved and many complications resulted therefrom. As a result it was decided to discontinue this method of operation as of December 1st."

The Chicago Motor Club offers rewards for information leading to the arrest and conviction of auto thieves who take members' vehicles. These rewards are to be paid to police as well as to private persons. The plan was approved by the State's Attorney, the Commissioner of Police, and the Director of the Chicago Crime Commission.

sixty days after the filing of proof of the theft. This allows ample time to recover and return most "stolen" automobiles. It allows time to make a careful investigation. It probably deters the filing of numerous fraudulent claims.[32] The companies have in some localities instituted a system of recording and interchanging information about insured persons who file more than one claim for loss of an automobile through theft.[33]

2. The Moral Hazard in Insurance

It will be noted that the last two measures described are designed to prevent the filing of fraudulent claims. They concern the behavior of owners of automobiles, many of whom conspire with thieves.[34] The one secures payment of insurance; the other finds easy access to automobiles and obtains, in

---

[32] Cf. "Everyone has observed how the fire losses have decreased since the companies decided to defer loss payments until 60 days after the filing of proof. This may merely be a coincidence but a good many people in the business think that it is a question of cause and effect and that the dropping off in fire losses indicates that a good many more claimants were dishonest than was generally supposed.

"It is interesting that automobile theft losses have also fallen off since the companies decided to defer loss payments for 60 days. The falling off in automobile losses is the more significant because it comes at a time when the automobile season is opening up and normally an increase rather than a decrease in losses would be expected." President Thomas T. North of North Adjust. Co., in the National Underwriter (April 14, 1933) 4.

[33] "Heretofore, there has been no check on repeaters, although anyone with experience in the business knows that they account for no small proportion of the automobile loss payments. . . .

"I believe that the arrangement, which has been instituted in Chicago, should be extended throughout the country. My idea would be to have the country zoned and loss information collated for each zone. This information could be available between the different zones and thus if a gang or individual should change their or his base of operations, the fact would be soon revealed." Id. 1.

[34] "There are two types of assureds, who will appear most frequently on any list of repeaters. There is one sort of person who welcomes a loss and therefore leaves his car unlocked or parks it in unpoliced and dark places and in every conceivable way, without actually indulging in collusion, offers his car to thieves. . . .

"The other frequent type of repeater is out to skin the insurance company. He may operate in various ways. For instance, he may buy an old car and cause it to be over-insured and then actually conspire to have it stolen or else leave it in places where he hopes it will be stolen. . . . There are also careless persons, who probably do not belong in either class, who are found among the repeaters. . . . They may habitually leave their cars unlocked." Id.

addition, payment for rendering these services. Again, many owners destroy or hide their automobiles and present claims for insurance. In a quarry in the east, about fifty hidden automobiles were found. The capacity of the quarry finally became exhausted; the last car driven into it protruded and was noticed.

This problem of moral hazard touches the whole field of interests protected by insurance. Although it is practically impossible to secure much in the way of quantitative data, it is certain, nonetheless, that in every type of theft insurance the number of fraudulent claims is enormous. If the opinions of private investigators, police, officials of insurance companies, and other well-informed persons are to be credited, fraudulent claims comprise from twenty-five to fifty per cent of all claims filed. Claims for alleged thefts, combined with similar ones for alleged burglaries and fires,[35] constitute a problem which cuts deep. They reveal a phase of automobile theft which defies any easy "solution." They emphasize the need for insurance companies to take measures to discover poor risks.[36] They affect

---

[35] *Cf.* P. W. Kearney, *$200 a minute for Arson, New York Herald-Tribune,* April 23, 1933. See the monograph, Manual for the Investigation of Automobile Fires, Including State Arson Laws, published by the National Automobile Theft Bureau (3rd ed. 1950).

"A majority of such [questionable] claims result from the premeditated and wilful burning of property. . . . The prevalence of this vicious practice throughout the nation indicates both a disregard for the law and a lack of fear of detection . . ." *Id.* 5.

[36] A Chicago newspaper reporter (*Chicago Herald-Examiner,* July 24, 1933) was informed by a police official that the insurance companies were so careless that they would issue a policy on a non-existent vehicle. The reporter, to test this, telephoned an insurance company, gave fictitious serial and motor numbers and was informed that the policy would be mailed forthwith. Police officials in Chicago recommended that insurance companies be required to determine that the automobiles actually exist, that the alleged owner has title to it and that it is worth the value placed upon it. A representative of the insurance companies maintained that a careful investigation is made before any money is paid to cover alleged losses. But the National Automobile Theft Bureau in the 1932 Annual Report of its Governing Board stated:

"Companies must be more particular in the underwriting of their business in the Chicago territory.

"The loss reports received in the Bureau cover hundreds of cases where old worn-out automobiles are insured for excessive amounts and in the hands of parties whose financial condition, location and employment, or lack of employment, would not entitle them to insurance. No Police Department or Organization such as your Bureau, can possibly protect you from losses in hundreds of cases such as are now being reported to the Bureau."

the cost of theft insurance to the community as a whole. The companies themselves, although some of them have been losing money for several years upon their total business, make, almost all of them, substantial profits on theft insurance.[37] But fraudulent insurance claims are so numerous that it is debatable whether the benefits derived from spreading the risk are not outweighed by its evil consequences.[38]

Insurance has become so deeply ingrained that it is hardly worth while to challenge its alleged value even if it were possible to consider the problem dispassionately. Yet it seems clear that theft insurance is about as harmful to some as it is beneficial to others because it provides temptations for many thousands of persons who are thereby led to commit crimes; it taxes the resources of the honest to support the dishonest; and it renders assured persons who have received payment for their losses indifferent as regards the detection and prosecution of thieves. General adoption of the plan instituted in Cook County for discovering repeated claimants, and more rigid, intelligent regulation of the sale of insurance might lessen some of these evils.

Other aspects of the effects of insurance are most evident in the theft of accessories rather than in theft of entire automobiles. It has been suggested that theft of accessories was initiated by the owners of automobiles to defraud insur-

---

[37]   AUTOMOBILE INSURANCE IN THE UNITED STATES

Totals of	Year	Net Premiums	Losses Paid	Ratio of Losses Paid to Premiums Written
automobile	1931	$432,029,766	$280,380,908	64.9
insurance in	1930	524,484,209	352,896,399	67.2
the U. S.	1929	556,029,491	300,961,610	64.1

Compiled by The Insurance Year Book Service, The Spectator Company, and taken from Facts and Figures of the Automobile Industry (1931) 67; *id.* (1932) 77.

The Chicago Motor Club shows losses on theft insurance in 1932. The National Underwriter (Apr. 14, 1933) 20.

[38] A number of insurance officials consulted by the writer do not carry theft policies. They stated that a large percentage of honest persons do not carry such insurance, but they evinced the belief that all dishonest ones are amply covered.

ance companies.[39] In any event, owners are frequently involved, along with criminal receivers, thieves, insurance adjusters, and police. The behavior of these groups varies so greatly that we can here describe only a general pattern. One or more of the above groups may be involved; sometimes all. An automobile owner conceals his car or strips its parts; he does this himself or he conspires with a thief or an insurance adjuster. The adjuster's duty is to investigate the claim and, if necessary, to have the automobile repaired. He purchases or supervises the purchase of parts. If his intentions are criminal, he patronizes a criminal receiver or he conspires with the owner himself, who, having concealed the accessories, sometimes replaces the very same parts after the claim has been paid.

Sometimes police participate in this criminal behavior. Thus in Chicago the Mayor announced that there was connivance between members of the police department and insurance adjusters.[40] Similar accusations are common. Numerous automobiles have been stripped after they had been recovered in good condition by the police.

These criminal depredations have been aided for a number of years by the shortsighted policy of insurance companies. Far from questioning the purchase of repairs from disreputable dealers, they have themselves sold automobiles to salvage-buyers and wreckers.[41] In both ways the insurance companies have encouraged auto theft. They have also been substantial buyers in the market of stolen accessories. They have allowed motors to come into the possession of receivers who buy wrecks in order to have motors which can be legally registered. When

---

[39] "This business of stripping cars seems to have started with the assured either working in collusion with the thieves or dismantling the car himself. An assured, for instance, might drive his car in an alley or in a barn, strip it and hide the parts. The loss would be reported and the car would later be found in a stripped condition. The insurance company would pay the cost of rehabilitation and the assured would merely replace the old parts. In many cases, the assured would buy new parts from a conniving dealer and after the loss was settled would return the parts to the dealer, get credit for them, and replace the old parts. Of course, the practice developed until the stripping of cars became highly organized." Thomas T. North, *op. cit. supra*, n. 32.

[40] *Chicago Herald-Examiner*, July 16, 1933.

[41] These automobiles are acquired by the companies either after the assured has been paid his loss; or they are wrecks which are not worth repairing.

such a reconstructed automobile is turned into the market, it is protected by a certificate of title, *bona fide* serial and motor numbers, and a bill of sale.

Within recent years the insurance companies have recognized the harmful effects of their methods.[42] Instead of allowing their adjusters to purchase parts indiscriminately, it is proposed to patronize only authorized dealers.[43] Thus in the early part of 1933, insurance companies organized a central salvage bureau in Chicago. Where the vehicle can be repaired, this bureau will purchase the parts and do the work itself. Where the vehicle cannot be repaired, the bureau will remove all usable parts, cut up the remainder of the machine and sell it as scrap metal.

These measures are illustrative of the participation of lay groups in the wider aspects of the law-process. The relative effectiveness of such activities as compared with those of public officials cannot be definitely determined. However, it is quite probable that these lay organizations are not only the most effective of all in the prevention of theft but, also, that the activities of the officials are considerably influenced by these non-public groups.

V. National and Uniform State Legislation

In 1919 the United States Congress passed the National Motor Vehicle Theft Act. Representative Dyer, who sponsored it,[44] pointed out that there was very wide demand for such a law; that state laws were inadequate because thieves took automobiles across state lines where they had associates to re-

---

[42] Annual Report of The Governing Board of the National Auto Theft Bureau (1932).

[43] *Cf.* "That this system has not produced better results is probably due to the fact that it was assumed that all authorized dealers are entirely above suspicion. . . . Discrimination must still be used." Thomas North, *op. cit. supra,* n. 32.

To prevent dishonesty in these quarters, it has been suggested that the dealers be required to secure and apply a certified factory invoice for all parts purchased for specific jobs. The purchase by the dealer is to be non-returnable to prevent his using stolen parts and sending back the ones he ordered.

[44] H. R. Report of the Committee on the Judiciary, No. 312 (1919), to accompany H. R. 9203.

ceive and sell; that the losses resulting were very large and the situation was getting worse; that insurance rates were advancing so rapidly that it was difficult for owners of cheaper cars to obtain theft insurance; that the cost of insurance had increased 100 per cent on the cheaper cars within one year. The purpose of the law was to suppress crime in interstate commerce and he pointed out that the power granted Congress under the commerce clause was adequate.[45]

The bill was adopted October 29, 1919.[46] In 1925 the Supreme Court, in Brooks v. United States, held the Act (the Dyer Act, as it came to be known) constitutional.[47] Eleven years after

---

[45] In support he quoted the United States Supreme Court in the case of Pensacola Telegraph Company v. Western Union Telegraph Company, 96 U. S. 1 (1877).

[46] "Whoever shall transport or cause to be transported in interstate or foreign commerce a motor vehicle, knowing the same to have been stolen, shall be punished by a fine of not more than $5,000, or by imprisonment of not more than five years, or both. Whoever shall receive, conceal, store, barter, sell, or dispose of any motor vehicle, moving as, or which is a part of, or which constitutes interstate or foreign commerce, knowing the same to have been stolen, shall be punished by a fine of not more than $5,000, or by imprisonment of not more than five years, or both. Any person violating this section may be punished in any district in or through which such motor vehicle has been transported or removed by such offender." 41 Stat. 324, C. 89; U. S. Code Ann., tit. 18, Crim. Code and Crim. Proc., sec. 408. The present law is stated in sections 2312 and 2313, tit. 18.

[47] 207 U. S. 402. Chief Justice Taft stated:

"It is known to all men that the radical change in transportation of persons and goods effected by the introduction of the automobile, the speed with which it moves, and the ease with which evil minded persons can avoid capture, have greatly encouraged and increased crimes. One of the crimes which has been encouraged is the theft of the automobiles themselves and their immediate transportation to places remote from homes of the owners. Elaborately organized conspiracies for the theft of automobiles and the spiriting them away into some other state, and their sale or other disposition far away from the owner and his neighborhood, have roused Congress to devise some method for defeating the success of these widely spread schemes of larceny. The quick passage of the machines into another state helps to conceal the trail of the thieves, gets the stolen property into another police jurisdiction and facilitates the finding of a safe place in which to dispose of the booty at a good price. This is a gross misuse of interstate commerce." 438–9.

The report of the Attorney General of the United States for the fiscal year 1932 shows that during that year the federal government operating under the Dyer Act recovered 3322 stolen motor vehicles valued at $416,644.75. From the enactment of this law in October, 1919, to 1932, 31,343 stolen motor vehicles, valued at $21,716,836.20, have been recovered in cases in which the Bureau of Investigation participated.

the passage of the law, Representative Dyer stated that he was very much dissatisfied with its administration by the courts particularly because young boys were being sentenced to the federal prisons; [48] and he threatened to submit a bill to repeal the act entirely unless it was administered more humanely.[49]

Since 1920, insurance companies and other interested organizations have vigorously advocated the adoption by the states of uniform legislation regarding automobile theft. The need and the demand for uniformity of such laws led to the drafting of a model law, the Uniform Motor Vehicle Administration, Registration, Certificate of Title, and Anti-Theft Act, by the National Conference on Street and Highway Safety. In 1926 the law was approved by this Conference and was subsequently endorsed by the National Conference of Commissioners on Uniform State Laws, the National Crime Commission [50] and the American Bar Association. It was revised in 1930, 1934, 1938, and again in 1944. Between 1919 to 1933 twenty-six states and the District of Columbia adopted laws identical with or based upon the uniform act.[51] The initiation of this legis-

---

[48] "Arrests and prosecutions under the Dyer Act, however, include a surprisingly large number of youthful joy-riders who take cars for temporary use." Report to the Section of Cr. Law and Criminol. of the A. B. A. Ass'n. 51st Ann. Meet. July 25–7, 1928, at 4.

[49] "The district attorneys and the courts have been sending many of these young men to the penitentiary, and I want to call your attention to this letter which I have received from the superintendent of prisons of date January 24:

'Out of the 450 Federal boys in the National Training School here in Washington, nearly 200 are violators of the Dyer Act, with the ages distributed as follows:

'Two boys 12 years of age, 6 boys 13 years of age, 19 boys 14 years of age, 31 boys 15 years of age, 64 boys 16 years of age, 48 boys 17 years of age, 19 boys 18 years of age, 1 boy 19 years of age, and 1 boy 22 years of age.

'I have before me now for parole consideration the cases of four youngsters sent from middle district of Tennessee to the Missouri Reformatory at Boonville, ages, respectively, 12, 13, 14 and 15 years of age.' " 72 Cong. Rec. (Feb. 5, 1930) 2494.

[50] Mimeographed Report (May, 1931) 18 pp. The Act is part of a Uniform Vehicle Code (U. S. Gov't. Prtg. Off. 1945).

[51] Arizona, California, Colorado, Delaware, Florida, Idaho, Illinois (1934), Indiana, Maryland, Michigan, Minnesota, Missouri, Montana, Nebraska, New Mexico, North Carolina, North Dakota, Oklahoma, Oregon, Pennsylvania, South Dakota, Utah, Virginia, West Virginia, Wisconsin, Washington (1933) and the District of Columbia. See Helen Wood, *The Texas Certificate of Title Act* (1951) 5 Southwestern L. J. 423.

lation followed shortly after the adoption of the Dyer Act, partly, no doubt, because federal officials took the position that the central government could deal with only a small portion of the problem and that ultimate responsibility must rest with the states.[52]

The method used to identify and transfer real estate was copied even to the recording of all encumbrances against the automobile on the certificate of title and the delivery of the instrument to the person holding the first lien, in strict analogy with the delivery of a deed to the first mortgagee.[53]

The basis of the law is the requirement of registration of each motor car in the state. In applying for a certificate the owner of a motor vehicle must supply information as to the state of the title, the make and type of vehicle, including the motor and serial numbers. The vehicle commissioner, after ascertaining that the applicant is, in fact, the true owner of the vehicle, must issue a certificate of title. When an owner sells or transfers his automobile he must endorse and deliver the certificate of title to the transferee who, upon receipt thereof, presents it to the motor vehicle department with an application for a new certificate.[54]

---

[52] "The theft of automobiles presents a perplexing problem that can be effectively and permanently solved by quite obvious means within the power of the States." Officials of the Bureau of Investigation, quoted in Legislative Bulletin of the American Automobile Association (Dec. 24, 1924). *Cf.* The Report of the National Crime Commission (May 25, 1931).

[53] See Art. 5 of the Uniform Act.

[54] It is interesting to note the effect the law has sometimes been held to have upon civil transactions. In Endres *v.* Mara-Rickenbacker Co., 243 Mich. 5 (1928), plaintiff sued the above named defendant and one Pushkin who had purchased a second-hand automobile from the above company, which was delivered to him prior to the receipt of the certificate of title and registration. Two days after the sale the defendant Pushkin negligently collided with plaintiff's car and plaintiff brought action against Pushkin and the automobile company. The court held that the sale was void, that the automobile was the property of the company at the time of the damage, and that the company was therefore liable.

The court's decision was based upon section 4 of Act. No. 46, Pub. Acts (1921) which made it a crime to sell a motor vehicle without attaching a certificate of title. Neither this statute nor any other in the state provided that the sale or transfer without such compliance was void or fraudulent.

In Bos *v.* Holleman De Weerd Auto Co., 246 Mich. 578 (1929), plaintiff brought an action in assumpsit against the defendant to recover the purchase

Failure to utilize a system of identification based on serial and motor numbers makes it impossible to check applications for registration. The uniform act therefore provides for a cross index by motor and serial number of all cars registered. This system is permanent whereas identification by reference to registration or ownership is temporary and changing. The dissemination of information identifying stolen automobiles throughout the country facilitates the recovery of such automobiles and the detection of thieves.[55] The uniform law is thus designed to decrease the criminal disposal of automobiles, to protect innocent buyers, and to eliminate fictitious defenses by criminal receivers of such property.[56] It is claimed, also, that the Uniform Motor Vehicle Anti-Theft Act stabilizes the used car market because it requires the licensing of all dealers in second-hand automobiles and parts and requires such dealers to keep records of all transactions. Again, it is claimed that the law reduces insurance rates approximately 30 per cent.[57] Insurance companies have reduced the rates in several states which adopted the uniform act, and they held out this inducement to other states to pass such legislation.

Finally, it is alleged that the adoption of the uniform act will prevent those states which do not, at present, have such laws, from being made the dumping ground for vehicles stolen in other states. This was one of the arguments which led to the

---

price paid for an automobile. After having used the car for approximately three months and not being able to secure a certificate of title, plaintiff returned the car to the defendant and sued to recover the purchase price. The court held that the sale was void because in violation of the above statute and entered judgment for plaintiff for the full amount of the purchase price plus the interest upon it.

And see H. F. Lusk, Effect of Registration and Certificate of Title Acts on the Ownership of Motor Vehicles (1941) Indiana Business Studies, No. 21.

[55] For statements from officials of states which have adopted the uniform act that auto thefts decreased and that percentage of recoveries increased as a result, see Insurance Bulletins, Nos. 13 and 22, issued by the Chamber of Commerce of the United States.

[56] A few states require that a card identifying the owner shall be fixed to the automobile and protected by a seal.

[57] A Proposed Motor Vehicle Anti-Theft Act for Illinois prepared by the Chicago Motor Club.

adoption of the act in Illinois. It was shown that the adjoining states had adopted the uniform act and that automobiles stolen in these states were brought into Illinois where it was easy to register and sell them.

There are definite indications of the effectiveness of the Uniform Act to deter the theft of automobiles. For example, in Chicago, 29,158 automobiles were reported stolen in 1931, 35,-233 in 1932, and 27,891 in 1933. Then in 1934, the figure dropped sharply to 12,993. In 1935 it went to 6,727, and in 1936, it was 3,527. The annual average for the decade 1940–1950 was 3,176, which is 88.62% less than the 1933 figures. Something very important must have happened in Chicago to effect the sharp decline beginning in 1934. Several significant things occurred there in 1934. A specialized Auto Theft Court was organized. The activities of the Stolen Auto Section of the Police Department were expanded and a corresponding, specialized division was established in the State's Attorney's Office. And in that year, also, on January 1, 1934 the Uniform Motor Vehicle Anti-Theft Act went into effect. Although the Director of the Chicago Crime Commission emphasizes the other changes, he recognizes that the Uniform Act was "a most effective means of further curbing the operations of automobile thieves." [58]

Whatever appraisal may be made of the relative effectiveness of the various changes adopted in Chicago in 1934, it seems evident that legal controls substantially altered a serious situation and in large measure achieved desirable results. This must give pause to uncritical acceptance of the thesis that criminal behavior is merely and inevitably a reflection of a total "culture" —unless legal controls are included, and in that case the correlation can be more precise. At the same time the persistence of theft of automobile accessories suggests that criminal conduct may simply have been diverted into other, safer channels.

---

[58] Letter of June 20, 1951 from V. W. Peterson, Director, Chicago Crime Commission. The writer is also indebted to Mr. Peterson for the recent Chicago statistics set forth above.

Indeed, not only theft of automobile accessories, but the frequency of similar types of crime would need to be known to support definite claims regarding the "total" effect of the new legal controls. This does not imply that we must shut our eyes to plain evidence of a sharp decline in certain types of criminal behavior and to the persuasiveness of a causal relation between that and certain legal reforms.

CHAPTER SEVEN

EMBEZZLEMENT

I. The Social Problem

Although embezzlement can be studied from many perspectives, an investigator who is guided by legal meanings has a definite sphere of relevance marked out for him. As we shall see, however, its ramifications are wide, and the problem investigated is nonetheless social. A study of violation of financial trust in a sense that is both legal and social cannot, however, be greatly influenced by the nuances of refined legal definitions, e.g. those concerning larceny by servant and the complexities of modern statutes which fuse embezzlement with larceny. We shall focus on embezzlement as it is usually defined in criminal law—the conversion of legally possessed property—but related offenses, laws, and practices which are socially important will need to be considered.

Certain phases of embezzlement are significant for all perspectives—its frequency, the kinds of offenders and the economic losses involved. Unfortunately, it is impossible to discover the relevant facts very precisely. The embezzlers won't confess, their employers are similarly silent in inordinate numbers, and the available statistics are little more than random samplings. Yet, a good deal of information on these questions is available, and investigation leads to a few definite conclusions which are sufficiently precise for purposes of legal control. Let us set out the principal conclusions first, then describe some of the supporting data.

The most distinctive facts regarding embezzlement are (1) the very high frequency of the offense and (2) its incidence in all strata of society. The discomforting likelihood, plainly indicated as one probes the data, is that if everyone was not sometime in his life an embezzler, at least a large percent of all types of person in every profession, vocation, social and economic status, has sometime committed embezzlement. Larceny is also frequent but the trespass involved limits its incidence among adults to persons usually identified with the "criminal classes" although, of course, individuals of socially approved groups sometimes steal. Receiving stolen property is definitely déclassé. Only in criminal fraud is the "white collar" offender equally prominent. There, however, manual laborers, lacking the necessary wit or inclination, are not represented in anything like their numbers found in embezzlement. For, though embezzlement has been regarded as a white collar crime,[1] the fact is that embezzlers are representative of all the "classes." It is impossible to determine the precise proportions; and the bonding of the more responsible jobs and the greater amounts involved there weight the recorded data toward obscuring the countless undetected petty embezzlements that undoubtedly occur.

Our first task is to fill the above general observations with concrete data in order that embezzlement may be more realistically apprehended. Suggestive information is found in cases reported in the newspapers: [2]

A woman, entrusted with her friend's funds for investment purposes, converted almost $15,000. 7/18/13

A hotel clerk took $200. 8/3/13

A postal clerk on a U.S. battleship embezzled government funds. 8/9/13

A bookkeeper took $8000. 8/17/13

The vice-president of a Texas bank embezzled $120,000. 9/6/13

The president of an export company embezzled almost $4000. 9/7/13

---

[1] E. H. Sutherland, White Collar Crime (1949) 231; 1001 Embezzlers 5 (pub. by U.S.F.&G.Co. 1943).

[2] The following cases were selected from the much more numerous items collected by my former colleague, the late Edwin Sutherland, and I am greatly obliged to Mrs. Sutherland for permission to use her husband's voluminous files on the subject. Unless otherwise stated, the reports are from *The New York Times.*

A cashier, employed at $20 per week, embezzled $50,000. 9/9/13

The assistant paymaster of a United States cruiser converted government property. 9/18/13

The director of a large bank took $650,000. 9/20/13

A public official took $2645. 9/20/13

A probation agent was charged with embezzling $475. Minneapolis Journal 3/25/27

A real estate and mortgage broker was sentenced 1–10 years for embezzlement. Minneapolis Journal 7/22/27

Twelve bank employees embezzled over 3½ million dollars in 2 years. Literary Digest 12/7/29, p. 82–84.

A company treasurer was found guilty of taking $87,000. 1/10/31

The brother of a former Attorney General of the United States, convicted of misapplying bank funds, was sentenced to 10 years imprisonment. 2/4/31

A Brooklyn lawyer was charged with embezzling $5000 from the estate of a disabled war veteran, the total shortage being $60,000. 2/4/31

A Newark lawyer embezzled $17,500 and was sentenced to 2 years in the penitentiary. 2/11/31

Kentucky bankers were charged with the embezzlement of $2,000,000 and misapplication of $7,000,000. 2/28/31

A Bible salesman took money collected from purchasers. 3/5/31

Several bankers had a shortage of $2,000,000. 3/5/31 [3]

A real estate operator embezzled more than $2,000,000. 3/18/31

---

[3] "Defalcations have been the largest single cause of insured bank failures. Of the 415 banks requiring the financial aid of the [F.D.I.] Corporation since its inception 17 years ago, 120—more than one out of four—were wrecked by dishonest employees . . . These widespread irregularities by bank employees are not new to the banking business, but our study shows that they are increasing at an alarming rate." *Integrity, Are You Protecting This Risk Asset?* An address by E. H. Cramer, Chief, Div. Research and Statistics, F.D.I.C., April 10, 1951.

The treasurer of a Virginia orphanage converted its funds. 4/9/31

State funds taken by public employees were fines collected from motor vehicle violators. 4/11/31

The manager of a building and loan association took $1,-000,000, pleaded guilty, was sentenced 30–60 years. 4/17/31

An Illinois county auditor took $65,000; on discovery, he committed suicide. 5/6/31

A clerk in a water department took $10,000, pleaded guilty. 5/6/31

A clerk in a city tax department took $4700. 5/9/31

An employee of a bonding company took $18,000 over a period of 3 years. 5/21/31

A borough collector disappeared with $1500. 6/4/31

A clerk in a welfare department took $207,000. 6/10/31

An American Legion official was sentenced to 6–15 years for taking $2500 from a fund for the care of orphans of war veterans. 6/19/31

An official embezzled $1050 from a county tuberculosis sanitarium. 6/19/31

The president of a corporation embezzled $125,000. 6/24/31

An accountant took $18,000 from the corporation employing him. 6/25/31

A clerk in a ticket agency took $18,000. 7/25/31

A local banker pleaded guilty to embezzlement of $250,000; his sentence was 3–6 years. 7/27/31

The manager of the coupon department of a Chicago bank took $3,500,000. Sentenced 10–100 years; paroled after serving 15 years. 9/2/31 [4]

Two church officials took $60,000 of the church's money. 10/22/31

A broker's assistant cashier took $2000. 11/1/31

---

[4] "The largest embezzlement which has come to our attention was created over a period of eight years by a Secretary-Manager of a Building and Loan Association and amounted to $10,811,000." R. T. Wood, *Millions Under Bond* (monograph pub. by American Surety Co.).

An Army lieutenant took U.S. property. 11/5/31

Clerks in an Alimony Bureau took $27,000 in a 5-year period. 12/5/31

The treasurer of a fraternal order took between $60,000 and $70,000. 12/6/31

The cashier of a corporation took $54,000. 12/21/31

A University treasurer was charged with embezzlement. Chicago Tribune 6/9/32

A state receiver of a building pleaded guilty to embezzling over $1000. Chicago Tribune 12/30/32

Chicago city garbage collectors who converted the city's gasoline to operate their own automobiles, said, "Everybody is doing it." Chicago Tribune 6/18/33

" . . . former bursar of the University of Manitoba, and a pillar of the_____church who was convicted of million dollar defalcations which halved the university's endowment fund and damaged the diocese finances . . ." Chicago Tribune 10/6/33

The treasurer of a college fraternity embezzled $32,000. Chicago Tribune 9/12/34

A Kentucky mayor, a clergyman, a county judge and four others were indicted for embezzling over $122,000 federal relief administration funds. Chicago Tribune 9/26/34

Women embezzlers, reported in the newspapers 1933–35, held the following positions: investment counsellor, secretary to woman's club, banker, cashier of realty concern, secretary to railroad supply house, cashier of association, treasurer of law enforcement division of the W.C.T.U., treasurer of schools, cashier of a hospital, cashier of American Dental Association, secretary for teachers' retirement fund, partner in realty company, and several who merely acted for their husbands.

"Charge_____looted union of $500,000." Chicago Tribune 4/5/35

A Kansas banker was found guilty of embezzling $63,000 and was sentenced to 36–60 years; he committed suicide. Chicago Tribune 6/7/35

A Navy paymaster embezzled $20,000 of Government funds. Indianapolis Star 2/21/36

A W.P.A. timekeeper was charged with embezzlement. Indianapolis Star 12/17/36

In 1938 Richard Whitney, former President of the New York Stock Exchange, embezzled large sums and was sentenced to 5–10 years for grand larceny in New York. The psychiatric report stated that an intelligence test showed Whitney rated so high that only "1 per cent of the people of the world could score as well." [5] Judge Owen W. Bohan said: "Your course in the last six years, has been a course of thefts and larcenies, of frauds and misrepresentations, of falsifications of books and financial statements covering losses of several millions of dollars . . . I can see nothing in your record to mitigate the circumstances . . ." Combined liabilities of Whitney and his firm amounted to $11,000,000. 4/13/38

An elevator operator of a New York department store was accused of merchandise thefts totalling $5000. New York Herald Tribune 10/5/38

Seventy-three persons, including many officials, were indicted for embezzling W.P.A. funds in New Mexico. Indianapolis Star 10/21/38

A jewelry store clerk embezzled property valued at $3000. He pleaded guilty and was sentenced to 1–10 years. Indianapolis Star 5/19/39

A Vatican library bookkeeper embezzled $30,000. Sentenced to 4 years and 4 months, he was pardoned by the Pope after serving about six months. Indianapolis Star 5/20/39

A New York broker took $60,000 and pleaded guilty. Indianapolis Star 5/28/39

A Kansas City city manager was indicted for embezzling $365,000. Indianapolis Star 6/30/39

Louisiana scandals of 1939, concerning the University President and Governor. Time Magazine 7/10/39. Saturday Evening Post Editorial 8/26/39[6]

---

[5] C. A. Murchison reports that embezzlers have the highest I.Q. of any class of criminals. Criminal Intelligence (1926) 58–62.

[6] "A similar study by the Fidelity and Casualty Company for the period 1932 to 1947 showed that of the losses of $5,000 or more on public official

A Michigan Bishop was paroled after serving 9 months for embezzling church funds. Indianapolis Star 7/6/40

A warehouse foreman, an order filler, and an order checker took $155,000 worth of meat from the warehouse of a meat-packing company. New York Times 7/14/40

In St. Louis, over $100,000 was taken from the treasury of a labor union. Indianapolis Star 11/8/41

Dock workers of an oil company embezzled over $1,000,000 in fuel oil. New York Times 4/19/42

A Michigan Supervisor of a Social Security Bureau embezzled almost $7000 in state-owned postage stamps. Indianapolis Star 4/22/42

A transfer clerk and a stock clerk in the warehouse of a large department store took $250,000 worth of merchandise. New York Times 11/29/42

An employee stole drugs and surgical supplies from a hospital. Newark Evening News 4/9/43

An assistant sales manager took $57,000 worth of coffee, tea, and rice in five years. New York Times 4/30/43

F.B.I. Director scores plant pilferers who have stolen nails, flashlights, tools, materials and equipment from industrial plants. New York Times 2/14/44

A Justice of the Peace embezzled $2500, was fined $500 and sentenced to 1–5 years. Indianapolis Star 4/2/44

Four employees of a wholesale tea and coffee firm were accused of stealing $10,000 worth of tea and coffee. New York Herald Tribune 5/4/44

A counterman was held in theft of $15,000 worth of butter from a restaurant. New York Sun 5/12/44

A jeweler's messenger was held in $10,000 theft of gems from his employers. New York Times 6/9/44

Eight men, including a captain of railroad police, were accused of stealing 6,500,000 pounds of scrap metal worth $650,-

---

bonds, 82% of the gross losses were attributable to dishonesty. A study by the Hartford Accident and Indemnity Company showed that 87.5% of its losses on public official bonds was due to dishonesty." Jules Backman, Surety Rate-Making (1948) 169.

000 from a railroad over a five-year period. New York Times 6/10/44

A filling station attendant embezzled $108 and was sentenced to 2–20 years. Indianapolis Star 9/22/48

The head of a collection agency was charged with embezzling $2500. Indianapolis Star 10/24/48

A labor union officer pleaded guilty to embezzling $1000 in union dues. His 2–20 year sentence was suspended. Indianapolis Star 11/7/48

"A 'model citizen' and former bank head today pleaded guilty to embezzling $49,000 over a 17-year period." Indianapolis Star 11/18/48

A mother embezzled her son's (a disabled veteran) guardianship funds. Indianapolis Star 4/29/49

A nurse took $20,000 from a Pennsylvania State Nurses' Association. Indianapolis Star 5/29/49

A truck driver who collected and kept about $300 was sentenced 2–20 years, fined $50, and disenfranchised for 5 years. Bloomington (Indiana) World-Telephone 11/2/49

A J.P.'s shortage was about $4000. Indianapolis Star 5/18/50

Half a million dollars' worth of merchandise was stolen from Montgomery Ward & Co. by truck drivers and warehouse employees. New York newspapers 6/26–27/51

A night clerk at the Y.M.C.A. hotel was arrested for embezzlement of $1100. The New York World Telegram and Sun 6/29/51

A renowned bacteriologist embezzled over $34,000 in university funds in 13 years; when discovered, he committed suicide. New York Times 8/25/51

An Army sergeant, veteran of 13 years service, embezzled $10,000 in Army theatre funds. New York Times 8/26/51

A public relations man took $93,000 in funds collected for the Sister Elizabeth Kenney Foundation. New York Times 8/31/51

The assistant cashier of a bank took $550,000 from the bank in 22 years. Fort Wayne Journal Gazette 9/14/51

A West Virginia bank teller, over a four year period, stole $363,410. Indianapolis Times 9/24/51

In one year almost $3,000,000 was embezzled by officers of seven banks in western Pennsylvania and West Virginia. New York Times 10/1/51

"The Federal Bureau of Investigation announced today the arrest of 120 persons in two months . . . accused of stealing more than $1,000,000 in goods from the armed forces.

"F.B.I. agents picked up trusted Federal employees with years of service . . ." New York Times 10/12/51

Officers of a Pittsburgh employees' credit union embezzled more than $300,000. Indianapolis Times 10/24/51

One may suspect the typicality of the above data because an event must have "news value" before it finds a place in the press. "Comparatively few embezzlements get into public print,"[7] and this raises questions regarding those reported. For example, embezzlements of small amounts by clerks, salespersons, and laborers are not sufficiently interesting to warrant publication; and it is also known that most defalcations of bonded embezzlers are not published.

Studies of the latter[8] disclose a very wide occupational distribution: branch managers of groceries, clothing, shoe, liquor, dairy and other stores, salesmen of products and services of all kinds, executive officers, treasurers, secretaries, auditors, bookkeepers, cashiers, clerks, stewards, buyers, paymasters, collectors, drivers and delivery men, laborers, attorneys, postal clerks, service men, superintendents of hospitals and apartment buildings, ticket sellers, warehousemen, watchmen, stock and shipping clerks, union officials, treasurers and assistant treasurers, foremen, laborers, and various others.[9] The women embezzlers were mostly employed in offices, and some were branch or office managers, and there were also store clerks, waitresses, and even a maid and a charwoman were represented. The bonded embezzler described in these studies is

---

[7] 1001 Embezzlers 10 (U.S.F.&G.Co. 1943).

[8] The following text is based on two studies by the U. S. F. & G. Co. on 1001 Embezzlers, 1943 and 1950.

[9] ". . . a private detective placed in a bank in order to develop certain information stole $500 from the bank." R. T. Wood, *Millions Under Bond* (monograph pub. by American Surety Co.).

"employed in every type of business."[10] "He is a regular fellow, a normal individual . . ."[11] "Again, the list includes employees of every degree of importance—from warehouse watchman to president."[12] "Every class of occupation is represented among the 1,001 embezzlers."[13] The same findings are met in a later study.[14] They are widely accepted among experienced officials of surety companies.[15] It should be noted again, however, that we do not know the *percent of each type of person (or vocation) who embezzles.* E.g., although an occasional college president, teacher, or clergyman embezzles, the percentage of embezzlers found in each of these groups is probably much lower than that in other vocations.

An index of the economic loss resulting from embezzlements is provided in statistics on the cost of fidelity insurance and on insured losses (amounts paid the insured) due to embezzlement. In 1925 almost $34,000,000 was paid in premiums and that amount rose to more than $45,000,000 in 1929. In 1925 the insured losses due to embezzlement were almost $13,000,000 and they rose to almost $21,000,000 in 1929.[16] However, as the Reporter for the Commission which published the above figures observed, they are not a valid index of the total of such losses because most defalcations are not covered by insurance and even the insurance that is carried covers only a fraction of the loss sustained. More recent figures are much larger. For 1950 the three types of surety company operating in this coun-

---

[10] 1001 Embezzlers (1943) 5.

[11] *Id.* 6.

[12] *Id.* 9.

[13] *Id.* 17.

[14] *E.g.* "All types of business are represented." *Id.* (1950) 9. ". . . in positions of every degree of importance, from handymen to heads of establishments." *Id.* 11. " 'White collar' men and men in shirt sleeves, office women and those of more humble status." *Id.* 15, 17.

[15] A writer with considerable experience in fidelity insurance reports: "The confidential files of surety or bonding companies contain confessions of persons from every walk of life. Investigation reports constitute irrefutable proof that dishonesty has no respect for position, salary, age, marital status, or education. It is oblivious of race, creed, sex and color." W. K. Mendenhall, *Bank Losses*, reprint p. 2, from Feb. 1947 National Auditgram.

[16] Nat'l. Com. on Law Obs. and Enf. no. 12, June 24, 1931, pp. 396, 415.

try reported that net premiums earned by them were $45,000,-000, $2,087,546 and $6,181,488 and from these respective sums the following losses, stated in percentages of premiums earned, were paid to insured persons: 29%, 46.7%, and 32.3%.[17]

So far as the total direct economic loss is concerned, little more is available than the guesses of experienced observers. Thus, we are told that "it is estimated that employers in the United States lose $200,000,000 yearly through employe dishonesty"[18] and that "a surety company recently announced that $2,000,000 currently is being embezzled on every single business day,"[19] which would bring the total to over half a billion dollars annually.[20] In any event, it is very probable that the annual losses due to embezzlement are so great that only experienced financiers can comprehend their enormity.

Certain important findings emerge: embezzlement is very frequent, widespread, and costly in economic loss and in damage to other values which are important in any society. Embezzlers are found in all strata of society, vocations, and professions. Although embezzlement often extends over a period of years, professional criminality is rarely met.[21] Embezzlers are older than most other offenders.[22] There are, of course, many other facts about embezzlers but those stated above seem to be most significant for purposes of appraising legal controls.

Without idealizing past economic organizations, e.g. guilds and small enterprises, or overlooking the frequency of crimes of violence in earlier periods, one must recognize that embezzle-

---

[17] Jour. of Commerce, August 14, 1951.

[18] 1001 Embezzlers 3 (U.S.F.&G.Co. 1943).

[19] Lester A. Pratt, *I Catch Bank Embezzlers*, Colliers, Nov. 20, 1948, p. 51. K. H. Wood, Secy., U.S.F.&G.Co., said a million dollars a day is "an understatement." The Rotarian, July 1951, p. 11.

[20] R. T. Wood, Manager, Fidelity Dept., American Surety Co., states: "The total amount of embezzlements each year is variously estimated at from $200,-000,000 to $405,000,000. . . ." *Millions Under Bond* (monograph pub. by American Surety Co.).

[21] For an interesting account of a professional embezzler, see St. Clair Mc-Kelway, *Annals of Crime—The Wily Wilby* (Jan. 1, 8, 1949) *The New Yorker*.

[22] Only 1.1% of those arrested for embezzlement and fraud in 1950 were under 18 years of age. 6.4% were under 21, while for auto theft 46.7% and for burglary, 40.7% were under 21. Unif. Cr. Rep. 1950, Vol. 21, Table 42, p. 111.

ment and other crimes against property not involving violence seem to have greatly increased in modern times.[23] When economic units were small and their owners had a direct interest in the business, sole custody of the cash, and were in immediate contact with all the employees, dishonesty was apt to be discovered quickly and vigorously discouraged. These conditions stand in sharp contrast to contemporary commercial and industrial enterprise, e.g., enormous capital investments, corporate organizations directed by managers—with owners distant, disinterested, and scattered among thousands of unknown persons, indeed, with even the managers far removed from the daily conduct of the employees. Even the symbols of traditional working relationships dissolve in the abstractions of huge corporate enterprise *vis a vis* solitary depersonalized wage earners.[24] Under such conditions, loyalty to an employer becomes unreal and devitalized, while prevention tends more and more to depend on mechanical devices, checks, and audits emphasizing the tacit canon that no man is trustworthy. The problem is actually more complex because enlightened personnel policies of many corporations have provided substitutes for the traditional methods of enlisting honest, loyal work. Yet modern business as a whole confronts a serious problem in this regard.[25]

---

[23] *Cf.* Sutherland, Principles of Criminology (4th ed. 1947) 38. Even short-range changes are indicated. *E.g.* ". . . at present there seems to be more danger from the trusted officer and the employee than from the burglar. Formerly the greatest danger was to be apprehended from the skilled burglar, who could blow open the vault doors, 'crack' the safe, and make off with the money; but now it is the skilled financier or bank clerk who coolly and quietly abstracts or misapplies the funds, falsifies the accounts, and makes away with millions where the burglar got thousands." A. R. Barrett ("An Ex-Government Examiner of Failed Banks") *The Era of Fraud and Embezzlement*, 14 The Arena (Boston, 1895) 197.

[24] *Cf.* F. W. Lanfrentz, *Defalcations*, 24 Jour. of Accountancy, 254–261.

[25] "There is a pronounced certainty of loss . . . This certainty is supported by many studies. For example, 62% of bank employees in a midwest city handling cash admitted, after undergoing a polygraph (lie detector) test, that they stole small or large sums of money. One chain store concern discovered that in one district 76% of its employees took money or merchandise, or both. Its annual loss from employee dishonesty amounted to $1,500,000." Jules Backman, Surety Rate-Making 60 (1948), citing Scott, Clothier, Mathewson and Spriegel, Personnel Management 1941, p. 190.

It is an easy "solution" of difficult problems to point to the economic organization and competitive character of American society as "the cause" of crimes against property, and thus to assert or imply that legal controls are unimportant. Without being diverted into a lengthy discussion of fundamental theories of history and culture, we need, in order to understand the problem of embezzlement and appraise legal controls correctly, to consider some facts regarding embezzlement in Russia.

Newspaper reports have long indicated that embezzlement is a serious problem in Russia. The doubts that may be raised regarding such reports are dissipated on reference to source materials. They reveal an interesting situation, highly significant for legal sociology.

Writing in 1933, N. Krylenko,[26] after referring to various recent trials in Moscow, Leningrad, and other cities, states: "These were trials of embezzlers and marauders in the supply organizations and in the co-operative system . . . today it is impossible to find anywhere a single co-operative or government store free from pilferers, marauders, thieves, speculators, rascals, embezzlers etc . . . In Moscow five death sentences were passed on people of just this type . . . in Leningrad there were two such sentences and the same number in Kharkov . . . What does this mean? It means that at present there is a channel through which the class enemy penetrates our midst . . . He is aided by 'disinterested' assistants, who of course never put anything into their own pockets, or, well, just a trifle, don't you know! These include Communists, who hold jobs at vital nerve centers of trade, supply or the co-operative system and who 'disinterestedly' assist the thieves and connivers in misappropriating Soviet goods . . ."[27] He then discussed the Decree of August 7, 1932 which imposed the capital penalty for theft of public property, with allowance for discretionary commutation

---

[26] Revolutionary Law, pub. in Moscow and Leningrad 1933 (monograph 39 pages).
[27] Id. 18.

to ten years' imprisonment and confiscation of property.[28]

The Russian penal law on embezzlement has recently been discussed at length by Professor John Hazard.[29] "The interest of Soviet legislators, courts, and authors in the crime of embezzlement has grown with the years . . . Authors link it with treason. Some of the highest penalties permitted by the criminal code apply to it. The constitution itself castigates it . . . 'Persons committing offenses against public, socialist property are enemies of the people.' In the Soviet lexicon there can be no greater condemnation."[30] It is quite clear, as Professor Hazard's study reveals, that embezzlement is frequent and widespread,[31] and the available data do not suggest any political motivation, although the crime of embezzlement was for some years "the most common of all crimes committed by officials . . ."[32] The cases are apparently ordinary crimes against property—the crucial difference being that Russian State-owned property is involved.[33] Although statistics are not available, one learns from an instruction issued by the Office of the Prosecutor of the U.S.S.R. on May 5, 1936 "that he had much information on a large number of embezzlements and thefts from agencies of voluntary public organizations . . . The circular says that in 1935

---

[28] Decree of the Central Executive Committee and the Council of the People's Commissars of the U.S.S.R. "The Central Executive Committee and the Council of People's Commissars of the U.S.S.R. consider public property (state, collective farm and co-operative) the foundation of the Soviet order; it is sacred and inviolable, and whoever does violence to public property must be deemed an enemy of the people, in view of which the ruthless struggle against embezzlers of public property is the foremost duty of the Soviet authorities." *Id.* 38.

[29] *Soviet Socialism and Embezzlement* (1951) 26 Wash. L. Rev. & St. Bar J. 301.

[30] *Id.* 301–302.

[31] Professor A. Trainin, a leading Russian legal scholar, writing of the earlier period of the Soviet Republic, states that economic crimes were numerous in 1922, and in 1923 they rose 450% above their former rate, occupying first place among all crimes. He concluded: ". . . one-third of all crimes in Soviet Russia consist of economic crimes." A. Trainin, *Les Crimes et Délits Economiques,* (1925) Revista Pénale at 470.

[32] Hazard, *op. cit.* 304.

[33] Collective farm and cooperative property were held the equivalent of "state property" in judicial interpretations of the statutes. Hazard, *op. cit.* 310, 316.

alone there were taken from *Osoviakhim* by embezzlement or
theft 1,750,000 rubles. It criticizes the work of the prosecutors
and declares that during 1935 there were 518 indictments for
embezzlement or theft within the *Osoviakhim*, but that conviction of only thirty-nine persons resulted. It is noted that
special growth of these offenses is found [in certain named
republics and provinces]."[34] In spite of the avowal, at least in
the early periods, of theories of nonpunitive treatment of criminals, the sanction for embezzlement in Russia has sometimes
been the capital penalty and, if it is not that now, it is certainly
one of the most severely punished crimes.

The crime-in-relation-to-culture thesis must, accordingly, be
formulated in terms sufficiently wide to include at least both
the Russian and the American socio-economic situations. A
rather loose theory, suggested by experienced surety officials,
is that anyone will embezzle when temptation is great and concealment is easy. A theory carefully formulated and tested by
D. R. Cressey is that embezzlement occurs when (a) a pressing
"non-shareable" financial problem (b) concurs with opportunities to embezzle without detection and (c) "rationalization" of the conversion, not as subsequent justification but as a
cause *preceding* the conversion, e.g. in terms of its being a
temporary "borrowing."[35] None of the extant studies has much
to offer regarding the diminution of embezzlement, though the
better ones warn against the likelihood that a solution can
easily be found. But where serious problems exist, the persons

---

[34] Hazard, *op. cit.* 312.
The New York Times, Feb. 6, 1952, reports: "A major wave of embezzlements, automobile thefts and similar crimes in Soviet Georgia has resulted in a
wholesale purge of top Communist and Government officials in that area, diplo-
matic sources report."

[35] Donald R. Cressey, Criminal Violation of Financial Trust (Ph.D. Thesis,
Indiana University) 1950. Cressey summarized his theory as follows: "Trusted
persons become trust violators when they conceive of themselves as having
a financial problem which is non-shareable, have the knowledge or awareness
that this problem can be secretly resolved by violation of the position of
financial trust, and are able to apply to their own conduct in that situation
verbalizations which enable them to adjust their conceptions of themselves
as trusted persons with their conceptions of themselves as users of the entrusted funds or property." Cressey, *The Criminal Violation of Financial Trust*
(1950) 15 American Sociological Review 742.

immediately involved deal with them in various ways. So far as they are concerned, their practices are more or less adequate solutions.

II. THE PRACTICES OF EMPLOYERS AND SURETY COMPANIES

Public attitudes have long condemned the conduct of thieves and "fences." These offenders' values are opposed to those of the community. There is no serious conflict among members of the community regarding the desirability of reducing the rate of larceny and criminal receiving by enforcement of the law.

In embezzlement we confront important differences. They result from the wholesale violations among all strata of the community, aggravated by a consensus of opinion regarding the values involved, i.e., the embezzlers recognize that they are violating their own values. More important is the fact that when detected, they are treated sympathetically by those in control. Thus, in sum, embezzlement is wrong; everybody, including most embezzlers, recognize that,[36] and there is no basic challenge to the rightness of the prevailing standards. But, far from rigorous law-enforcement by the "dominant class" when its property interests are criminally appropriated, we encounter condonation and wholesale avoidance of legal coercion. In sharp contrast to what we find regarding *known apprehended* thieves and criminal receivers (against whom there is ample evidence for conviction), in the case of the embezzlers, there is such lack of law-enforcement as practically to nullify the legal controls.

All of the relevant literature as well as letters to the writer from experienced observers and oral statements made to him agree that ". . . the embezzler . . . is seldom prosecuted."[37] A

---

[36] "The embezzler . . . has no philosophy to support him in his trial and punishment." Sutherland, Principles of Criminology (4th ed. 1947) 200. ". . . the trust violator, unlike the confidence man or the professional thief, violates his own code of values. As a member of society and particularly as a trusted person he accepts certain standards of behavior, including an ideal of honesty . . ." Cressey, Criminal Violation of Financial Trust (Thesis, *op. cit.*) 206.

[37] R. Walton, Amer. Surety Co. publication, 1932.

contemporary investigator reports that "... perhaps most of the embezzlement cases are disposed of through the discharge of the employee without the initiation of prosecutive action. Some companies have a definite policy against prosecuting dishonest employees."[38] Almost 50 years ago another investigator said: "One of the first sure conclusions reached after a study of embezzlements is that the larger number of them are never made public. The employer is sorry and doesn't prosecute; restitution is made, or promised, and the thing is hushed up."[39] This indicates that we do not confront an unusual or post-war situation.

The best available sources of information on this question are the executives of surety companies, who have had wide experience in this field for many years. Accordingly, the writer on April 6, 1951 wrote to twelve large surety companies and, later, to three national associations of surety companies, asking for data on (1) the administration of the criminal law on embezzlement and (2) the percentage of known embezzlers who were prosecuted. In this latter connection, the writer ventured to suggest that relatively few embezzlers were prosecuted and that employers often avoid prosecution, preferring restitution. Eleven replies were received.

The replies, written by some of the ablest surety company executives in the country, included the following statements:

(1) "... it is our considered opinion, based on claim cases that less than 1% of embezzlers are prosecuted by their employers."

(2) "From our day to day experience in handling fidelity claims, we know very definitely that there are far more embezzlers who escape prosecution than are actually prosecuted ... We dare say that three out of four embezzlers are not prosecuted."

(3) "As a matter of fact, it [prosecution] is rare ... where

---

[38] V. W. Peterson, Operating Director, Chicago Crime Commission, Why Honest People Steal 12 (Pub. by Chicago Crime Commission 1947).

[39] Alfred A. Thomas, *The Temptation of Employees Who Handle Money* 15 (Pub. Nat'l. Cash Register Co. 1905).

many thousands of dollars is concerned and the case is one of public knowledge, there is prosecution, but this is an unusual situation rather than the usual."

(4) "From our experience in the case of private or commercial employers as distinguished from banks or Government agencies, we find it the very rare case where the employer prosecutes . . . from my experience over a long period of years in handling claims involving embezzlements, I should judge that one in 100 employers would prosecute."

(5) The other correspondents said they had no data or statistics on the questions asked, one saying he could not even venture a guess, but none of them challenged the suggestion that very few known embezzlers are prosecuted.

In the present study, that will be regarded as an established fact; and on that premise, we proceed to consider the reasons for this interesting phenomenon. We shall first present a number of operating influences and shall later venture certain generalizations regarding them.

1. The embezzler does not fall within the popular conception of "criminal." That is obviously true of the white collar embezzlers, including bankers and public officials who, far from suggesting criminal types, are regarded as models of success to be imitated. And the embezzler in shirt sleeves, the truckdriver and warehouse employee, though they do not evoke such wide imitation, are respected members of their group. All are distinguished from the prototype of the "criminal" to whom otherness and malevolence are attributed.

2. Important consequences result. Psychologically, the principal reaction is easy identification with the embezzler; indeed, if he is the employee of a large corporation, as is probably the case,[40] it is much easier for most persons to identify themselves with him than with his employer, a "soulless entity." This situation must be contrasted with those represented in crimes of violence and even with simple larceny where identi-

---

[40] "The ordinary case of embezzlement is a crime by a single individual in a subordinate position against a strong corporation." Sutherland, White Collar Crime (1949) 231.

fication with the offender is marginal or dependent on unusual sensitivity, and where normal identification is apt to be with the victim.

3. With regard to the employer, it should be noted that, although it is an exaggeration to say that the "typical embezzler" is the old trusted employee,[41] this is sometimes true; and in many more instances he has been employed in the same firm for several years. Despite the relative impersonality of modern business, there are degrees of personal attachment ranging from friendship to an appreciation of the symbols of protection that motivate the managers of many large organizations. The manager's loyalty to the corporation is offset by his immediate relations with, and concern for, the employee.

4. Embezzlement is often, though not always, an expression of a serious personal problem, and the motive is sometimes a good one. This factor coalesces with, and augments, the preceding ones. In sum, it is easy to understand, to identify oneself with and, thus, to condone the conduct of persons who resemble us and who were sorely beset by difficulties that trouble many decent persons.

The situations and attitudes described above do not always exist or, if present, they are not invariably the dominating factors. Frequently, the impersonal relations of modern business prevail over sympathetic attitudes. A trust has been violated, expected loyalties have been trod upon. Instead of touching family needs, the motive is often the pressure of debt resulting from gambling or worse, practices which, however common, are condemned. Moreover, if the offender is left unpunished, will that not encourage defalcation by other employees? In light of the undoubted operation of these attitudes and policies, explanation of the infrequent prosecution of known embezzlers must include other factors than those discussed above.

---

[41] "More than four-fifths (85.2 per cent) of the embezzlers were employed less than five years in their bonded positions when their embezzlements were discovered. . . .

"From the point of view of amount of loss, the long-time trusted employees tend to embezzle the largest sums. . . ." E. Redden, Embezzlement 53 (Ph.D. Thesis, Univ. of Chicago 1939).

5. Many employers avoid prosecution because of the cost of investigation and the inconvenience and uncertainty of trials. Cases of embezzlement extending over a period of years and, often, less continuous defalcations require detailed, costly investigations to gather the facts and reduce them to forms necessary for presentation as evidence in a courtroom.[42] These costs are not covered by insurance (nor are they insurable at present); hence the employer confronts a direct, often large, out-of-pocket expenditure. Besides, there are the loss in time, including that spent in court, the inconveniences resulting from seemingly interminable continuances, the "tying-up" of the books and records of the company and, finally, the uncertainties of criminal trials resulting from the protections available to the accused and the officials' and juries' leniency. Many employers, intent on rigorous law-enforcement and willing to make the necessary sacrifices, have met only disappointment and frustration after prolonged trials. Having suffered or having heard about such experiences, they are apt to be deterred from the prosecution of embezzlers.

Fear of reprisal by suit for false arrest or malicious prosecution is also alleged to be an important influence. The fact, however, seems to be that although employers express such apprehension, there is little, if any, ground to support it. Unfounded opinions are sometimes potent, and several executives of surety companies, with whom the writer corresponded, referred to the possibility of such reprisal as a deterrent to the initiation of prosecution by employers. At least one surety company instructs its field agents: "No warrant should be sworn out by a company representative," indicating a like wariness. The only rational basis of this policy is advice of cautious counsel whose mere reference to the possibility of a suit for damages carries weight.

The question seemed of sufficient importance to engage the attention of Miles F. McDonald, District Attorney of King's

---

[42] These problems are discussed by B. Kostelanetz, *The Auditor Meets the Thief* (July 1951) 21 The N. Y. Cert. Pub. Accountant 458.

County, New York who, on May 22, 1950, addressed a meeting of the American Management Association on the subject of embezzlement.[43] Mr. McDonald said, "There are a lot of companies which are afraid of unlawful-arrest lawsuits, yet I personally have never seen a successful unlawful-arrest suit in a case of this kind."[44] He advised employers to refer cases of embezzlement to the prosecuting attorney who would either file an information or, in a doubtful case, present the facts to a grand jury, allowing arrest to follow the return of an indictment. The actual infrequency of damage suits and the availability of these simple protective measures and of abundant proof of reasonable grounds for initiating prosecution suggest that fear of reprisal is actually a minor influence or that, apart from other much more potent factors, such influence would be negligible. The fact is that employers are already persuaded on other grounds not to initiate prosecution. When their lawyer mentions the possibility of a suit for damages, that is used as little more than confirmation of a decision that has already been made.

6. A much more direct, potent influence (in addition to expense, inconvenience, and uncertainty of trial) is the employers' dislike of the publicity regarding embezzlement in their establishment. This is particularly emphasized with reference to banks and other institutions whose good will is dependent on public confidence in the honesty of the staff. Even when prosecutions are actually started, the reports given newspapers grossly understate the amounts embezzled. Several correspondents adverted to the "adverse effects on the business of publicity," suggesting that this consideration is not limited to banks. A different aspect of adverse publicity is suggested by one correspondent who notes that businessmen are deterred from prosecution if the embezzler in their employ received a small salary or if he took the money to meet an emergency, e.g. to pay for his wife's operation. In such situations, public criti-

---

[43] Published in *Controls and Coverages against Dishonesty Loss,* Insurance Series No. 85, by the American Management Association, New York, 1950.
[44] *Id.* 15.

cism and even animosity might be directed against the company which initiated a criminal prosecution. Thus, in many instances it is simply sound business to forego the prosecution of embezzlers.

7. A more selfish, indeed, a rather startling influence is the fear, not of a suit for damages but of the discovery of illegal practices carried on by the employer himself. This is a delicate and an obviously difficult factor to uncover; yet there are reasons to believe that it is not an insignificant one. An experienced surety company executive informed the writer of a prosecution for embezzlement of $100,000, in the trial of which defense counsel showed that the management of the business "had in fact engaged in activities which, to say the least, were subject to eye-brow lifting." In another trial, the embezzler (by his own confession) was acquitted and, so the writer was informed, the president of the complaining company was himself indicted for offenses disclosed in the embezzlement trial. This sort of thing is, of course, rare, but it may nonetheless be an important factor in deterring the prosecution of employees whose work has provided opportunities to discover unsavory facts about the business. The late E. H. Sutherland came to the considered conclusion that directors and other officers so frequently engage in criminal conduct as to provide a pattern that is merely imitated by employees.[45] We need not resolve that question here. More often, sharp practices may have been discovered by the embezzling employee; indeed, under present circumstances of detailed, far-flung regulations carrying punitive sanctions, it would not be surprising if many technical violations occurred.[46] The embezzler uses his knowledge of these facts as a kind of extortion—the threat of exposure if the

---

[45] White Collar Crime (1949).

[46] ". . . a clever criminal defense lawyer can blow up, let us say, the necessary working of a woman employee over a limited number of hours to get out a rush order on occasion, which at the time the employee is perfectly willing to do, seeing the reasonableness of it. We know of many bank cases where, on prosecution, the court has severely castigated the banker for not paying the embezzling employee enough money." From the letter of a surety company executive to the writer.

management initiates prosecution for the embezzlement. Or, despite the absence of such facts, he will threaten to lie about the employer in ways that may seriously embarrass him.[47]

8. Perhaps the most important of all the factors influencing the employer's conduct is restitution. The practice of foregoing prosecution where restitution is made or arranged for is so frequent and widespread that it tends to reduce embezzlement to a merely private transaction, the defalcation being viewed as damage that can be fully repaired by the payment of a certain sum of money—like a breach of contract. Restitution pervades and defines the entire meaning of embezzlement.

Restitution is obviously in the financial interest of the employer, client, or other victim of the crime as well as that of the surety company which must otherwise make good the defalcation. From a purely economic viewpoint, it is a matter of indifference to the employer who carries sufficient insurance, whether the loss is compensated by the embezzler himself or his family or by the surety company which has underwritten the bond.

Several surety company executives in their letters, noted above, emphasized the failure of employers to initiate prosecution because of the influence of restitution. One correspondent stated: "It has occurred to us time and again that an insured is more interested in getting its money back from the bonding company than spending time in court." Another wrote that ". . . employers prefer to make an agreement with the dishonest employee rather than prosecute . . ."[48] Victims of em-

---

[47] "Frequently, by way of afterthought the defense of the employee takes the form of a counterfeited attack upon his employer. For example, the employee may claim that he was not actually stealing the money but was merely taking it as part of his employer's plot to evade income taxes; or, the employee may claim that the diverted sums were used to bribe politicians, police, labor officials, or others; or sometimes an accused calmly asserts that his immediate boss was committing the larceny and the employee was just a helpless conduit." Kostelanetz, *op. cit.* 460.

[48] The Director of the Chicago Crime Commission wrote to the author on July 2, 1951: "Frequently too, the employer feels that by dealing directly with the offending employee he can work out some arrangement for restitution, which might not be possible if criminal prosecution were commenced."

bezzlement naturally and properly want to recover compensation; and most of them seem to be willing to forego prosecution if that is necessary. Others, who make no agreements to withhold prosecution, simply lose interest in criminal proceedings once restitution has been made. They've recovered their loss—why bother with a troublesome criminal trial? Thus, it is not restitution alone, nor the omission to prosecute which raises serious questions but, instead, the interrelation of these factors.[49]

Although only a small portion of the potential market is covered by insurance, the sale of fidelity bonds runs into the millions. The surety companies, next to the employers, are accordingly the parties most interested in embezzlement. What is their practice regarding restitution ("salvage") and prosecution?

While the effect of restitution on employers' conduct is relatively simple, its influence on the surety companies is rather complex. In an effort to arrive at definite knowledge of the surety companies' practices regarding prosecution where salvage is involved, the writer raised the question in a second letter, written May 12, 1951, to the executives of surety companies who had replied to his first letter, noted above.[50] All recipients answered this letter, and some interesting phases of the problem began to emerge.

---

[49] There are other unfortunate derivatives of restitution. *E.g.* Cressey reports the case of a bank teller who, having already embezzled from the bank, and being apprehensive of early detection, embezzled an additional very large amount so that he would be in a good position to bargain with the bank when the defalcations were discovered. Ph.D. Thesis *op. cit.* 170.

Cf. Train, True Stories of Crime From the District Attorney's Office (1935) 157–187, reports the case of a criminal lawyer who advised his client to "take $125,000 more," then dickered with the bank with the result that the lawyer got $25,000, the bank the rest, and the embezzler was let go.

[50] In his letter of May 12th the writer stated: "An interesting problem has been raised in my mind concerning the attitude of surety companies toward restitution by employees instead of prosecution. Some of my informants point out that the surety's financial interest favors restitution and that the limitation of loss is the surety's primary obligation. On the other hand, other informants insist that their company prefers prosecution since that will act as a deterrent, and they add that the employer's distaste for the inconvenience of prosecution is the only reason for the infrequency of prosecution."

Most of the writers insisted that the surety companies favor prosecution, *never* allowed restitution ("salvage") to influence them in any way except to report the fact to the court without recommendation and, in fact, invariably forego salvage if it is at the expense of prosecution. Some of these letters bore unmistakable signs of awareness of the "correct" behavior.

One surety company official, without specifying his company's practice with regard to prosecution, said, "where a surety company is called upon to pay a loss and can obtain full restitution from an employee prosecution is not likely." Another writer quoted his company's instructions to its field agents: "The Adjuster should ascertain from the insured if the loss has been reported to the police, and whether or not the insured intends to prosecute the defaulter. No advice should be offered in connection with the matter. If the question is raised by the insured, he should be advised to consult his own attorney."

Thus, we find (1) usual insistence on prosecution at the expense of salvage, (2) an occasional contradiction of that, and (3) a circumspect, noncommittal position.

In evaluating these statements, we must remember that premium rates are lower if losses are diminished, and that "without salvage, surety rates would have to be much higher."[51] The assumed easy alternative—raising the rate of premium—is rigorously limited by actual market conditions in the surety field, e.g., the resistance of many businessmen to any fidelity insurance (in the opinion of surety company officials, only 10–15 percent of the potential market is now insured), the present substantial cost of such insurance, and the competitive nature of the surety business. These and other factors place definite limits on the rate of premiums that the market will tolerate. There can be no doubt that the surety companies are anxious to salvage as much as possible, and that they are motivated to that end by a desire to maintain the lowest possible rates in order to sell more fidelity bonds. The surety companies also recognize the unwillingness of the insured to prosecute as well

---

[51] Backman, *op. cit.* 90.

as the dependence of successful prosecution on his vigorous cooperation. The surety companies adjust to their situation by concentrating on salvage. They are in a business that quite properly seeks a profit. They can hardly be expected to play the role of reformers of the mores of employers and public. But the outside observer, while he may sympathize with their situation, may find in the surety relationship to embezzlers the most accessible fulcrum to apply needed reforms.

The emphasis of surety company executives on the fact that the companies are in business to make a profit reveals a perspective that is challenging. The implication is that there is no obligation to aid law-enforcement except, of course, where that will aid salvage; and this attitude must surely operate in some, perhaps many, cases in avoidance of prosecution. The surety company's position seems to be that it is not a law-enforcing agency—a mere truism since the surety companies are obviously not public officials appointed to enforce the criminal law.[52] Yet, with questionable consistency, surety company officials assert that law-enforcement is the employer's problem.[53] But the employer is just as much a private person as is the surety company, and if the company is justified in pursuing its profit without restraint, why not the employer? Surely the fact that he is more immediately involved, is in direct contact with the embezzler, and that his testimony is essential do not restrict

---

[52] The activities of surety companies in cooperating with police and other authorities in cases where an embezzler has absconded are illustrated in St. Clair McKelway, *Annals of Crime—The Wily Wilby*, The New Yorker, Jan. 1, 8, 1949. *E.g.* when a snapshot of the embezzler had been discovered, "The Travelers Insurance Company delightedly made thousands of copies of the snapshot . . . and began mailing them to police departments, hotels, railroads, airports, and its branch offices, all over the United States and Canada. . . ." *Id.* Jan. 8 issue. After the embezzler had been apprehended and while confined in the Tombs, "he made a bargain with the Travelers Insurance Company that was as original as his methods of embezzlement. He offered to tell the company where it could find around three hundred thousand dollars of the stolen money if it would give him ten thousand dollars for himself . . . [The company] mulled over Wilby's proposition for several weeks and finally accepted it." The insurance company gave the embezzler a certified check for $10,000.

[53] "The surety ordinarily will not prosecute the thief. It considers that as a problem for the insured." Kostelanetz, *op. cit. supra*, n. 42 at 462.

the duty of law-enforcement to him. Nor does the fact that employers dodge their obligation condone like conduct by the surety companies.

The practice of the surety companies is complicated by the fact that prosecution often aids salvage. Thus, an experienced observer reports that "As a general rule, it is probably accurate to say that surety companies get a far more substantial measure of restitution when a prosecution is pending . . . particularly on the eve of sentence." [54] This would account for the fact that in some cases the surety companies urge prosecution. When salvage is not recoverable out-of-court, it is only good business to press for prosecution and hope that the judge will enforce restitution.

There are, however, certain restraints on the pursuit of salvage via court action, e.g., the criminal courts must not be used as collection agencies,[55] although it is problematical how effective that rule is. On the other hand, in securing salvage without court action, there are also certain restraints. The surety companies have been warned that there is such a crime as compounding a felony.[56] Much more potent, if the reports of appellate cases are any index,[57] is the fact that agreements made under duress or for a promise not to prosecute cannot be enforced.[58] If the surety wants agreements enforced, the only safe thing is to "promise a defaulter only this, and nothing more that he [the surety] will state to the Prosecuting Officer and to the Court, the *unadorned* fact that restitution has been made." [59] One may therefore assume with confidence that the surety companies do not openly agree to forego prosecution in consideration of salvage. Not a word is uttered to that effect.

---

[54] *Ibid.*

[55] E. A. Shure, *Problems in Effecting Restitution, as Related to Duress and the Criminal Law,* an address delivered before the Surety Company Claim Men's Forum, January 16, 1946.

[56] Kostelanetz, *op. cit.* 461.

[57] An examination of the digests of criminal cases on compounding a felony in the American Digest System, 1926 to date, discloses about half a dozen cases, none of them involving embezzlement or an insurance company.

[58] Shure, *op. cit.*

[59] *Id.* 4.

No promises are made except to report to the court the fact that restitution has been made. Perhaps the offender is also informed that judges are apt to be influenced favorably by restitution. In short, the policy of good business calculation is—salvage immediately or, failing that, get an agreement to make restitution and get it in a contract that is enforceable, not one that may be thrown out of court and possibly subject the moving party to the discomfort of knowing he is compounding a felony.

Whether and to what extent this happens in cases where salvage is secured without prosecution is unknown. It would be unfair to assert or to suggest that clever adjustors convey the threat of prosecution in subtle ways that can never be proved against them. But we know what the surety companies' attitude is regarding salvage. We have seen at least an equivocal stand regarding prosecution. Perhaps we also know a little about human nature as it is often revealed in such situations. The reader is entitled to draw his conclusions regarding the relationship between salvage and prosecution in such cases— where the plain, if unpalatable, choice is prosecution *or* salvage. Do a few or many or all the surety companies, realizing that their business is closely involved "in the public interest," let the salvage go rather than hold out illegal promises, evade prosecution, or indulge in other questionable practices?[60] The emphasis on salvage, the denial of any obligation to aid law-enforcement, and the facile transfer of that duty to the insured —without at the same time requesting or aiding him to discharge it—raise serious doubts.[61]

If the social investigator reflects on this aspect of the embezzlement problem he is bound to doubt that insurance is an unmixed boon. The influence of insurance as a criminal motive, e.g. in arson, the criminal disposal of automobiles, and homi-

---

[60] E. H. Sutherland in his files reports an interview with the manager of a surety company, who stated: "We can't get restitution if we shove them up, and that's our business." And see *supra* p. 313.

[61] *Cf.* the rather harsh judgment of the surety companies in *Note* (1939) 39 Col. L. Rev. 1203, which, however, is softened at 1204.

cide is unavoidable, though it can be diminished.[62] More serious, because it is much more remediable, is the operation of insurance to discourage law-enforcement, e.g., as regards jewel thieves, criminal receivers, and embezzlers. This engenders corresponding attitudes and rationalizations nullifying law-enforcement, as well as anti-social practices ranging from self-seeking expediency to definite criminality. The consequences are undoubtedly far-reaching. Serious tensions and weakened morale result when some offenders are relatively and regularly immune from prosecution while others, for adventitious circumstances of employment or coverage, are treated as criminals, e.g., among the former, employees who make restitution or are bonded, as against those who cannot raise the funds, and employees of the Post Office. Such conflicting practices and attitudes are potent determinants of the character of legal institutions. They are also major factors to be weighed in any program of reform.

Criminal prosecution, although it is only one of many indices of a legal institution, is especially important because, among other reasons, it represents the recorded conduct of a powerful, strategically placed official, responding to various stimuli, pressures and situations. An opportunity is presented to illustrate an important phase of legal sociology by articulating some of the theories employed in the above inquiry regarding prosecution. Their validity rests on the data described above and in other parts of this book, and thus varies in degree of probability. Generalization beyond those data, as in some of the following propositions, raises questions of further verification. Subject to the indicated qualifications, the following theories are presented in partial explanation of the problem: *What determines the rate of prosecution of known offenders* (their being in custody and the availability of sufficient evidence to convict held constant)? All of the following theories need to be qualified, also, to take account of their interrelations with each other.

---

[62] A. Manes, *Insurance Crimes* (1945) 35 J. Crim. L. 34.

1. The rate of prosecution varies directly in proportion to the gravity of the harm.

2. The rate of prosecution varies directly in proportion to the extent and intensity of sustaining mores.

3. The rate of prosecution is in inverse proportion to the degree and extent of psychological identification of the public with the offender. Some doubt arises from the claim of certain psychoanalysts that there is widespread identification with criminals whose punishment is insisted on as an escape from feelings of guilt. But the facts of the embezzlement situation indicate that this has only marginal significance. We identify easily with the trusted employee, a respected member of the community, and we disapprove his defalcation; yet, as seen, prosecution of his type is rare.

It is possible to formulate this theory in terms of the offender's "class status"; but the controversial issues that arise, e.g. whether there are "classes" in America, suggest difficulties which are avoided in the above formulation. It also escapes other difficulties such as the frequent prosecution of bankers and, on the other hand, the lack of any evidence tending to prove that laborers, servants, and other manual workers are more frequently prosecuted for embezzlement than are members of the so-called "white collar" classes.

4. A specific variation of 3, which allows the use of more objective data, is that the rate of prosecution depends on the relationship of the *victim* to the offender. Are they friends or strangers? If the former, how long have they known each other? Are they members of the same social, religious, political groups, and so on? The victim is especially important not only because his initiative is usually required to start prosecution but also because his attitude greatly influences both public and official attitudes, though there are of course definite limits and exceptions to this.

5. The rate of prosecution varies directly in proportion to the advantage to be gained from it by the complainant or, the rate is in inverse proportion to the disadvantages that will be sustained by him. E.g., in embezzlement, if prosecution will enforce restitution which cannot otherwise be obtained, the

tendency will be to prosecute. But in many cases the *quid pro quo* of salvage is precisely, not to prosecute. On the other hand, if there is nothing to be gained by withholding prosecution and nothing to be lost by prosecuting, e.g. an automobile thief or a burglar, the rate of prosecution rises.

6. The rate of prosecution varies directly in relation to the amount of publicity given an offense.

7. The rate of prosecution varies directly in proportion to the influence exerted by organized groups. For example, the Furriers' Association and the Jewellers' Security Alliance are positive influences on prosecution. That of insurance companies is often a negative influence. Semi-public organizations, such as crime commissions, undoubtedly stimulate prosecution. And, finally, the influence of specially trained investigatory forces, e.g. post-office inspectors, bank examiners, and the F.B.I. is considerable.

8. The rate of prosecution varies inversely in proportion to the number of known offenders, i.e. the more numerous the known offenders are, the lower is the rate of prosecution. This suggests, e.g. that the rate of prosecution of known criminal receivers will be higher than that of known embezzlers (always holding constant the availability of sufficient evidence to convict).

Most of these theories find some support in data presented in this book. However, as in all social research, the question of "sufficient" verification remains open, and there are complex interrelations among the variables. Perhaps some future investigator, armed with financial and other resources that were not available to the writer, will be able to subject these and other theories advanced in this book to more precise, detailed study.[63]

III. Administration of the Criminal Law

We have found that the dominant practice is not to prosecute known embezzlers. Let us now examine the exceptional cases

---

[63] The writer has discussed some of the relevant theories and methods in General Principles of Criminal Law (1947) 560–566, in Living Law of Democratic Society (1949) ch. 3, and in the Introduction of this book.

where the legal apparatus is put into operation. What happens when prosecution is initiated?

The Judicial Criminal Statistics issued by the Bureau of the Census contained significant data on this subject, despite the lumping of fraud with embezzlement.[64] The figures for these offenses reveal the following patterns:

1. A higher percent of the prosecutions for these offenses (embezzlement-fraud) was disposed of without conviction than in the prosecution of most serious crimes.[65]

2. A higher percent of these prosecutions was dismissed *by the State* than the percent of prosecutions so dismissed regarding almost any other charge.[66]

3. From 1933–1944, except for those convicted of auto theft and receiving stolen property, a higher percent of those convicted of embezzlement-fraud was placed on probation or given suspended sentence than in convictions of any other serious crime.

The typicality of the statistical pattern represented in these national data is confirmed by other data, e.g., the mortality tables in the Illinois Crime Survey. Statistics on the disposition of prosecutions in Illinois show that a far higher percent of prosecutions for embezzlement and fraud was eliminated in the preliminary hearing than was true of any other crime. In Chicago and Cook County over 70% of the prosecutions (these figures again include fraud) was eliminated in preliminary

---

[64] The long neglect of judicial statistics continues to impose serious difficulties in studying the administration of the criminal law. A beginning was made in the direction of collecting national data by the Bureau of Census in 1933, but it was discontinued in 1945. See Sellin, *The Uniform Criminal Statistics Act* (1950) 40 J. Cr. L. 679.

[65] *E.g.* table 6, p. 12, Jud. Cr. Stat. 1933 shows only manslaughter to have a higher percentage. The same pattern recurs in 1934, table 37, p. 31, and in 1943, table 5, page 5. For most years, from 1933–1944, embezzlement-fraud ranks second or third in this regard. Usually manslaughter and aggravated assault and, occasionally, another serious offense had a higher percentage of cases disposed of without conviction.

[66] *Id.* After 1936 forgery-counterfeiting exceed embezzlement-fraud, and after 1942 burglary and auto-theft also exceed embezzlement-fraud in this regard.

hearings.[67] For Illinois, index figures on such disposition range from 147 for Embezzlement-Fraud to 52 for Robbery. The disparity in Chicago and in Cook County would presumably be even greater.[68] More recent statistics for Cook County, 1946 through 1950,[69] disclose a still lenient disposition of prosecutions which, *having survived preliminary hearing,* were assigned for trial to the criminal courts of Cook County. During those five years, there was a total of 118 such prosecutions for embezzlement.[70] In the disposition of those prosecutions by the county courts, 50 convicted embezzlers were placed on probation, and there were dismissals and acquittals in 28 cases. Accordingly, in a total of 78 cases (66%) there was no punitive treatment.[71]

The New York City Police Department in its annual reports has published statistics on violations of financial trust although, technically, "larceny" is usually the correct charge. The fact-situations are sufficiently like embezzlement to render the following court findings significant.[72]

---

[67] The Illinois Crime Survey 62–63 (1929).

[68] Von Hentig, in a study of embezzlement in Chicago, 1926, found that 81.26% of the embezzlement cases were eliminated before trial, and that Jud. Cr. Stat., 1936–40, show that only 21.8% of the convicted embezzlers were imprisoned as compared with 63.1% for robbery, 41.9% for burglary, 28.4% for larceny, and 90.5% for all major crimes. Hans Von Hentig, Crime: Causes and Conditions (1947) 66 and 72.

[69] They were kindly supplied by V. W. Peterson, Director of the Chicago Crime Commission.

[70] Cook County includes Chicago which, alone, has a population of approximately 3,500,000. Additional data, supplied by Mr. Peterson, reveal that the embezzlements known to the police during 1946–50 were much fewer than the indictments returned by grand juries, *e.g.* in 1946, the police "knew" of only 4 embezzlements while grand juries returned 45 indictments. In 1947 the police "knew" of only 1 embezzlement while the grand juries returned 39 indictments. The figures for 1948 are respectively 26 and 42; for 1949, 18 and 20; and for 1950, 10 and 29.

[71] See footnote 79 p. 146 *supra.*

[72] Beginning in 1944, the earlier "larceny" was divided into grand and petty larceny, but the figures given in the text below combine them throughout the entire period. In 1940, the Annual Reports added "Embezzlement" but the figures show only a handful of cases in that category. The limitations on these statistics for many purposes are therefore serious. Unfortunately, this is a rather typical situation regarding criminal statistics which, in this country, remain in a highly unsatisfactory condition.

From 1935 to 1947 inclusive:

(a) 7938 "dishonest employees" (other than servant) were tried, and 4059 or 51% of them were convicted and of these, 2256, representing 28% of those tried, received some punishment or corrective treatment.[73] In 54 cases of short term employees, 19% of those tried received some punishment or treatment.

(b) 1141 "dishonest servants" were tried, and 658 or 58% of them were convicted, and of these, 355, representing 31% of those tried, received some punishment or corrective treatment.

(c) 128 "dishonest trustees, bailees, attorneys," etc. were tried, and 72 or 56% of them were convicted, and of these, 35, representing 27% of those tried, received some punishment or corrective treatment.

(d) 1437 "dishonest friends" were tried, and 581 or 41% of them were convicted and of these, 354, representing 25% of those tried, received some punishment or corrective treatment.

(e) 74 "dishonest relatives" were tried, and 23 or 31% of them were convicted, and of these, 13, representing 17% of those tried, received some punishment or corrective treatment.

All of the above statistics point in a single direction—the relative leniency of criminal law administration in embezzlement cases throughout the entire process from preliminary hearing to the trial determining guilt, and thence to the sentencing of those convicted.

Competent students of the problem agree that the administration of the criminal law in embezzlement cases is unusually lenient.[74] Several of the surety company executives who corresponded with the writer, and others in conversation, alluded to the clemency of the courts, one correspondent stating, "We find that the courts are quite lenient with embezzlers when

---

[73] The figures include those sent to a hospital as well as those imprisoned. Obviously, the per cent of those tried who were acquitted or received no institutional treatment was 72%.

[74] William Ashdown, *The Psychology of Embezzlement,* The Bankers Magazine, April 1926, 519–25. Cf. *Bank Wrecking and Clemency* (June 1911) 92 The Nation 547–8.

successful prosecution does take place, and we find it the rule rather than the exception for the embezzler to be granted probation." Indeed, several letters stressed the fact that it is difficult to get the authorities to initiate prosecutions. "We are told by some of our insureds," wrote one surety company executive, "that it is a waste of time to report losses to the authorities." Another emphasized what is commonly known among prosecutors, namely, that a contested embezzlement trial is a very difficult legal assignment. "On many occasions where employers have brought the embezzlement to the attention of the prosecutor he has not acted, for to obtain a conviction it required too much effort on his part."

That judges are exceptionally lenient in embezzlement cases and have accepted restitution as sound treatment or as an adequate substitute for such treatment is evidenced in numerous newspaper reports. The major operating influences seem to be (1) the desire of the victims to obtain restitution and their willingness and that of the court to dismiss the prosecution or suspend sentence if restitution is made; and (2) very unfortunate circumstances affecting the embezzler or his family which stimulate forgiveness or leniency.

In an embezzlement case involving more than half a million dollars, the defendant was sentenced to 30 months' imprisonment. "'His life has been blasted by his dishonesty and his family has been disgraced,' said Judge Collins in explaining why the punishment was light . . . 'In addition, I understand he is using $26,000 to make partial restitution.'" New York Herald Tribune 1/11/30

"Judge Desort continued an application for probation until February 26 in order to investigate the assets of ——— available for restitution." Chicago Tribune 2/2/32

"The charge against him [embezzling $7,150] was dismissed late in the afternoon. . . . The case was dropped when he made a property assignment and promised to restore the funds on the installment plan . . ." Chicago Tribune 7/7/32

"———, former paying teller . . . appeared yesterday in the Criminal court and asked that he be given probation on charges of embezzling $33,000 in funds of patrons of the bank. Chief

Justice John Prystalski pointed out that ———— had not yet entered a plea and refused to entertain the request unless all complainants in the case recommended probation.

"Eleven of the 13 complainants said they had recovered their losses and were willing that he should be put on probation. Mrs. ————, an aunt of the defendant, and Miss ————, asked prosecution, saying restitution had not been made in their cases. Judge Prystalski continued the case until Dec. 19 to allow ———— to negotiate with Mrs. ———— and Miss ————." Chicago Tribune 11/18/32

"————, former teller . . . was placed on probation yesterday by Chief Justice John Prystalski of the Criminal court. He was charged with embezzling $33,314 from customers of the bank. He pleaded guilty some months ago, but Judge Prystalski held up a probation motion until after restitution was made to all of ————'s victims." Chicago Tribune 3/14/33

"———— who was charged with embezzling $2,535 . . . was granted a year's probation yesterday . . . in the Criminal Court. ———— has made restitution and has no previous record of dishonesty." Chicago Tribune 5/4/33

"Judge Inch suspended sentence in the case of ————, and placed him on probation for one year, or until he pays the $517 over-draft. ———— told the court that he would call at the office of the United States Attorney today and pay the $517." New York Times 4/20/34

"Embezzlement charges against ———— were dismissed in Chicago after he had saved every penny of the $26,000 involved and returned it to the company. His employer said he was considering rehiring ————. The judge, in dismissing the charges for lack of prosecution, suggested that ———— be given the post of treasurer of the concern." Indianapolis Star 2/17/41

A former bank teller who embezzled $15,000 received a suspended sentence and probation in a Federal District Court. The District Attorney told the court that the defendant had paid back $2200 "and had indicated a desire to make full restitution." Indianapolis Star 7/9/43

A suspended three year sentence was imposed on the assistant manager of a Farm Loan Association who embezzled $5,200 in government funds, and pleaded guilty in a District Court. The defendant "told the court she had repaid more than half the amount and promised to produce the remainder within 30 days." Indianapolis Star 4/18/44

In New York the assistant manager of a bank embezzled almost $900,000 and was sentenced to three years' imprisonment. The sentence could have been 45 years in addition to a fine of $30,000, but he helped recover all the money taken except $6,000. Indianapolis Star 7/7/49

A former Justice of the Peace was sentenced 1–5 years for embezzling $1,500. "The sentence, however, was suspended by the court. Arrangements have been made to repay shortages in his accounts as a justice." Indianapolis Star 2/25/50

". . . postal clerk drew a two-year suspended sentence [in a U.S. District Court] . . . after a probation report noted that he had made restitution of the $400. . . ." [Defendant] "said he had sold his home to pay back the money. . . ." He was placed on probation for three years. Indianapolis Star 9/15/50

"————, 43 years old, who embezzled $87,533 from the Northwestern Mutual Life Insurance Company, was spared a prison term today when his wife testified that 'I drove him to it.'

"Circuit Judge Gerald J. Boileau sentenced ———— to 10 years in prison on his guilty plea, but stayed the sentence and put him on 10-year probation.

"The judge then ordered probation, and told ———— he must make full restitution.

"————, who said he embezzled the money while working as an auditor, already has paid back all but $29,000 by surrendering his assets.

"Under terms of the probation he must repay at least $10,000 of the remainder during the 10-year period." St. Louis Post Dispatch 4/15/51

A salesman embezzled $375 from his employer, was fined $25 plus costs, given a suspended sentence of 2–20 years, placed on probation, and ordered to repay the money embezzled. Bloomington (Indiana) Daily Herald-Telephone 5/4/51

As has been stated, restitution, itself, is not only an object of normal desire on the part of those who have sustained damage; it is also a commendable reparation of economic harm. Restitution may be desirable for other reasons. In some states there is provision for its use in "compromise" of certain misdemeanors, but it is usually stipulated that the agreement must be approved by a magistrate.[75] The French and other civil law systems permit the question of damages to be adjudicated in the same trial in which criminal guilt is determined.[76] At least since Bentham, restitution has been discussed with reference to sound peno-correctional programs.[77]

Accordingly, when a judge grants probation or a suspended sentence, and restitution has been made or promised, the pertinent question is this—Has he merely adopted the lay viewpoint of most employers—in fact functioning like a collection agency? Or has he conducted a careful pre-sentence hearing and, in the light of that, did he determine that a sound peno-correctional program should require restitution? Unfortunately, the available data indicate that the former attitude prevails in most courtrooms.[78] Such superficial sentencing strengthens

---

[75] N. Y. Code Cr. Proc. Sec. 664. Similar statutes are found in about a dozen states. See *Note* (1939) 39 Col. L. Rev. 1194–5, fn.50 for the citations.

[76] In Nebraska upon conviction of embezzlement, in addition to a prison sentence a fine may be imposed which is treated as a judgment favoring the complainant. Nebr. Comp. Stat. (1929) No. 28–550.

[77] A new and potentially very important use of restitution as part of the penalty for violating the Federal Food, Drug, and Cosmetic Act has recently been suggested. S. M. Levine, *Restitution—A New Enforcement Sanction* (July 1951) 6 Food, Drug, Cosmetic Law 503.

[78] The writer of the *Note, Restitution and the Criminal Law* (1939) 39 Col. L. Rev. 1185, in referring to the courts, reports that ". . . the testimony of many persons actively engaged in criminal law is that the promise or act of restitution is often a factor in the granting of a suspended sentence." On the other hand, when writing of the probation department of New York County, he states that recommendations to suspend sentence are not influenced by restitution. "Indeed, it is said that offers of restitution are frequently rejected." But if, on other grounds a suspended sentence is decided on, in many instances "it is thought desirable to require the defendant to make restitution or reparation as one of the educational features of the probation." *Id.* 1198. From Jan. 1, 1927 to Dec. 31, 1936 the Probation Dept. of the N. Y. Co. Court of Gen. Sess. collected $594,811.11. *Id.* 1199 fn. 69. See I. E. Cohen, *The Integration of Restitution in the Probation Services* (1944) 34 J. Cr. L. 315.

the lay attitude in its interpretation of embezzlement—that only a private economic loss is involved. Even such court procedure is, however, preferable; it at least requires consultation with an official and instead of a secret "deal," the hearing is public.

In any event, there are persuasive grounds to conclude from the above discussion that (1) prosecutors do not initiate proceedings in many cases of embezzlement reported to them; (2) they dismiss a relatively high percentage of the prosecutions they did initiate; (3) acquittals are very frequent; and (4) judges are quite apt to suspend sentence and grant probation to convicted offenders if restitution has been made or arranged. These official practices undoubtedly influence employers and surety company executives who might otherwise report embezzlement cases and cooperate in the trial of embezzlers. On the other hand, we have also met avoidance of prosecution by employers for other reasons. And, in the background of all the current practices, lay and official, are widespread undetected embezzlements involving a large part of the population which, except in rare cases, seems indifferent to the punishment of embezzlers.

The legal sociologist cannot often perform experiments to test the precise operation of specific variables but he can observe similar processes and make apt comparisons among them. Such an area in the field of embezzlement—that occurring in the Post Office—may be compared very significantly with the general situation described above. The salient fact, as stated by the manager of a surety company, is that "The post office probably has the lowest rate of embezzlement of any business. This is because they are scared to death of the relentless pursuit of the offender by Uncle Sam. They are watched, checked and prosecuted if they go wrong. And there is no sympathy at all about it. There are very few cases of embezzlement in post offices and that is the reason the rate is low." [79]

Whatever the causes may be, it is widely believed that among the 500,000 United States postal employees the rate of

---

[79] From the report of a conference with E. H. Sutherland.

embezzlement is much lower than in other vocations. The following statistics, though fragmentary and lacking any comparative data, are rather striking. "During the fiscal year 1951, a total of 531 postal employees were apprehended for the theft of mail and of this number, about 125 were temporary employees hired during the Christmas season only. A total of 448 were convicted during the fiscal year. During the same period, 144 postal employees were apprehended for the embezzlement of postal funds and 121 were convicted. . . . Invariably these offenses are reported to the proper United States Attorney. In connection with these statistics it should be borne in mind that the postal service has a force of about 500,000 employees (which is increased considerably during the Christmas season) employed at about 42,000 post offices." [80] Even if the rate were equally low or even lower in certain groups, e.g., teachers or clergymen, the significance of the post office data would not diminish because its employees are more typical representatives of the general population. We shall proceed on the premise that the above opinion regarding the embezzlement rate among postal employees is valid, and confine inquiry to a consideration of the probable causes.

Postal employees come within the Civil Service, are required to pass the usual examinations, and enjoy various advantages. For example, the position provides security both in tenure and in retirement, and it carries the prestige of government employment. For these and other reasons, the positions are much sought after, and many postal employees have had to wait several years before being appointed. Accordingly, status, security, including pension, and perhaps a higher *esprit de corps* set off that vocation from many other comparable types of employment.

While the above differentiae concern matters of degree, there are other aspects of postal employment which are unique. A professional police force, consisting of 815 trained inspectors, is in service to prevent theft of mail, apprehend the offenders,

---

[80] Letter to the writer from C. C. Garner, Chief Post Office Inspector.

including postal employees, and institute and aid prosecution of offenders. The United States Postal Inspectors are regarded as a well-organized, effective police force. The inspectors, who periodically check the accounts of postmasters and conduct many other investigations, are required to report all crimes to the United States District Attorney, who makes the decision regarding prosecution. So far as Post Office officials are concerned, the policy is to prosecute but it is not harsh nor unmindful of mitigating circumstances. Moreover, the practice is entirely uninfluenced by restitution, although restitution undoubtedly influences the sentence.

In the decade 1942–1951 a total of 3558 embezzlement cases, involving 3658 postal employees, were terminated. 3390 defendants were found guilty, 48 not guilty, 70 nolle prosequi, and 128 quashed or dismissed (5 "other" dispositions).[81] This indicates very rigorous law-enforcement in comparison, e.g., with comparable facts in New York and Cook County.[82]

The following instance was reported to the writer as typical of post office policy. A detected embezzler proceeded to make restitution and, after considerable sacrifice by his family, he returned the entire equivalent of a substantial sum of money he had taken. The regional postal inspector nonetheless filed a complaint, the District Attorney initiated prosecution, and the embezzler was tried and convicted. The Court, informed of the restitution, imposed a suspended sentence. This terminated employment and waived the rights to pension though not to the accumulated amount paid into the fund by the defendant. In this latter connection, it may be added that postal employees sometimes transfer accumulated payments in the pension fund to compensate for their defalcations. This may influence the initiation of prosecution—it would be strange, indeed, if it never tipped the scales even in meritorious cases—but mitigation of sentence, not escape from prosecution, is asserted to be the principal effect. Uncle Sam, unlike ordinary employers, is

---

[81] Communication from U. S. Dept. of Justice, 10/19/51. Data on sentences imposed are not available.

[82] See *supra* pp. 320–322.

not too greatly moved by the prospect of repairing a financial loss caused by embezzlement.

One of the more interesting phases of postal inspection is the presence of hidden booths in the large post offices, from which an inspector can observe the employees without being seen by them. A regional Postal Inspector, in charge of the force in a large city, informed the writer that such observations were unusual, that there was no general inspection of employees, but only those suspected were watched. He noted with much persuasiveness, so far as this writer is concerned, that with a total national force of 815 inspectors who devote only one-third of their time to the detection of all crimes against the mails, it would be impossible to engage in any general preventive watching. At the same time, the fact that inspection is known to be possible would seem to provide an important deterrent in some post offices. Thus, in sum, the causes of the relatively low rate of embezzlement by postal employees are at least partially explained by the above factors operating in improved methods of prevention and detection, and in regular prosecution of the known offenders.

Embezzlement in banks also provides significant data for comparative purposes. Despite occasional opinions that defalcations are very common in banks,[83] the rate is probably lower than in most businesses.[84] The banks, even more than the post office, provide "prestige" jobs. Other, more definite factors are operative, e.g. the bank examiner who may call to inspect the records any time. Bank examiners must notify the directors, the District Attorney and the F.B.I. of all acts which may be violations of law. In critical situations they must telephone or telegraph the Washington office of the Federal Deposit Insurance Corporation, which may request the F.B.I. to send an agent immediately to the bank involved. In the meantime, the Examiner, following detailed instructions, continues to prepare

---

[83] See notes 3, 23, and 25 *supra*.

[84] "It is impossible to emphasize too strongly the fact that only a small percentage become embezzlers." W. K. Mendenhall, *Bank Losses* (reprint p. 7 from Feb. 1947, National Auditgram).

the case for further investigation and proceedings.[85] This aids discovery and efficient law-enforcement.

Statistics on the administration of the criminal law in cases of embezzlement and related defalcations committed in insured non-member banks [86] show that from the adoption of the Banking Act in 1935 through December 1950, 2017 reports of such offenses were forwarded to United States district attorneys.[87] Of these, 263 have not yet been disposed of—at least, no information regarding them was received. Of the remaining 1754, there were convictions in 741 cases and, of these, probation or suspended sentence was granted in 316 cases. Punitive treatment was imposed in 24+% of the cases. An additional 84 offenders, 4%, were prosecuted in State courts, with no data as to their final disposition available. In 4%, the grand juries returned "no bills" and 836 cases, 48+%, were "closed without prosecution." [88] Department of Justice statistics, apparently overlapping with those stated above, show that in the decade 1942–1951, 2331 cases involving violations of the National Bank and Federal Reserve Act were terminated in district courts. Of 2766 defendants, 2180 were found guilty, 78 not guilty, 216 nolle prosequi, 220 quashed and there was "other" disposition in 10 cases. Data on sentences imposed are not available.[89] These figures indicate much more rigorous enforcement than in the typical business situations.

---

[85] The above is based on a letter, dated May 11, 1951 from Edward H. De Hority, Asst. Chief, Division of Examination, Fed. Dep. Ins. Corp., and from mimeographed detailed instructions to bank examiners.

[86] Memorandum of May 31, 1951 from N. C. Bakke, Associate Gen. Counsel, F.D.I.C.

[87] The Washington office states: "We report all such apparent irregularities regardless of the amount involved, restitution, failure to place responsibility, or extenuating circumstances." *Id.*

[88] "The reasons usually given by the United States Attorneys for closing the files without prosecution are, primarily, no criminal intent shown, no substantial amount involved, no financial loss to the bank, or inability to identify the offender." Letter from N. C. Bakke, 10/5/51. "The closing of cases for want of prosecution is usually due to the disappearance or death of witnesses, the insufficiency of evidence or the death of a defendant." Letter from U. S. Dept. of Justice, 10/19/51.

[89] Source: Communication from U. S. Dept. of Justice.

In the banks, as in the Post Office, we find direct govern-
mental participation—investigation by expert examiners who
also assist in the preparation of the cases. Although bankers
wish to avoid publicity and, *a fortiori*, prosecution of their employees, the presence of the bank examiners who communicate
evidence of defalcation to district attorneys and the F.B.I. is
an important countervailing factor. Again, a professional police
organization, in this case the F.B.I., functions to collect the
necessary evidence and apprehend offenders. Again, the government pays the cost of investigation and preparation of the
cases for trial. In both situations there is a legal duty to report
offenders. In the absence of more comparative data than are
now available, any conclusions must be quite tentative. On the
basis of the presently known data, the clearly indicated conclusion is that the above factors are important influences which,
in part at least, account for the relatively lower rate of embezzlement in banks and the Post Office.

Embezzlement provides an excellent opportunity to appraise
penological theories.[90] Even when pertinent questions are thus
limited, serious disagreement is met among informed persons.
For example, one surety company executive, with whom the
writer corresponded, thought prosecution in embezzlement
cases acts as a substantial deterrent: "It is the fear of punishment that keeps individuals in line." Several other experienced
surety company executives doubt that even certain prosecution
and severe sentences would make "lasting impressions on
others." They have noted "successive defaults in the same organization and even in the same family"; and the conviction of
the first offenders apparently had no deterrent effect whatever
on the later ones. Other executives think vigorous, certain law-
enforcement would be an important deterrent. There was wide
agreement on only one point—in the present circumstances of
lax law-enforcement, the major deterrent is the fear of loss of

---

[90] "The statistics of embezzlement are highly important from the point of
view of a theory of crime . . ." E. H. Sutherland, Principles of Criminology
(4th ed. 1947) 36.

employment and social standing through exposure as an embezzler. Only the Post Office experience (and to some extent that of banks) is available to indicate that efficient law-enforcement deters embezzlement. As noted, competent observers associate the low embezzlement rate in the Post Office with the practice of regular prosecution of offenders. But the supporting data and the relevant facts permitting necessary comparisons and appraisals are too incomplete to establish the validity of these opinions regarding deterrence.

The theory of rehabilitation, presented as the *only* sound objective of criminal law, meets a severe test in embezzlement cases. The reason for this was indicated in the remarks of Judge Woodward when he sentenced the officers of the H. O. Stone Co. in Chicago some years ago: "You are men of affairs, of experience, of refinement and culture, of excellent reputation and standing in the business and social world." One could easily underline this aspect of the penological problem by recalling the Whitneys, college presidents, clergymen, and many other prominent, well educated, highly esteemed persons occupying executive positions in business or government who are found among the embezzlers. If these persons are normal and unusually competent, what is the function of corrective treatment with regard to them? Or, is it to be assumed that all of these offenders suffered from serious mental disturbances? [91] Even if that assumption is seriously entertained, where is the needed therapeutic knowledge? It is only human to imagine that sufficient knowledge of rehabilitation is available and that competent personnel can be found to man all the administrative boards. It is easy for even able laymen, while recognizing that they can neither reform maladjusted persons nor discover when they cease to be dangerous, to assume that there are experts in sufficient number who can do those things. Unfortunately, that is not true, and the difference between actual knowledge and the knowledge we want very much to have is often painfully great.

---

[91] "Undoubtedly individual differences between employees may be found, but the persons who occupy positions of financial trust are seldom psychopathic, feebleminded, residents of deteriorated slum areas, or in other ways personally or situationally pathological." Sutherland, *id.* 36.

So, too, with regard to personnel. It should also be recognized that with reference to many crimes, including embezzlement, one encounters not a public "lust for vengeance" which blocks rational treatment of offenders but, instead, public indifference to the destruction of important values.

These various difficulties suggest that an important, though certainly not exclusive, place in any adequate treatment program for embezzlers must be reserved for the moral instruction provided by just punishment. What is basic in this viewpoint is the importance of careful public evaluation of the offender's conduct—with congruent consequences. This implies that the punishment is deserved in the sense that the offender is a normal adult who could and should have controlled his criminal drives.

Except for purposes of analysis or emphasis, it is futile to isolate just punishment by insisting that it must be considered wholly apart from deterrence and reformation. This is evident when one considers not only the dependence of much actual deterrence on the belief that punishment is the community's rational response to harmful action but also that just punishment is intelligible by normal offenders—hence its utility in correction should not be arbitrarily dismissed. In short, isolating just punishment from the other objectives of criminal law is tantamount to asserting that education (or any other valuable experience) is not worthwhile *except* insofar as it leads to *future* desirable consequences. When just punishment is defended, what is meant in this connection is that understanding the moral situation and the values involved in criminal harm is itself important. But only a thorough skeptic would doubt that such education has influence on character formation and future conduct. In the light of these considerations, and especially of the characteristics of embezzlers, the pertinent difficult questions in the development of treatment programs concern the wise integration of all the sound objectives of criminal law.[92]

---

[92] See Hall, General Principles of Criminal Law (1947) e.g., pp. 130, 245, 421, 535, and *Science and Reform in Criminal Law* (1952) 100 U. of Pa. L. Rev. 787.

IV. REFORM

1. *Prevention by Employers*

Improvement in the methods of prevention of embezzlement is being explored by many business organizations in cooperation with surety companies.[93] Suggestions range from simple matters, such as insistence on vacations by cashiers, unannounced rotation of employees in key positions, and provision of an Employees' Loan Fund to very complicated accounting procedures. Internal checks and audits, improved stock inventory, intricate registers and other recording devices, control of the books, systematization of receipts and payments, electric eyes and recording locks—these indicate some of the more complex preventive methods. There is a sizable literature on the subject.[94] Certainly the elimination of opportunities to embezzle is important. But, as in other areas of theft, clever offenders keep abreast of the times, and the ingenuity employed to defeat elaborate systems of prevention is remarkable.[95] The technological phase of embezzlement thus parallels that of larceny.

There is need to improve the selection of key employees and, even more, to maintain sufficient contact with them to know when they run into serious personal problems. This is difficult in large organizations. The "blanket bonds" which have largely superseded individual bonding discourage investigation of employees' past records. Neither the surety companies nor the employers make more than perfunctory inquiries. Perhaps it is impracticable to investigate large numbers of

---

[93] A. F. Lafrentz, *Loss Prevention* (an address to Insurance Accountants Ass'n of N.Y.)

[94] A. E. Keller, Embezzlement and Internal Control (1945); I. H. Dearnley, Fraud and Embezzlement (1933); V. Z. Brink, *Internal Check* (March 1939) Jour. of Accountancy, reprinted as monograph by American Surety Co.; T. D. Davidson, *The Accountics of Fidelity Bond Claims* (address before Surety Co. Claim Men's Forum, 12/15/1943).

[95] The careful controls of the Mergenthaler Linotype Co. of New York and the methods used by a $60-a-week cashier to steal $800,000 are described in detail by District Attorney Miles F. McDonald, *Case Study of a Prominent Dishonesty Loss,* pub. in Insurance Series No. 85, Amer. Management Ass'n 1950.

employees, but improvements in this direction could be made with reference to certain positions.

A rather ambitious preventive program was recommended by District Attorney McDonald, when he was asked, "How can an organization check on the personal habits of its employees who are in a position to steal large sums from the company?" Mr. McDonald replied:

"The only way that can be handled, I think, is by creating a department of the firm similar to the Inspector General's Department of the Army. Such a department might consist of one or two men, who should have an independent office, in no way connected with the firm at all, and to be known only to, say, the president of the firm.

"These men should make general inspection tours of the homes, and in an undercover method observe the habits of all the employees that handle funds. The job calls for a man who is trained in this type of work—someone who has had FBI training or special training in detection.

"But this problem has to be handled absolutely independently. These investigators cannot be known to any employee of the firm. They must never come to the company's offices—they must never be seen. Their reports should be filed perhaps with the one company officer who knows about them, by mail, at his home—not through the firm at all."[96]

This proposal amounts to a policing of employees by a professional force, as is done, e.g. in the Post Office. There, however, government employment is involved, and the policing is tolerable in view of the government's obligation to protect the mails. It is doubtful whether similar controls would be tolerated in private business as a daily condition of general employment. But such surveillance might be feasible at cer-

---

[96] *Id.* 16.

tain times or with reference to important positions and there may be some businesses where it could be used more widely.[97]

2. *Substantive Law*

In the context of the social problem of embezzlement, the practices of law-avoidance, and the lenient administration of the law by prosecutors and judges, the substantive criminal law seems almost irrelevant. When an ordinary paring knife is ignored, why discuss the refinements of a complete set of surgical instruments? Moreover, the relations of substantive law to social actualities have been discussed throughout this book.

In this regard, there are certain aspects of the embezzlement problem which impose greater difficulties in the way of reform of the substantive law. There is, e.g., a lack of clear lines of empirical differences suggesting apt legal controls. For example, the social situation comprising theft for consumption is clearly and significantly different from theft for sale, just as criminal receiving separates into lay and dealers' conduct, while joy-riding differs plainly from "real" larceny of an automobile. These and other important empirical differences evidently require correspondingly differentiated legal controls and sanctions. But when we turn to embezzlement, we find only vague differences in conduct and social harm to serve as dubious guides to the reform of the relevant substantive law. There are, to be sure, many differences in personality, motivation, and conduct. But while these factors are important in any wise administration of the law, they do not readily denote differences of such social import as to mark clear lines for reform of the *substantive* law.

The numerous detailed laws on embezzlement, defalcation, misapplication, kiting etc., would seem to provide an array of instrumentalities sufficient for any prosecutor's purposes. Where

---

[97] There are now national protective organizations which use "shoppers" and in other ways test the honesty of employees of large businesses.

these legal complexities combine with the niceties of larceny and fraud to raise further difficulties, including procedural hazards, problems are met which, of course, deserve attention on their own merits, i.e. as problems within the substantive and procedural law.[98] These, however, are not the sort of problems with which this study is particularly concerned. We shall merely call attention to certain of the more pressing substantive law problems, and shall then return to the question raised above—the suggestiveness of the social data for substantive reform.

It is axiomatic that the substantive law should at least not impose obstacles to sound administration. It should, in fact, facilitate the solution of acute problems met in court. Even a casual reference to the substantive law of embezzlement, however, meets such a proliferation of statutes that handling them is fraught with difficulty. A job of clearing away much of the growth by generous repeals and organizing the remainder is plainly indicated. Sometimes embezzlement is treated as a form of larceny and carries the same sanctions. In other states, the crimes are different, and sanctions may be widely apart. Larceny by bailee is sometimes treated as embezzlement, sometimes as larceny—again with very different consequences. Many statutes are distinguished in terms of the vocation of the offender, but it is impossible to discover rational bases for the substantial differences in punishment that are often found. For example, in Massachusetts a bank officer may be imprisoned less than two and one-half years, while an employee in the State's treasury may be imprisoned for life.[99] Sentences for felonious embezzlement vary widely in different states—e.g. not exceeding five years in Pennsylvania [1] to 2–20 years in Indiana.[2] Some states have made procedural progress in join-

---

[98] E.g. R. E. Carlson, *The Relationship Between Embezzlement and Larceny in Illinois* (1949) U. of Ill. Law Forum 715.
[99] Ann. Laws of Mass. (1932) Vol. 9, ch. 266, sec. 52 and sec. 50.
[1] Purdon's Penna. Stat. Ann. (1939) Title 18, secs. 4807, 4815.
[2] Ind. Ann. Stat. (Burns, 1933) Title 10–1704.

ing embezzlement, larceny, and fraud in a single offense, theft, carrying a uniform punishment;[3] but this is open to serious question if embezzlement is generally regarded as a lesser offense. There are difficult questions regarding the required *mens rea*, e.g. when the intention must be to deprive permanently.[4] There is also the problem whether one or many embezzlements are committed in a series of defalcations.[5]

In embezzlement, unlike parallel conduct in larceny and criminal receiving, a long series of defalcations does not connote professional criminality. Moreover, the embezzler whose defalcations extend over a period of years, if he is an "old employee," is often less severely condemned than the grab-and-run embezzler who takes a small sum. Thus, mores and business practices are frequently at odds with more rational standards regarding the offenders' conduct and the extent of harm perpetrated in these situations.

Although reform, especially of penal legislation, is limited by popular attitudes, it should be possible to make at least some beginnings in desirable directions. For example, the degree of trust, as shown in the relative importance of the position held, seems to be one valid criterion to guide reform. Another is the amount taken, for despite doubts regarding the extant legislation, it seems likely that if the differences in amounts converted were substantial, that would justify the

---

[3] A. W. Scott, Jr. *Larceny, Embezzlement and False Pretenses in Colorado —A Need for Consolidation* (1951) 23 Rocky Mt. L. Rev. 446; J. Scurlock, *The Element of Trespass in Larceny Under the Statutes* (1949) 22 Temple L. Q. 253.

[4] See 52 L.R.A. (n.s.) 1914, 1018–1022.

[5] A postmaster was convicted of embezzlement on two counts and sentenced to Leavenworth for seven years. The United States District Attorney "told Judge Cant the government could have pressed charges on 54 other counts of the same nature." In sentencing the defendant, the judge said, " 'You could have been prosecuted on many other charges, enough to confine you in jail for several times the length of your life.' The total stolen by [the defendant] in all the 56 thefts was $538." Minneapolis Journal 3/28/30. See *Note—Charging One Theft as Several Larcenies, A Series of Thefts as a Single Larceny* (1942) 40 Mich. L. Rev. 429.

current division into major and petty offenders.[6] Embezzlement by public officials might also be considered as more serious than that committed by private individuals. Violations of trust in areas where insurance by victims is not obtainable or, at least, is not usual, e.g. real estate and other independent operators, might be treated as more serious than "ordinary embezzlement." There are other bases for differentiating the embezzlement of independent agents. Some European codes distinguish such embezzlement from that of an employee who has mere custody of property [7] on the ground that the former is wholly entrusted with the property whereas the employee is under surveillance and various checks on his honesty are maintained. On the other hand, servants in homes and relatives who embezzle property of little value might be prosecuted only on the complaint of the victim.[8]

3. Lay Practices and Administration

The most salient feature of the entire embezzlement situation is the widespread practice of private justice—private individuals deciding who shall be prosecuted, who condoned, and what, if any, sanctions shall be applied. There has always been private participation in the administration of criminal justice, and it will and should continue to play an important role. Thus, it is a commonplace that police are dependent on the assistance of private citizens and that prosecutions cannot be successful unless complainants and other witnesses cooperate with the State's Attorney. On the other hand, the penalties for failure to respond to the hue and cry in past epochs and the crimes of misprision and accessory after the fact indicate a

---

[6] This distinction is supported in the typological classification of embezzlers by E. Redden, Embezzlement (Ph.D. Thesis, U. of Chicago 1939). "The Little-Fellow Embezzler who withholds small amounts . . . any amount under ten dollars." Id. 31, "The Picayune, under $100 embezzler, who embezzles a small amount, usually a series of small amounts, the total of which is less than $100." Id. 34.

[7] German Criminal Code of 1871, sec. 246. The Swiss Federal Criminal Code, Art. 140, 30 J. Cr. L. Supp. 52 (1939).

[8] German Criminal Code of 1871, sec. 247. Swiss Federal Criminal Code, Art. 140, #3.

recurrent problem in this regard. In embezzlement we find wholesale avoidance of legal process exhibited in a congeries of sharp, sometimes criminal, practices.

Where such widespread persistent practices in respectable quarters oppose common avowals of policy and accepted law, we may be certain that no easy reform is possible. The plain indication is that deeply rooted causes are operative, challenging the feasibility of proposed reforms, indeed challenging the need for any reform. Certainly it is arguable whether the present situation is not, after all, the best one among practicable alternatives. It is even possible that the described practices and the attitudes they engender, as well as their consequences, are socially desirable, that, in effect, we have an enlightened private individualization of treatment which avoids the crudities of exposure and punishment and, in sum, is superior to official administration of the criminal law. The logic of this position would require us to turn back the pages of history to the mid-eighteenth century. It would return embezzlement to the private law of contracts from which it has never been fully extricated. This might eliminate many inner conflicts and the compounding of felonies involved in the current practices.

Most students of the criminal law would, it may be hazarded, reject such a proposal. The harms caused by embezzlement are very substantial, the conduct is immoral, and sustaining mores are certainly not completely lacking. The fallacy involved in the either/or position—that prosecution should be initiated in every case of known violation or that criminal law should never be applied—is obviously untenable. It ignores, e.g. the enormous range of sound discretion which often requires that there shall be no prosecution. The less extreme position that if only a few of the known violators who ought to be prosecuted are prosecuted, the law should be repealed, is oblivious to the existence of difficult problems met throughout the entire process of law-enforcement. It would have either perfection or nothing at all. It also rests on the invalid premise that the criminal law is intended to control only "bad people," and that it has no function to perform regarding "good people." The grounds for rejecting these positions cannot be presented here.[9] But certain pertinent observations must be made. For example, there are always degrees of tension and many gaps between a legal order, public attitudes, sound policy, and the practices of enforcement. Logic and "technical" violations are sometimes dominated by experience and custom, e.g. the use of the employer's stamps, stationery and telephone, "padding" expense accounts, and the maid's consumption of choice household items. There are conflicts and inconsistencies throughout the entire law-process and, as regards some offenses, the opposition between mores and moral judgments is acute.

Yet few would deny that many of the private practices described above are opposed to the values of a sound legal order. Few would deny that sound individualization of treatment of offenders is not likely to be achieved by fortuitous exculpations. Until a thoughtful defense of the current practices is presented, it will be assumed that they are unsound, and that legal reform should aim precisely at their elimination, the inculcation of law-enforcing attitudes, and the substitution of official, for lay, administration of the criminal law. With regard to the feasibility of implementing this policy, it must be recognized, despite the weaknesses and conflicts that presently obtain, that substantial sustaining mores are sometimes operative, indeed, occasionally, very severe sentences are widely approved. Sound mores can be strengthened and expanded. The indicated principal direction of reform is therefore toward more effective law-enforcement—not, of course, in any narrow sense, but in a defensible sense, i.e. one in which expert competence to use power wisely, take account of case histories, and so on, is available.

In order to encourage employers to report embezzlements to the authorities, they must be persuaded that official investigation will be efficient and entail a minimum loss of time, and

---

[9] Hall, Living Law of Democratic Society (1949) 99–100.

that the authorities will arrive at sound decisions. This suggests
the need for many reforms which, although they are of great
importance, are not our immediate concern. We seek specific
reforms directly related to the above study of embezzlement.

We have found that the expense entailed in preparation for
trial deters many employers from reporting embezzlement cases
to the prosecuting attorney. Accordingly, the surety companies
should explore the possibility of insuring the costs of investigation, accumulation of evidence, and counsel fees. No reason
known to the writer or stated by any of the surety company
officials, to whom the suggestion was made, renders the proposal impracticable.

As we have seen, however, more serious factors than these
financial costs operate in avoidance of law-enforcement. To
overcome them something more effective than the obligation of
citizenship is required. An earlier form of surety bond, now
universally discarded, required prosecution as a condition
precedent to payment of the insurance. It was abandoned because of resistance by the insured and the willingness of some
surety companies to write bonds without such a limitation on
payment of the insurance. In a competitive market, only 10–15
percent of it insured, the restrictive clause was doomed.

It is worth considering, however, whether such a provision
should not be legally required. Since prosecution is within the
State's Attorney's discretion and, also, in view of the surety
companies' policy to pay the insurance even though sufficient
proof of guilt to convict is lacking, such a requirement would
need to be limited to the reporting of the offense to the State's
Attorney. The sanction would be civil—the loss of the amount
insured. Compliance of the surety companies would be essential. This would involve periodical examination of their files
and difficult questions regarding sanctions. Moreover, it would
continue to depend upon a very numerous class, the employers,
for performance of the desired act—reporting defalcations to
public officials. These difficulties raise doubts as to the feasibility of such a law.

Feasibility of enforcement increases as legal control (a) is limited with reference to the number of persons bound, (b) is simplified with regard to the conduct required and proof of violation, and (c) is implemented by serious, yet reasonable, sanctions. Accordingly, the most important single reform, in the writer's opinion, would be a specific application of misprision, i.e., *require the surety companies to report to the State's Attorney when notice of criminal defalcation is received by them from the insured.* Although the insurance companies cover only a small percentage of all embezzlements, their absolute coverage is so large that their compliance with the indicated law would have great effect.

The feasibility of enforcement of such a narrower law, as compared with the very serious difficulties that would undoubtedly be met if the duty to report were imposed on all employers, is an important consideration. The modern demise of misprision[10] is closely related to its very wide reference. In modern conditions, including the rise of a professional police force, it is impossible to enforce misprision on the entire population. But a specific application of misprision to certain persons and situations presents quite a different question.[11]

The advantages of the proposed reform over statutes on compounding a felony are equally manifest. It is exceedingly difficult to prove compounding a felony, and even if prosecutors

---

[10] *Note, Existence of Common Law Offense of Misprision of Treason and Felony in Modern Law* (1941) 7 Univ. of Pittsburgh L. Rev. 246.

[11] ". . . banking institutions . . . are required to inform the authorities of defalcations." Kostelanetz, *op. cit.* 461.

Section 10(b) of the Federal Deposit Insurance Act (Title 12, U.S.C. Section 1820 (b)) provides in part that the "Board of Directors shall appoint examiners who shall have power . . . to examine any state nonmember bank. . . . Each such examiner shall have power to make a thorough examination of all of the affairs of the bank and in doing so he shall have power to administer oaths and to examine and take and preserve testimony of any of the officers and agents thereof, and shall make a full and detailed report of the condition of the bank to the Corporation. . . ."

"It is under the authority of the above quoted section that an officer of the bank is required to answer certain questions among which is the question to which you refer." Letter to writer, Nov. 27, 1951, from Norris C. Bakke, Associate General Counsel, F.D.I.C.

Cf. U.S. Code, 1946 Supp. IV, tit. 18, sec. 4.

were anxious to enforce that law, they would face practically insuperable difficulties.[12] In contrast, compliance with the proposed law and, consequently, proof of its violation are reduced to simple, almost mechanical checks—although the differentiation of sanctions with reference to reckless and intentional violations would require greater effort by the public officials. The proposed law would be circumvented by some employers who, under severe pressure, decided to pocket their loss or to deal only with the defaulting employees rather than report the defalcation to the surety company. But it is unlikely that many businessmen would surrender the advantages, indeed, the necessities, of their insurance. The employer would only notify the surety company of the defalcation; the surety company, an outside party, would report the case to the public authorities.

The required report to the Attorney General or the local State's Attorney might be specified as due "not later than 30 days after receipt of notice of the defalcation." This would allow ample time to persuade offenders to make or agree to make restitution. It would eliminate the possibility of reference to prosecution as a bargaining influence, but it would not affect the promise to report restitution to the prosecutor and the Court, if prosecution were later initiated.

---

[12] In New York City during 15 years, from 1935–1949 inclusive, there were only 36 trials for compounding felonies and misdemeanors, in which there were convictions in 9 cases and some punitive treatment imposed in 4 cases. New York City Police Dept. Annual Reports.

APPENDIX

THE PROPOSAL TO PREPARE A MODEL PENAL CODE [1]

I have selected for discussion what I regard as the most important problem relevant to the proposed project, namely, the theory of the research and the methods of conducting it. It must be evident that these are the basic overall questions which will confer worth-while distinctiveness on the final product. In order to give you some definite frame of reference on which to hang my remarks, may I say that the specific problems which I think should be the first ones undertaken are: (1) Mental Disease, (2) Intoxication, (3) Sex Crimes, (4) Theft (Larceny, Embezzlement, Fraud, Receiving Stolen Property), (5) Petty Offenses—Strict Liability, and (6) Juvenile Delinquency.

The theory of the proposed research can be described in different ways, but all formulations would include: (1) intensive study of certain social problems; it would be necessary to utilize all of the known methods of research that could profitably be applied and to draw on the existing knowledge in all the relevant sciences and disciplines; (2) study of the relevant law; in first instance, this is the law of the books—the statutes, decisions, and regulations; but a thorough understanding of this body of law would include a knowledge of the forces that brought it into existence, the relevant patterns of culture, how the law actually worked, what its effects were, and what changes were made in it by legislation, judicial techniques, public opinion, and expert criticism; and (3) the research would include the answers to many legal questions which the extant literature of science and the social disciplines provides.

For example, scientific and social research on alcoholism reveals great diversity in personality types, much mental disease, and sharply differing situations. As knowledge increases, the nature of the relevant social harms changes not only because

---

[1] This paper was presented at the Round Table on Crimes at the Association of American Law Schools' annual meeting, December 29, 1950. Reprinted, with permission, from 4 J. of Leg. Educ. 91 (1951).

empirical knowledge reveals them more fully but also because our evaluations of certain situations as harms are themselves influenced by our factual understanding. A draftsman who "defines" harms on the basis of thorough knowledge of the relevant social problems, including personality components, will stand on relatively firm ground. He will define in terms of actual facts and behavior; and he will have ideas regarding what is significant in the actual problems, which would form the basis for sound legislation.

Equally important in the institution of adequate legal controls is knowledge of how the past relevant law has functioned and how it functions now. For example, when it was required that a thief must have been convicted before the receiver of stolen goods could be prosecuted, certain unfortunate consequences occurred. When penalties are severe, certain subterfuges and fictions are indulged to evade the plain letter of the law. When there is no law defining the taking of an automobile for a "joy-ride," radical interpretations of an auto-larceny statute are common. Where "legal provocation" is greatly restricted, juries arrive at strange factual findings in order to assure desired results. Thus studies of the administration of past and present laws are essential to the discovery of sound substantive laws and to the demonstration of their soundness (two quite different matters). Such studies test the validity and efficacy of past and present controls. Generalized, this knowledge reveals the conditions of effective legal control.

In order to keep the potentially limitless problem of administration from getting out of hand, it would be necessary to restrict it by (1) separating administration from procedure, and largely ignoring the latter, and (2) confining it to certain limited categories, e. g., (a) statistical analysis of the administrative process, (b) official administration (judge, jury, lawyers), (c) public opinion, and (d) private agencies. The factors studied would vary, depending on the problem and, within each, the investigation would be confined to a sampling sufficient to sustain definite conclusions regarding the operation of the law and the reasons for its success or failure.

Paralleling the investigations of the selected social problems, the substantive law, and its administration, would be investigations of the relevant types of treatment, correction, punishment, and other reliefs and remedies. This research would supplement the above factual studies especially as regards problems of personality, and it would be concerned with the methods of treatment, results, predictions, and so on. It would be desirable to have one member of each research group, engaged in studying relevant social problems, also assigned to a research group studying treatment. He could thus bring to that group important information which would guide the development of the treatment program.

Throughout the research numerous scientific problems would be formulated in detail. Specific issues would be raised. Definite answers would be given. Methods of analysis and research personnel would be determined and selected with reference to the nature of each inquiry. In each investigation, the legal problems would be the central points of interest, and this implies direction of the research by legal scholars who are also social scientists.

Thus, to summarize: each project would include (a) historico-socio-legal analysis of a particular problem; (b) restatement of the existing relevant law together with an analysis and commentary on it; (c) careful description of the functioning of the law; the process of change: legislation, judicial techniques, prosecutor's practices, private organizations, and so on; (d) a summary of available empirical knowledge brought to bear on the relevant, specific legal problems; and (e) recommendations for improvement of the law and its administration.

To assure the success of the project, there should be set up a *Council on Methods* which would formulate the theory of such research in detail. It would be especially concerned with the theory of socio-legal investigation, the integration and use of the relevant knowledge derived from the sciences and disciplines, a critique of methods, and a model study to guide the various researchers.

The emphasis on methods should not terminate in generalizations formulated by persons who remained outside the actual research. The members of the Council on Methods should be closely associated with the research groups. Each research group should deliberate on the methods to be employed in the solution of its particular problem. Its program should be pointed at and stated in terms of the particular problem to be studied. Each group would submit its formulation of methods for criticism by the Council. A member of the Council should be assigned to parallel the actual conduct of the research by pertinent inquiries regarding the methods employed, the recording of the data to permit verification, the significant formulation of conclusions, and so on. In short, the objective must be not debate on methods, but the *use* of the best methods, the assurance that these are known and employed so far as possible and feasible. The articulation of the methods to be used will help enormously if only because it will facilitate self-criticism. It will also help to support the conclusions finally reached and to defend them against unsound criticism. The information acquired in the various researches noted above would become the basis of various drafts of laws on each major type of social problem. After passing the critical scrutiny of the group which carried on a particular investigation, each draft would go (a) to a Committee on Legal Controls for general review and (b) to a central Drafting Committee for improvement in form and interrelation with the other proposed enactments. Thus a Code would emerge as a natural product of the various detailed investigations. It would be significant and defensible by references to the relevant specific researches.

The Code should not be stressed in the early stages of the work. Scholars in various sciences and disciplines can be united in cooperation if the dominant bond is scientific in the sense of discovery of what happened and what goes on now. Although it would be fatuous to imagine that value-judgments could be excluded from any part of the work, it is also noteworthy that whereas disagreement commonly attends broad programs of reform, there is often agreement on specific factual problems and even on specific reforms if they are considered directly in relation to detailed factual studies.

Finally, and most important, a new type of literature could be invented—an integration of law, science, and social discipline. This literature would be the product of the socio-legal research carried on in the ways indicated above and of the distinctive character of the objectives sought. It would include a record of the empirical knowledge relied upon, the policies adopted and the reasons supporting them, and the specific conclusions reached. These records would constitute the ultimate bases of the proposed Code. The various parts of this record would be submitted to experts in different fields for specific criticism. In final form, they would for the most part represent a consensus of expert opinion. Anyone who examined the Code could refer to the relevant empirical and legal knowledge and the policies relied upon. Criticism could be specific and significant.

For example, the group studying certain harms committed by intoxicated persons and proposing a series of laws, to be part of the Code, would write an appropriate summary of the relevant knowledge on alcoholism, including the types of personality involved, the various diseases met, the relevant psychiatric and social data, and so on. These would be written not in the form of a treatise but succinctly with direct reference to the problems of legal control. Upon completion, this summary of the relevant empirical knowledge would be submitted to many experts for their comments and criticism. Where a consensus of the experts could not be obtained, that fact would be stated.

Similar methods and checks would be used regarding the studies of administration and the analyses of policy. We would know where we stood with reference to the best knowledge available. And, as a result of the completion of the above studies, there would be created an organization of persons qualified to carry on socio-legal research and to codify the results.

If adequate facilities are made available the objectives outlined above can certainly be attained. That accomplishment would have very great significance for similar endeavors in many fields. The approaches to the problems, the methods of research, the provision of a validating record of empirical knowledge and the grounds of policy, the relation of the Code to such determinate data, the creation of an organization which had demonstrated its effectiveness—these and other benefits would result. The long range effects cannot be precisely anticipated, but their importance cannot be doubted. Those who direct the project should be mindful of the larger implications of its successful completion.

———

The plan of research, outlined above, represents a synthesis of ideas relevant to the general application of the methods employed in *Theft, Law and Society* and in the writer's studies on intoxication and mental disease.[2] The purpose was to construct a bridge between theory and research, i.e. a plan or "model," specifying very briefly the best methods of formulating and conducting the research, analysis, and drafting in order to produce the soundest code of criminal law. Accordingly, it should not be understood to require a group of persons or even one person to fulfill each indicated function. The model would serve its purpose if only one scholar undertook the entire task of supplying the code. In short, the number of researchers and draftsmen engaged in the project, the financial subsidy, and other practical questions of undoubted importance in the execution of the plan, are not relevant to its validity.

To test its validity, it would be necessary to consider, e.g., whether important methods or techniques or aspects of organization are not included in the model or are not provided for in the best way possible. No doubt amendments and corrections can be made, and it is equally probable that improvements would be suggested in the course of using the model in actual research.

If, as suggested, a Council on Methods were appointed, the first task assigned each member might well be to draft his "model" of the research required to produce the best code of

———

[2] General Principles of Criminal Law (1947) Chapters 13 and 14.

criminal law. The availability of half-a-dozen such models would, in effect, pool the experience of socio-legal researchers and lead to the construction of the master model. As indicated above, such a plan, properly used, would not inhibit investigation in any way but, instead, would guide it until, under the stimulation of the actual research, better methods were discovered.

The basic theoretical problem in penal codification concerns the relations of the desired code to the knowledge upon which its validity depends, e.g., to a sociology of criminal law. Instead of relying only on general discussions of this problem which, suggestive as they may be, are often remote from actual investigation of definite problems, it would be very helpful if, in addition, several detailed analyses of specific socio-legal researches were made available. This does not imply any depreciation of theory; instead, it seeks more pointed, critical, relevant theory.

Finally, an equally important, though unnoticed, problem concerns the need to preserve in the research the essential difference between scientific, i.e., relatively disinterested, inquiry and reform of the criminal law. Both are needed. But, it is submitted, neither a sound code nor important knowledge of the criminal law will be provided if science and reform are indiscriminately intermingled.'

---

3 *Cf.* Hall, *Science and Reform in Criminal Law* (1952) 100 U. of Pa. L. Rev. 787.

STATUTES ON (1) BENEFIT OF CLERGY, (2) NON-CLERGABLE OFFENSES AND (3) TRANSPORTATION AND OTHER PENALTIES—1276 to 1857

4 Edw. 1, St. 3, c. 5 (1276) The Statute of Bigamy	"Men twice married, whom the Bishop of Rome hath excluded from all Clerks Privilege . . . shall not henceforth be delivered to the Prelates, but Justice shall be executed upon them, as upon other Lay People."
9 Edw. 2, St. 1, c. 16 (1315)	"The Privilege of the Church being demanded by the Ordinary, shall not be denied to a Clerk that hath confessed Felony."
18 Edw. 3, St. 3, c. 2 (1344)	Bigamy. ". . . the justices shall not have the cognizance or power to try the bigamy by inquest, or in other manner; but it shall be sent to the spiritual court . . ."
25 Edw. 3, St. 3, c. 4 (1350)	Secular as well as religious clerks convicted of treason or felony not touching the King or royal family, shall have benefit of clergy, and shall be delivered to the Ordinary. ". . . whereby they shall be safely kept and duly punished . . ."
4 Hen. 7, c. 13 (1487)	Persons "lettered," but not within holy orders who have once had clergy shall not have clergy for subsequent offences.
12 Hen. 7, c. 7 (1496)	If any lay person murder lord or master, he shall not have clergy upon conviction or attainder; execution as though he were no clerk.
4 Hen. 8, c. 2 (1512)	With the exception of those in holy orders, clergy denied in cases of murder or felony in churches, etc., murder or robbery of person on the king's highway or in house, someone being there and put in fear.
23 Hen. 8, c. 1 (1531) Made perpetual by 32 Hen. 8, c. 3 (1540)	Except those within holy orders (i.e. "of the orders of sub-deacon, or above") clergy denied to those committing petit treason, wilful murder, robbing holy place, robbery in person's dwelling, the person or family being therein and put in fear, robbery on highway; arson of dwelling house or barn having grain therein, or being accessory thereto before the fact. They shall "suffer death . . . as if they were no clerks."

356

25 Hen. 8, c. 6 (1533) Extended by 28 Hen. 8, c. 1 § 6 (1536)	Made buggery felony without benefit of clergy.
27 Hen. 8, c. 17 (1535)	Servant embezzling master's goods over value of 40s. shall lose clergy and sanctuary. This had been made a felony in 1529, and was "revived" in 5 Eliz. c. 10, 3 (1562).
28 Hen. 8, c. 1 (1536) Made perpetual by 32 H. 8, c. 3 (1540)	§ 7. Those within holy orders shall henceforth be subject to same penalties as those who are not, specifying various felonies regarding which certain earlier statutes had preserved their privilege, ". . . any provision or exception specified in any of the said acts, or any other usage or custom of this realm, to the contrary thereof notwithstanding."
37 Hen. 8, c. 8 (1545) Cf. 1 Edw. 6, c. 12, 2 & 3 Edw. 6 c. 33, 31 Eliz. c. 12	§ 2. Stealing a horse etc. excluded from benefit of clergy, ". . . and shall suffer death . . . as they should have, if they were no clerks."
1 Edw. 6, c. 12 (1547)	§ 10. Clergy and sanctuary abolished for murder, breaking of house if person therein and put in fear, robbing a person on highway, stealing horses etc., feloniously taking goods from chapel or church. § 12. Clergy and Sanctuary allowed in all other felonies as in time of 1 Hen. 8.
§ 14 Repealed, 4 & 5 Vict. c. 22.	§ 14. In every case, including those mentioned in this act, except murder or poisoning, Lords of Parliament shall have clergy but only once, though they cannot read.
5 & 6 Edw. 6, c. 9 (1552)	Burglary in any part of a house, or booth or tent in any fair or market, persons being within in another part; offender excluded from clergy, even if the persons be asleep.
4 & 5 P. & M. c. 4 (1557)	Any person who commands, hires, counsels any person to commit petit treason, murder, robbery, in dwelling-house, or highway robbery, or burns dwelling or barn having grain therein, excluded from clergy.
8 Eliz. c. 4 (1565) Repealed, 48 Geo. 3	§ 2. Clergy denied to person who feloniously takes goods, money or chattels from person of another without the latter's knowledge.
18 Eliz. c. 7 (1576)	§ 1. Rape and burglary excluded from clergy. § 4. Carnal knowledge of female under 10 declared felony without benefit of clergy.

31 Eliz. c. 4 (1589) c. 12	Embezzlement of military supplies made felony. § 5. Accessories before and after felony of horse-stealing denied clergy.
39 Eliz. c. 9 (1597)	Clergy withdrawn from principals and accessories before the fact in the taking away, etc., any woman against her will, who has lands or goods, or is heir apparent to her ancestor.
c. 15	Clergy denied for felonious taking in the day-time money or chattels of value of 5s. or more, in a dwelling-house or out-house, though no person be therein.
2 Jac. 1, c. 8 (1604)	Clergy denied to one who stabs another who has not first struck him, and the stab results in death within 6 months, though malice afore-thought cannot be proven.
21 Jac. 1, c. 6 (1623)	"Whereas by the laws of this realm the benefit of clergy is not allowed to women convicted of felony, by reason whereof many women do suffer death for small causes"—Women convicted of felonious taking of money or goods above value of 12 pence and under 10s., or being accessory, it not being burglary or highway robbery or private stealing from person, shall have clergy as men do, and be branded and may be imprisoned not over a year.
18 Car. 2, c. 3 (1666)	Excludes "great, known and notorious thieves" from clergy. However, on conviction, they may be transported "into any of his Majesty's dominions in America, there to remain, and not to return."
31 Car. 2, c. 2 (1679) Habeas Corpus Act	§ 14. Provided always, and be it enacted, That if any person or persons lawfully convicted of any felony, shall in open court pray to be transported beyond the seas, and the court shall think fit to leave him or them in prison for that purpose, such person or persons may be transported into any parts beyond the seas.
3 W. & M. c. 9 (1691) Made perpetual by 6 & 7 Wm. 3, c. 14 § 1 (1695)	§ 1. Any person who shall rob any other person or feloniously take goods or chattels in any dwelling-house, the owner being therein and put in fear, . . . or shall comfort, aid, etc. any person to commit said offenses, or to break any dwelling-house, shop or warehouse thereunto belonging, or therewith used, in the daytime, and feloniously take money, goods, or chattels of value of 5s. or more, although no person shall be in such place, . . . shall not have benefit of clergy.

10 & 11 Wm. 3, c. 23 (1699)	Every person . . . that shall by night or in the day-time, . . . in any shop, warehouse, coach-house, or stable, privately and feloniously steal any goods of the value of five shillings or more although such shop, warehouse, . . . be not actually broke open by such offender, and although the owners, or any other person be or be not in such shop, warehouse . . . or shall assist, hire . . . any person to commit such offense, . . . shall be excluded from the benefit of clergy.
5 Anne, c. 6 (1706)	§ 6. If any person be convicted of a felony for which he should have had his clergy, he shall not be required to read, but shall be punished as clerk convict as if he had read like a clerk.
12 Anne, c. 7 (1713)	§ 1. Any person who feloniously steals money, goods, chattels, of value of 40s, or more from any dwelling or out-house, whether he broke in or not, and whether or not there was a person in such house, shall be denied his clergy. § 2. Not applicable to apprentices under 15 years.
4 Geo. 1, c. 11 (1717)	§ 1. Provides for transportation in cases of robbery, larceny, etc., where party has prior thereto been denied benefit of clergy. Covers receivers— 14 years transportation. Persons guilty of clergable larcenies to be transported for 7 years instead of being branded or whipped.
9 Geo. 1, c. 22 (1722)	§ 1. Any person, armed and disguised, who . . . shall unlawfully hunt deer . . . take or steal fish out of pond or river . . . felony, . . . death without benefit of clergy . . . appear in hare warren etc., or unlawfully rob such warren . . . felony . . . death without benefit of clergy.
2 Geo. 2, c. 25 (1729)	§ 1. Forgery made felony without benefit of clergy. § 3. Steal or take by robbery any chose in action —punishable as if he had taken other goods of the same value.
4 Geo. 2, c. 32 (1731)	Any person who steals, any lead, iron bar, iron gate, or iron rail, fixed to any building, etc. guilty of felony, punishable by transportation for seven years. Receivers with knowledge incur same punishment.
14 Geo. 2, c. 6 (1741)	If any person feloniously drive away sheep or other cattle . . . or kill with intent to steal the carcase . . . or shall assist therein, . . . felony, and . . . denied benefit of clergy.

15 Geo. 2, c. 13 (1742)
§ 12 repeated in 35 Geo. 3, c. 66 § 6 (1795) and in 37 Geo. 3, c. 46 § 6 (1796)

§ 12. If any officer or servant of Bank of England being entrusted with note, bill, dividend warrant, bond, deed or security, shall secrete, embezzle or run away with it, he shall be guilty of felony, suffer death as felon without benefit of clergy.

15 Geo. 2, c. 27 (1742)

If a person in possession of cloth or other woolen goods that have been stolen in night-time from racks, tenters, or having been left out to dry, cannot give satisfactory account of how he acquired it or produce the party from whom he received it, or a witness, he shall be deemed to have stolen the goods. Shall pay treble damages to owner, in default of which, be imprisoned for 3 months until he pay.
Second offense—6 months imprisonment in addition to treble damages.
Third offense—Felony—transportation for 7 years.

18 Geo. 2, c. 27 (1745)

Stealing linen or cotton goods, etc. or assisting— shall suffer death without benefit of clergy.

24 Geo. 2, c. 11 (1751)

§ 3. If any officer or servant of South-Sea Company shall secrete or embezzle any note, bill, etc. . . . guilty of felony, . . . death without benefit of clergy.

c. 45

Any person who feloniously steals the value of 40s. from ship, . . . upon any navigable river, port of entry or discharge, or in creek belonging thereto, or steals same from wharf or key adjacent to navigable river etc., shall be denied benefit of clergy.

25 Geo. 2, c. 10 (1752)

Any person who unlawfully takes black lead from a mine shall be deemed guilty of felony, punishable by one year imprisonment and publicly whipped, or transportation up to 7 years.

26 Geo. 2, c. 19 (1753)

If any person steal goods or other effects from ship in distress or wrecked, . . . guilty of felony, . . . death without benefit of clergy.

29 Geo. 2, c. 30 (1756)

Every person who shall buy or receive lead, iron, copper, brass, bell-metal or solder, knowing it was stolen; . . . shall, upon conviction, be transported for fourteen years.

30 Geo. 2, c. 24 (1757)

All persons who by false pretences shall obtain from another money, goods, wares or merchandise, with intent to defraud, etc. shall upon conviction be fined and imprisoned or pilloried, or whipped, or transported for seven years.

2 Geo. 3, c. 28 (1761)	§ 12. Any person who buys or receives any part of cargo, goods, stores belonging to ship in Thames, knowing same to have been stolen, shall be transported for 14 years as felons are. (Although principal felon not convicted.)
5 Geo. 3, c. 14 (1765)	§ 1. If any person enter park, . . . and shall take, . . . any fish, or shall buy or receive same, knowing of unlawful taking, shall be transported for 7 years.
c. 25	§ 17. If any officer, etc. of Post Office shall secrete, embezzle or destroy any letter, packet, with which he is entrusted or which comes into his hands by virtue of his employment, containing bank note, bank post bill, bill of exchange, etc. . . . shall . . . suffer death as felon.
6 Geo. 3, c. 36 (1766)	Any person who in night-time spoils . . . or carrys away any beech, oak, ash . . . tree; or . . . root, shrub or plant of value of 5s. in night-time, . . . felony, . . . and may be transported for 7 years. Buying and receiving same—same punishment.
7 Geo. 3, c. 50 (1767)	§ 1, 2, 3. Enlarged 5 Geo. 3, c. 25 and added "without benefit of clergy."
10 Geo. 3, c. 48 (1769)	Every person who shall buy or receive jewels, gold or silver plate, or watch, knowing they were stolen, shall be guilty of a felony if such goods were taken by robbery or burglary, and may be convicted before the principal felon, and shall be transported for fourteen years.
16 Geo. 3, c. 30 (1776)	Changes punishment for deer hunting, etc., to forfeiture of £20 for first offenders; 7 years transportation for subsequent offenses. Penalizes illegal possession of deer unlawfully taken.
19 Geo. 3, c. 74 (1779)	§ 1. Offenders sentenced to transportation shall be transported beyond the seas elsewhere than America. § 3. Where any offender entitled to benefit of clergy and liable to be burnt in the hand, the court may instead impose a moderate fine or order him to be whipped. Branding practically abolished. § 4. Court may imprison such offenders for a term of not over one year; or hard labor in house of correction for 6 months to 2 years. § 27. Provides for discretion in courts (except in petty larceny) to sentence male person to ship to be kept at labor in cleaning the Thames for a term of one to five years in lieu of 7 years transportation; one to seven years in lieu of 14 years transportation.

21 Geo. 3, c. 68 (1781)   Adds copper, brass, bell-metal, utensil or fixture; punishment, 7 years transportation, or 1 to 3 years hard labor and public whipping.

c. 69   Every person who shall buy or receive pewter in any form, knowing the same to be stolen . . . shall be transported like felons up to 7 years, or imprisoned for 1 to 3 years at hard labor and be whipped.

39 Geo. 3, c. 85 (1799)   If any clerk or servant shall by virtue of his employment receive any money, goods, bond, bill, banker's draft, or other security or effects on the account of his master or employer and shall fraudulently embezzle, secrete, or make away with the same or any part thereof, he shall be deemed to have feloniously stolen the same and punished by transportation up to fourteen years.

40 Geo. 3, c. 89 (1800)   Any person knowingly selling, delivering, or receiving or concealing war, naval or victualling supplies marked with the king's brand, shall be deemed receiver of stolen goods with knowledge of the theft and shall be transported for 14 years, unless he can produce certificate of naval officer.

48 Geo. 3, c. 129 (1808)   § 1. Repealing 8 Eliz. c. 4. § 1 and § 2 *re* benefit of clergy as to those taking privately from person of another.
§ 2. Every person who shall at any time or in any place whatsoever feloniously steal any money, goods or chattels from the person of another, whether privily or not, but without . . . robbery, or who shall be present, aiding or abetting, shall be liable to transportation for life or for term not less than 7 years or be imprisoned not exceeding 3 years with or without hard labor.

52 Geo. 3, c. 63 (1812)   If any banker, merchant, broker, attorney or agent with whom any bill, warrant or order for payment of money, bank receipt, . . . embezzle, etc. . . . guilty of misdemeanor. Transportation up to fourteen years or such other punishment as may be inflicted for misdemeanor.

1 Geo. 4, c. 117 (1820)   § 1. Repeals 10 & 11 Wm. 3, c. 23 § 1 as to the taking of goods under value of £15.

§ 2. Persons who privately and feloniously steal goods, wares or merchandise of the value of 5s. to £15 in any shop, warehouse, coachhouse or stable, shall be liable to be transported for life or any term not less than 7 years, or be imprisoned with or without hard labor for any term not exceeding 7 years.

4 Geo. 4, c. 48 (1823)

Whenever a person be convicted of a felony except murder, and shall by law be excluded from benefit of clergy, the court may abstain from pronouncing judgment of death.

7 & 8 Geo. 4, c. 28 (1827)

§ 6. *"And be it enacted, That Benefit of Clergy, with respect to Persons convicted of Felony, shall be abolished; . . ."*
§7. *"And be it enacted, That no Person convicted of Felony shall suffer death, unless it be for some Felony which was excluded from the Benefit of Clergy before or on the First Day of the present Session of Parliament, or which hath been or shall be made punishable with Death by some Statute passed after that Day."*

9 & 10 Vict. c. 24 (1846)

§ 1. In all cases where the court is empowered or required to sentence to transportation exceeding 7 years, it may award such sentences for not less than 7 years or imprisonment for any period not exceeding 2 years, with or without hard labor.

16 & 17 Vict. c. 99 (1853)

Penal Servitude Act of 1853.
1. No person shall be sentenced to transportation who would not have been liable to be transported for life or 14 years or upwards.
2. In place of transportation for less than 14 years, penal servitude as below shall be awarded.
3. Any person liable to 14 years to life transportation, may be so sentenced or kept in penal servitude.
4. Instead of 7 years transportation, 4 years penal servitude; instead of 7 to 10 years transportation, 4 to 6 years penal servitude; instead of 10 to 15 years transportation, 6 to 8 years penal servitude; instead of over 15 years transportation, 6 to 10 years penal servitude; instead of life transportation, life penal servitude.

20 & 21 Vict. c. 3 (1857). Amending 16 & 17 Vict. c. 99, repealing 1, 2, 3, 4 of that act, and making the rest part of this act.

2. No person shall be sentenced to transportation; any person who prior to this act might have been transported shall be kept in penal servitude for a term of the same duration as the transportation; provided that where the offender could have been sentenced to transportation or imprisonment, he may now be sentenced either to penal servitude for the same term or to the same period of imprisonment. In any case where 7 years transportation had been provided, the court may pass sentence of penal servitude for not less than 3 years.

PENAL LAW SEC. 1308

Buying, receiving, concealing or withholding stolen or wrongfully acquired property

A person who

1. a. Buys or receives any property knowing the same to have been stolen or obtained in any way under circumstances which constitute larceny or who conceals, withholds, or aids in concealing or withholding any property, knowing the same to have been stolen, or appropriated wrongfully in such a manner as to constitute larceny under the provisions of this article, if such misappropriation has been committed within the state, whether such property were so stolen or misappropriated within or without the state; or

b. Being a dealer in or collector of junk, metals or second hand materials, or the agent, employee or representative of such dealer or collector, buys or receives any wire, cable, copper, lead, solder, iron or brass used by or belonging to a railroad, telephone, telegraph, gas or electric light company, or any machinery, machine equipment, machine attachments or parts of a machine, or any metal in the form of ingots, ingot bars, wire bars, cakes, slabs, billets or pigs, without ascertaining by reasonable inquiry that the person selling or delivering the same has a legal right to do so; or

c. Being a dealer in or collector of second hand books or other literary material, or the agent, employee or representative of such dealer, or collector, buys or receives any book, manuscript, map, chart, or other work of literature, belonging to, or bearing any mark or indicia of ownership by a public or incorporated library, college or university, without ascertaining by reasonable inquiry that the person selling or delivering the same has a legal right to do so; or

d. Being engaged in the business of supplying a service involving the furnishing, renting or hiring out to others for personal, trade or business uses, of clean laundered articles of property, or the agent, employee or representative of such person, buys, receives, conceals or withholds or aids in the concealing or withholding of any such property bearing any mark or indicia of ownership by another person engaged in such business, without ascertaining by reasonable inquiry, that the person selling or delivering the same has a legal right to do so,

Is guilty of a misdemeanor if such property be of the value of not more than one hundred dollars; and

Is guilty of a felony if such property be of the value of more than one hundred dollars; or, regardless of the value of such property, if it was purchased for resale or by a dealer, or if the defendant has been previously convicted of the crime of buying, receiving, concealing or withholding stolen property as herein defined, and is punishable by imprisonment for not more than ten years, or by a fine of not more than one thousand dollars, or by both such fine and imprisonment.

2. The purchase, receiving, concealing or withholding by any person engaged in any supply business aforementioned, or by his agent, employee or representative of any merchandise or property of the nature and character of the merchandise or property used in such business, bearing any mark or indicia of ownership of another person so engaged in such supply business, without the latter's express consent, shall create the presumption that such merchandise or property was bought, received, withheld or concealed by the former knowing the same to have been stolen or misappropriated. This presumption, however, may be rebutted by proof.

3. A person who being a dealer in or collector of junk, metals, or any other merchandise or property, or the agent, employee, or representative of such dealer or collector, fails to make reasonable inquiry that the person selling or delivering any stolen or misappropriated property to him has a legal right to do so, shall be presumed to have bought or received such property knowing it to have been stolen or misappropriated. This presumption may however be rebutted by proof. As amended L.1914, c. 93; L.1916, c. 366; L.1920, c. 570; L.1921, c. 429; L.1926, c. 707; L.1928, c. 354; L.1938, c. 513; L.1940, c. 443; L.1943, c. 180, eff. June 1, 1943.

STATE OF WISCONSIN

IN SENATE, NO. 784, S.

April 26, 1951—Introduced by LEGISLATIVE COUNCIL.

343.22 RECEIVING STOLEN PROPERTY. (1) Whoever intentionally receives or conceals stolen property may be penalized as follows:

(a) If the value of the property does not exceed $100, a fine of not more than $200 or imprisonment for not more than 6 months or both.

(b) If the value of the property exceeds $100, imprisonment for not more than 10 years.

(c) If the actor is a dealer in stolen property, he may be imprisoned not more than 25 years regardless of the value of the property.

(2) A dealer is one who buys and sells stolen property. Possession by the actor at the time of arrest of other stolen property having a minimum value of $100 is prima facie evidence that he is a dealer in stolen property.

LEGISLATIVE COUNCIL COMMENT:

One of the most important things about the new section is the criteria used in determining the amount of the prescribed penalty. Although some differentiation is made on the basis of the value of the property, the principal distinction is between the lay and the professional receiver. The latter is given a more severe penalty on the ground that he is a greater threat to society. Dealing in stolen property has become a profitable business and an encouragement to thieves. The thief who steals for his own consumption steals much less than the one who steals in large quantities because he knows where he can get rid of his loot easily.

Subsection (2) defines a dealer as anyone who buys and sells stolen property, i.e. a person in the business of dealing in stolen property. Obviously, the term dealer does not include someone who at one time in his life buys or sells a stolen article. The second part of the subsection provides that if the receiver has other stolen property worth at least $100 in his possession at the time of arrest, it is prima facie evidence that he is a dealer. Possession of this amount of other stolen property is good evidence that the property, which the actor is charged with receiving, is not the only stolen property he has bought or sold.

Analogous legislation. No other state has a section similar to this one in all respects. A number of states have attempted to provide greater penalties for the dealer in stolen property by prescribing a greater penalty for repeaters and persons convicted of several acts of receiving stolen property within a specified time. See Fla. Stat. §811.18 (1949); Hawaii Rev. Laws §11559 (1945); Ill. Stat. c. 38, §493 (1934); Maine Stat. c. 119, §11 (1944); Mass. Anno. Laws c. 266, §62 (1933); Mich. Comp. Laws §750.535 (1948); N. Y. Penal Law §1308 (1944) (also covers person who purchases for resale).

References. People v. Jaffe, 185 N. Y. 497, 78 N.E. 169 (1906).

Clark and Marshall, *Crimes* 498 (4th ed., Kearney, 1940).

Hall, *Theft, Law and Society* 125 (1935).

INDEXES

TABLE OF CASES

INDEX OF NAMES

SUBJECT INDEX

References are to Pages

A

ADMINISTRATION OF CRIMINAL LAW
    conflicting forces within, 177, 274, 275
    contemporary, 142
    discretion, 142-144
    distinctive problem of, 150, 151 (See JUDICIAL FUNCTION)
    preparation of Model Penal Code, 350
    reconstruction of legal categories, 262
    relationship to social and legal problems, 262

ADMINISTRATIVE PRACTICES (See DISCRETION IN CRIMINAL LAW ADMINISTRATION; WAIVER OF FELONY)
    cases illustrating, 119-132
    eighteenth century, 118, 133
    judges', 118-126
    juries', 126-130
    prosecutors', 131, 132
    summarized, 141

ASPORTATION (See TAKING AND ASPORTATION)
    element of larceny, defined, 166, 259, 260
    illustrated, 260, 261

ATTITUDES (See PUBLIC OPINION; SOCIAL ATTITUDES)
    effect on law, 68, 69
    judges', change in, 50, 51
    public, and misrepresentation, 66
    toward embezzlement, 300, 301, 304

AUTOMOBILE THEFT
    Administration of the Law
        arrests, 262-266; and size of city, 263-265; trends, 264, 265
        disparity with substantive law, 274, 275
        illustrated in Chicago, 265-275, 287; Chicago Crime Commission, 267-275
        judicial interpretation of statutes, 259, 262
        lay participation, 275-278
        relation to social and legal problems, 262
        under Dyer Act, 283, 284
    As Legal Problem, 256-262
        analysis of, 256, 260
        animus furandi, 259
        definition, 240
        Federal legislation, 282, 283
        need for subdivision, 261, 262
        registration of title requirement, 285, 286

379

References are to Pages

C

CAPITAL PUNISHMENT
avoidance by jury, 126-130
avoidance by prosecutors, 130, 131
eighteenth century, 117
in Russia, for embezzlement of public property, 301, 302
nullification by eighteenth century courts, 118-126
simple larceny, device for avoiding, 120, 121
statutory mitigation of, 139

CARRIERS' CASE, Chapter 1
animo furandi, in taking subsequent to bailment, 5
bailment
terminated by breaking bulk, 5
what constituted, 4
bales, contents of, 19
Bracton, emphasis on *animo furandi,* 7
breaking bulk, 5, 9, 10
case history, method of research, Introduction, viii–ix, xvi, xviii
change from medieval to modern world, 20
conjunction of legal sanctions with political and economic conditions, 31
Crown influence, 17, 18
decision, 9
opposing points of view, 4
economic conditions, 18, 19
Edward IV, personal interest in commerce, 28
Exchequer, 4
existing law, 4
common law, 5
law of nature, 5
stare decisis, 5
foreign trade
legislation and treaties, 27
prevalent difficulties, 23, 24
industry, wool, 30
judges, Crown influence on, 16
larceny by servant, emergence of, 31
mercantile class, connection with Crown, 22
merchandise involved, 29
Mirror of Justices, 7
new law, 12
political conditions, 14-18
procedural aspects, 4ff
safe conduct, for alien merchants in 15th century England, 24
Star Chamber, influence of Crown, 17
Stephen, on Carrier's Case, 7
summarized, 33
transportation, need for regulation in 15th century England, 22-24
Year Books, at time of Carrier's Case, 5

References are to Pages

References are to Pages

D

DEALERS (See RECEIVING STOLEN PROPERTY)
diligent inquiry required, 211-216
New York rule, 211-213, 220; applied, 212-216
special class in receiving stolen property legislation, 213

DEALING IN STOLEN GOODS (See RECEIVING STOLEN PROPERTY)
altering goods to avoid identification, 160
bankrupts as source of goods, 159
competition and organization, 163, 164
correlation to general market conditions, 161, 162
difficulty of conviction, 189-199
distinguished from non-professional receiving, 155, 216-218, 219
early statutes on, 76
emergence as result of economic change, 70
Federal legislation, 225-232
habitual offender laws, 155, 156
informer, 201, 202
legislation requiring diligent inquiry, 211-216
movement and marketing of goods, 160, 161
New York legislation, 220-223
non-standard business operation, presumption of guilt, 224, 225
organization, 156, 157
recommended legislation, 219, 220
relation to dealers in second-hand goods, 162, 163
thief-receiver relationship, 196
transportation and international trade, 162
types of merchandise, 160

DISCRETION IN CRIMINAL LAW ADMINISTRATION (See JUDICIAL
FUNCTION; PROSECUTING ATTORNEY; WAIVER OF FELONY)
advantages, 149; disadvantages, 274
basic problem, 150
by jury, 142, 143
by magistrates, 144
by prosecutor, 142, 144
characteristics, 273-275

E

ECONOMIC AND SOCIAL CONDITIONS (See CARRIER'S CASE)
Anglo-Saxon, 20
effect on law of criminal fraud, 69
effect on law of embezzlement, 65, 66
effect on law of receiving stolen property, 70, 71
effect on subject-matter of larceny, 101, 102
eighteenth century, 63, 77
banking, growth and development in England, 64
effect on law of theft, 65, 66
capitalism, Weber's theory of development, 64
colonial expansion, double purpose, 62, 63
Commercial Revolution, and economic enterprise, 62

References are to Pages

References are to Pages

References are to Pages

References are to Pages

References are to Pages

References are to Pages

References are to Pages

References are to Pages

References are to Pages

References are to Pages

References are to Pages

W